tune no.

meter (p.88)

date of earliest source

incipit

no. of voices in earliest source

analysis of structure (see p.88)

see footnote below

Sources in chronological order (see pp. 55-81)

41.   1 1 2 3 2 1   7 1 5   3 2 1   7 1 2   1 2 3 4

SM   4v   H H F H

1779

Tune	Key	Text	Voices	Tune name(s)
A43	a	b	382	NORWICH / PS. 24
A47	a		382	NORWICH
A47a	a	b	382	NORWICH / PS. 24
A51	a	c	382	NORWICH
A54	a		382	NORWICH
A56	a		382	NORWICH
A57	a		382	NORWICH / PS. 24
A57.2	a		382	NORWICH / PS. 24
A60	a		382	NORWICH
A61	a		382	NORWICH
A62	a		382	NORWICH
A67	a		382	NORWICH
A70	a		382	NORWICH
A74	a		382	NORWICH / PS. 24
A80	a		74	NORWICH
A84	a		382	NORWICH
A85	a		382	NORWICH / PS. 24
A87	a		749	NORWICH
A89	a		382	NORWICH
A91	a		382	NORWICH
A62.3	a		382	NORWICH
A92	a		382	NORWICH
A95	a		382	NORWICH / PS. 24

key

texts (see pp. 439-63)

tune name(s)

b Brownson
c Hibbard

composer attributions

Detroit Studies in Music Bibliography

General Editor
Bruno Nettl
University of Illinois at Urbana-Champaign

NICHOLAS TEMPERLEY AND CHARLES G. MANNS

Fuging Tunes
in the
Eighteenth Century

DETROIT STUDIES IN MUSIC BIBLIOGRAPHY NUMBER FORTY-NINE

INFORMATION COORDINATORS, INC.   DETROIT   1983

Copyright © 1983 by Nicholas Temperley and Charles G. Manns

Printed and bound in the United States of America
Published by
Information Coordinators, Inc.
1435-37 Randolph Street
Detroit, Michigan 48226

Book design by Vincent Kibildis
Composition by Elaine Gorzelski

Library of Congress Cataloging in Publication Data
Temperley, Nicholas.
Fuging tunes in the eighteenth century.
(Detroit studies in music bibliography ; no. 49)
Includes indexes.
1. Hymns, English — 18th century — Bibliography.
I. Manns, Charles G., 1949-   . II. Title.
III. Series: Detroit studies in music bibliography ; 49.
ML128.H8T45 1983   016.7839   83-10782
ISBN 0-89990-017-8

CONTENTS

PREFACE

T HE FUGING TUNE was an artifact of the country psalmody practice which grew up
in Britain and America in the eighteenth century. In an effort to supersede the folk
tradition of metrical psalm singing, known as the Old or Usual Way, members of a parish
congregation were taught to sing music from notes. At first these singers were supposed
to lead the whole congregation in the plain old psalm tunes in two- or three-part harmony,
but as they became more accomplished they began to sing more elaborate music. The
fuging tune evolved in those Anglican parish churches that lacked organs, and from there
it spread to Congregational and Baptist churches in England and North America.

Long considered beneath serious notice, the fuging tune has recently attracted
attention and even revival in the United States. The first scholars who examined fuging
tunes believed them to be a strictly American phenomenon,[1] but it was later realized
that they had originated in England.[2] There has never been a comprehensive study of
the subject, so that writers have sometimes fallen wide of the mark when they have had

---

[1] See, for instance, Hamilton C. MacDougall, *Early New England Psalmody* (Brattleboro, 1940),
pp. 95-98; Carl E. Lindstrom, "William Billings and His Times," *The Musical Quarterly* 15 (1939): 479-97.

[2] See Irving Lowens, "The Origins of the American Fuging Tune," *Journal of the American
Musicological Society* 6 (1953): 43-52, reprinted in Lowens, *Music and Musicians in Early America*
(New York, 1964), pp. 237-63; J. Murray Barbour, *The Church Music of William Billings* (East Lansing,
1960), pp. 67-79; Richard Crawford, preface to James Lyon, *Urania* (New York, 1974), p. xviii, n. 17;
Karl Kroeger, "The Fuging-Tune Revisited," unpublished paper delivered at the National Meeting of
the American Musicological Society, Washington, November 5, 1976; Nicholas Temperley, *The Music
of the English Parish Church* (Cambridge, 1979), pp. 170-76. The English origin of the fuging tune
was certainly known to Oscar Sonneck: see his *Francis Hopkinson and James Lyon* (Washington, 1905,
reprint 1967), pp. 148-63. See also Temperley, "The Origins of the Fuging Tune," *Royal Musical
Association Research Chronicle* 17 (1981): 1-32.

to generalize about fuging tunes. It was primarily for this reason that we decided to chart the earlier history of the genre in full detail, by preparing an analytical Census of all examples that could be found in printed sources up to the year 1800. The Census has, indeed, yielded new and often surprising facts about the origins, growth, and dissemination of fuging tunes, and has revealed sharp differences between the English and American subspecies and between practices of individual composers and compilers. It has also located the original sources of many tunes previously known only in later collections. These matters are discussed in the Historical Account, pages 3-54.

This work is also offered as illustrating a method of indexing which we believe could be profitably extended to cover all psalm and hymn tunes, of whatever complexity, in the Anglo-American repertory, or indeed in any repertory. The method is essentially simple, lends itself easily to computer storage and retrieval, and is designed to detect relationships between tunes which might otherwise pass unnoticed. Our analysis of tune structure (see page 88) suggests a way of classifying the ornate tunes of the eighteenth and nineteenth centuries.

Unfortunately our method is not compatible with the one chosen by Kate Van Winkle Keller and Carolyn Rabson for their recently published index of Anglo-American tunes from secular sources of a similar period.[3] We did consider following their system. But their decision to exclude all notes before the first downbeat of a tune, though it can be justified for secular songs and dances, does not work well for hymn tunes, which are based on a strict textual meter rather than a strong musical beat. In a psalm or hymn tune, every syllable of the text is a fundamental unit, whether represented by one or by more than one note in the tune; tunes are classified by meters, and texts are interchangeable only if the lines agree exactly in their syllabic length and stress pattern. We designed our method to fit these basic facts.

We decided for practical reasons to exclude manuscript sources from consideration. They are often hard to date, and usually appear to be copied from printed sources. We feel confident that printed editions were the primary mode of dissemination: for example, it was by the sale and later reprinting of certain popular English psalmody books that the fuging tune and parochial anthem were introduced into the American colonies in the 1750s and '60s.

Our terminal date of 1800 is also a practical limitation. Bibliographical control of printed sources is reasonably complete up to 1800. For British sources, we have been able to build up in the Psalmody Archive at the University of Illinois an extensive microfilm collection of editions, the vast majority of which we traced through the *British Union-Catalogue of Early Music*. For American sources, the American Antiquarian Society's microcard reproductions of editions listed in Charles Evans's *American Bibliography* could be supplemented, whenever necessary, by other editions which have been located by a group of scholars working in this area. But the 1800 limit is, of course,

---

[3] Kate Van Winkle Keller and Carolyn Rabson, *The National Tune Index* (New York, 1980).

an artificial one, falling perhaps just after the high tide of the fuging tune. The genre continued to flourish in Britain, the United States, and Canada in the early nineteenth century, and has survived to this day in the shapenote music of primarily Baptist communities in the southern states. The detailed study of this later history would be a large-scale project in itself, and might well involve far greater difficulties than any we have encountered. At least we hope that our Census will allow the ready identification of any eighteenth-century tunes found in post-1800 sources.

The fuging tune is hard to define precisely, and any historical conclusions about it must depend to a certain extent on the definition adopted. Earlier definitions[4] have tended to revolve around a "model" type of fuging tune which is frequently found in American psalmody books. British tunes, however, do not follow this pattern at all closely, and we therefore adopted a more general definition. We define a *tune* (i. e., a psalm or hymn tune) as a piece of music intended for strophic repetition with a sacred metrical text. (Thus anthems, set pieces, chanting tunes, and canons, all of which are

---

[4] Lowens (1964), pp. 240-41, followed by Richard Crawford in *Andrew Law, American Psalmodist* (Evanston, 1968), pp. 15-16. Our definition will include many tunes which Crawford would term "tunes with extension" (*Andrew Law*, p. 16). Kroeger, in "The Fuging-Tune Revisited," proposed a widening of Lowens' definition but still did not encompass all tunes with imitative entries producing text overlap.

FALMOUTH from William Tans'ur, *The Royal Melody Compleat: or, The New Harmony of Sion,* 3rd ed., London 1764-65 (Source P155.3), p. 60. (Newberry Library, Chicago, 7Q.190. *Reproduced by permission.*)

[60] *The Royal Melody Compleat : Or,*

Falmouth Tune. PSALM XXIX. Compofed in *Four Parts.* W. T.

Un—to the living LORD.

Un—to the living LORD.

Un—to, un—to the living LORD.

Old *Verfion.*

Verfe 1. GIVE to the LORD ye *Potentates,*
Give ye with one Accord :
All *Praife* and *Honour,* Might and Strength,
Unto the living LORD.

Verfe 2. Give Glory to His holy Name,
And honour Him alone :
Worfhip Him in His Majefty,
Within His holy *Throne.*

Verfe 3. His Voice doth rule the *Waters* all,
As He himfelf doth pleafe :
He doth prepare the *Thunder-claps,*
And governs all the Seas.

Verfe 4. The Voice of GOD, is of great Force,
And wond'rous excellent :
It is moft *mighty,* in Effect,
And moft magnificent.—*&c.*

— *To Father, Son, &c.* —

To *Falmouth*

found in country psalmody collections, are excluded.) *A tune is fuging if, in at least one phrase, two or more voice parts enter non-simultaneously, with rests preceding at least one entry, in such a way as to produce overlap of text* (i. e., two syllables sung simultaneously). The music example on page ix shows a typical fuging tune which answers to all these characteristics. The music example, *below,* on the other hand, shows a tune which is highly ornate but not fuging. Although the voices enter successively there is no point at which they produce any overlap of text. The distinction is an important one, because a frequently repeated ground of objection to fuging tunes was the fact that, by obscuring the text, they interfered with the religious thoughts of the worshippers.[5]

*   *   *

The research for this project was done at the University of Illinois at Urbana-Champaign between 1975 and 1980. It was planned by Nicholas Temperley, and carried out with the help of his research assistants Thomas McGeary, Charles G. Manns and Laurie Ryan; Charles G. Manns continued as an independent collaborator. We are deeply indebted to the Research Board, School of Music, and Music Library of the University of Illinois for the financial support that has made this work possible. Special thanks are due to Richard Crawford for giving freely of his vast knowledge of American sacred music publications in this period.

---

[5] See, for instance, Temperley, pp. 211-12; Crawford, *Andrew Law,* p. 183n.

We also express our gratitude to Karl Kroeger and Irving Lowens for generously allowing free use of their earlier work on fuging tunes; to Leonard Ellinwood and his assistant, Elizabeth Lockwood, at the Dictionary of American Hymnology for help in identifying texts; to Gillian Anderson, Sheila Craik, Roger Duce, Oliver Neighbour, Denys Parsons, Watkins Shaw, and Ruth Wilson for examining sources not directly available to us; and to Patty Manns and Barbara Young for typing parts of the original manuscript. Finally we wish to thank the many libraries which have made materials available on loan or on microfilm, more particularly the British Library, London; University Library, Cambridge; Birmingham Public Library; National Library of Scotland, Edinburgh; Glasgow Public Library; Manchester Public Library; Library of Congress, Washington; Newberry Library, Chicago; and Yale University Library.

The information in this index will eventually be incorporated into a more comprehensive, computerized index of all psalm and hymn tunes associated with English texts from sources dating from the Reformation to about 1820. We are currently at work on this Hymn Tune Index at the University of Illinois at Urbana-Champaign, under a research grant from the National Endowment for the Humanities.

Urbana, Illinois
March, 1983

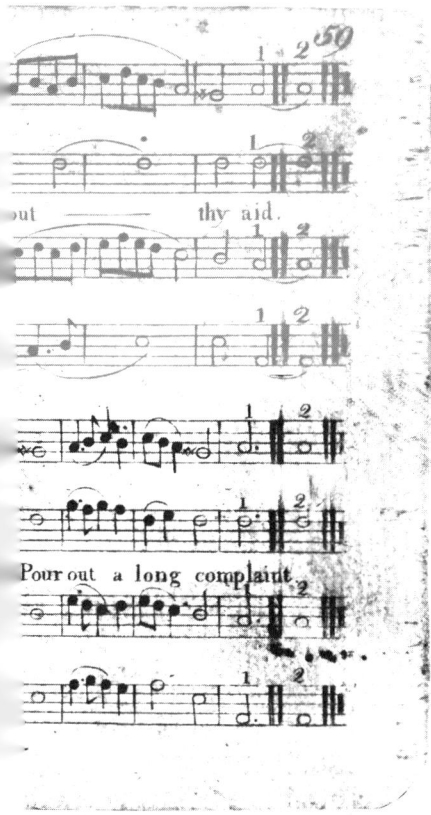

Bottom half:
NORWICH (tune 41) from Andrew Law,
Select Harmony,
New Haven 1779 (Source A47), p. 59.
(Newberry Library, Chicago,
Case VM.2116.L415.
Reproduced by permission.)

Census
of
Fuging Tunes

HISTORICAL INTRODUCTION

By Nicholas Temperley

Origins of the Fuging Tune (1690-1745)

THE FUGING TUNE was the last stage in a process. Elaboration of metrical psalm singing had begun with the introduction of singing from notes in English parish churches near the end of the seventeenth century. Before that time, singing had been congregational, monophonic (or heterophonic), and, in most churches, unaccompanied; after generations of neglect, and in the absence of any guidance from professional musicians, it had reached that slow, arhythmic, dissonant heterophony that was known as the Old Way of Singing.[1]

Contrapuntal settings of psalm tunes, sometimes known as "reports," had indeed existed in earlier times in both England and Scotland,[2] though it is quite unlikely that they had ever been used in public worship to any great extent.[3] This school of polyphonic psalm singing made its last appearance in the Scottish Psalter of 1635, a book which was never reprinted and indeed became obsolete for use in church when in 1650 the Church of Scotland adopted a new metrical version of the psalms.[4] There is no historical thread

---

[1] Described more fully in Nicholas Temperley, "The Old Way of Singing: Its Origins and Development," *Journal of the American Musicological Society* 34 (1981): 511-44.

[2] English examples in *The Whole Psalmes in Foure Partes* (London: John Day, 1563); John Cosyn, *Musike of Six, and Five Partes* (London, 1585); William Damon, *The Psalmes of David in English Meter* (London, 1579). For Scottish examples see Kenneth Elliott, ed., *Music of Scotland 1500-1700,* Musica Britannica, 15 (London, 1957): 134, 136.

[3] Nicholas Temperley, *The Music of the English Parish Church,* 2 vols. (Cambridge, 1979), 1: 72-73.

[4] Millar Patrick, *Four Centuries of Scottish Psalmody* (London, 1949), pp. 90-95.

connecting this earlier polyphonic practice with the eighteenth-century fuging tune; nor is the latter linked in any direct way with Continental developments.

The reform of psalm singing in the Church of England around 1700 has been described elsewhere.[5] It was closely bound up with the high-church devotional movement, expressed in the formation of religious societies of young men in many parishes to meet for devotional purposes under the direction of the clergyman. The societies took it upon themselves to improve the quality of public worship, and to this end they employed singing teachers to teach them to sing from notes, generally in two or three vocal parts (tenor/bass or alto/tenor/bass). In churches that could not afford an organ, the group of young men became in effect a voluntary choir, and it soon advanced beyond its initial purpose of leading the congregational singing. As Arthur Bedford wrote in 1711, "The *good Effects* of *Divine Musick* are evident from many Places in the Country, where the Inhabitants learn to sing *Psalms* in *Consort,* tho' from a mean *Artist:* And if it is thus with *Psalms,* the meanest Part of *Divine Musick,* what might we expect from finer *Composures,* taught by such, who are better skill'd in so noble a *Science?*"[6]

There was no lack of musicians, publishers, and teachers ready to take up such a challenge, and in the early decades of the eighteenth century an astonishing quantity of new church music was provided for parish choirs. Their first book, generally, had been John Playford's *The Whole Book of Psalms . . . in Three Parts,* published in 1677 but attaining its greatest popularity between 1695 and 1730.[7] This included the whole of Sternhold and Hopkins's metrical psalms, set out with tunes which were almost entirely the ones that had been used for generations. Virtually no new tunes had been added to the English repertory since Ravenscroft's book of 1621. In the 1690s, however, composers began to write new tunes, which were printed in a series of books catering to the new developments. Prominent among them were Henry Playford's *The Divine Companion* (1701); Tate and Brady's *A Supplement to the New Version of the Psalms* (1700, greatly expanded in 1708); and John Bishop's *A Set of New Psalm Tunes* (1710). In all these books, trained professional musicians provided tunes, often of fine quality, which distilled the current style of art music into a form sufficiently simple for a country congregation to sing when led by a rehearsed and literate choir. Henry Playford went one step further by including anthems explicitly designed for parish choirs, as well as hymns with figured-bass accompaniment for domestic use.

These developments were eagerly taken up by a new breed of country singing teachers, who travelled from parish to parish, selling their books and assembling temporary "singing schools" in which they taught volunteers how to use them. This was the pattern that was to form the basis for the rise of the fuging tune in both England

---

[5] Temperley, *Parish Church,* 1: 100-105, 141-62.

[6] Arthur Bedford, *The Great Abuse of Musick* (London, 1711), p. 229.

[7] See Nicholas Temperley, "John Playford and the Metrical Psalms," *Journal of the American Musicological Society* 25 (1972): 331-78, esp. pp. 373-75.

and America. One of the earliest of these teachers whose name is known was Daniel
Warner, who worked in the area around Oxford and published a series of psalmody
books beginning in 1694. The book which formed the model for later publications
was *The Psalm-Singer's Compleat Companion,* published by Elias Hall, another
psalmody teacher, in 1706. It contained metrical psalms, hymns, and a few anthems,
with the tenor part (written in the G clef) carrying the tune, supported by a vocal bass,
and a subordinate alto part; some pieces in the book also have a soprano part. Hall
was active in Lancashire, which, together with the West Riding of Yorkshire and the
North Midlands, was the cradle of the developments to come.

The singing master, who was very often his own bookseller and sometimes his own
engraver, was self-appointed, and generally lacked formal schooling or musical training.
At first he compiled his books chiefly from the works of the Playfords, but as time went
on, country composers emerged with their own tunes and anthems. Though they evidently
modeled their work at first on the professionals, it soon took on a singular quality of its
own, in which, at best, an attractive freshness and vigor compensates for the lack of skill
in harmony and counterpoint.

As the country choirs became a recognized and popular institution, they began
to sing not only anthems at the end of the service, but new and difficult psalm tunes to
replace the plain old ones that everybody knew. These met with opposition, from
clergymen who saw that the singing was becoming a performance for its own sake rather
than an aid to worship, and from older members of the congregation who did not like
being reduced to silence. But the pleasure and self-satisfaction of the singers furthered
the pecuniary interest of the teacher-compilers. With this double motivation, country
psalmody flourished mightily throughout the eighteenth century and into the nineteenth.
As the singers grew more sure of their position, their tunes became more flamboyant.

The first sign of elaboration was in the use of melismas. Old psalm tunes had
normally had only one note to a syllable: occasionally one or two syllables would carry
a pair of notes, and there was an increase in these small melismas in Playford's 1677
collection. The new tunes of the *Supplement to the New Version* and the *Divine
Companion* were more systematic in their use of melismas, and were often in triple
time (Example 1, page 6). This tendency could be taken a step further by adding
an "Alleluia" at the end of each line of the text. The first tune in which this was done
was the Easter Hymn from *Lyra Davidica* (1708), an anonymous collection that cannot
be decisively linked with the Church of England. This hymn and tune (Example 2,
page 7) has remained a popular favorite ever since, and supplied a model for further
elaborations later on. Its two- and three-note melismas differ from earlier ones in that
they do not always move by step to a passing note, but may join two harmony notes a
third or even a fifth apart.

Another innovation was the repeating line, generally the last, which extended the
form of the typical common-meter tune. Perhaps this suggested the idea of having only
one vocal part sing the line the first time, answered by the rest or by the whole choir or
congregation. One of these "repeating tunes" is *Adeste fideles,* still a popular favorite

EXAMPLE 1. *St. John's Tune*   Psalm 92 [New Version]

How good and plea - sant must it be, to thank the Lord most high!

And, with re - pea - ted Hymns of praise, his Name to mag - ni - fy!

With ev' - ry Mor - ning's ear - ly Dawn, his Good - ness to re - late;

And of his con - stant Truth, each Night, the glad Ef - fects re - peat.

— From *A Supplement to the New Version of Psalms,* 6th ed. (1708)

EXAMPLE 2. *The Resurrection*

Je-sus Christ is Risen to-day   Hal-le-Hal-le-lu-iah   Our tri-um-phant Ho-ly day

Hal-le-Hal-le-lu-iah

etc.

— From *Lyra Davidica* (1708)

(drawn from an English Catholic source of the 1740s).[8] A short step from this was to
have some lines of the text allocated exclusively to individual parts or pairs of parts:
probably the first tune with this feature was one by John Bishop.[9] There were hazards
in using this method for a strophic tune. The subdivision of the text might work very
well in one verse, but not so well in another, and the words uttered by some of the
singers might not make sense. However, if this was a point for clerical objections,
it does not seem to have troubled either the singers or the composers unduly. The
voices could even come in one at a time, building up to a climax (Example 3, page 8).

With this kind of effect the tune was beginning to sound very much like a
performance for an audience, and was coming closer in character to an anthem or "set
piece." The final step in this direction was taken when some sections of the tune were
sung in counterpoint, so that different parts of the text actually overlapped. When this
happened, a true fuging tune had been born. At first, the imitation and text overlap were
cautious and unobtrusive; perhaps clerical objections to obscuring the text acted as a
brake, especially when combined with the difficulty of chopping up the text in a way
that suited all verses of a hymn or psalm. It was not until the late 1740s that the fully-
fledged fuging tune, with a section in four-part imitative counterpoint, got under way.

---

[8] The tune was composed by J. F. Wade, an English Catholic in exile at Douay (France),
and survives in a manuscript source of the 1740s: it was first published in 1782. See J. Stéphan,
Adeste Fideles (Buckfast Abbey, 1947); Erik Routley, *The English Carol* (London, 1958), p. 147.
    [9] Reprinted, Temperley, *Parish Church,* 2: 104.

EXAMPLE 3.   Psalm 119, The 5th Part [Old Version]

— From John Bishop, *A Supplement to the New Psalm-Book* (1725)

As with the other developments, the archetypes for the fuging tune were written by professional composers, and the possibilities for imitating them were taken up by country psalmodists some time later. The first tune that answers to our definition, **670**, was by Robert King, organist of St. Martin-in-the-Fields, London, and it was contributed to Henry Playford's *Divine Companion* (1701), where it takes the form of a vocal duet with continuo accompaniment, intended no doubt for home use (Example 4a, *below*). When this book was heavily plundered by most of the country psalmody collections that followed, King's tune, shorn of its bass figures, was taken into the repertory as an early model for the fuging tune: it even reached an American collection (A22) as Psalm 50 (Example 4b, page 10). Its shape, with the fuging section reserved for the repeated last line, may have guided the later development of the genre.

The other archetype, **106**, is from the second edition of John Chetham's *Book of Psalmody* (1722). Though the book is a country collection, emanating from the West Riding of Yorkshire, this anonymous piece has clear signs of being written by an accomplished professional (which Chetham himself was not). It ingeniously gets over the problem of strophic repetition by choosing two successive pairs of verses from Psalm 24 which have almost identical words. The setting begins with a duet for tenor and bass in triple time, then changes to split common time with an alternating question-and-answer duet, setting off the women's voices against the men's and modulating to the dominant key; it ends with a triumphant line for the full chorus. It sounds more

EXAMPLE 4a. An Hymn Set by Mr. Robert King for Two Voc.

—.Tune **670**, from Source P51

like a set piece than a tune, but the imitative element is confined to one short passage (mm. 13-15). The tune had great influence. It reappeared in different forms in later collections, sometimes with greatly increased imitation and text overlap.[10] It also spawned several later fuging tunes, one of which, **858**, was the only one in the first edition of John Arnold's influential collection, *The Compleat Psalmodist* (1741).

EXAMPLE 4b.   Psalm 50

— Tune **670**, from Source A22

---

[10] The original (1722) and "fugalized" (1744) versions are reprinted in Temperley, *Parish Church*, 2: 108, 110.

TABLE 1. PRINTED FUGING TUNES UP TO 1745

Source	Date	New Tunes No.	Fuging Section	Origin	Old Tunes No.
P51	1701	670	2 duet lines	By Robert King	
P51.2	1707				670
P51.3	1709				670
P51.4	1722				670
P71.2	1722	106	1 duet line	Anonymous	
P86	1724				106
P89	-1725				670
P80.B	c1725				670
P80.C	c1725				670
P86.4	1731				106
P104	1731-	597	2 lines of 4-part imit.	By Arthur Bedford	
D1	1733	653	1 line of 4-part imit.	By Arthur Bedford	
P88.3	1733	857	1 duet line	Derived from 106	
		860	1 line with "late entry"	Influenced by 106	
P107	c1733				106,860
P111a	1736				106
P117	1740	858	1 line with "late entry"	Derived from 857	
P118	1740				857
P111a.7	1741				106
P118.2	1741				857
P120	1741	911	1 line with "late entry"	Anonymous	857,860
P123	1744	828	1 duet line	Influenced by 106	106*
P124	1745	383	3-part imit. in 1 line	Anonymous	
P125	1745	993	4 duet lines	By John Broderip	
P126	c1745	567	1 duet line	By John Alcock	

*In a "fugalized" version, with 3 duet lines containing imitative entries.

Until about 1745 the development of the fuging tune was dominated by these two archetype tunes and their derivatives, as can be seen in Table 1, *above,* which lists all known printings of fuging tunes up to that date. Few books contained more than a single specimen. Of the twelve different tunes, five were by named composers. King, Broderip and Alcock were organists; Bedford was a clergyman and polemical writer, who believed passionately in the moral value of music, and tried his hand at composition. His tunes were intended for the private devotions of religious societies, and were set to hymn texts not used in Anglican worship, but they are forward-looking in the fact that they contain lines with actual four-part imitation of a rather rough variety. Bedford's could be called the first tunes that are fuging in the fullest sense.

Most of these early tunes have only two-part imitation, either in lines with only two voices, or where one voice has a "late entry" and then catches up with the others. Apart from Bedford's tunes, only **383**, printed by John Bellamy (who conducted a singing school at West Redford, Nottinghamshire), attempts anything more than two-part imitation. But this, though an interesting experiment, was never reprinted.

It is fair to say, then, that up to 1745 only tentative moves had taken place in the development of the fuging tune, however significant they may appear in retrospect. I have called the few examples that had gained any popularity "archetypes" rather than "prototypes," in the sense that they were not yet in a form that would become standard. Though undoubtedly fuging tunes by our definition, with imitative entries producing text overlap, most of them employed only a mild or marginal amount of imitation.

Establishment of a Genre (1745-1765)

I N THE LATER 1740s there is a sudden lurch forward. For the first time, several country psalmodists produce books containing substantial numbers of fuging tunes which appear to be of local origin, and which embody sections of full four-part imitation.

At this stage the country psalmodists do not appear to have emulated cathedral or other professional music. There was, after all, a considerable body of parochial anthems already in use, going back some three decades, whose general harmonic and melodic style was similar to that of homophonic psalm tunes of country origin. They were largely based on common chords, with a preference for root-position triads or open fifths; the treatment of dissonance was free and unsystematic, with seemingly casual false relations and clashing passing notes; parallel fifths and octaves were not uncommon; the tenor was normally the leading melodic part, with occasional solos or duets for other voices; single words were sometimes repeated or drawn out into long melismas for illustrative effect. Many of these anthems contained one or two passages of four-part imitation. Two good examples that had been many times reprinted are *By the rivers of Babylon,* probably by Robert or James Barber (1723), and the anonymous *Great is the Lord* (c. 1730).[11] The passage "If I forget thee, O Jerusalem" from *By the rivers of Babylon* could well have been a model for the fuging sections of British fuging tunes of the mid-century. The only remaining technical problem was to incorporate this type of counterpoint within the confines of a strophically repeated tune with a metrical text. The prototypes already discussed, up to and including Bedford's two specimens, can be seen as attempts to deal with this problem.

---

11 These anthems are reprinted in Temperley, *Parish Church,* 2: 85-95; see especially p. 94.

Because several collections are undated, it has been difficult to know where the credit for the primary development of the fuging tune should be bestowed. Four pioneering psalmodists, all working in different parts of the country, seem to share the honors: Michael Beesly, James Evison, William East, and Joseph Watts. If we were to go by imprint date, Evison could claim priority, for his *Compleat Book of Psalmody,* with four fully fuging tunes, is dated 1747. But there is good reason to believe that Beesly was the real originator.

Two of the three psalmody books that Beesly published were "collected" by himself. They were sold (according to the title pages) by booksellers at Oxford, Newbury, Reading, Gloucester, and Winchester. All are undated. One, however, is called *A Collection of 20 New Psalm Tunes Compos'd with veriety of Fuges after a differant manner to any yet Extant,* and indeed the tunes in it are all fuging, though two of them were not in fact new. The only copy is in the British Library, where it is assigned a date of [c. 1760] ; I followed this date in my book *The Music of the English Parish Church* (where the book is numbered PC 177), but I now have reason to emend it, and assign a new number (129a). The fact that one of the tunes in the book is also printed in Abraham Milner's *The Psalm Singers Companion* with the name BEESLY strongly suggests that Beesly printed it before Milner, whose book is dated 1751. But more compelling evidence comes from the comparison of tunes found both in Beesly's *Collection* and in Evison's *Compleat Book* of 1747 (**88, 326, 402, 948**). In each case Evison made a number of changes in the music which tidied up anomalies, smoothed dissonances, removed consecutives and so on. It is scarcely credible that these alterations could have been made in the opposite direction. Thus Beesly's book probably dates from about 1746—or even earlier. It seems that the claim made in its title (cited above) is almost literally true. He did not claim to have composed the tunes he printed.[12]

It is significant that one of the only two existing models for a tune with four-part imitation, tune **597** (by Arthur Bedford), was reprinted in Beesly's book (and in no other). But about half of the new tunes use a new principle not borrowed from Bedford. They have one line, usually the last, in four-part imitation, generally in voice order (BTAS or SATB). The voices enter at one-measure intervals, and the third and fourth voices have the same subject, answer and countersubject that have just been sung by the first and second, often with little or no additional counterpoint (Example 5, page 16). This simple procedure, analogous to a stretto, clearly simplified the problem a great deal for the untrained contrapuntist. It was adopted by many later composers, and as it seems to be the "differant manner to any yet Extant" claimed by Beesly on his title page, I will call it the Beesly technique. Other tunes in the book try out various other methods of imitation, usually with little success. It is apparent that the composer(s) had difficulty in handling more than two voices. In most of the tunes the tenor and bass make good music, but the upper voices introduce anomalies.

---

12 For more detailed discussion see Temperley, "The Origins," pp. 7-16.

Seven of the fuging tunes printed in Beesly's *Collection* were also printed by William Knapp in *New Church Melody* [c. 1752]; these include the very popular tune POOL(E) (**1112**). Five of the seven use the Beesly technique. They were later attributed to Knapp, but though Knapp's book may have been the source for later compilers, Knapp himself makes no direct claim to have composed them; indeed he confesses that "Some of the Anthems and Psalm-Tunes are not entirely of my own composition." Two other tunes from Beesly's *Collection* were to be popular for a long time: **141** (later called SHOREHAM or PSALM 150) and **948** (later called CRANLEY). Beesly's other two books are *A Book of Psalmody* and *An Introduction to Psalmody*. They make no claim to originality, and on internal evidence appear to date from about 1751 and 1756 respectively.

Evison seems to have been active in the southeast. Copies of *A Compleat Book of Psalmody* have been found in a number of Sussex churches, and Evison was evidently a collaborator of Starling Goodwin, an organist and writing master at Maidstone, Kent, who wrote a dedicatory poem for the book. There are four fuging tunes in the 1747 edition, nine in 1751, and twelve in 1754. Three of the ones in the first edition are tidied-up versions of Beesly's, though even in their revised versions the fuging sections often make little sense. The one new tune (**345**) is more competently written.[13] Later editions of Evison's book add more tunes on similar lines.

East had a singing school at Waltham, Leicestershire, and the booksellers listed on the title pages of his books were located in that county and the neighboring ones (Derbyshire, Nottinghamshire, Lincolnshire, and Rutland). The first edition of *The Voice of Melody,* dating from about 1748, contained only one fuging tune, but in 1750 it was extended to two volumes with a spectacular expansion to twenty-eight fuging tunes. *Sacred Melody* (1754) is the only one of East's in which *all* the tunes are fuging: it contains, in the words of the title page, "A Curious and Select Number of Psalm-Tunes, in the Fugeing, Syncopating and binding taste"—this is probably the first use of the word *fuging* in this connection. Further examples were included in his

---

[13] To avoid misunderstanding I wish to emphasize that these and similar judgments on the composers of fuging tunes are not made on the basis of criteria applicable to art music of the eighteenth century. Although the psalmody books often contained introductions stating rules of composition derived from art music (such as the ban on consecutive fifths and octaves), and although some compilers attempted to follow these rules, I do not condemn tunes because these rules are broken, or because they contain nonfunctional dissonance, progressions not used in art music, etc. My criterion is a more general one that applies to any polyphonic music, whatever the style: a successful composer must be able to control the harmony and the individual melodic lines at the same time. The harmonic style of country psalmody can be judged from the many two-part tunes, or from homophonic tunes in three and four parts. When the introduction of contrapuntal entries leads to a breakdown of this harmonic style, it is clear that the composer's technique is inadequate to the situation. (For further discussions of the style of country psalmody see Temperley, *Parish Church,* 1:190-96, and J. Murray Barbour, *The Church Music of William Billings* [East Lansing, 1960], pp. 66-69.)

Collection of Church Musick, published about 1755.[14] In all East printed at least
fifty-three new fuging tunes and perhaps as many as fifty-five, so that in quantity he
was the most important of the pioneers. Some of his tunes were attributed to other
country composers—two to William Costall of Caythorpe[15] (who was also the engraver
of *The Voice of Melody*); one each to Broderip and Knapp; thirteen to John Everet,
of Grantham, Lincolnshire, who later compiled his own collection, published by East
in 1757. Others were lifted from other country psalmodists, with what appears to be
a deliberate attempt to disguise them: for instance **143** and **178** are obviously cribbed
from **948** and **402** respectively, but they are assigned new texts, and their opening
measures are altered.

In tunes borrowed from Beesly or Evison, East shows his superior technical skill
by tidying up some of the faulty passages in the original tunes. Many of the anonymous
examples first printed by East have the now popular four-part imitation in voice order
at one-measure intervals, often, but not necessarily, using the Beesly technique. Others,
including most of Everet's, are more ambitious and elaborate in their plan, sometimes
with overlapping fuging sections. One of the most remarkable is Everet's tune **868**. It
has several contrasting sections, four out of five of them fuging; many "choosing notes"
(the alto part often divides); and some beautiful suggestions of sixteenth-century harmony.
East did not claim to have composed any tunes himself. None of his products became
enormously popular, though many were reprinted. (Table 2, pages 18-19, lists the most
popular fuging tunes in the repertory.)

Watts described himself on the title page of *A Choice Collection of Church Music*
(1749) as "of Fennycompton, in the County Warwick," and his book was also sold by
"Mr. Calcut, Banbury, Oxon." It contains nine fuging tunes, some taken from Beesly
with virtually no alteration, others new: one Watts claimed as his own, the rest are
unattributed. Of the four pioneers he achieved the distinction of producing the greatest
favorites: **192** (Example 6, pages 16-17: most commonly called OTFORD) and **1060**
(later NEWBURY). Both, moreover, are of a plan that would later be almost standard,
particularly in America. One is HHFH, the other HEHF;[16] in both, the fuging section
has four voices entering at one-measure intervals; there are consecutive fifths and octaves
and bare-fifth cadences; the counterpoint produces harsh non-functional dissonance.
These tunes have all the earmarks of the developed fuging tune, and in view of their
popularity and early date, they have a better claim than any others to have set the style.

---

14 Edith B. Schnapper, ed., *The British Union-Catalogue of Early Music,* 2 vols. (London,
1957), gives a date of [c. 1750] for this work. But it is made up in great part of sheets of two earlier
publications (P137 and P151), the later of which has an imprint date of 1754. Accordingly, we
have emended the date to [c. 1755].

15 He is so described in the list of subscribers to P151. There is a Caythorpe in Nottinghamshire
and another in Lincolnshire, both some twenty miles from Waltham.

16 See page 88 for an explanation of structural abbreviations.

EXAMPLE 5.   Psalm 5 [New Version]

Lord, hear the voice of my Com-plaint, of my Com - plaint,

Lord, hear the voice of my Com - plaint, of my Com-plaint,

Lord, hear the voice of my Com-plaint, Com - plaint,

Lord, hear the voice of my Com - plaint,

— Tune **1042**, from Source P129a

EXAMPLE 6.   Psalm 8th Ver. 1st [Old Version]

O God our Lord, how won - der - ful are thy works

16

EXAMPLE 6—*Continued*

Thy fame sur-mounts in dig - - -

Thy fame sur-mounts in

ev' - ry where; Thy fame sur-mounts in dig - ni - ty, thy fame sur-mounts in

Thy fame sur-mounts in dig - ni - ty, thy fame sur - mounts in

- - ni - ty the high-est heav'ns that are. are.

dig - ni - ty

dig - ni - ty the high-est heav'ns that are. are.

— Tune **192**, from Source P135

TABLE 2. THE THIRTY-ONE FUGING TUN

Tune No.	Name(s), (Composer if known)	Meter
1060	STROUD, (NEW) NEWBERY, CUDHAM	CM
192	CANTERBURY, OTFORD	CM
115	BEESLY, CHARLESTOWN	CM
948	CRANLEY	CM
106	BERWICK	CMD
670	GAINSBOROUGH (R. King)	8^6
690	YARMOUTH	CM
860	LONDON NEW	$6^4\,4^4$
125	OXFORD, WROTHAM	CM
350	KNOWL (Knapp?)	8^6
458	BROMLEY (R. Broderip)	LM
1042	HAM-PRESTON	CM
141	MAPHAM, SHOREHAM	LM
381	KNIGHTON	CM
402	BRIDGWATER	LM
345	DARKING	CM
846	DOWN	CM
974	BRABROOK	CMD
382	ST. NICHOLAS'	CM
1033	CREEKMOOR	CM
1112	POOLE (NEW)	LM
1161	HAM WORTHY	CM
219	——	CM
222	MILE END (NEW) (Davis)	LM
272	HARBRO' NEW	CM
320	SANDWICH NEW (Knapp?)	CM
348	CORFE CASTLE (Knapp?)	CM
475	GREENWICH, ST. THOMAS'S	LM
843	DERBY (Stephenson)	CM
867	SOUTHWARK	668668
1002	WARWICK (Stephenson)	CM

For an explanation of abbreviations in the Structure column, see page 88.
When a letter is printed in italics it indicates that the line of music referred to repeats
an earlier phrase of the text. In the Name(s) column, the earliest British name
is given first, followed by any other names commonly used in British sources.

Structure	Probable First Compiler, Date	Number of Printings			
		P	D	S	Total
HEHF	Watts, 1749	36	1	1	38
HHFH	Watts, 1749	28	7	2	37
HHHH*F*	Beesly, c1746	13	5	-	18
FHFF	Beesly, c1746	16	-	-	16
HHHFHHHH	Chetham, 1722	14	-	-	14
HHHHFF	H. Playford, 1701	14	-	-	14
HFHF	Watts, 1749	13	1	-	14
HHHEHHHF	Holdroyd, 1732	14	-	-	14
HHHH*F*	Watts, 1749	13	-	-	13
FHEHHHO	Knapp, c1752	13	-	-	13
HHH*OFOF*	T. Williams, 1789	8	4	1	13
FEFE	Beesly, c1746	13	-	-	13
EFEF	Beesly, c1746	11	-	-	11
FHE*E*HH	Beesly, c1746	11	-	-	11
HHHF	Evison, 1747	11	-	-	11
HHHH*HF*	Evison, 1747	10	-	-	10
HHFO	A. Williams, 1763	7	3	-	10
HHF*HFHFHFHFH*	*Gospel Magazine*, 1774	3	7	-	10
EEHF*H*	Evison or Beesly, c1751	8	1	-	9
FH*H*FHH	Beesly, c1746	9	-	-	9
HHOF	Beesly, c1746	9	-	-	9
EFHFH	Beesly, c1746	9	-	-	9
HHHF*H*	Watts, 1749	8	-	-	8
FHHF	Addington, 1786	3	5	-	8
EFH*H*FH	Addington, 1786	3	5	-	8
HHHF*O*	Knapp, c1752	8	-	-	8
HHFF	Knapp, c1752	8	-	-	8
HHHF	R. Cook, c1770-5	6	2	-	8
FHF*FFF*	Stephenson, c1758	8	-	-	8
FHHHFFF	Addington, 1786	3	5	-	8
FHF*FF*	Stephenson, 1760	8	-	-	8

After 1750 a number of other psalmodists made their own contributions. William Knapp, glover and parish clerk of Poole in Dorset, had already published a popular *Sett of New Psalms and Anthems* in 1738. In his second book, *New Church Melody* (1753),[17] he included seven of Beesly's fuging tunes and eleven new ones, suggesting in the preface that most of them were his own; we have assumed that all those not found in earlier publications were composed by Knapp. Many of his tunes use the Beesly technique. He was more skillful than many of these early psalmodists: on the whole, his counterpoint works, even in four parts.

William Tans'ur, the eccentric poet, bookseller, theorist, and composer, played a less important part in the overall development of the fuging tune than has generally been suggested. Only three of his nine psalmody collections include fuging tunes. Those in *The Royal Melody Compleat,* Book II (1755), were important in America for a time because this book was reprinted by Daniel Bayley at Boston in 1767, but they soon afterwards dropped out of the repertory. They are all claimed as Tans'ur's own, and share one characteristic: the fuging section is an optional "Chorus," which repeats the last two lines of text after a homophonic tune, complete in itself, has ended on a full cadence in the home key.[18] They are technically poor, and almost limited to root-position harmony.

John Arnold included the occasional fuging tune[19] in some of his own compilations, put out from his headquarters at Great Warley, Essex, but the bulk of those he published were in *The Leicestershire Harmony* (1759), the whole of which, according to its title page, was "composed . . . by an Eminent Master of the County of Leicester." Some of these tunes are very long, almost set pieces, but despite the "eminence" claimed for their composer, they make little harmonic sense. Arnold himself later professed to be rather scornful of fuging tunes, for he wrote in the preface to *Church Music Reformed:*

> Most of the Tunes which are now published, being Productions
> chiefly of Country Singing Masters, . . . plainly prove that
> such Composers are not acquainted with that Species of Music,
> which is proper for Parochial Singing, as their Tunes mostly
> consist of what they call Fuges, or (more properly) Imitations;
> and are, indeed, fit to be sung by those only who made them.[20]

Joseph Stephenson's first fuging tune, PSALM 3 (**843**), turned out to be a great favorite, which was reprinted forty-five times up to 1800. It appeared as an appendage to *An Anthem Taken Out of the 44 Chap. of Isaiah,* published to celebrate the victories of Frederick the Great of Prussia at Rossbach and Leuthen (1757) in the Seven Years'

---

[17] The first edition of this work is undated, but it was advertised in the *Salisbury Journal* (no. 810, 3 September 1753) for publication on 24 September. I am grateful to Betty Matthews for this reference. The second edition is dated 1754.

[18] For an example see **217**, reprinted in Temperley, *Parish Church*, 2: 112.

[19] One of these, **1018**, lost its "fugue" when reprinted in American collections, and so these later appearances find no place in our Census.

[20] See, for example, **990**, reprinted in Temperley, *Parish Church*, 2: 43.

War. Set to an otherwise unknown paraphrase of Psalm 3, the common-meter tune has no less than three fuging entries using the Beesly technique. In his *Church Harmony Sacred to Devotion* (3rd edition, 1760), Stephenson did not reprint this tune, but provided twenty-four other new ones, all claimed as his own; a number of them were popular, and two (**302, 1002**) were in the "favorite" category, particularly in America, where they were known as PSALM 34 and MILFORD (Andrew Law named the latter, no doubt, after his birthplace at Milford, Connecticut). Stephenson came from Poole, and may well have been influenced by Knapp; the latter wrote a commendatory letter to the reader as a foreword to *Church Harmony.* In the great majority of his tunes Stephenson uses the Beesly technique. He claims on the title page to pay special heed to word setting, and on the whole this claim is borne out (e. g. in **220**). Stephenson was more musical and literate than some of his country colleagues.

Several lesser "masters" of the fuging tune also emerged in this period, but for whatever reason, their tunes did not find much favor with later compilers. Uriah Davenport produced a dozen specimens, but none venture beyond the old-fashioned "duet" and "late entry" types of fuging section. Jonas Pratt provided only two, but they are highly fugal. J. French (his first name is not known) published eight new tunes, several of which use the Beesly technique; Benjamin West preferred to experiment with more irregular forms of imitation, but his technique was not equal to the task.[21] (Neither French nor West, it seems, was connected with his American namesake.) A collection by two Leicestershire schoolmasters, William Barnes and William Carpendale,[22] contains fifteen new fuging tunes of some complexity, but none of them appears in any later book. Other compilers, such as Abraham Adams and Matthew Wilkins, contented themselves largely with reprinting fuging tunes from earlier collections.

All the books so far considered were designed for Anglican parochial use, and it was in parish churches, certainly, that the fuging tune developed. Of the main dissenting bodies, the Congregationalists and Presbyterians had followed the Anglican movement

---

[21] See, for example, **990**, reprinted in Temperley, *Parish Church,* 2: 43.

[22] This book (P186a), hitherto unknown, was identified by Karl Kroeger in 1981. We are indebted to Dr. Kroeger for supplying a photocopy of the copy he discovered at Nottingham Central Library, and for providing supporting information. A proposal to publish the book by subscription appeared in *The Leicester and Nottingham Gazette* on 24 December 1762, and the same paper on 12 February 1763 carried an announcement of expected publication on Lady Day (25 March). The preface is signed "W. Barnes" and dated "Long Clawson, March 21^t, 1763." It includes the following statement: "The Author of half thereof (my particular Friend lately deceasd [i.e. William Carpendale]) and my self had each of us Compos'd several Psalm Tunes & Anthems, not with a design of making them public: only with a view to practise them in our own Choirs; till a Year or two ago, we (at the desire of some of our Acquaintance) corrected them in order for publication, but in the mean time my friend died. After his decease his friends gave me all his Tunes with permission to publish them at discretion." There is nothing to indicate which tunes are by Barnes and which by Carpendale. It is more than likely that other local searches, similar to the one carried out by Kroeger in the North Midlands, would turn up other local psalmody books not so far recorded.

for regular singing from notes early in the eighteenth century,[23] but their Calvinist tradition was opposed to elaborate music or the formation of choirs, and the tune supplements to Isaac Watts's psalms and hymns remained conservative and strictly monophonic or homophonic until late in the century. The Baptists were still engaged in controversy over the validity of any kind of singing in worship.[24]

Nevertheless, several enterprising compilers tried to make their books attractive to Anglicans and dissenters alike, and were careful to respect the prejudices of the latter. Thus John Hill, in *A New Book of Psalmody* (c. 1757),[25] included a number of Isaac Watts's hymns and psalm paraphrases, which only dissenters would have used in worship. But it is noteworthy that all ten of the *fuging* tunes in the book are set to psalms from the New Version of Tate and Brady, and are thus for Anglican use. Similarly James Hewett's *Introduction to Singing* (1765) takes most of its texts from Watts, but its three fuging tunes have Old Version psalm texts. On the other hand Abraham Milner's book of 1751, though dominated by conservative settings of old psalm tunes, has also a few fuging tunes (none of them new), some with texts of Dr. Watts. These are the earliest examples of such a conjunction, the next being in Caleb Ashworth's *Collection of Tunes* (c. 1760).

The most important early collection of this "ecumenical" kind is *The Universal Psalmodist* of Aaron Williams (1763). Williams was himself a dissenter, and is said to have been clerk to the Scottish Church at London Wall (in the City of London). He offered his book to "all Country Churches as well as . . . the Congregations and other Religious Societies in London and Westminster." In his preface he quotes Dr. Watts, attacks the choirs of charity children (a peculiarity of Anglican town churches), but praises "those little country societies, the design of which is to promote a regular method of singing," and asserts that "if the congregation would take the trouble to learn as they do, they might sing with them with great pleasure and delight."[26] His collection contains only three fuging tunes, but both the new ones (PENBURY, **352**, and DOWN, **846**) are assigned to hymns by Isaac Watts, and were to be reprinted in America with those texts.

By 1765, then, the character of the fuging tune was decisively established. It was a product of the country parish church, whose elaborate four-part imitative counterpoint was suited to the self-appointed choirs who performed there; but it was to be copied in other Protestant churches in England, in the American colonies, and even, to a small extent, in Scotland.

---

23 Louis F. Benson, *The English Hymn: Its Development and Use* (Richmond, Va., 1915), pp. 89-90. See W[illiam] L[awrence], *A Collection of Tunes, Suited to the Various Metres in Mr. Watts's Imitation of the Psalms of David* (London, 1719).

24 Benson, pp. 91-100. For evidence of the continuance of the controversy in the late eighteenth century see Gilbert Boyce, *Serious Thoughts on the Present Mode and Practice of Singing in the Public Worship of God* (Wisbech, 1785).

25 The date [c. 1730] assigned to this work in Schnapper is much too early. By means of research based on the List of Subscribers we have arrived at a range of years [1754-61]: any date within this range is possible in terms of the contents of the book.

26 Aaron Williams, *The Universal Psalmodist* (London, 1763), p. iv.

The Later British Fuging Tune (1765-1800)

A FTER THE EARLY 1760s the British fuging tune divides into three streams: the traditional parish-church type; the kind used in dissenting chapels and in Scotland; and the "reform" tune written by professional composers with the intention of raising musical standards.

Fuging tunes of the traditional kind continued to be popular (Table 2, pages 18-19), and were now often accompanied by instruments. We can gain a vivid idea of the situation at the turn of the century from one of the "reformers," William Gresham, organist of Dunstable:

> In many country Churches, I have frequently heard some of
> the worst portions of the Psalms, from Sternhold and Hopkins'
> version, sung in ill-constructed Fugues, replete with disallowances
> or false concords, with the words so broken, and words and
> half-words repeated and jumbled together in a manner seemingly
> more calculated to raise the idea of a Catch Club, than to inspire
> Devotion; and the Congregation, being excluded from joining,
> by the nature of the Music, are often obliged patiently to hear
> this jargon. . . . The usual manner of executing the four Parts
> in country Churches is very singular; for the Air, or principal
> Part, is uniformly sung by Tenor Voices, and the other two
> Parts, which should be Accompaniments to the Air and Bass,
> are sung by Treble and Counter-Tenor Voices; and are thereby
> frequently made too predominant; and, for want of sufficient
> Voices, the Treble is often omitted, and the Counter made
> completely to overpower the Air, by being played on a Clarinet
> or two, and in the Treble Octave.[27]

The repertory of fuging tunes sung in this traditional manner probably remained more or less unaltered. There was a sharp decline, in the 1760s and '70s, in the production of *new* fuging tunes, as Table 3, page 26, clearly shows; and although the production picked up again towards the end of the century, the new tunes were mostly of the "reform" variety, to be discussed below.

The principal books after 1765 representing the traditional parochial fuging tune were those published by John Harrott (1769, 1770), Richard Cook (c. 1770, 1775), Tans'ur (1772), John Ivery (1773), Elizabeth Wilkins (c. 1775), John Crompton (1778), John Barwick (c. 1783), John Valentine (c. 1785), William Dixon (1789), and Joseph Key (c. 1800). These books can be identified as Anglican in intention by (among other things) their almost exclusive use of texts from the Old and New Versions.

Several of these books, however, merely reprinted the established repertory, as did the later editions of such earlier books as Chetham's, Arnold's, Adams's, and

---

[27] William Gresham, *Psalmody Improved* (London, [1797]), pp. v-vi.

Knapp's. The only ones containing substantial numbers of new tunes were Harrott (1769), with eleven; Barwick, with eighteen; Valentine, with thirteen; and Key, with ten. These tunes can be said to continue the earlier tradition in all its variety, with very little tendency to standardization: both Harrott and Barwick, for instance, used many different structures and techniques of imitation. There are signs, however, of a gradual change in the style, even among these traditionalists, towards the *galant* idiom of current art music.

This can be partly explained as being due to the introduction of instruments.[28] A cello or bassoon to double the bass line had already been quite common in the 1740s; now other instruments were added, and by about 1770 a small band accompanying the singers was not unusual. Harrott states on the title page of his 1770 book that the "psalm-tunes, Hymns & Anthems" in it are "adapted to the most proper keys for the Bassoon, Hautboy &c." The book contains three very elaborate fuging tunes, one of which (**1072**) has a three-part instrumental symphony and an independent bass for bassoon. References to instruments are also made by Valentine (who provides symphonies and instrumental basses) and Key, while John Arnold in *A Supplement to the Complete Psalmodist* (1777) mentions the use of "violins, oboes, clarinets, vauxhumanes &c."

The alto and tenor parts, now usually printed in the G clef to be sung an octave lower, were frequently doubled at the written pitch (in the "treble octave," as Gresham put it) by clarinet and oboe respectively, while the treble part was doubled at the unison. This encouraged women and children to sing the "tune" or tenor part an octave higher, and the balance and relationship among the voices began to change.[29] Instead of the clear dominance of tenor and bass parts, there was now a preponderance of higher parts

---

28 For details of the introduction of instruments see Temperley, *Parish Church*, 1: 148-51, 196-201.

29 The doubling of parts at the upper or lower octave was suggested as early as 1677 by John Playford, who was the first to print the tunes of the psalms in the G clef and said that "All *Three Parts* may as properly be sung by Men as by Boys or Women" (*The Whole Book of Psalms . . . Compos'd in Three Parts, Cantus, Medius, & Bassus* [London, 1677], fol. A4r). How far this was followed in the early eighteenth century is doubtful: Abraham Barber objected to Playford's practice, "for there is not one Voice of any Boy in One Hundred, can reach the high Notes . . . The *Treble* is no leading Part in the *Psalm* Tunes, but the *Tenor,* and Sung as the General Part" (*A Book of Psalm-Tunes,* 6th ed. [York and Wakefield, 1711], p. viii). Thus the tenor in the choir continued to sing the tune, reinforced by the congregation, in which, no doubt, male voices predominated. The steady trend towards art music led to many attempts to imitate cathedral practice by placing the tune in the treble part (for statistics on this point see Temperley, *Parish Church*, 1: 368-81); several prefaces drew attention to the change, and cautioned against doubling the tune in the tenor (e.g. [Arthur Bedford], *Divine Recreations* [London, 1736-37], 1: 4). But, evidently, the men did not so readily give up the privilege of singing the tune, so that octave doubling tended to result. It was further encouraged by the use of instruments. James Williams Newton, who placed the tune in the treble, objected to certain "improprieties" in psalm singing: "The treble part is frequently sung in full chorus by a *tenor* voice . . . To introduce a German flute, as an accompanyment to the tenor voice is a practice much to be condemned;

widely separated from the (vocal or instrumental) bass, a texture characteristic of the *style galant.* By the end of the century, indeed, the G clef had become thoroughly ambiguous, and in some tunes the tenor and treble parts had changed places.

It can be said that although many older fuging tunes retained their popularity in parochial use—the archetypal **106**, for instance, kept its place in successive editions of Chetham's *Book of Psalmody* until 1811—the creative period for this type of tune had ended, and there had been a change in taste towards treble-oriented tunes of a different kind.

Among dissenters, on the other hand, fuging tunes were on the rise. There was a gradual breaking down of resistance, as some authoritative figures showed their acceptance of the fuging tune; and a growing output of fuging tunes designed for dissenters' use. "Ecumenical" books continued to appear. Samuel Pearce's *Sacred Music* (c. 1776) has many hymns and psalms of Dr. Watts set to two- and three-part tunes with solos (some marked for women's voices), but not to fuging tunes; it also has thirty-one new fuging tunes, mostly four-part, set to psalms in the Old and New Versions and one or two hymns for Christmas and so on. They are indexed together, and the title page refers to "Churches, Dissenting Congregations, and other Societies." Similarly with the anonymous *Musica Sacra* (1783). William Dixon, on his title page of 1789, says that "all [his tunes] are adapted to the versions of the Church of England, & to render the Book more generally acceptable [and hence, he might have added, more profitable], several of them are also accommodated to the Words of Dr. Wattes's Psalms & Hymns." John Beatson printed about 1780 *A Complete Collection of All the Tunes Sung by the Different Congregations in Hull,* and John Dalmer did the same thing for Bath (c. 1788). Each included five fuging tunes.

The breakthrough for the dissenting bodies came when their own leading clergymen sanctioned books containing fuging tunes. Caleb Ashworth, a Congregational minister at Daventry (Northamptonshire), has already been mentioned in this connection. Stephen Addington was another Congregational minister, at Spalding (Lincolnshire), Market Harborough (Leicestershire) and then at Miles Lane, London. His *Collection of Psalm Tunes for Public Worship* was probably first published in 1777:[30] the third

because the German flute is an octave above the part it accompanies; and, for that reason, it is always too distinguishable" (*Psalmody Improved* [Ipswich, 1775], p. xiv). By the 1780s the three upper parts, all written in the G clef, were often being sung or played in both octaves: see Thomas Billington, *The Te Deum, Jubilate . . .* (London, 1784), pp. 3-4; William Gresham, *Psalmody Improved* (London, [c. 1797]), p. vi. The dissenting practice of alternating women's and men's voices in the tune naturally encouraged them to sing in octaves when they sang together, and this practice carried over when the tune was chorally harmonized. Isaac Smith explained this point in his preface (see p. 27 below). See also the preface to Aaron Williams, *The New Universal Psalmodist* (London, 1770). For some further discussion of these points see Temperley, *Parish Church,* 1: 184-90.

[30] The *Leicester Journal* carried the following advertisement on 23 September 1777: "Just Published. A Collection of Tunes for Publick Worship . . . by Stephen Addington. Printed for the Author & sold by him at Market Harborough. . . ." We are indebted to Dr. Karl Kroeger for this information.

TABLE 3. FUGING TUNES PRINTED BEFORE 1801

Decade	Printed in Great Britain				Printed in America (A)	Total
	P	D	S	Total		
Part A. All printings of fuging tunes in distinct editions						
1701-1710	3	. .	. .	3	. .	3
1711-1720	. .	. .	. .	. .	. .	. .
1721-1730	3	. .	. .	3	. .	3
1731-1740	8	1	. .	9	. .	9
1741-1750	87	. .	. .	87	. .	87
1751-1760	308	1	. .	309	. .	309
1761-1770	197	1	1	199	51	250
1771-1780	187	5	. .	192	119	311
1781-1790	218	22	1	241	807	1048
1791-1800	226	92	23	341	2047	2388
1701-1800	1237	122	25	1384	3024	4408
Part B. Printings of new fuging tunes						
1701-1710	1	. .	. .	1	. .	1
1711-1720	. .	. .	. .	. .	. .	. .
1721-1730	1	. .	. .	1	. .	1
1731-1740	3	1	. .	4	. .	4
1741-1750	53	. .	. .	53	. .	53
1751-1760	166	1	. .	167	. .	167
1761-1770	38	. .	1	39	4	43
1771-1780	66	2	. .	20	20	88
1781-1790	109	17	. .	126	155	281
1791-1800	150	43	1	194	395	589
1701-1800	587	64	2	653	574	1227

In Part A, each tune is counted once each time it was printed in a distinct edition of which a copy survives. A "distinct edition" is one which is listed in the List of Sources, whether its contents are listed there separately (as in the case of P134 and P134.2) or not (as in the case of P148 and P148.2). When a tune is printed twice in the same edition (e.g. in P148) both printings are counted. Thus each line representing a source in the Census counts once in this table. For undated editions, the printing is assigned to the most likely decade.

In Part B, each tune is counted once only, in the decade in which it was (most probably) first printed. The reason why the total, 1227, is less than the number of the last tune in the Census (**1239**) is that the Census contains five "ghosts" (deleted numbers) and seven tunes which, though separately numbered, have been treated here as "versions" of other tunes.

edition, the earliest to survive, is dated 1780, and states firmly that it is "Adapted to Dr. Watts's Psalms and Hymns." It was a highly successful book, gaining many supplements and reaching a 13th edition by 1799, with a gradually increasing number of fuging tunes including several new ones. Ralph Harrison, minister of Cross St. Unitarian Chapel, Manchester, published a successful *Sacred Harmony* in 1784. It too went into several editions, and was an important source for dissenting, Scottish and American compilers. Finally, the Baptist minister John Rippon, whose authoritative *Selection of Hymns . . . Intended to be an Appendix to Dr. Watts's Psalms and Hymns* had appeared in 1787, gave his name to a musical companion published about 1792 (probably compiled by Thomas Walker) with twenty fuging tunes, including thirteen new ones.

Thus each of the three leading bodies of English dissenters now possessed at least one authorized collection with fuging tunes in it.[31] There was now no bar to the production of other collections by and for dissenters, such as those of Isaac Smith (and his successor S. Major), Thomas Williams, and William Mason of Cambridge, all of which contributed popular fuging tunes.

Some of these collections include a good crop of the more popular Anglican fuging tunes, with new texts and often new names, and quite frequently reduced to three or even two voices. Indeed, a preference for the texture of two trebles and bass (or at least two parts in the G clef and one in the F clef) is shown early in dissenters' books: it is used throughout by Addington, his successor S. Hawes, Thomas Williams, and Mason, and is predominant in Rippon. Fugal imitation is usually much less extensive than in Anglican tunes, confined perhaps to one late or early entry in one line. The cadences are notably square and forthright. The dissenters made a specialty of "repeating" tunes, not necessarily fuging, in which a line was sung once by women and then repeated louder by the full choir. Sometimes the echo effect applied to part of a line or even a single word. We can find this idea adapted to fuging tunes, when a word is bandied to and fro several times between one part and another: for instance, in tunes **854** and **867** (Example 7, page 29).

Many of these characteristics are related to a cardinal difference between dissenting and Anglican practice. Dissenters gave little encouragement to performances by choirs in worship. They wanted the whole congregation to sing (led, if possible, by rehearsed singers). Aaron Williams's remarks on this point have already been quoted, and Gresham's comments show how the congregation was excluded in Anglican churches. Harrison said that Part 2 of his *Sacred Harmony,* with the fuging tunes, was for choirs, "yet . . . not altogether beyond the attainment of congregations." Isaac Smith said in his preface: "It is much to be wished that every congregation would appoint an hour or two, some evening every week, to practice such tunes as may be thought proper."

---

[31] English Presbyterians in the course of the eighteenth century had tended to split into two streams: one passed through Socinianism to Unitarianism, the other, rejecting this trend, joined forces with the Congregationalists.

He explained: "Over the Tenor is written Loud, Soft, &c. &c. . . . as they are now commonly sung in several places, in, and about, London. By *Loud*, I mean the strains in which men and women sing in full chorus; by *Soft*, when the women and boys only sing. But as the women in most congregations are not accustomed to sing loud by themselves, it will be best for the men softly to accompany them . . . ; and the women and boys singing in the Octave . . . above, will render the melody equally pleasing."[32]

With the whole congregation joining in, it is no wonder that dissenters tended to simplify the "fuging" element in their tunes, and to emphasize broad and simple effects, including those that set off male and female voices. Some dissenters, indeed, still disapproved of fuging tunes altogether. As Benjamin Cuzens put it in *The Portsmouth Harmony*, "the customs of places differ from each other; and Singers at different places are of different tastes and opinions; some are delighted with very sprightly, airy, fuge tunes, others with midling, and others with more grave & solemn ones."[33]

The effect of the Methodist movement on the history of the fuging tune was complex. The form did not suit John Wesley's ideal of heartfelt popular singing: he objected to "the repeating the same word so often (but especially while another repeats different words—the horrid abuse which runs through the modern church-music)."[34] During the lifetime of the Founder, Wesleyan Methodists appear to have respected his wishes. Relatively few Wesleyan hymns will be found in the Index of Texts in this volume. James Leach was the first Wesleyan compiler to use fuging tunes, but his *New Sett of Hymns* of 1789, though its tunes have varied texture, scrupulously avoids text overlap. Only in his *Second Sett*, published after Wesley's death, did Leach include fuging tunes; typically they have one line with the voices entering imitatively in pairs, but there are a few with full three- or four-part imitation. In fact they are like other dissenters' tunes. Leach made it clear that he intended congregational participation, but only those who could read music were to sing the "other parts": the rest were to stick to the tenor.

The Calvinistic Methodists, followers of George Whitefield and Selina, Countess of Huntingdon, seem to have entertained no objection to fuging tunes, and even produced some original ones. This group was closely allied to the Evangelical party within the Church of England, and collections like Andrew Loder's of 1798 were designed to suit either. Other Evangelicals, however, disapproved of fuging tunes, and a book such as *The Psalms of David* (1790) by Edward Miller carefully avoided counterpoint and text overlap. William Jackson of Exeter, whose *Hymns in Three Parts* (1768) was "*not* published for the Use of any particular Sect or Congregation" (though he himself was an Evangelical Anglican), stated his opinion that "the Music of the Hymn admits not of Fugue, Repetition or Division."

---

[32] Isaac Smith, *A Collection of Psalm Tunes* (London, [c. 1780]), pp. 3, 11.

[33] Benjamin Cuzens, *The Portsmouth Harmony* (London, [c. 1800]), pp. i-ii.

[34] Temperley, *Parish Church*, 1: 209.

EXAMPLE 7. Jersey Psalm 45. Dr. W. C.M.

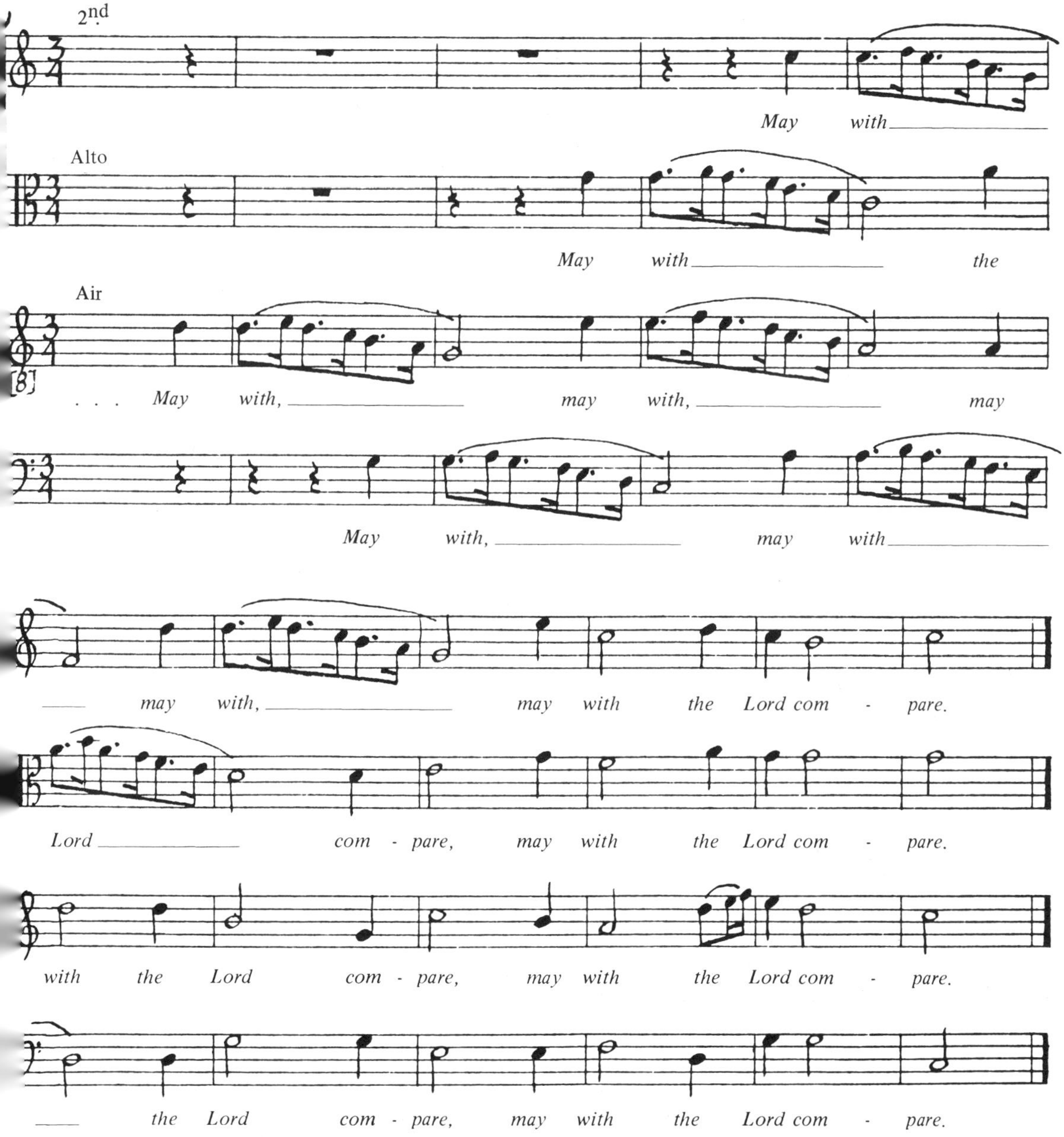

– Tune **213**, from Source D6

In Scotland, as might be expected, fuging tunes made only a token appearance in the eighteenth century, and that only in Episcopal churches or in private domestic use. The true Presbyterian remained implacably opposed to anything that treated scriptural words so lightly. Only two fuging tunes clearly originate in Scottish sources. One of them (**227**), printed by a recent immigrant from England, is a derivative of the archetypal tune **106**. The other (FORFAR, **1038**), printed by Laurence Ding, appears to be a genuine Scottish artefact.

The "reform" type of tune was in a sense a continuation of the early archetypes composed by professionals: it sought to substitute for the country tune a product more correctly written, according to the rules of art music at the time, and more elegant. The "improvement" of country psalmody gained momentum after 1790, when it was publicly acknowledged that the superior singing of the Methodists was attracting large numbers away from the Established Church. "Reform" tunes are notable for their correct voice-leading, smooth part-writing, and avoidance of such striking characteristics of country psalmody as open fifth chords, unresolved accentual dissonances, and consecutive fifths and octaves. They often recall Handel or, later, the pre-classical style. In many cases they are designed to be sung with organ accompaniment.

As in earlier times, leading organist-composers were called on to provide models. John Stanley wrote one for Christopher Smart (**609**), Charles Burney for John Crompton (**856**), Thomas Greatorex for Ralph Harrison (**1165**). Hugh Bond and John Marsh each printed one of their own. The earliest large collection of "reform" tunes was *The Food of Devotion,* printed about 1775 by one D. Senior of whom practically nothing is known; it contains twenty-two tunes of Senior's own authorship, all unica. The collections of Thomas Tremain and Matthew Cooke are of this type, too. Of greater significance was William Dixon's *Psalmodia Christiana* (1789): Dixon commissioned a number of leading composers to provide some twenty-two out of fifty-one fuging tunes he printed, but most of the others came from country collections, so that his book was (unusually) a roughly equal mixture of the two streams.

Samuel Arnold and John Callcott's ambitious *Psalms of David* (1791), on the other hand, was a comprehensive effort at reform, as the preface makes very clear. The authors themselves were two of the most eminent musicians of the day. They printed no less than seventy-five fuging tunes, the largest number in any British collection, and every one of them was newly composed or adapted: Arnold himself adapted twenty-one, mostly from the works of Handel. Some of the composers (e. g. Luffman Atterbury) carefully showed how the tunes were to be adapted to subsequent verses of the psalm in such a way that the fuging section did not make nonsense of the text. This was an entirely new refinement.

William Tattersall's *Improved Psalmody* (1794) was an equally ambitious venture, this time by a low-church clergyman of independent means who acknowledged the help of two distinguished professional musicians, William Parsons and Benjamin Cooke. Tattersall made a clean break with tradition by selecting his texts entirely from a little-known but "elegant" version of the psalms by James Merrick. Despite this obstacle his book won considerable popularity. He asserted that the best model for parish psalmody was the glee, and among the well-known composers of glees whom he commissioned to provide tunes for his book were William Shield, Samuel Webbe, Arnold and Callcott. He even induced Josef Haydn to contribute six tunes. Since three of them are fuging by our definition, Haydn finds a place in our census, where, it must be confessed, he is something of a giant among pygmies.[35]

In the later eighteenth century, then, the English fuging tune was largely taken out of the hands of the country singing teachers and the parish-church choirs. They had had their day, but now it was the turn of dissenting clergymen and trained organist-composers to make fuging tunes more respectable. Though it is certain that the older fuging tunes survived well into the nineteenth century, both in print and in performance, this was, indeed, a survival, not a continuing creative development.

Introduction of Fuging Tunes to the American Colonies (1761-1782)

A S ONE MIGHT EXPECT, the progress of psalmody in the colonies tended to follow developments in the mother country, often at an interval of a generation or so. The earliest colonists probably brought the old way of singing with them, and a knowledge of the early psalm tunes. Regular singing, through the teaching of notation to a religious society of young men, first appeared in the Anglican churches of Maryland just before 1700, under the supervision of Dr. Thomas Bray, a leading figure in the corresponding movement in England.[36] From there it spread to Anglican churches elsewhere in the colonies, probably reaching the King's Chapel, Boston, by 1710.[37] As in England, churches in the larger towns acquired organs when they could.[38] The first American fuging tune (703), by Francis Hopkinson, appears in a publication of 1763 "For the Use of the United Churches of Christ Church and St. Peters Church in Philadelphia," which was printed in anticipation of the introduction of organs there.[39] It is a cautious

---

[35] One of Haydn's tunes is printed in Temperley, *Parish Church,* 2: 50.

[36] Mason Martens reported his discoveries in an unpublished paper, "Tate and Brady's *New Version* of the Metrical Psalms and Its Introduction into the American Colonies," delivered at a meeting of the American Musicological Society, Washington, D. C., 1976.

[37] An Anglican religious society was founded in Boston in 1704: see William S. Perry, ed., *Historical Collections Relating to the American Colonial Church,* 5 vols. (Hartford, 1973), 3: 76-79. Tate & Brady's metrical psalms were first imported in London editions, then reprinted at New York in 1710; a Boston edition with tunes was printed "for the Use of His Majesty's Chapell of America" in 1713. See also Temperley, "The Old Way," pp. 538-39.

[38] King's Chapel, Boston, acquired one in 1714; St. Philip's, Charleston, in 1728; Christ Church, Philadelphia, probably in the same year, and a larger one in 1766; Trinity, Newport, R. I., in 1733; and so on. (Information from Mason Martens, who kindly supplied me with a copy of his paper cited in n. 36 above).

[39] [Francis Hopkinson], *A Collection of Psalm Tunes* (Philadelphia, 1763), pp. iii-iv.

EXAMPLE 8.   The 4th Psalm

Have Mer - - cy Lord & hear, have Mer - - cy

Have Mer - - cy, Lord, and hear, have Mer - - cy,

Have Mer - cy, Lord, have Mer - - cy,

Lord, and hear.

Lord, and hear.

— Tune **703**, from Source A18

Lord, and hear.

affair, of the "late entry" type found in some of the earliest English fuging tunes (Example 8, *above*).

    The absence of music printing, and indeed the rarity of printed books of any kind, in the southern and middle colonies make it difficult to chart the progress of psalmody in the churches there before 1760. But the sudden appearance of James Lyon's *Urania*, published at Philadelphia in 1761, suggests that a number of English country psalmody collections had already been circulating; for its contents, including all six of its fuging tunes, are largely drawn from such sources.[40]

---

[40] Richard Crawford's preface to the Da Capo reprint of *Urania* (New York, 1974) contains a wealth of valuable and detailed information about *Urania* itself, its sources, and its influence on later American publications.

Though Lyon himself was a Presbyterian minister,[41] he dedicated his book "To The Clergy of every Denomination in America," and the list of subscribers contains the names of clergymen of various denominations, including that of Dr. William Smith, Provost of the College and Academy of Philadelphia and later a leading figure in the formation of the Protestant Episcopal Church. The contents of the book reflect Lyon's wish to cater to several sects. The psalm tunes are untexted, though they are arranged in four parts with the tune in the tenor, as in Anglican collections. The six fuging tunes, in particular, were more likely to find easy acceptance in an Anglican church than in any other at this date. The anthems, the first examples of this genre to be published in America, must also be regarded as primarily intended for Anglican use.[42] But at the end of the book are fourteen hymns, with texts mostly from Watts and Wesley, in the three-voice or two-voice format favored in general by Congregational and Methodist societies. The book is thus of the "ecumenical" variety, comparable to those of Abraham Milner (1751) or John Hill (c. 1757), though nothing in it is likely to have appealed directly to Scottish Presbyterians.

In the Congregational churches of New England, regular singing was introduced, amid lively controversy, around 1720.[43] The institution of singing schools at about this time was the agency by which the new skills were taught, and the schools became a powerful social tradition in New England life.[44] At first the meetings were generally conducted by ministers, and included sermons: they may be regarded as the Congregational equivalent to the devotional meetings of the Anglican religious societies. The stimulus towards improvement in singing may well have been the music at the King's Chapel, which was possibly the first experience of orderly singing for many Bostonians.[45]

The tune supplements printed in New England between 1720 and 1760, for use with Watts's *Psalms and Hymns* or Tate and Brady's *New Version,* were influenced by

---

[41] See Oscar G. T. Sonneck, *Francis Hopkinson and James Lyon* (Washington, 1905), pp. 121-24.

[42] This statement includes Lyon's own piece "The Lord descended from above," though Lyon did not designate it an anthem, doubtless because its text is metrical. The text, is, in fact, from the Old Version of Sternhold & Hopkins, a version not used by any sect in America, other than the Church of England, since the mid-seventeenth century.

[43] There is a good account of this controversy in Gilbert Chase, *America's Music from the Pilgrims to the Present* (New York, 1955), pp. 22-40. For a list of accounts see David P. McKay and Richard Crawford, *William Billings of Boston: 18th-Century Composer* (Princeton, 1975), p. 10n.

[44] Accounts of the singing school movement are given by Allen P. Britton, "Theoretical Introductions in American Tunebooks to 1800," Ph.D. diss., University of Michigan, 1949, and Alan Buechner, "Yankee Singing Schools and the Golden Age of Choral Singing in New England, 1760-1800," Ph.D. diss., Harvard University, 1960.

[45] Cotton Mather wrote in his diary in 1718: "The psalmody is but poorly carried on in my flock, and in a variety and regularity inferior to some others. I would see about it" (cited Buechner, p. 63). Judge Sewall wrote on March 16, 1721: "At night Mr. Mather preaches in the schoolhouse to the young musicians . . . House was full and the singing extraordinarily excellent, such as has hardly been heard before in Boston. Sung four times out of Tate and Brady" (Buechner, p. 79).

Playford's books, and also by tunebooks used by London dissenters.[46] They contain a number of the early psalm tunes, and a few newer ones of a slightly more ornate character, generally set out for three voices—counter or medius, tenor, and bass. Towards the end of that period, some tunes were printed whose long melismas and varied texture suggest a breaking away from the austerity of the old tradition (Example 9, *below*).[47]

EXAMPLE 9.   136 Psalm Tune

... For God does prove   His_____   bound-less love

Our   con - stant friend,

Shall_____   ne - ver end.

— From Thomas Johnston's tune supplement to Tate & Brady (1755)

There is some evidence that English country psalmody collections were circulating in New England in the 1750s,[48] and their anthems and fuging tunes may have been

---

[46] For instance Lawrence's *Collection* (see n. 23 above), as surmised by Robert Stevenson, *Protestant Church Music in America* (New York, 1966), p. 21; and Simon Browne, *Hymns and Spiritual Songs* (London, 1720)—see Irving Lowens, *Music and Musicians in Early America* (New York, 1964), pp. 52-53.

[47] From Thomas Johnston's tune supplement to Tate and Brady's *New Version* (Boston, 1755). For details of the music in these collections see David K. Stigberg, "Congregational Psalmody in Eighteenth Century New England," M. M. thesis, University of Illinois, 1970.

[48] Crawford, *Urania,* preface, p. i. John Arnold added to the 5th edition (1761) of his *Compleat Psalmodist* the information that it was "for the Use of all Churches . . . throughout his Majesty's Dominions of Great Britain, Ireland, and Plantations abroad."

performed in the singing schools, even if not admitted in church. The first fuging tunes
published in New England appeared in three books printed in 1764, and all came from
different sources. Daniel Bayley printed a version of the earliest, archetypal tune **670**,
headed "PSALM 50." (This makes it almost certain that he took it from a little-known
source, Francis Timbrell's *The Divine Musick Scholar's Guide,* the only book in which it
is set to Psalm 50, New Version. See Example 4b, page 10). Josiah Flagg took one tune
(LAINDON, **246**) from Arnold's *Compleat Psalmodist,* retaining its Old Version text,
and two others (PENBURY, **352**, and NEWBURY, **1060**) from Aaron Williams's
Universal Psalmodist, with new texts from Watts's Hymns. And the 1764 edition of
Thomas Walter's *Grounds and Rules of Musick* includes a Tans'ur fuging tune without
text. Flagg went to yet another source, Stephenson's *Church Harmony,* for the solitary
fuging tune in his next collection. None of these tunes are among the six chosen by Lyon.
The next incursion of fuging tunes into the region was by means of Daniel Bayley's
American editions of the Anglican Tans'ur and the dissenting Williams. Further British
sources of fuging tunes published in New England are Knapp's *New Church Melody,*
first tapped in Bayley's *New Universal Harmony* (1773), and Arnold's *The Leicestershire
Harmony,* in Stickney's *Companion* of 1774—but Stickney may have taken the tunes
originating in the latter source from Lyon's *Urania.* Arnold's book was certainly used
as a direct source for Andrew Law's *Select Harmony* (1778, 1779).

Most of the early borrowings from English books tend to retain the original text,
whether it be from the Old or New Version, Dr. Watts's Psalms or Hymns, or an
anonymous source (as KRYNSON [KEYNSON], **876**). This may reflect the technical
difficulties of adapting a fuging tune to a different text, but it also suggests that the
music was not much used in the Congregational churches of the area. It may have
been chiefly for the delight of the singing schools. (I shall return to this point later.)
The English psalmodists whose tunes "caught on" best were Beesly, J. Arnold, and
Stephenson (see Table 6, page 42), who were perhaps jointly responsible for establishing
the "standard" (though by no means universal) type of American fuging tune. No such
standard type ever became prevalent in Britain.

This standard type was first identified by Irving Lowens. It was normally a four-
liner (SM, CM or LM were most common), beginning with two homophonic phrases.
The fuging section would start with the third phrase, and the last would either continue
in fuging texture or close in plain homophony. Thus the structure in abbreviated form
is HHFH, HHFF, HHFO, or some variant of these. Another common type is a
six-liner (HHHHFF or similar). The fuging section has four parts entering at one-measure
intervals, most frequently in voice order (BTAS is the favorite, but SATB is also quite
common), with "tonal" answers approximately half an octave apart. The typical figure
of imitation is a four-note phrase with an upbeat (of variable length), followed by three
quarter notes, the first of them being on the first beat of a measure (as in Example 10,
page 36). There are certainly scores, perhaps a hundred American tunes that follow
this pattern more or less closely, and they seem to derive, in particular, from a tune first
published probably by Joseph Watts (**125**) and a couple of Stephenson's (PSALM 34, **302**,

EXAMPLE 10.　CXXII Ps.

& there our Vows & there our Vows & Ho - nours　Pay.

& there our Vows & Ho - nours　Pay.

& there our Vows & Hon,　　& there our Vows & Ho - nours　Pay.

& there our Vows & Ho - nours　Pay,　　& there our Vows & Ho - nours　Pay.

— Tune **355**, from Source A39

and MILFORD, **1002**).[49]　Knapp also came near it several times, and consolidated the Beesly technique which easily combines with the standard form.

　　William Billings was the first of the New England tunesmiths to produce original fuging tunes. His first three efforts, in *The New-England Psalm-Singer* (1770), are far from the standard model; instead they follow Tans'ur in providing a fuging "chorus" tacked on to an already complete homophonic tune. All have fugal entries in voice order starting with the bass, but the interval of imitation is the octave or unison, either at 1½ or 2 measures. The tunes are unusually sonorous, with "choosing notes" (divided parts) and generally full harmony. Billings's three texts are interesting: one is from the Old Version, one from the New, and the third is an original verse of his own. Only with his second collection of 1778 does he begin to use predominantly Isaac Watts texts for fuging tunes.

　　The three 1770 tunes are unica, and only two of the eleven 1778 tunes (BETHLEHEM, **935**, and MARYLAND, **405**) achieved much popularity. The one original tune in Stickney's book of 1774 was PSALM 122 (**355**) by the Anglican

---

[49] Lowens suggested that **302** and **1002** by Stephenson "served as actual prototypes for Billings's work and perhaps for that of other early American composers as well," and made a direct comparison between **302** and Edson's LENOX (**15**) (Lowens, pp. 240, 247-48).

Amos Bull,[50] but with a text by Watts. Its meter is 668668, its structure H H F H H F; both fuging sections are of the "American standard" type, one in downward voice order, the other BTSA (Example 10, *opposite*). It is Andrew Law's *Select Harmony*, however, that decisively establishes this type. Five of the eight original tunes in the two editions of 1778 and 1779 conform more or less to the standard design, and of these, four achieved notable popularity: Deaolph's PSALM 136, Alexander Gillet's FARMINGTON, Abraham Wood's WORCESTER, and a tune of doubtful authorship, NORWICH. This last is the most often reprinted of all the American tunes so far mentioned, and is shown on page ix of this book.[51]

By the time of the Declaration of Independence, the American fuging tune was fairly launched. Sprung from an Anglican seed, it flourished chiefly in Congregational ground. Though they followed English models closely, the American composers already gave the fuging-tune concept a different character by selectivity in their choice of models. By establishing a standard form, they created stronger expectations in the listener, which certainly played a part in the phenomenal popularity that fuging tunes were to achieve in the 1790s.

The American Heyday (1783-1800)

I N 1801 Dr. William Bentley of Salem, whose diary has been an important source of information about American life in this period, wrote "the history of our Psalmody" in a letter to a German historian, and summarized his remarks in his diary.

> I then noticed the progress of music from the single part
> to Tenor, bass & medius. The work of Tansur & the
> improvement by Williams. The singing of appropriate tunes
> to Psalms interrupted by the new Version. The Selection
> of Tunes. The change by Billings, his Reuben & other books.
> The works of Holyoke, Kimball, & Holden, & the numberless
> publications which have appeared in New England, which
> I did not presume to enumerate.[52]

---

[50] Ruth Wilson has discovered that Bull had been parish clerk of Holy Trinity, New York. See also Ruth Mack Wilson, *Connecticut's Music in the Revolutionary Era* (Hartford, 1979), pp. 52-55.

[51] Andrew Law at first attributed the tune to Brownson, but did not repeat the attribution, and Brownson did not include it in his own collections. (I am grateful to Richard Crawford for pointing out that the Brownson attribution is suspect.)

[52] *The Diary of William Bentley, D. D.* (Salem, Mass., 1907), p. 371. By "the singing of appropriate tunes to Psalms" Bentley meant the custom of associating each tune with a particular psalm, often reflected in tune names such as PSALM 34. He contrasts this with "the Selection of Tunes" in which tunes are provided to fit any text of the right meter. Billings's "Reuben" was his first publication, *The New-England Psalm Singer*. See Hans Nathan, *William Billings: Data and Documents* (Detroit, 1976).

The end of the War of Independence in 1783 saw the beginning of a long boom in American psalmody publication which in sheer quantity far exceeded anything that Britain had experienced.[53] In this huge output, fuging tunes played a substantial part (see Table 3, Part A, page 26). Out of 154 American publications of sacred music of all kinds which Richard Crawford dates between 1783 and 1800, 103 contain some fuging tunes, ranging from one in Law's *Rudiments of Music* (1783) to 88 in Shumway's *American Harmony* (1793). There was evidently a situation of keen commercial rivalry among several publishers, particularly in New England, where the great majority of these books originated. This is reflected in the contents of many of the books, which tend to be anthologies of the most popular music in current use. In Crawford's view it was these large anthologies, like Law's *Select Harmony,* Jocelin's *The Chorister's Companion,* and *The Worcester Collection* (compiled by various hands) that were chiefly responsible for shaping the American psalmody of the time.[54] To a far greater degree than in England, the same tunes were reprinted over and over again. The "core repertory" which Crawford has established (the one hundred pieces most often reprinted) includes early English psalm tunes like OLD 100TH, as well as plain and ornate fuging tunes, set pieces, and anthems, both British and American, from various dates in the eighteenth century.[55]

The large number of psalmody publications is partly to be explained by the probably limited area of distribution of many books (Andrew Law's were perhaps exceptional). It was a time when local amateur printers, using engraved plates, could command an adequate market for the sale of perhaps a couple of hundred copies. In Connecticut alone, which Crawford has identified as a particularly important area in the development, six different imprints are found in this period: Cheshire, Danbury, Hartford, Middletown, New Haven and Simsbury.[56] (By contrast, the majority of British publications have a London imprint, even when they are clearly of country provenance.) The situation quickly altered after the turn of the century when professional printers took the lead, printing from type and producing large runs.[57]

Table 4, *opposite,* shows how the proportion of British tunes among all those printed in American books dwindled from 92% in 1761-65 to 8% in 1796-1800: naturally, the War of Independence produced a steep decline. It may be noted, however, that the number of British tunes printed in America continued to rise; what caused the proportion to decline was the immense increase in the printing of American tunes (see Table 3,

---

[53] The only British precedent that comes to mind is the publication of at least sixty-six distinct editions of Sternhold & Hopkins's *Whole Book of Psalms* in the decade 1631-40.

[54] Richard Crawford, "Psalmody. II. North America," *The New Grove Dictionary* (London, 1980), 15: 345-47. For a discussion of *The Worcester Collection* see Karl Kroeger, "The Worcester Collection of Sacred Harmony and Sacred Music in America," Ph. D. diss., Brown University, 1976.

[55] Richard Crawford, "Connecticut Sacred Music Imprints, 1778-1810," *Notes* 27 (1971): 445-52, 671-79. See also Crawford, *A Bibliography of Sacred Music Printed in America Through 1810* (Worcester, Mass., 1983).

[56] Crawford, "Connecticut," pp. 447-52.

[57] Crawford, "Connecticut," pp. 674-75.

TABLE 4. BRITISH FUGING TUNES IN AMERICAN PRINTED SOURCES

Half-Decade	Total Printings of British Fuging Tunes in America	The Same as a Percentage of All Tunes Printed	British Tunes Printed for the First Time in America
1761-1765	12	92%	10
1766-1770	36	92%	9
1771-1775	58	95%	6
1776-1780	31	53%	7
1781-1785	81	33%	6
1786-1790	81	15%	12
1791-1795	106	11%	13
1796-1800	81	8%	9
1761-1800	486	16%	72

Part A, page 26). Table 5, pages 40-41, lists the thirty fuging tunes most often printed (anywhere) before 1801, and it shows clearly how many more American reprintings there were than British, of both British and American tunes. Indeed, the list would have most of the same tunes in much the same order if it was based on American sources alone: only **1060** and **192** would be drastically displaced. Table 6, page 42, shows the original sources of the sixty-nine British fuging tunes discovered in American publications.

The situation also encouraged the printing of new music; the financial investment in a publication was moderate, and the publisher could often wait until subscriptions were adequate before going into production. A psalmodist with a moderate teaching "connection" or public could hope to achieve at least local success for his tunes. Because there was much borrowing of material from one compiler to another, a successful tune could quickly spread over the whole New England area and even beyond it. Thus we find during this "boom" period an unprecedented number of original fuging tunes (see Table 3, Part B, page 26), some of which soon became established favorites.

In this period, it seems that American psalmody had come to exist independently of worship. The singing school, as already pointed out, had long been a social institution in its own right,[58] and it is hardly surprising that some compilers now indicate that their

---

[58] Crawford, "Psalmody," p. 346; Lowens, pp. 282-83.

TABLE 5. THE THIRTY FUGING TUN

Tune No.	Usual Name(s)	Meter
302	PS. 34, GUILDFORD	CM
1060	STROUD, NEWBURY	CM
15	LENOX	666688
41	NORWICH	SM
337	GREENFIELD	8^6
1002	MILFORD	CM
187	BRIDGEWATER	LM
845	STAFFORD	SM
571	BRISTOL	LMD
1160	WORCESTER	SMD
843	PSALM 3	CM
968	SHERBURNE	CM
405	MARYLAND	SM
807	MONTAGUE	LMD
1057	GREENWICH	LMD
1148	OCEAN	CMD
192	CANTERBURY, OTFORD	CM
760	RAINBOW	CM
1112	POOL(E) (NEW)	LM
238	PSALM 136	666688
935	BETHLEHEM	CM
254	RUSSIA	LM
303	MONTGOMERY	CMD
96	CALVARY	CM
1102	WASHINGTON	LM
1131	VICTORY	CM
268	WALPOLE	CMD
613	NAPLES	LM
1101	PHILADELPHIA	SM
943	PSALM 46	8^6

For an explanation of abbreviations in the Structure column, see page 88. When a letter is printed in italics it indicates that the line of music referred to repeats an earlier phrase of the text.

Structure	Composer	Number of Printings				
		P	D	S	A	Total
HHFO*H*	Stephenson	6	1	-	72	79
HEHF	anon., -1749	36	1	1	40	78
HHHHFF	Edson	-	-	-	58	58
HHFH	uncertain	-	-	-	58	58
HHHFFH	Edson	-	-	-	58	58
FHF*FF*	Stephenson	8	-	-	49	57
HHFF	Edson	-	-	-	55	55
HHFE	D. Read	-	-	-	53	53
HHHHFFFH	Swan	-	-	-	51	51
HHHH*HH*EEF*FF*HH	Wood	-	-	-	47	47
FHF*FFF*	Stephenson	8	-	-	38	46
HHF*FFFF*	D. Read	-	-	-	46	46
HHHH*FFF*	W. Billings	-	-	-	45	45
HHHHFFO*H*H	Swan	-	-	-	45	45
HHHHFFOO	D. Read	-	-	-	45	45
HHHHFFHH	anon., 1786	-	-	-	43	43
HHFH	anon., -1749	28	7	2	2	39
HHFF*EH*	Swan	-	-	-	38	38
HHOF	anon., c1746	9	-	-	26	35
HHFHFF	Deaolph	-	-	⋮	33	33
HHHH*FFFE*	W. Billings	-	-	-	32	32
HHFO*H*	D. Read	-	-	-	31	31
HHEHFHF*H*H	Morgan	-	-	-	31	31
FOFE	D. Read	-	-	-	30	30
HH*HFFFF*H	W. Billings	-	-	-	30	30
HHHF*H*	D. Read	-	-	-	29	29
HHHHHHEF	Wood	-	-	-	27	27
HHFF	D. Read	-	-	-	27	27
HHHH*FO*	W. Billings	-	-	-	27	27
HHFHHH	Chandler	-	-	-	26	26

TABLE 6. SOURCES OF BRITISH FUGING TUNES PRINTED IN AMERICA

Part A. By original publication

Source No.	Original British Source (in chronological order)	No. of Tunes
P51	H. Playford, *Divine Companion*, 1701	1
P129a	Beesly, *Collection of 20 New Psalm Tunes*, c.1746	6
P130	Evison, *Compleat Book*, 1747	1
P135	Watts, *Choice Collection*, -1749	3
P137	East, *Voice of Melody*, II, 1750	1
P142	Tans'ur, untitled, c.1750	2
P145a	Beesly, *Book of Psalmody*, c.1751	1
P148	Knapp, *New Church Melody*, 1752	3
P153	Davenport, *Psalm-Singer's Pocket Companion*, 1755	1
P155	Tans'ur, *Royal Melody Compleat*, 1755	4
P163	J. Arnold, *Psalmist's Recreation*, 1757	1
P168	Stephenson, *An Anthem*, c.1758	1
P169	J. Arnold, *Leicestershire Harmony*, 1759	9
P171	Stephenson, *Church Harmony*, 3/1760	8
P155.2	Tans'ur, *Royal Melody Compleat*, 2/1760	1
P189	A. Williams, *Universal Psalmodist*, 1763	2
P198	Harrott, *Rutland-Harmony*, 1769	1
P242	Beatson, *Complete Collection*, c.1780	1
P253	Harrison, *Sacred Harmony*, 1784	4
P257	Valentine, *Thirty Psalm Tunes*, c.1785	4
P269	T. Williams, *Psalmodia Evangelica*, 1789	3
D12	Rippon, *Selection of Psalm and Hymn Tunes*, -1791	3
P291	S. Arnold & Callcott, *Psalms of David*, 1791	11
	TOTAL	72

In cases where primacy could not be established, the more likely first source has been listed.

Part B. By composer

Composer / No. of Tunes		Composer / No. of Tunes	
Anonymous	26	King, Robert	1
Arnold, John	1	Knapp, William (?)	3
Arnold, John (?)	1	Milgrove, Benjamin	1
Arnold, Samuel	5	Stephenson, Joseph	9
Broderip, John	1	Tans'ur, William	7
Callcott, John Wall	5	Taylor, Rayner	1
Graun, Karl Heinrich*	1	Valentine, John	4
Greatorex, ?Thomas	1	Walker, Thomas	2
Handel, George Frederick*	1	Williams, Thomas	1
Heighington, Musgrave	1	TOTAL	72

*Adapted

music is "Designed for the Use of Singing Schools in America" (as Daniel Read has it on the title page of *The American Singing Book,* 1785) without mention of use in church. Many later collections imitated this phrase, or expanded it to "Singing Schools and Musical Societies" (Kimball, Belcher), while others, as if in contrast, offered tunes "adapted to public worship" (Jenks, *New England Harmonist*) or claimed as "Suitable for Divine Worship" (Belknap, *The Evangelical Harmony*).

More compelling evidence on this point can be found in the contents of the books. American collections had not usually followed the common English practice of designating specific verses of a psalm or hymn for use with each tune, and printing the subsequent verses beneath the tune. They had continued the practice of the early eighteenth-century untexted tune supplements, designed for binding in with a book of metrical psalm texts. Thus when Daniel Bayley prepared his edition of Tans'ur's *Royal Melody Compleat* in 1767, he omitted the additional verses which Tans'ur had set out under each tune. Even if a tune was named "Psalm So-and-So," no verses were specified, and the tune could easily be used with another text in the same meter.

Many fuging tunes, however, were designed to fit specific texts, often with a substantial amount of "word-painting." By the 1780s, it was more and more usual in American psalmody books to find a single verse underlaid, with no indication of its provenance, and no additional verses set out. This would hardly be convenient for worship, when normally several verses of a psalm or hymn would be required. It was clearly intended for "singing schools and musical societies," where, with no religious object in view, the members could sing the tune to fasola syllables, or to the words set out, repeating them as often as they wished until they tired of the music.[59]

We know that as early as 1766 a singing school or society associated with the New South Church, Boston, had become sufficiently secularized to shock one young lady, who felt moved to express her dismay in an open letter to the *Boston Gazette.* She found "a large company, in all the spirit of gaiety, professedly convened for amusement, or instruction in the use of the voice . . . yet employed in uttering nothing but the most solemn addresses to the Deity, in prayers, confessions, praises. . . . The most devoted sentences of the inspired *Psalmist* paraphrased . . . dwelt upon the singers lips, the whole evening; interrupted now and then by a cheerful joke, a glass of wine, or the repeated *plaudits* of the hearers."[60]   The cardinal point to note here is that the psalm texts were still used even when the singing had no religious purpose.

We cannot assume, then, that the elaborate fuging tunes we find in print were commonly used in worship. Books that were officially designed for church services in

------

[59] If this was indeed the practice, it could of course be argued that such pieces no longer qualify as fuging *tunes,* since they do not fulfill the prerequisite of strophic repetition. We have, however, included in the Census any piece that goes through one verse in a standard meter and hence could be used strophically.

[60] *Boston Gazette,* March 10, 1766; cited Nathan, p. 14.

this period generally contain much plainer tunes.[61]   And indeed, as Oliver Holden said in the preface to *The Union Harmony* (1793), "Fuging music in general is badly calculated for divine worship; for it often happens that music of this description will not admit of a change of words without injuring the subject." According to John Hubbard, the "chaos of words" produced by the "common fugue" had by 1808 led many of the clergy "almost . . . to omit music in public worship."[62]

The American fuging tune of the 1780s and '90s must therefore be regarded as essentially secular in character and purpose, even when it has a sacred text. Composers no longer had to worry very much about possible religious objections to the obscuring of the text, or to inappropriate levity in the setting of solemn words. Anything that was enjoyed in the singing schools would sell, and they could concentrate on making their music lively, enjoyable to sing (rather than elevating to listen to), and challenging to the singers.

American composers found this situation quite favorable to the further development of the fuging tune. A standard type had been established, by selective imitation of English models, and was by this time quite familiar in the singing schools. There was a demand for more; singers probably enjoyed the challenge of tackling new music, provided it did not depart too far from what they expected; local engravers and publishers could print and distribute music without too much difficulty. A number of composers took advantage of the opportunity.

At the head of the list was William Billings, who created more fuging tunes (forty-two by our count)[63] than any other composer, English or American, in the eighteenth century. Not many of these, however, became general favorites. Although Billings accounts for eight of the one hundred items in Crawford's "core repertory,"[64] only one of these (MARYLAND, **405**) is a fuging tune. Billings is the only American psalmodist whose music has been treated in a book-length study, by J. Murray Barbour.[65]   The distinguishing characteristic of his mature style is originality: he is rarely content merely to follow a pattern, and his tunes use all manner of structures

---

61 See, for instance, Andrew Law's *A Collection of Hymn Tunes* (Cheshire, [1783]), which was bound together with *A Collection of Hymns for Social Worship:* the hymns, many of them by Watts or Wesley, are assigned to specific tunes, many of them by Martin Madan, Felice Giardini etc. and taken from Madan's "Lock Hospital Collection." For the Episcopal Church see *Tunes Suited to the Psalms and Hymns* which was attached to *The Book of Common Prayer . . . As Revised and Proposed to the Use of the Protestant Episcopal Church* (Philadelphia, 1786). Neither contains any fuging tunes.

62 "Many respectable clergymen in New England, have been almost determined to omit music in public worship. To their great sorrow, they have observed, that the effects of a most solemn discourse, were often obliterated by closing with improper music" (John Hubbard, *An Essay on Music* [Boston, 1808], p. 19; quoted McKay & Crawford, p. 194).

63 Lowens, using a slightly different definition of the term, arrived at total of thirty-six.

64 Professor Crawford kindly allowed me to see this, in advance of his forthcoming publication, *The Core Repertory of Early American Psalmody* (Madison: A-R Editions, forthcoming).

65 J. Murray Barbour, *The Church Music of William Billings* (East Lansing, 1960). Barbour treats the fuging tunes chiefly in the chapter "Counterpoint and Harmony," pp. 66-99.

and modes of imitation. He had a taste for sonority, expressed not only in his unusually frequent use of "choosing notes" to make chords of up to eight notes,[66] but in his habit of holding on the last note of a phrase in an imitative passage to provide a harmonic background to what follows (Example 11, page 46). In some tunes he extended the fuging section to such an extent that the piece gives the effect of an anthem: this term has even been used by Lowens to describe the tune CREATION (**260**).

Lowens has pointed out that "Billings's fuging-tunes are not really . . . typically American," in the sense that they rarely use the standard formula that Lowens has identified as probably derived from Stephenson.[67] I agree with this conclusion, yet I would not go on to conclude with Lowens that Billings's techniques are "markedly similar to those used by his English contemporaries." Though Billings shares with English psalmodists the absence of consistent use of the standard formula, I do not see any strong positive resemblance between the two styles. It seems to me rather that Billings's unshakable individuality caused him to shy away from any standardization, while his superior talent enabled him both to achieve a late mastery of his materials and to venture successfully into musical realms previously unexplored.

Next in order of quantity comes Daniel Read, who was responsible for thirty-five original fuging tunes in printed collections up to 1800.[68] Lowens has asserted, with good reason, that Read's "music and compilations" were even more important than those of Billings "in establishing the high popularity of the American fuging-tune."[69] His fuging tunes include more of the "standard" type than any other composer's. Six of them are in Crawford's "core repertory." The largest single group of his pre-1800 tunes is in *The American Singing Book* (1785), and they show a strong standardizing tendency. Whatever the meter of the verse, he tends to "fugue" the penultimate line, starting off with the bass voice with the standard figure and bringing in the others in voice order, or occasionally BTSA. Typically the harmony in this passage is static, the "point of imitation" being largely on the notes of the tonic chord (Example 12, page 47). This is true of four of the five tunes in this collection which became favorites (CALVARY, AMITY, LISBON, NAPLES). Two others that never "caught on" with the public (NORTON and HUMAN FRAILTY) are also examples of the standard type, but differ in that the point of imitation is a rather unusual phrase which gives rise to fast-moving harmonies during the fuging section. One might conclude that the static harmony was a help to people learning a new tune, and contributed to the popularity of these tunes. The fifth "favorite" from this collection (VICTORY, **1131**) is interesting in another way. It is non-standard, with a fuging section that is little more than a

---

[66] Barbour, p. 122.

[67] Lowens, p. 238; cf. also p. 240.

[68] Lowens states correctly that Read, as well as Holyoke, Jenks and French, wrote more fuging tunes than Billings in their entire careers (p. 248, n. 10). All these, however, were active after 1800, whereas Billings died that year.

[69] Lowens, p. 160.

EXAMPLE 11. Heath   Words Anon.

A - wake & see the new born light_____ Sprang from the dark -

A - wake & see the new born light_____ Sprang

A - wake & see the new born light

A - wake & see the new born light_____ Sprang from the

-some womb of Night,   Sprang from the dark - some

from the dark - some womb of Night,_____ Sprang from the dark - some

Sprang from the dark - some womb of Night,

dark-some, *sprang from the* dark - some womb *of* Night,_____

— Tune **756**, from Source A40

EXAMPLE 12. Lisbon   [Dr. Watts] 14th Hymn   2d Book

Wel - come *to   this   re - sto - ring breast And*

Wel - come to this re - sto - ring breast And these   re -

Wel - come *to   this   re - sto - ring breast And these re - joi* -   -   -

Wel - come *to this re - stor - ing breast And these*   re - *joi - cing eyes, and   these*   re -

these re - joi - cing   eyes.   *eyes.*

joi - cing   eyes.   *eyes.*

-        *cing   eyes.*   *eyes.*

joi - cing   eyes.   *Wel -*   *eyes.*

— Tune **591**, from Source A63

"delayed entry" plus the effective repetition of the word *sound*. This experimentation with word-painting is not uncommon with the American psalmodists, particularly in anthems. Its use here suggests that this tune was not really intended for strophic repetition, and this is borne out by the fact that it is set to the *last* stanza of Dr. Watts's Psalm 27, 1st part.

Jacob French's *New American Melody* (1789) has twenty-two new fuging tunes which he claims as his own compositions, whereas the same compiler's *The Psalmodist's Companion* (1793) carries no such claim of authorship. None of French's tunes became very popular; many were unica. He often used the standard formula for the fuging section, but many of his tunes have a homophonic section complete in itself followed by a fuging "chorus" repeating the last two lines of text; this feature no doubt comes from French's teacher, Billings, who took it from Tans'ur. ATTENTION (**174**) begins with an unusual fuging section: opening "fugues" are rather rare in American tunes. French's texts are chosen from a wide variety of sources, some of which we have not been able to trace; one or two, such as that of ATTENTION, have no clear religious content. Evidently many of these tunes were intended for social use, although the title page refers to "A new and complete body of Church Musick suited to all Metres usually sung in Churches . . . The whole . . . for the use of Singing Societies."

Thomas Lee's *Sacred Harmony,* of uncertain date (c. 1790-96 according to Crawford), is worth special mention. Its dozen new fuging tunes, mostly unattributed, show a strong tendency to a second "standard" type, an eight-liner with a structure of HHHHFHHH (or something similar). The second edition of the same work (c. 1791-96), compiled jointly with Daniel Willard, has thirteen more new tunes, all anonymous and unica, but these are mostly four-liners of the pattern HHFH, apart from a few very long ones. These two books represent an obscure corner of the fuging-tune repertory of some independent interest.

Jacob Kimball, in the preface to *Rural Harmony* (1793), disclaims professional skill as a composer, but aspires to originality in the music, which includes nineteen fuging tunes (INVITATION, **908**, had been published before with attribution to Kimball). He seems to favor Long Meter or 888888 in his texts, and to make the *last* line fuging, in both respects differing from "standard American" practice. Some have greatly extended fuging sections reminiscent of Billings (e. g., HILLSBOROUGH, **190**). BOXFORD (**749**) is in three vocal parts, but the tenor divides in 3 to provide a slightly absurd contrast in the last line, suggested by the text. WOBURN (**64**), however, attains beautiful simplicity, as each voice holds the last note of the point of imitation to build up an open-fifth chord.

Shumway's *The American Harmony,* already mentioned as the largest collection of fuging tunes on record, includes at least twenty-four new ones by various composers. Those claimed as Shumway's own are often greatly extended. He has his own preferred structural pattern for a four-line text: HHFFHH (or similar), with the third and fourth lines sung first fugally, then homophonically (WESTMINSTER, **113**; LAMBERTON, **398**; and others). Another large anthology, *The Columbian Harmony* by Joseph Stone and Abraham Wood (also 1793), has at least thirty-six new tunes. Many are attributed to one of the compilers, and although both tend to follow the standard formula, one clear distinction exists between their otherwise similar styles: whereas Wood prefers to bring his voices in order order (BTAS), Stone consistently favors BTSA.

Supply Belcher claims authorship of all twenty-six fuging tunes in *The Harmony of Maine* (1794).[70] Many are of the standard type or near it, but even more frequently he writes a six- to eight-line tune with fuging sections in the middle, like Shumway. Belcher's composing technique is shaky. Even allowing for misprints, it is hard to make sense out of many of his progressions, and in this respect he is a throwback to some of the early English psalmodists like Evison and West. All the tunes in this collection except **891** are unica.

Nathaniel Billings's *The Republican Harmony* contains fuging tunes of his own composition, many of which are of the standard kind, and well written of their type. In some tunes he prefers, like some of his predecessors, to join two stanzas of a four-line text to make an eight-line tune (CMD, like BLESSING OF THE SPRING, **841**, or SMD, like SUPPLICATION, **562**). This scheme naturally allowed for more variety in the placing of the fuging section, but Billings still generally uses the conventional type of imitation.

Of the other composers producing substantial numbers of original fuging tunes, Stephen Jenks and Daniel Belknap tend to favor the standard formula, though with occasional minor whimsicalities: Jenks uses an exotic key, F sharp major, for one of his (LIBERTY, **1099**); Belknap has one tune "for seven voices" (SSATBBB), though it is really in only five parts, the two lower basses sticking to an untexted drone bass. Belknap's texts are often isolated verses chosen for their special references to music, song or dance, or for their imagery (snow, fire and so on); again it is obvious that he is thinking of the musical society rather than the church, though the title page claims that the contents are "suitable for Divine Worship." Jacob Kimball, who printed nine new fuging tunes claimed as his own in *The Essex Harmony* (1800), uses the standard formula most of the time (though sometimes combining parts to reduce the imitation to three or even two entries).

Timothy Swan was a composer who attained his greatest popularity only after his own collection had been published in 1801. Before 1800, only eight fuging tunes by Swan had been printed, but of these no less than three were among the twenty most popular tunes (Table 5, pages 40-41). All three date from 1783: RAINBOW (**760**) and BRISTOL (**571**) appeared on adjacent pages in Brownson's *Select Harmony* and MONTAGUE (**807**) in Stickney's *Gentleman and Lady's Musical Companion*. Swan tended to prefer the "standard American" pattern. He generally chose striking texts full of imagery, especially for the fuging passages which thus take on a word-painting function. In RAINBOW, for "The sea grows calm at thy command And tempests cease to roar," Swan not only brings in the four voices in descending order, but also (most unusually) has them fade out in the same way, leaving the basses holding a solitary low C ("cease to roar").

---

[70] One of them, however (**891**), had already been printed in three earlier collections without attribution.

Towards the end of the century some signs are evident of a "reform" movement in American psalmody similar to that which was already far advanced in Great Britain. Law introduced a type of hymn tune that Crawford has aptly called "solo style hymnody,"[71] using among other sources Martin Madan's *Collection of Psalm Tunes* (London, 1769: the "Lock Hospital Collection") and Thomas Butts's *Harmonia Sacra* (London, [c. 1760]). Crawford has concluded that changes in the economics of printing "contributed to the decline of American sacred composition early in the nineteenth century and helped an imported European repertory to supersede a native music," and there were certainly some American psalmodists at the time who perceived things in that way. Law spoke of the "dignity and the ever varying productions of Handel, or Madan, and of others, alike meritorious" being "supplanted by the pitiful productions of numerous [American] composuists, whom it would be doing too much honor to name";[72] Holden wrote that "it is to be lamented that among so many American authors so little can be found well written or adapted to sacred purposes."[73] Yet in the perspective of an Anglo-American tradition it seems unrealistic to present the undoubted conflict as one between "American" and "European" styles. After all, both the "country" and the "reform" styles originated in Great Britain; both were adopted in America, at first with difficulty, but at last with full confidence and individuality. Lowell Mason and Thomas Hastings americanized the "reform" style as much as William Billings and Daniel Read americanized the "country" style. The distinction was one of social class and education, not of nationality; it reflected the unstoppable trend toward urbanization, not a failure of patriotic vigor.

As far as fuging tunes are concerned, the "reform" style, though it had deeply affected British efforts, had barely scratched the surface of American composition before 1800. Samuel Holyoke, a leader of the movement, disapproved of fuging tunes: "for the parts, falling in, one after another, each conveying a different idea, confound the sense, and render the performance a mere jargon of words."[74] Several of the "reform" fuging tunes published in Arnold & Callcott's *Psalms of David* were reprinted in American books (A153, A161, A203), and some of the dissenters' tunes for two trebles and bass were also taken over by American compilers (for instance **854**, **924** and **1077** from Rippon). But there are almost no fuging tunes of the "reform" type to be found among original American compositions of the eighteenth century, perhaps because there were as yet no American composers who had mastered the art of writing imitative counterpoint in a style that was correct by the standards of European art music. The nearest thing is perhaps the tune SHIRLEY (**698**) by Jacob Kimball, which he published in *The Essex Harmony* (1800). It is in three vocal parts only, either SSB or STB (the G clef is

---

71 Richard A. Crawford, *Andrew Law, American Psalmodist* (Evanston, 1968), p. 264.

72 Andrew Law, *The Musical Primer* (New Haven, 1780), preface; cited Chase, p. 130. In the 1793 edition Law specifically recommended "European" composers as models.

73 Oliver Holden, *The Union Harmony* (Boston, 1793), preface.

74 Samuel Holyoke, *Harmonia Americana* (Boston, 1791), preface.

ambiguous); the first part has four phrases of mellifluous homophony in 3/2 time,
and the second part, in common time, though using the "standard" American formula,
is remarkably "European" in its harmony and counterpoint.

   Karl Kroeger has assembled evidence that in the closing years of the century
instrumental bands were associated with the singers in some American societies, and
even in church.[75] Nathaniel Gould, writing in the mid-nineteenth century, said that bass
viols had begun to be used in singing schools "about the commencement of Billings'
career" but were considered unfit for use in church until around the beginning of the
nineteenth century. Bentley admitted instruments to his church at Salem, Massachusetts,
in 1796, and at the Thanksgiving Service on November 30, 1797 his band consisted of
"2 Bass Violins, 3 German flutes & 6 violins." Kroeger points out that several American
collections of the 1790s provide for instrumental symphonies and separate instrumental
basses: he cites Holyoke's *Harmonia Americana* (1791), Holden's *Union Harmony* (1793),
and Billings's *Continental Harmony* (1794) and *Massachusetts Compiler* (1795) as "among
the earliest." This practice, already well established in Britain, seems to have been well
under way in New England in the 1790s, in singing schools if not in churches. But its
effect on the character of the fuging tune was marginal until the first decade of the
nineteenth century.

English and American: A Comparison

I N THE COURSE of the eighteenth century, over twelve hundred different fuging tunes
were printed, roughly half of them originating in England and half in New England.
(The numbers originating in Scotland and in other parts of America are insignificant.)
It is not possible to draw a well-marked distinction between the two, and the majority
of examples could probably have been written in either country. The most striking
difference is in the part played by the fuging tune in musical life in the two countries,
and any differences in style seem incidental to that. Nevertheless, our analysis does
point up certain national differences in the character of fuging tunes.

   In England the fuging tune was, from first to last, considered as an adjunct to
worship. For this reason it flourished first in Anglican parish churches, as a consequence
of the movement to improve psalmody, but entered only gradually into dissenting worship
because of Calvinist or Wesleyan objections to the form and the manner of its performance.
Commercially motivated efforts to appeal to members of more than one religious sect
had to take account of the customs and prejudices of each. There was little demand for
fuging tunes as social music: other types of music filled this function. "Reform" fuging

----

   [75] Karl Kroeger, unpublished paper, "The Church Gallery Orchestra in New England."
Dr. Kroeger was kind enough to provide me with a copy of this paper, which is my source for the
information in this paragraph.

tunes made great headway in the last quarter of the century, not least because many thought that praise offered to God in church ought to be of the highest class and quality.

In America, objections to the use of the fuging tune in worship were perhaps as strong or stronger, and in many places they prevailed. But the form flourished nevertheless, because the singing school, instead of being (as in England) merely a temporary expedient to train a parish choir, had become a leading social institution. Towards the end of the century there was a thriving free market in psalmody collections which was largely independent of religious bodies. The reform movement at first made little headway in the absence of professionally trained American composers; but after 1800 many Americans learned to imitate this style.

Consequently, the English fuging tune developed very slowly, as country composers labored to master the difficult technical problems it posed. Composers working in different localities found their own solutions to these problems, and no prevailing or standard type was ever established, though the "Beesly technique" came near to it. As conditions altered—as instruments were added to parish choirs, as dissenting congregations took up the form, as professional composers weighed in with improvements—the style and technique changed to meet each new situation. The captive audience of the church or chapel congregation generally accepted whatever was provided for its edification. In Britain, forty-seven percent of all fuging tunes printed were new (653 out of 1384), as Table 3, page 26, shows.

Meanwhile, when the fuging tune crossed the Atlantic, some examples proved specially well suited to the needs of both composers and singers in the American colonies. The Beesly technique offered a method of dealing with the unfamiliar problem of imitative counterpoint, and when it was carried out with predictable rhythmic motives and static harmony, the result proved quite easy to sing. In the free market situation of the singing school or musical society, the "best" kind of fuging tune was established by a process of repeated selection. Though originality and innovation were possible, the central tradition was determined directly by what the singers wanted. Only nineteen percent of fuging tunes printed in America were new (574 out of 3024).

The type of fuging tune that caught on best in America, as we have already seen, was one that began with a closed homophonic section of two or four lines and continued with a "fugue." Table 7, *opposite,* shows, indeed, a difference among national and religious preferences in this regard. In English parochial tunes, the most popular type began right off with a fuging section for the first line of text, but a fair proportion had their first fuging section with the second, third or fourth line of text. Among Dissenting and Scottish tunes there is a clear preference for the *fourth* line. In the case of American tunes, however, well over half the total of 574 tunes have their first fuging section with the third line, and the fifth is the next most common—which fits well with Lowens's observation.[76] Less than one American tune in ten has a "fuge" in the first two lines,

---

76 Lowens, p. 247.

TABLE 7. FUGING TUNES BY STRUCTURAL TYPE

Source Category	Which Line of Text is the First to be Treated Fugally								Total
	1	2	3	4	5	6	7	8+	
Part A. By numbers of tunes									
P	177	99	133	135	14	9	14	6	587
D+S	8	8	13	28	4	4	0	1	66
P+D+S→A	19	5	21	19	3	3	2	0	72
A	39	9	319	52	109	10	24	12	574
Total (P+D+S+A)	224	116	465	215	127	23	38	19	1227
Part B. As percentages of each source category									
P	30.2	16.9	22.7	23.0	2.4	1.6	2.4	1.0	
D+S	12.1	12.1	19.6	42.4	6.1	6.1	0.0	1.5	
P+D+S→A	26.4	6.9	29.2	26.4	4.2	4.2	2.8	0.0	
A	6.8	1.6	55.6	9.1	19.0	1.7	4.2	2.1	
Total (P+D+S+A)	18.3	9.5	37.9	17.5	10.4	1.9	3.1	1.5	

For each tune, the question asked is this:
When the first fuging phrase occurs, which line of the verse text is being sung?
The answer can be found by looking up the tune in the Census,
and seeing what number appears above the first F in the grid at the right.
In this table, tunes are sorted in columns according to the answer to this question,
and in rows according to the source category of the earliest source, P, D, S, or A.
P+D+S→A means "tunes originating in English parochial, Dissenting,
or Scottish sources that were reprinted in American sources before 1801."
For an explanation of the total number of tunes (1227), see the note to Table 3, page 26.

compared with nearly half the English parochial tunes. Of the 72 British tunes later selected for publication by American compilers, there is also a preference for the third line, though it is only marginally ahead of the first and fourth.

The greater commercial dissemination of psalm tunes in America helps to account for other differences. Tune names in England were generally of local significance only, and when a compiler took over a tune from a book used in another part of the country, he often gave it a new name: the extreme case is tune **475**, which acquired six different names in as many printings. Many English tunes were anonymous, and were freely altered by later compilers. By contrast, in American books, fuging tunes, whether of British or American origin, soon acquired a fixed form, name, and composer attribution (correct or otherwise), which then remained largely unaltered through many subsequent printings. (For instance tune **1060**, about equally popular in both countries, has seven names and five variants of incipit or structure in 36 British sources; in 40 American sources it has just two names and no variants.) Local variation had less place in the organized American system of singing schools linked by a flourishing tunebook industry.

Of the two situations, the American was more conducive to creative achievement. Composers have generally worked best where strong conventions are built into their audience's expectations, and can be stretched, delayed, or occasionally denied in a new composition, but not destroyed. Such conditions barely existed in England, but they were created in America by the strong singing-school environment. Although some fine specimens of fuging tunes can be found in both English and American sources—sometimes in obscure books that never attracted much notice at the time—it was only in the American heyday of 1783-1800 that a "school" of fuging tunes took shape.

LIST OF SOURCES

T HIS LIST comprises all printed sources known to the compilers that contain fuging tunes and were published with English-language texts between 1700 and 1800. It is divided into four categories:

English Parochial Sources (P)

English Dissenting Sources (D)

Scottish Sources (S)

American Sources (A)

Later editions of the same book with identical fuging-tune content are indexed by means of decimal points. Thus P51.2 means "P51, 2nd edn.," and is listed under P51 here. After each source is a list of the fuging tunes it contains, the numbers referring to the Census.

Tunes marked with an asterisk (*) have been identified as *original* in the source concerned, on the basis of:

1. unique printing in this source; or
2. a claim by the compiler, not contradicted by appearance in an earlier source; or
3. clear primacy of publication date; or
4. where the two earliest sources have the same or uncertain publication date, an acknowledgment, by one, of the other as the source for the tune.

Where there is not enough information to establish primacy for one source, the tune is marked with the sign (+) in two or more sources, one of which was the earliest.

ENGLISH PAROCHIAL SOURCES

These are described in greater detail in Nicholas Temperley, The Music
of the English Parish Church *(Cambridge, 1979), pp. 364-90, where the
same numbers are used. Subsequent editions are designated as follows:
P155.2 means "the second edition of P155" (whether or not it is called the
second edition); P176.A and P176.B refer to two editions of P176 whose
chronological sequence could not be determined. P182a was omitted from
the list in Temperley (1979); some other items have been renumbered here.*

P51   Playford, Henry. *The Divine Companion,* 1701. 2nd edn., 1707. 3rd edn.,
         1709 (reissued 1715). 4th edn., 1722.
         670*

P71.2   Chetham, John. *A Book of Psalmody,* 2nd ed., 1722. *See also* P86, P111a.
         106*

P80   Timbrell, Francis. *The Divine Musick Scholar's Guide.* (Various unique
         copies, [c. 1725].) Copy "B": Trinity College, Glasgow, 39.C.4. Copy "C":
         British Library, A.980.a.
         670

P86   Chetham, John. *A Book of Psalmody,* 3rd edn., 1724. 4th edn., 1731.
         See also P71.2, P111a.
         106

P88.3   Holdroyd, Israel. *The Spiritual Man's Companion,* 3rd edn., 1733. 4th edn.,
         1746. 5th edn., 1753.
         857* 860

P89   Broom [e], Michael and John. *Michael Broom's Collection of Church Musick,*
         [Collection I, -1725].
         670

P104   Pearson, William. *The Second Book of the Divine Companion,* [1731-].
         [2nd edn.], *The Divine Companion,* [c. 1745].
         597*

P107   Broom [e], Michael. *Michael Broom's Collection of Church Music,* [Collection
         II, 79 leaves, c. 1733].
         106 860*

P111a   Chetham, John. *A Book of Psalmody,* 6th edn., 1741. 7th edn., 1745.
        8th edn., 1752. 9th edn., 1767. 10th edn., [1779]. 11th edn., 1787.
        See also P71.2, P86.
           106

P117   Arnold, John. *The Compleat Psalmodist,* 1741.
           858*

P117.2 ————. 2nd edn., 1750. 3rd edn., 1753. 4th edn., 1756.
           402 858 948

P117.5 ————. 5th edn., 1761. 6th edn., 1769.
           246 325⁺ 948

P117.7 ————. 7th edn., 1779.
           106 246 948 1060

P118   Sreeve, John. *The Divine Music Scholar's Guide,* 1740. 2nd edn., 1741.
           857

P120   Buckenham, John. *The Psalm-Singer's Devout Exercise,* 1741.
           857 860 911*

P123   Green, James. *A Book of Psalmody,* 10th edn., 1744. 11th edn., 1751.
           106 828*

P124   Bellamy, John. *A System of Divine Musick,* 1745.
           383*

P125   Broderip, John. *A New Set of Anthems and Psalm Tunes,* [1745].
           993 *

P126   Alcock, Dr. John [the elder]. *Psalmody,* [c. 1745].
           567*

P129a   Beesly, Michael. *A Collection of 20 New Psalm Tunes,* [c. 1746].
        (Formerly P177.)
           88* 115* 141* 212* 226* 326* 381* 473* 531* 597 675* 818* 860
           948* 970* 1033* 1042* 1112* 1161* 1175*

P130   Evison, James. *A Compleat Book of Psalmody*, 1747.
              326 345* 402* 948

P130.2   ———. 2nd edn., 1751.
              125 141 192 326 345 402 690 948 1060

P130.3   ———. 3rd edn., 1754. 5th edn., 1769.
              125 141 184* 192 326 345 382+ 402 690 948 1034* 1060

P134   East, William. *The Voice of Melody*, [Book I], [c. 1748]. *See also* P137.
              370*

P134.2   ———. 2nd edn., Waltham, 1750.
              219 267* 378* 419* 465* 670 860

P135   Watts, Joseph. *A Choice Collection of Church Music*, 1749.
              66* 88 125+ 192+ 219+ 288+ 326 670 690+ 1060+ 1175

P136   Broderip, John. *A Second Book of New Anthems and Psalm Tunes*, [-1750].
              (Reissued, [1764].)
              897*

P137   East, William. *The Voice of Melody*, Book II, 1750. *See also* P134.
              56* 60* 125 142* 143* 178* 192 326 370 426+ 444* 451+ 463* 470*
              648* 690 739* 993 1060 1073* 1092*

P142   Tans'ur, William. [Untitled collection of church music: British Library,
              shelfmark A.1232.f], [c.1750].
              357* 456+ 719+

P143   Hinton, Simon. *A Collection of Church Musick*, [-1751].
              670

P144   Milner, Abraham. *The Psalm Singers Companion*, 1751. 4th edn., [c. 1765].
              115 192 288 670 1060

P145a   Beesly, Michael. *A Book of Psalmody*, [c. 1751]. (Formerly P176.A.)
              88 115 125+ 192+ 212 219+ 288+ 326 382+ 426+ 451+ 473 597 690+ 818
              860 948 1060+ 1175

P148   Knapp, William. *New Church Melody,* [c. 1752] . 2nd edn., 1754. 3rd edn., 1756. 4th edn., 1761. 5th edn., 1764.

> 169* 236* 320* 348* 350*(2) 372* 381(2) 466* 675 734* 816* 876* 970
> 1033 1042 1112 1136* 1161

P149   Broome, Michael. *A Collection of Twenty Eight Psalm Tunes . . . ,* 1754.

> 993

P151   East, William. *The Sacred Melody,* 1754.

> 23* 27* 77* 135* 141 249* 263* 359* 446* 449* 459* 572* 604* 639*
> 677* 725* 735* 747* 868* 1044* 1174*

P152   Crisp, William. *Divine Harmony,* 1755.

> 193* 690 911 1060

P153   Davenport, Uriah. *The Psalm-Singer's Pocket Companion,* 1755. 2nd edn., 1758. 3rd edn., 1785.

> 121* 324* 399* 411* 447* 616* 619* 720* 871* 879* 881* 1079*

P155   Tans'ur, William. *The Royal Melody Compleat,* Book II, 1755.

> 137* 217* 297* 456⁺ 480* 719⁺ 736*

P155.2   ———. 2nd edn., 1760.

> 217 297(2) 456 480 719 736 859*

P155.3   ———. 3rd edn., 1765. *See also* A28, A30, A31.

> 217 297(2) 456 719 736 859 1045*

P155a   (Beesly, Michael?). *An Introduction to Psalmody,* [c. 1755] . (Formerly P176.B.)

> 125 320 690 858 1060

P156   Broome, Michael. *A Choice Collection of Twenty Four Psalm Tunes . . . With the Addition of Nine Psalm Tunes . . . ,* [c. 1755] .

> 993

P157   East, William. *Collection of Church Musick,* [c. 1755] .

> 23 55* 56 77 115 125 141 168* 178 192 211* 219 234* 249 263 266* 321*
> 359 365* 419 439* 444 446 449 457* 459 470 604 639 662* 677 690 695*
> 725 727* 735 739 785* 818 826* 860 868 941* 954* 1060 1073 1174

P158   Pratt, Jonas. *A Set of Anthems and Psalm Tunes,* [c. 1755].
            158* 1149*

P163   Arnold, John. *The Psalmist's Recreation,* 1757.
            246*

P164   Everet, Jonathan. *The Divine Concert,* 1757.
            39* 279* 299* 343* 356* 629* 660* 731* 832* 874* 955*

P166   Hill, John. *A New Book of Psalmody,* [c. 1757].
            12* 746* 823* 836* 909* 953* 1012* 1024* 1132* 1140*

P168   Stephenson, Joseph. *An Anthem Taken Out of the 44 Chap. of Isaiah,* [c. 1758].
            843*

P169   Arnold, John. *The Leicestershire Harmony,* 1759.
            105* 107* 147* 179* 247* 293* 499* 517* 527* 564* 622* 624* 642*
            663* 733* 812* 932* 996* 999* 1018* 1081* 1095* 1097*

P169.2   ———. 2nd edn., 1767.
            99* 105 107 147 179 247 293 499 517 527 564 622 624 642 663 733
            812 932 996 999 1018 1081 1095 1097 1185*

P170   French, J. *The Young Psalm Singer's Complete Guide,* 1759.
            54* 152* 230* 455* 477* 641* 1070* 1168*

P171   Stephenson, Joseph. *Church Harmony Sacred to Devotion,* 3rd edn., 1760.
            4th edn., [c. 1775].
            220* 240* 244* 262* 269* 281* 282* 302* 366* 367* 443* 448* 452*
            488* 489* 492* 521* 555* 592* 790* 794* 1001* 1002* 1178*

P173   West, Benjamin. *Sacra Concerto,* 1760. 2nd edn., 1769.
            138* 422* 621* 627* 668* 678* 990* 991*

P174   Adams, Abraham. *The Psalmist's New Companion,* 6th edn., [c. 1760].
            97+ 125 141 184 192 325+ 326 344* 345 382 402 690 860 948 1060

P174.10   ———. 10th edn., [c. 1775]. 11th edn., [c. 1785]. 12th edn., [c. 1795].
            97 125 141 184 192 325 326 344 345 382 402 690 860 948 1010+
            1042 1060

P175   Ashworth, Caleb. *A Collection of Tunes,* [Part I] , [c. 1760] . 2nd edn.,
          1765. 3rd edn., 1766. 4th edn., 1775.
            485* 1060

P176.A   *See* P145a.

P176.B   *See* P155a.

P177   *See* P129a.

P180   *A Collection of Psalm Tunes with a Thorough Bass,* [c. 1760] .
            106 828

P182a   Wilkins, Matthew. *A Book of Psalmody,* [c. 1760] .
            62* 192 259* 348 366 448 521 555 670 720 876 1002 1033 1042 1112 1161

P183   Catchpole, Robert. *A Choice Collection of Church Music,* 1761.
            46* 348 350 492 998*

P186a   Barnes, William and Carpendale, William. *Harmonia-Sacra-Nova,* (1763).
            1224* 1225* 1226* 1227* 1228* 1229* 1230* 1231* 1232* 1233* 1234*
            1235* 1236* 1237* 1238*

P189   Williams, Aaron. *The Universal Psalmodist,* 1763. 2nd edn., 1764. 3rd edn.,
          1765. *See also* A31.
            352* 846* 1060

P189.4   ———. 4th edn., 1770.
            352 846

P191   *A Collection of Melodies to the Psalms . . . According to the Version of
          Christopher Smart,* 1765.
            609* 907*

P192   Hewett, James. *An Introduction to Singing,* 1765.
            219 326 382

P198   Harrott, John. *The Rutland-Harmony,* 1769.
            27 47* 77 115 143 175* 178 179 192 219 243* 263 279 299 343 356
            359 408* 439 449 459 461* 527 622 639 677 725 727 731 735 741* 744*
            747 818 832 868 874 941 955 1017* 1060 1174

P200   Harrott, John. *The Divine Vocal and Instrumental Concert,* 1770.
        1008* 1072* 1177*

P204   Cook, Richard. *Kentish Psalmodist's Companion,* [c. 1770].
        97+ 350 475+ 816 1042 1136 1179+

P210   Tans'ur, William. *Melodia Sacra,* 2nd edn., 1772.
        184 297 357 456 719 736

P212   Ivery, John. *The Hertfordshire Melody,* 1773.
        62 105 107 219 246 286* 345 349* 402 517 622 639 663 689* 843 932

P220   Cook, Richard. *The Psalmodist's Companion,* [c. 1775].
        193 320 350 475+ 690 816 843 941 1010+ 1033 1042 1136 1161 1179+

P226   Senior, D. *The Food of Devotion,* [c. 1775].
        623* 630* 638* 643* 646* 681* 737* 751* 752* 923* 1005* 1083*
        1100* 1116* 1117* 1120* 1121* 1122* 1123* 1125* 1129* 1130*

P227   Stephenson, Joseph. *The Musical Companion,* [c. 1775].
        843 1126*

P228   Wilkins, Elizabeth. *A Collection of Church Music,* [c. 1775].
        62 192 320 348 366 448 521 555 568* 720 793* 876 1002 1033 1042
        1112 1161

P230   Bond, Hugh. *Twelve Hymns and Four Anthems,* [c. 1776].
        172*

P231   Pearce, Samuel. *Sacred Music,* [c. 1776].
        19* 20* 25* 26* 58* 65* 79* 92* 189* 197* 198* 199* 200* 202* 203*
        237* 287* 317* 335* 341* 407* 425* 440* 505* 515* 586* 1000* 1142*
        1143* 1146* 1151*

P233   Arnold, John. *A Supplement to the Complete Psalmodist,* [1777].
        390*

P235   Crompton, John. *The Psalm Singer's Assistant,* 1778.
        62 125 141 192 325 344 402 485 492 689 690 839* 856* 860 996
        1060 1075*

P237   Roome, Francis. *The Harmony of Sion,* 1779.
         567 569*

P242   Beatson, John. *A Complete Collection of All the Tunes Sung . . . in Hull,*
         [c. 1780].
         30⁺ 36* 192 688⁺ 1060

P246   Smith, Isaac. *A Collection of Psalm Tunes,* [c. 1780].
         1060

P246.2   ———. A new edition with supplement, [c. 1782]. 4th edn., [c. 1784].
         192 1060

P246.5   ———. 5th edn., with additions by S. Major, [c. 1790]. *See also* P258.
         192 290⁺ 458⁺ 869* 1060

P249   *Musica Sacra: or, A Collection of Easy Tunes,* [-1783].
         182* 242* 1002 1060

P250   Barwick, John. *Harmonia Cantica Divina,* [c. 1783].
         180* 206* 229* 265* 273* 291* 339* 342* 373* 374* 526* 603* 748*
         904* 918* 937* 971* 997* 1025*

P253   Harrison, Ralph. *Sacred Harmony,* Vol. I, [1784]. [2nd] edn., [1786].
         4th edn., [c. 1795].
         31* 115 188* 192 231* 241* 243 267 302 366 411 436* 648 688⁺ 843
         1002 1060 1165*

P255   Marsh, John. *A Verse Anthem . . . Ten New Psalm Tunes,* [c. 1785].
         707*

P256   Tremain, Thomas. *Twenty Psalms,* [c. 1785].
         176* 684* 711* 712* 740* 1124* 1134*

P257   Valentine, John. *Thirty Psalm Tunes,* [c. 1785].
         18* 95* 131* 171* 264* 385* 848* 861* 951* 966* 1040* 1090* 1093*

P258   Harrison, Ralph. *Sacred Harmony,* Vol. II, [1786].
         51* 251* 358* 423* 598* 692* 772* 921* 1089* 1170*

P259   Harwood, Edward. *A Second Set of Hymns and Psalm Tunes,* (1786).
            6* 208* 468*

P263   Dalmer, William. *Twenty Psalms and Hymns,* [c. 1788] .
            3* 49* 680* 864* 895*

P264   Hill, John. *Hill's Church Music,* [1788-91] .
            1194*

P266   Dixon, William. *Psalmodia Christiana,* 1789.
            23 31 37* 81* 115 147 153* 183* 192 215* 243 245* 253* 258* 263
            279 290+ 302 340* 345 365 446 455 472* 475 477 604 625* 629 636*
            639 670 688 725 735 843 853* 922* 941 942* 946* 976* 992* 1027*
            1032* 1048* 1051* 1060 1086* 1112 1167*

P267   Harrod, W. *Select Psalms of David,* 1789.
            670

P269   Williams, Thomas. *Psalmodia Evangelica,* Vol. I, 1789. 2nd edn., (1790).
            3rd edn., (1792).
            241 458+ 467* 475 567 600* 846 886* 1169*

P270   Heron, Henry. *Parochial Music Corrected,* 1790.
            714*

P273   Collins, Thomas. *A Collection of Anthems and Psalms,* [c. 1790] .
            704*

P274   Cooke, Matthew. *Twelve Psalm Tunes,* [c. 1790] .
            122* 148* 645* 656* 673* 679* 713* 768* 1055* 1082* 1137* 1191*

P291   Arnold, Dr. Samuel, and Callcott, John W. *The Psalms of David,* 1791.
            1* 2* 9* 16* 17* 48* 108* 109* 111* 118* 120* 140* 154* 162* 167*
            173* 181* 210* 354* 516* 589* 606* 628* 644* 649* 654* 658* 661*
            664* 672* 674* 683* 685* 694* 696* 702* 716* 717* 722* 724* 726*
            745* 750* 753* 776* 863* 894* 912* 928* 944* 950* 983* 994* 995*
            1039* 1041* 1052* 1063* 1113* 1114* 1118* 1127* 1128* 1138* 1150*
            1152* 1153* 1158* 1162* 1163* 1172* 1187* 1188* 1189* 1192*

P292   Tattersall, William D. *Psalms Selected from the Version of . . . Merrick,*
          [1791].
              145* 1060 1069*

P293   Beaumont, John. *Four Anthems . . . ,* (1793).
              139* 900*

P297   Tattersall, William D. *Improved Psalmody,* Vol. I. In score, 1794. In parts,
          1795.
              4* 5* 21* 53* 119* 144* 150* 151* 155* 159* 163* 164* 165* 295*
              635* 640* 650* 651* 652* 657* 669* 676* 686* 693* 697* 699* 700*
              701* 706* 710* 721* 730* 738* 742* 775* 888* 925* 967* 969* 986*
              1031* 1050* 1108* 1133* 1144* 1190*

P303   Major, S. *Sacred Melody,* 9th edn., [c. 1795]. 10th edn., [c. 1796]. 11th edn.,
          [c. 1800]. *See also* P246.
              115 192 222 272 290 458 867 869 974 1060

P309   Broderip, John and Robert. *Portions of Psalms,* (1798).
              458

P310   Loder, A. *A Collection of Church Musick,* 1798.
              52* 682* 687* 708* 1135* 1147* 1193*

P313   FFitch, George. *The Country Chorister,* [1799].
              617*

P321   Harvey, William. *The Melksham Harmony,* [c. 1800].
              7* 24* 404* 558* 729* 933*

P323   Key, Joseph. *Five Anthems . . . Twenty Psalm Tunes,* Book III, [c. 1800].
              8* 160* 216* 280* 313* 396* 762* 824* 914* 1078*

P651   (Jacob, Benjamin.) *A Collection of Hymn Tunes . . . for the Use of Surry
          Chapel,* [1797].
              1064*

ENGLISH DISSENTING AND DOMESTIC SOURCES

This list is limited to English sources not *intended for use in parish churches; but it should be remembered that many sources in the P list above were used in dissenting meeting houses or in private houses as well as in parish churches. Such uses are designated by the code numbers 6 and 7 respectively in Temperley (1979). Further, dissenting or domestic books lacking fuging tunes are not listed here.*

D1	Bedford, Arthur. *The Excellency of Divine Music,* Appendix, (1733). *For domestic use and for Religious Societies.* 653*
D2	Knibb, Thomas. *A Collection of Tunes in Three Parts,* [1754-]. *For Calvinistic Methodists and other dissenters.* 1200*
D3	Knibb, Thomas. *The Psalm Singer's Help,* [c.1765]. (A revision of D2.) *For Calvinistic Methodists and other dissenters.* 1200
D4	*The Gospel Magazine,* June 1774. *1 hymn, for Methodist or domestic use.* 974*
D5	*The Gospel Magazine,* December 1779. *1 hymn, for Methodist or domestic use.* 239*
D6	Addington, Stephen. *A Collection of Psalm Tunes for Public Worship,* 3rd [and earliest surviving] edn., 1780. *For Congregationalists.* 192 213* 974
D6.6	———. 6th edn., 1786. 115 192 222* 272* 867* 974
D6.10	———. 10th edn., 1791. 115 192 222 272 867 974
D6.11	———. 11th edn. (rev. J. Murgatroyd), 1792. 12th edn., 1797. 115 192 222 272 340 458 846 867 974

D6.13   ———. 13th edn., 1799. *See also* D15.
         71* 115 192 222 272 340 349 386* 458 475 503* 867 952 974

D8   Mason, William, of Cambridge. *Congregational Singing,* [c. 1790].
         For Congregationalists.
         290+ 475 590*

D9   Radiger, Anton. *Four Setts of New Psalm Tunes in Score,* [c. 1790].
         For worship in general.
         103* 166* 487* 537* 718* 782* 878* 973* 1013* 1046* 1047* 1098*

D10   Banister, Charles W. *Twelve Psalm and Hymn Tunes,* 1792.
         For general domestic use or for dissenting worship.
         278*

D11   Haweis, Thomas. *Carmina Christo,* [c. 1792].
         For the Countess of Huntingdon's Connexion.
         952* 1020*

D12   Rippon, John. *A Collection of Psalm and Hymn Tunes,* [1792-].
         For Baptist worship.
         90* 132* 157* 172 192 213 239 302 363* 371* 458 467 556* 671* 829*
         854* 924* 988* 1060 1077*

D13   Hering, John Frederic. *Twelve Hymns in Four Parts,* (1795).
         For the Countess of Huntingdon's Connexion.
         984* 1037*

D14   Leach, Thomas. *A Second Sett of Hymns and Psalm Tunes,* 1798.
         For Wesleyan Methodists.
         1201* 1202* 1203* 1204* 1205* 1206*

D15   H[awes], S. *A Second Volume to Addington's Collection,* [1799].
         Sequel to D6, for Congregationalists.
         132 195* 375* 382 508* 667* 690 899* 988 1036* 1085* 1132 1150 1159*

D16   Cuzens, Benjamin. *The Portsmouth Harmony,* [c. 1800].
         For dissenting worship.
         34* 73* 362* 502* 618* 631* 1076*

D17   Porter, Samuel. *Twenty Five Odes, Hymn Tunes &c.,* [c. 1800].
         For dissenting worship or domestic use.
         368* 543*

SCOTTISH SOURCES

This list is limited to the small number of books
published in Scotland in which fuging tunes were found.
They were probably used only in Episcopal churches or in private.

S1   Moore, Thomas. *The Psalm-Singer's Delightful Pocket Companion,* [c. 1762].
      227*

S3   *A Collection of Sacred Music . . . for the Use of the Episcopal Chapel in*
      Glasgow, 1787.
      227

S5   Ding, Laurence. *The Beauties of Psalmody,* 1792.
      30+ 192 239 1038*

S5.2 ————. 2nd edn., 1800.
      30 239 1038

S6   Boyd, Henry. *A Select Collection of Psalm and Hymn Tunes,* 1793. 2nd edn.,
      [c. 1800].
      30 132 192 239 290 458 1060

S7   Peaston, William. *A Selection of Psalm and Hymn Tunes in Three Parts.*
      [c. 1800.]
      239

AMERICAN SOURCES

This list is based on an early version of Richard Crawford's bibliography
of American sacred music collections, which he kindly made available.
Every item listed separately by Crawford has been given its own
number, even if it is merely a later edition of another work so listed.
In a few cases, a later reissue of one of these has been separately entered.

A17   Lyon, James. *Urania,* 1761. [2nd] edn., [1767].
      125 141 345 517 948 1060

A18   [Hopkinson, Francis.] *A Collection of Psalm Tunes,* 1763.
      703*

A22   [Bayley, Daniel.] *A New and Complete Introduction,* 1764. [2nd] edn.,
          1765. [3rd] edn., 1766.
               670

A23   Flagg, Josiah. *A Collection of the Best Psalm Tunes,* 1764.
               246 352 1060

A24   Walter, Thomas. *The Grounds and Rules,* 1764.
               297

A26   Flagg, Josiah. *Sixteen Anthems,* [1766].
               302

A28   Tans'ur, William; (Bayley, Daniel?). *The Royal Melody Complete,* 3rd edn.,
          1767. [An edition of P155.]
               217 297 456 480 719 736 859 1060

A30   Tans'ur William; (Bayley, Daniel?). *The Royal Melody Complete,* 4th edn.,
          1768. [An edition of P155.]
               217 297 456 480 719 736 859 1060

A31   Bayley, Daniel. *The American Harmony,* 5th edn., 1769. [Contains edns.
          of P155 and P189.] 6th edn., 1771. 7th edn., 1771. 8th edn., 1774.
               217 297 302 352 456 480 719 736 790 846 859 1060

A33   Billings, William. *The New-England Psalm-Singer,* [1770].
               221* 431* 493*

A34   Gilman, John Ward. *A New Introduction,* 1771.
               297 456 790

A36   [Bayley, Daniel. *New Royal Harmony*], 1773.
               843 1112

A37   Bayley, Daniel. *The New Universal Harmony,* 1773.
               350 517 843 876

A39   Stickney, John. *The Gentleman and Lady's Musical Companion,* 1774.
          [2nd] edn., [c. 1780]. *See also* A54.
               297 302 352 355* 381 480 517 734 790 806* 843 846 859 1060 1112

A40   Billings, William. *The Singing Master's Assistant*, 1778. 2nd edn., [1779-80].
           3rd edn., 1781. 4th edn., [1786-9].
             40* 128* 307* 405* 482* 546* 756* 893* 935* 1101* 1102*

A41   Law, Andrew. *Select Harmony*, 1778. *See also* A43.
             141 238* 302 355 499 622 843 1060 1112 1160*

A43   Law, Andrew. *Select Harmony*, 1779. *See also* A41, A47a.
             41* 141 147 179 196* 238 301* 302 331* 355 499 622 755* 843 885*
             935 1002 1060 1095 1112 1160 1185

A44   Billings, William. *The Psalm-Singer's Amusement*, 1781.
             63* 308* 825* 1011*

A45   Law, Andrew. *A Select Number of Plain Tunes*, 1781.
             1060

A47   Jocelin, Simeon and Doolittle, Amos. *The Chorister's Companion*, 1782.
           See also A49, A87.
             15* 41 141 187* 302 337* 381 513* 622 843 845* 935 1002 1060 1101
             1102 1112

A47a   Law, Andrew. *Select Harmony*, [c. 1782].
             41 141 147 179 196 238 301 302 331 355 499 622 843 885 935 1112
             1160 1185

A49   Jocelin, Simeon and Doolittle, Amos. *The Chorister's Companion*, Part III,
           [1782-3]. *See also* A47, A87.
             405 540* 825 893

A51   Brownson, Oliver. *Select Harmony*, 1783.
             41 91* 124* 187 246 256* 302 311* 312* 337* 387* 395* 413* 513
             519* 541* 571* 588* 760* 773* 825 873* 875* 893 943* 968* 985*
             1068* 1101 1102 1145*

A53   Law, Andrew. *The Rudiments of Music*, 1783. *See also* A62a.
             15 517 557*

A54   Stickney, John. *The Gentleman and Lady's Musical Companion*, [1783].
           See also A39.
             41 238 246 302 331 350 352 355 381 517 734 790 806 807* 843 846
             917* 935 1101 1112 1160

A56   [Bayley, Daniel.] *Select Harmony,* [1784].
             41 147 179 187 238 246 301 302 331 350 352 355 381 499 517 622
             734 755 790 806 807 843 846 908* 917 935 1002 1101 1112 1160 1185

A57   [Norman, John?] *The Massachusetts Harmony,* [1784]. [2nd] edn., [1785].
             41 123* 238 302 355 443 492 517 592 790 843 935 959* 1002 1060
             1101 1112 1185

A59   *A New Collection of Psalm Tunes,* [c. 1784].
             302 1060

A60   Bayley, Daniel. *The Essex Harmony,* 1785.
             15 41 187 238 302 331 337 355 405 571 760 843 845 935 1002 1160

A61   Dearborn, Benjamin. *A Scheme for Reducing the Science of Music,* 1785.
             41 187 238 1112

A62   Brownson, Oliver. *Select Harmony,* [2nd edn.], [1785]. [3rd] edn., [1789-91].
             41 91 124 187 246 256 302 311 312 337 387 395 413 513 519 541 571
             588 760 773 825 834* 873 875 893 943 985 1068 1101 1102 1145

A62a   Law, Andrew. *The Rudiments of Music,* 2nd edn., [1785]. *See also* A53,
             A68, A106.
             15 126* 187 220 247 337 571 760 796* 807 845 932 968 1002 1057*
             1102

A63   Read, Daniel. *The American Singing Book,* 1785. 2nd edn., 1786. *See also*
             A80.
             11* 35* 70* 72* 94* 96* 127* 194* 306* 330* 391* 427* 557* 591*
             613* 614* 845 934* 936* 968 1009* 1131*

A65   Billings, William. *The Suffolk Harmony,* 1786.
             124 224* 474* 806

A67   [Langdon, Chauncey.] *Beauties of Psalmody,* 1786.
             15 41 126 187 194 337 359 405 513 571 760 777* 807 845 850*

A68   Law, Andrew. [8-page supplement to A62a], [1786].
             96 518* 591 1148*

A70   [Thomas, Isaiah?] *The Worcester Collection,* 1786. *See also* A91.
           15 41 91 96 123 187 238 256 268* 302 312 337 355 376* 395 405
           490* 519 540 613 760 825 834 843 845 893 917 934 935 936 943 968
           972* 985 1002 1009 1060 1101 1102 1112 1160 1171*

A71   [Thomas, Isaiah?] *The Worcester Collection,* Part III, 1786.
           283* 361* 514* 571 809*

A72   Doolittle, Amos and Read, Daniel. *The American Musical Magazine,*
           Nos. 1-12, [1786-7].
           204* 254* 268 382 514 528* 765* 784* 798* 917 930* 945* 1057

A74   *Sacred Harmony,* [1786-8].
           15 41 91 96 123 187 238 256 268 302 312 337 355 376 395 405 490
           517 519 540 613 760 807 825 834 843 845 893 917 934 935 936 968
           972 985 1002 1009 1060 1101 1102 1112 1171 1185

A77   Billings, William. *An Anthem for Easter,* [1787].
           481*

A79   Jocelin, Simeon. *A Collection of Favorite Psalm Tunes,* [1787].
           31 171 188 241 366 436 648 848 1093 1165

A80   Read, Daniel. *The American Singing Book,* 3rd edn. with *Supplement,* 1787.
           4th edn., [1793]. 5th edn., [1796]. *See also* A63.
           11 15 35 41 70 72 94 96 127 187 194 254 302 306 330 337 391 405
           427 513 540 557 571 591 613 614 804* 807 843 845 934 936 945⁺ 968
           1002 1009 1057 1131

A84   Bayley, Daniel. *The New Harmony of Zion,* 1788.
           15 41 96 123 147 179 187 238 268 301 302 331 337 352 355 405 499
           540 613 622 755 790 893 908 935 1002 1060 1101 1102 1112 1160
           1171 1185

A85   *The Federal Harmony,* [1788]. *See also* A98.
           41 91 96 123 187 194 238 254 256 268 302 312 337 355 376 395 490
           519 528 540 571 613 760 774* 784 807 808* 834 843 845 891⁺ 917
           932 934 935 936 938* 968 972 985 1002 1007* 1009 1101 1102 1112
           1160 1171 1185

A87   Jocelin, Simeon. *The Chorister's Companion,* 2nd edn., 1788. *See also*
        A47, A49, A117.
> 15 31 41 146* 171 187 188 241 243 277* 302 328* 337 366 405 436
> 519 540 571 648 804 843 845 848 935 1002 1060 1093 1101 1102 1165

A89   *A Selection of Sacred Harmony,* [1788]. *See also* A101.
> 15 41 187 302 337 405 571 760 845 885 935 1060 1101 1102 1160

A91   [Thomas, Isaiah?] *The Worcester Collection,* 2nd edn., 1788. *See also*
        A70, A71, A108.
> 15 41 91 96 123 187 194 238 268 302 331 337 355 395 405 571 613
> 760 807 825 834 843 845 891+ 893 917 932 934 935 936 943 968 972
> 985 1002 1057 1060 1101 1102 1112 1160 1164* 1171 1185

A92   Adgate, Andrew and Spicer, Ishmael. *Philadelphia Harmony* with *The
        Rudiments of Music,* [2nd edn.], 1789. 3rd edn., 1790. *See also* A103.
> 15 41 101* 187 302 337 405 519 571 760 807 845 968 1057 1060
> 1102 1148 1160

A93   French, Jacob. *The New American Melody,* 1789.
> 80* 102* 174* 292* 364* 388* 438* 441* 469* 577* 607* 637* 665*
> 778* 819* 870* 892* 920* 977* 1016* 1026* 1054*

A94   Wood, Abraham. *Divine Songs,* 1789.
> 757*

A95   Burger, John Jr. and Tiebout, Cornelius. *Amphion,* [c. 1789].
> 15 41 126 187 238 302 337 760 807 845 968 1002 1160

A96   Benham, Asahel. *Federal Harmony,* 1790. *See also* A111.
> 84* 98* 100* 256 285* 303* 430* 483* 632* 804 813* 833* 835* 842*
> 1110* 1180* 1182*

A97   Billings, William. *The Bird,* [1790].
> 1239*

A98   *The Federal Harmony,* 1790. *See also* A85, A109.
> 15 41 44* 96 129* 187 238 254 268 302 327* 337 376 420* 571 588
> 613 760 765 807 808 809 843 845 917 943 968 982* 985 1002 1007
> 1057 1112 1131 1139* 1160 1185

A101   *A Selection of Sacred Harmony,* 3rd edn., 1790. *See also* A89, A146.
        15 41 187 195 302 337 405 519 571 760 807 845 885 935 968 1057
        1060 1101 1102 1148 1160

A102   Lee, Thomas Jr. *Sacred Harmony,* [c. 1790-6]. *See also* A110.
        13* 539* 580* 582* 596* 599* 602* 769* 801* 882* 989* 1061* 1181*

A103   Adgate, Andrew. *Philadelphia Harmony* [Part I]; Part II, with *The
        Rudiments,* 4th edn. (A103), 1791. "4th" edn. (A103.4), 1796. 5th edn.,
        1797. 6th edn., 1799.
        15 41 101 187 256 285 302 303 337 405 430 519 571 760 807 822*
        835 842 845 935 968 1057 1060 1102 1148 1160

A105   Holyoke, Samuel. *Harmonia Americana,* 1791.
        552* 1003*

A106   Law, Andrew. *The Rudiments of Music,* 3rd edn., [1791]. 4th edn., 1792.
        See also A62a.
        15 41 147 187 238 247 250* 302 303 331 337 355 499 571 622 760
        796 807 885 932 968 1002 1060 1112 1148 1160 1185
        Note: 1107* replaces 968 in 106.4

A108   [Thomas, Isaiah?] *The Worcester Collection,* 3rd edn., 1791. *See also* A91,
        A147.
        15 41 96 123 187 238 268 302 308 331 337 355 395 405 571 613 743*
        760 807 834 843 845 917 934 935 936 943 968 972 978* 985 1002 1101
        1102 1112 1160 1164 1171

A109   *The Federal Harmony,* with *Appendix,* [c. 1791]. *See also* A98, A114.
        15 41 44 96 129 187 238 254 268 302 327 337 376 420 571 588 613
        760 765 807 808 809 843 845 908 917 943 968 982 985 1002 1007 1057
        1112 1131 1139 1160 1185

A110   Lee, Thomas Jr. and Willard, Daniel. *Sacred Harmony,* [2nd edn., c. 1791-6].
        See also A102.
        13 539 580 596 599 602 769 801 882 979* 989 1061 1148 1171 1181
        1207* 1208* 1209* 1210* 1211* 1212* 1213* 1214* 1215* 1216* 1217*
        1218* 1219*

A111   Benham, Asahel. *Federal Harmony,* 2nd edn., 1792. 3rd edn., [c. 1793].
        4th edn., [c. 1794]. 5th edn., [c. 1795]. 6th edn., [c. 1796]. *See also* A96.
        84 98 100 256 285 303 420 430 483 608* 632 634* 743 804 813 833
        835 842 919* 1110 1148 1180 1182

A113   Ely, Alexander. *The Baltimore Collection,* 1792.
       15 41 126 187 238 256 302 337 355 405 413 519 571 591 760 807 845
       968 1002 1160

A114   *The Federal Harmony,* 1792. Later edn. (A114.B), 1793. *See also* A109,
      A137.
       15 41 44 96 129 187 254 268 302 327 337 376 513 571 588 613 760
       765 807 808 809 843 845 908 917 943 982 985 1002 1007 1057 1112
       1131 1139 1148 1160 1185

A115   Holden, Oliver. *The American Harmony,* 1792.
       947*

A116   Jocelin, Simeon. *A Supplement to the Chorister's Companion,* 1792. *See also*
      A117.
       192 333+ 338+ 411 415+ 509+ 831+ 966

A117   Jocelin, Simeon. *The Chorister's Companion,* 2nd edn. with *Supplement,*
      [1792]. *See also* A87, A116.
       15 31 41 146 171 187 188 192 241 243 277 302 328 333+ 337 338+
       366 405 411 415+ 436 509+ 519 540 571 648 804 831+ 843 845 848
       935 966 1002 1060 1093 1101 1102 1165

A119   [Thomas, Isaiah?] *The Worcester Collection,* 4th edn., 1792.
       15 41 96 104* 123 204 254 268 302 308 331 336* 337 405 571 591
       613 743 760 765 807 808 843 845 865* 917 934 935 936 938 943 968
       978 1002 1007 1057 1101 1102 1112 1131 1148 1160 1164 1171

A121   French, Jacob. *The Psalmodist's Companion,* 1793.
       15 87+ 96 126 187 195 207* 225* 254 268 294* 303 323+ 327 329*
       337 377* 384* 484* 500* 571 591 613 620* 637 743 800* 803* 821*
       842 845 908 910* 938 943 964+ 968 977 1056* 1057 1131 1148 1184+

A124   Holden, Oliver. *The Union Harmony,* 1793.
       15 42* 59* 124 129 170* 238 254 268 284* 302 303 327 336 337 405
       544* 571 591 613 760 773 784 789* 807 808 809 845 908 938 943 981*
       1002 1004* 1057 1094+ 1119* 1131 1148 1160

A125   Kimball, Jacob. *The Rural Harmony,* 1793.
       57* 64* 133* 136* 190* 232* 394* 403* 424* 553* 601* 749* 799*
       814* 908 915* 926* 1019* 1094+

A128   Read, Daniel. *The Columbian Harmonist,* No. 1, (1793). *See also* A145.
          69* 185* 186* 209* 379* 400* 454* 471* 476* 494* 547* 548* 584*
          659* 723* 754* 781* 788* 795* 797* 889* 896*

A130   Sanford, E. and Rhea, John. *The Columbian Harmony,* (1793).
          15 41 187 268 302 337 405 705* 743 757 845 875 968 1002 1057 1101
          1102 1148

A131   Shumway, Nehemiah. *The American Harmony,* 1793.
          15 41 67* 96 113* 124 126 156* 174 187 195 201* 204 238 254 268
          283 296* 298* 302 303 308 309* 334* 337 355 361 393* 395 398* 405
          410⁺ 416⁺ 418⁺ 435* 441 453⁺ 474 490 512* 513 514 528 534* 536*
          554* 571 574* 594* 637 665 743 760 767* 798 802* 806 807 809 825
          842 843 845 875 883* 891 892 934 935 936 943 958* 968 977 1002
          1014* 1016 1053* 1057 1060 1102 1112 1148 1160 1166* 1184⁺

A132   Stone, Joseph and Wood, Abraham. *The Columbian Harmony,* [1793].
          32* 93* 110* 177* 218* 233* 252* 257* 268 276* 322* 346* 410⁺
          414* 416⁺ 418⁺ 421* 434* 453⁺ 483 490 495* 524* 542* 549* 551*
          566* 570* 571 573* 578* 579* 593* 605* 612* 615* 743 771* 791*
          840* 927* 1087* 1160 1173* 1182 1183*

A135   Belcher, Supply. *The Harmony of Maine,* 1794.
          22* 43* 76* 235* 351* 380* 412* 433* 496* 545* 576* 581* 585* 595*
          626* 715* 779* 844* 866* 891 957* 962* 1030* 1088* 1091* 1186*

A136   Billings, William. *The Continental Harmony,* 1794.
          29* 45* 130* 214* 260* 274* 360* 369* 428* 506* 525* 561* 759*
          766* 827* 849* 872* 887*

A137   *The Federal Harmony,* 8th edn., 1794. *See also* A114.
          15 243 302 337 405 571 845 908 1057 1112 1131 1139 1148

A141   Law, Andrew. *The Art of Singing: The Christian Harmony,* Vol. I, 1794.
          See also A142.
          147 250 331 709* 1002 1065* 1105*

A142   Law, Andrew. *The Art of Singing: The Musical Magazine,* No. 3, [1794].
          See also A141, A156.
          661

A144   Poor, John. *A Collection of Psalms and Hymns,* 1794.
        15 302

A145   Read, Daniel. *The Columbian Harmonist,* No. 2, [1794] . *See also* A128, A157.
        15 41 96 187 254 302 337 405 513 540 571 591 613 632 743 763* 804
        807 843 845 945 968 1002 1057 1103* 1131 1148

A146   *A Selection of Sacred Harmony,* 4th edn., 1794. 5th edn., 1797. *See also*
        A101.
        15 41 187 195 302 303 337 405 519 571 760 807 845 935 968 1057 1060
        1101 1102 1148 1160

A147   [Thomas, Isaiah?] *The Worcester Collection,* 5th edn., 1794. *See also* A108,
        A168.
        15 41 96 124 171 187 238 254 268 302 331 337 355 405 571 591 613
        743 749 757 760 807 843 845 908 916* 934 935 936 943 968 1002 1057
        1101 1131 1148 1160 1164

A148   Atwill [Atwell] , Thomas H. *The New York Collection,* 1795.
        15 41 187 238 254 268 302 327 337 387 389* 507* 513 560* 563* 773
        809 815* 842 845 890* 908 938 943 968 1002 1057 1148 1160

A149   Babcock, Samuel. *The Middlesex Harmony,* 1795.
        392* 1115*

A150   Billings, Nathaniel. *The Republican Harmony,* 1795.
        86* 174 195 228* 246 270* 303 391 413 416 445* 483 510* 513 562*
        773 780* 809 841* 847* 851* 877* 1015* 1056 1107 1176*

A152   Bull, Amos. *The Responsary,* 1795.
        355 460* 732* 783* 939* 1049* 1074*

A153   [Gram, Hans, Holyoke, Samuel, and Holden, Oliver.] *The Massachusetts
        Compiler,* 1795.
        10* 111 241 353* 458 716 916 924 1077 1223*

A156   Law, Andrew. *The Art of Singing: The Musical Magazine,* No. 4, [1795].
        See also A142, A161.
        658

A157   Read, Daniel. *The Columbian Harmonist,* No. 3 [1795] . *See also* A145, A172.
        611* 949*

A158   [Ranlet, Henry?]. *The Village Harmony,* 1795. *See also* A163.
            15 41 96 124 187 195 238 254 268 302 303 327 337 355 405 528 591
            743 765 784 808 809 843 845 865 917 936 943 964 968 1002 1057 1131
            1148 1160 1184

A160   Holden, Oliver. *The Union Harmony,* Vol. I, 2nd edn., 1796.
            15 124 129 238 248* 254 268 302 303 327 336 337 401* 571 591 613
            760 773 784 789 807 808 809 820* 845 844* 908 938 943 956* 961*
            968 981 1002 1043* 1057 1131 1148 1160

A161   Law, Andrew. *The Art of Singing: The Christian Harmony,* Vol. II, [1796].
            See also A156, A162.
            17 118 140 750 1052 1114

A162   Law, Andrew. *The Art of Singing,* Parts I; II, and III, [1796]. *See also*
            A161, A203.
            17 118 140 658 661 750 1052 1114

A163   [Ranlet, Henry?]. *The Village Harmony,* 2nd edn., 1796. *See also* A158, A175.
            15 41 64 67 96 124 187 191* 195 223* 238 242 254 256 268 284 302
            303 316* 318* 327 331 336 337 355 405 490 504* 528 552 571 591 743
            765 784 805* 807 808 809 843 845 898* 908 917 936 938 943 964 968
            972 1002 1019 1057 1131 1148 1160 1184⁺

A164   Griswold, Elijah and Skinner, Thomas. *Connecticut Harmony,* [c.1796].
            See also A182.
            13 87⁺ 303 323⁺ 409* 522* 528 583* 596 743 810* 837* 842 964⁺ 1003
            1028* 1057 1184⁺

A166   Belknap, Daniel. *The Harmonist's Companion,* 1797.
            74* 261* 289* 437* 442* 535* 538* 792* 811* 1021* 1141* 1156*

A167   Brownson, Oliver. *A New Collection of Sacred Harmony,* 1797.
            31 187 300* 323⁺ 330 483 486* 513 519 575* 613 632 757 769 791 813
            898 979 1023* 1029* 1060 1068 1131 1157*

A168   Holden, Oliver. *The Worcester Collection,* 6th edn., 1797. *See also* A147,
            A198.
            15 33* 41 59 96 124 205* 238 254 268 302 337 401 405 571 591
            613 757 760 789 807 808 820 843 845 884 908 916 934 935 936 938
            943 956 961 968 1057 1131 1148 1160 1164

A170   Mann, Elias. *The Northampton Collection,* 1797.
            15 41 84 187 254 268 302 303 331 337 405 571 591 613 743 757 760
            789 807 842 845 943 1003 1035* 1057 1131 1148 1160 1171

A171   Merrill, Richard. *The Musical Practitioner,* 1797.
            134* 305* 315* 855* 931* 960* 1006* 1106* 1111*

A172   Read, Daniel. *The Columbian Harmonist,* Nos. 1, 2, and 3, [1797]. *See also*
            A145, A180.
            15 41 69 96 185 186 187 209 254 302 337 379 400 405 454 471 476 494
            513 540 547 548 571 584 591 611 613 632 659 723 743 754 763 781 788
            795 797 804 807 843 845 889 896 945 949 968 1002 1057 1103 1131 1148

A174   *New Jersey Harmony,* 1797.
            15 87 96 101 126 254 268 303 323 337 418 483 528 591 594 596 809
            810 833 842 964 1028 1057 1148 1184

A175   [Ranlet, Henry?] *The Village Harmony,* [3rd edn., c. 1797]. *See also* A163, A181
            15 41 64 67 96 187 191 194 223 238 242 254 256 284(2) 302 303 316 318
            327 331 336 337 405 490 504 528 552(2) 571 591 743 765 784 799 805 807
            808 809 843 845 865 898 917 934 936 938 943 964 968 972 1002 1019
            1057 1131 1148 1160 1184

A177   Benham, Asahel. *Social Harmony,* [1798]. 2nd edn., [1799].
            68* 78* 82* 112* 116* 129 149* 450* 462* 464* 610* 786* 789 833
            852* 898 902* 913* 1058* 1062* 1067*

A180   Read, Daniel. *Additional Music to the Columbian Harmonist,* No. 2, [1798].
            See also A172.
            784 898 1197* 1198* 1199*

A181   [Ranlet, Henry?] *The Village Harmony,* 4th edn., 1798. *See also* A175.
            15 41 64 67 96 187 191 194 223 238 242 254 284 302 303 316 318 327
            331 336 337 405 490 504 528 552 571 591 601 743 765 784 799 805 807
            808 809 814 843 845 865 898 917 934 936 938 943 964 968 978* 1002
            1019 1023 1057 1131 1148 1160 1184

A181.5   [Ranlet, Henry?] *The Village Harmony,* 5th edn., 1800.
            15 41 64 67 96 187 191 194 223 238 242 254 284 302 303 316 318 327
            331 336 337 405 490 504 528 552 571 591 601 743 765 784 799 805 807
            808 809 814 843 845 865 898 917 934 936 938 943 964 968 975 1002
            1019 1023 1057 1131 1148 1160 1184 1195* 1196*

A182   Griswald, Elijah, and Skinner, Thomas. *Connecticut Harmony,* [2nd edn., c. 1798]. *See also* A164.
      13 87 303 323 406* 409 522 528 583 596 743 810 837 842 964 1003 1028 1057 1131 1184

A183   Benjamin, Jonathan. *Harmonia Coelestis,* 1799.
      302 458 600 886

A186   Howe, Solomon. *Worshipper's Assistant,* 1799.
      929* 1022*

A187   Jenks, Stephen. *The New-England Harmonist,* 1799.
      255* 275* 304* 314* 491* 498* 520* 633* 787* 898 980* 1109* 1154* 1220* 1221* 1222*

A188   Merrill, David. *Psalmodist's Best Companion,* 1799.
      41 64 191 397* 417* 511* 565* 634 799 810 975 1023 1071*

A189   Pilsbury, Amos. *The United States' Sacred Harmony,* 1799.
      14* 15 41 96 101 114* 117* 161* 187 238 254 277 301 302 303 327 331 337 355 405 523* 540 571 613 632 666* 743 774 789 805 806 807 809 838* 843 845 854 880* 893 908 964 968 987* 1002 1057 1059* 1060 1102 1148 1160 1180

A190   *The Boston Collection,* [c. 1799].
      15 96 124 187 254 302 303 327 337 405 552 571 591 613 760 784 789 807 808 809 845 893 934 938 943 956 961 968 982 1002 1043 1057 1131 1148 1160

A192   Belknap, Daniel. *The Evangelical Harmony,* 1800.
      74 75* 89* 261 310* 319* 327 437 442 529* 532* 533* 535 559* 587* 764* 901* 965* 1021 1115 1141 1156

A195   [Holden, Oliver.] *The Modern Collection,* 1800.
      15 42 170 223 254 268 302 458 497 528 552 591 728 758 784 789 799 808 820 884 908 938 961 964 968 1002 1023 1057 1119 1131 1160

A196   [Holden, Oliver.] *Plain Psalmody,* 1800.
      50* 83* 429* 497* 728* 758* 761* 830* 1084* 1096*

A198 Holden, Oliver. *The Worcester Collection,* 7th edn., 1800. *See also* A168.
    15 223 254 268 302 458 497 528 552 571 591 728 758 760 784 789
    799 808 820 845 884 908 938 943 961 964 968 1002 1023 1057 1131
    1148 1160

A200 Huntington, Jonathan. *The Albany Collection,* 1800.
    15 38* 84 126 187 254 303 323 337 436 513 563 571 743 757 796
    807 842 968 979 1002 1057 1060 1148 1155*

A201 Jenks, Stephen. *The Musical Harmonist,* 1800.
    28* 61* 85* 332* 347* 478* 501* 550* 655* 770* 800 850 862* 898
    963* 964 1066* 1099* 1104* 1240*

A202 Kimball, Jacob. *The Essex Harmony,* 1800.
    479* 647* 691* 698* 903* 905* 906* 940* 1080*

A203 Law, Andrew. *The Art of Singing,* 3rd edn., 1800. *See also* A162.
    17 118 140 147 250 331 658 661 709 750 1002 1052 1065 1105 1114

GUIDE TO CENSUS

How to Use

Access to the census of fuging tunes can be gained in one of three ways:

1. Through the *List of Sources,* which is chronologically arranged in four categories on pages 55-81. Under each source is a list of the fuging tunes it contains, identified by the tune numbers under which they can be found in the Census. (The Index of Persons at the end of the book incorporates compilers of the sources in this List.)

2. Through the *Indexes* at the end of the book, which list texts, tune names, and persons (composers, authors and compilers), each in alphabetical order. Again, the tunes are identified by the numbers under which they can be found in the Census.

3. By directly looking up the tenor incipit in the *Census* itself. The following steps should be followed:
   - Determine the key of the tune (the tonic, *do*), and call this note 1. The other six notes of the scale are then represented by 2 (*re*), 3 (*mi*), 4 (*fa*), 5 (*so*), 6 (*la*), 7 (*ti*).
   - Write down the numbers representing the first fifteen notes of the *tenor* part of the tune, defined as the voice part written in the second stave upwards.
   - Disregard octave register, accidentals, rhythmic values, rests, grace notes (i.e., notes printed small), and ornament signs.
   - If the part divides into two or more "choosing notes," choose the upper one.

     — Look up the resulting string of fifteen digits in its numerical
       order in the Census, and you should find either the details
       of the tune or a cross-reference. For an example, see the
       incipit for the tune entry no. **41**, pages 86-87.

The Census gives, for each tune, the following *details* in the first three lines:
tune number (boldface), tenor incipit, structure, meter, number of voices, date of
first printing, and composer (if known). Then follows a *table of sources* of the tune
in chronological order: each line gives the source (as abbreviated in the List of Sources),
followed by the reference number, key, reference letter, text (by number), and tune
name in that source. *Footnotes* give any composer attributions or significant variants
in the details of the tune as given.

The following sections explain the Census more fully.

What Is in the Census

Sources Consulted. All collections of religious music in English printed between 1700
and 1800 were potential sources, though books of cathedral music and monophonic
tunebooks were obviously of no practical value. Where the best available dating is
"c. 1800" the source was consulted. For English parochial sources (P) we were guided
by the numbered list in Nicholas Temperley's *The Music of the English Parish Church*
(Cambridge, 1979). For English dissenting or domestic religious music (D) and for
Scottish sources (S) we examined all relevant books listed in *The British Union-
Catalogue of Early Music,* ed. E. B. Schnapper (2 vols., London, 1957), or in *The
National Union Catalog: Pre-1956 Imprints* (685 vols., Washington, 1968-80), although
in these two categories we have listed only those sources in which we found fuging
tunes. For American sources (A) we used an early version of the list which will appear
in Richard Crawford's forthcoming bibliography of American sacred music publications
to 1810. Professor Crawford kindly allowed us to use an advance copy of this list:
we have numbered all items in it, but have listed only those containing fuging tunes.
All known pre-1801 editions of every source were taken into consideration.

Tunes Included. For inclusion, a piece must be all of these things:

    1. *Vocal polyphony.* It may include an instrumental bass or symphony,
       but it must have at least two parts, including a vocal bass.
    2. *Sacred.* Either a psalm or a hymn text is present or assigned, or it is
       clear from the context that the tune is mainly for use with such a text.
    3. *Metrical.* The text must be in a regular verse meter.
    4. *Strophic.* The music to be sung must consist of several stanzas of
       a text sung to the same tune, even if only one stanza is present.

5. *Fuging.* At least one phrase of the tune must have non-simultaneous vocal entries creating text overlap (for further discussion see "**Structure**," page 88).

Set Pieces. The most difficult frontier to establish is between the fuging tune and the "set piece," which we define as a through-composed (i.e., non-strophic) setting of a metrical text. We treated a fuging piece as a set piece (and hence excluded it from the Census) if either:

1. More than twelve lines of text are sung to one statement of the tune; or
2. The only designated text is exhausted by a single statement of the tune.

In some cases, a tune is repeated several times to different verses of the text, then followed by a musical "coda" sung to a special text such as a doxology or alleluia. If the main tune is fuging in such cases, we have included it. But "varied strophic" tunes, where the main tune is replaced by a contrasting tune for one or more stanzas of the psalm or hymn text, are regarded as set pieces.

Order of Tunes. The tunes are numerically ordered by tenor incipit, and this order is reflected in the boldface numbers. A few tunes, discovered after the rest had been numbered, were added at the end: cross-references to these have been inserted in the proper numerical places.

How the Tunes Are Described

For the sake of certainty, we defined "tenor" as the voice part written on the second lowest stave (disregarding any independent instrumental bass stave). In most cases, this voice is clearly the bearer of the main "tune," but towards the end of the eighteenth century this began to be in doubt, especially in British psalmody, as the soprano voice gradually took over the lead. In some collections the notation is ambiguous. The second lowest stave may actually represent the soprano voice, or may be for tenor or soprano at the singers' option. The same tune may be found in two collections with the voices printed in different order. We have stuck to our definition; but we have also cross-indexed the voice on the top stave, with a reference by number to the main tune entry, in the following cases:

1. All tunes in British collections between 1780 and 1800.
2. All other tunes in which the top voice seems to bear the "tune" or leading part.

Tenor Incipit. The first fifteen notes of the tenor part are listed in number form, as they are found in the earliest source of the tune. The numbers are those of the diatonic scale, counting upwards from the keynote, in any octave register and with or without an accidental. Grace notes and rests are disregarded; tied or repeated notes sung to a single syllable are counted only once.

EXAMPLE:

To look up the piece found on page 59 of Andrew Law's *Select Harmony* (1779)– reproduced on pages x-xi of this book:

1. Is it a "tune"? (A tune is a piece of music intended for strophic repetition with a sacred metrical text.)

    Yes.

2. Is it "fuging"? (In at least one phrase, two or more voice parts enter non-simultaneously, with rests preceding at least one entry, in such a way as to produce overlap of text.)

    Yes.

3. Is it in a printed source published before 1801? (Then it should be in the Tune Census.)

    Yes.

4. Determine the keynote of the tune.

    The last bass note: A.

5. Call this note 1. A = 1

6. Write down the numbers representing the first fifteen notes of the tenor part (the second stave from the bottom).

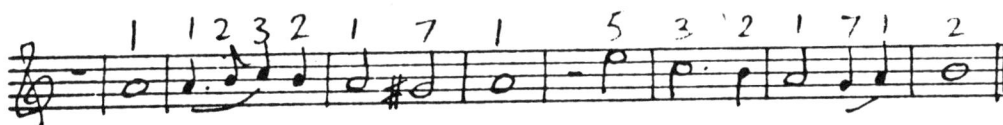

    (Disregard octave register, accidentals, rhythmic values, rests, grace notes, and ornament signs. If the part divides into two or more "choosing notes," choose the upper one.)

7. Now you have a string of fifteen digits. 1 1 2 3 2 1 7 1 5 3 2 1 7 1 2
    Look it up, in numerical order, in the Tune Census. (*See opposite.*)

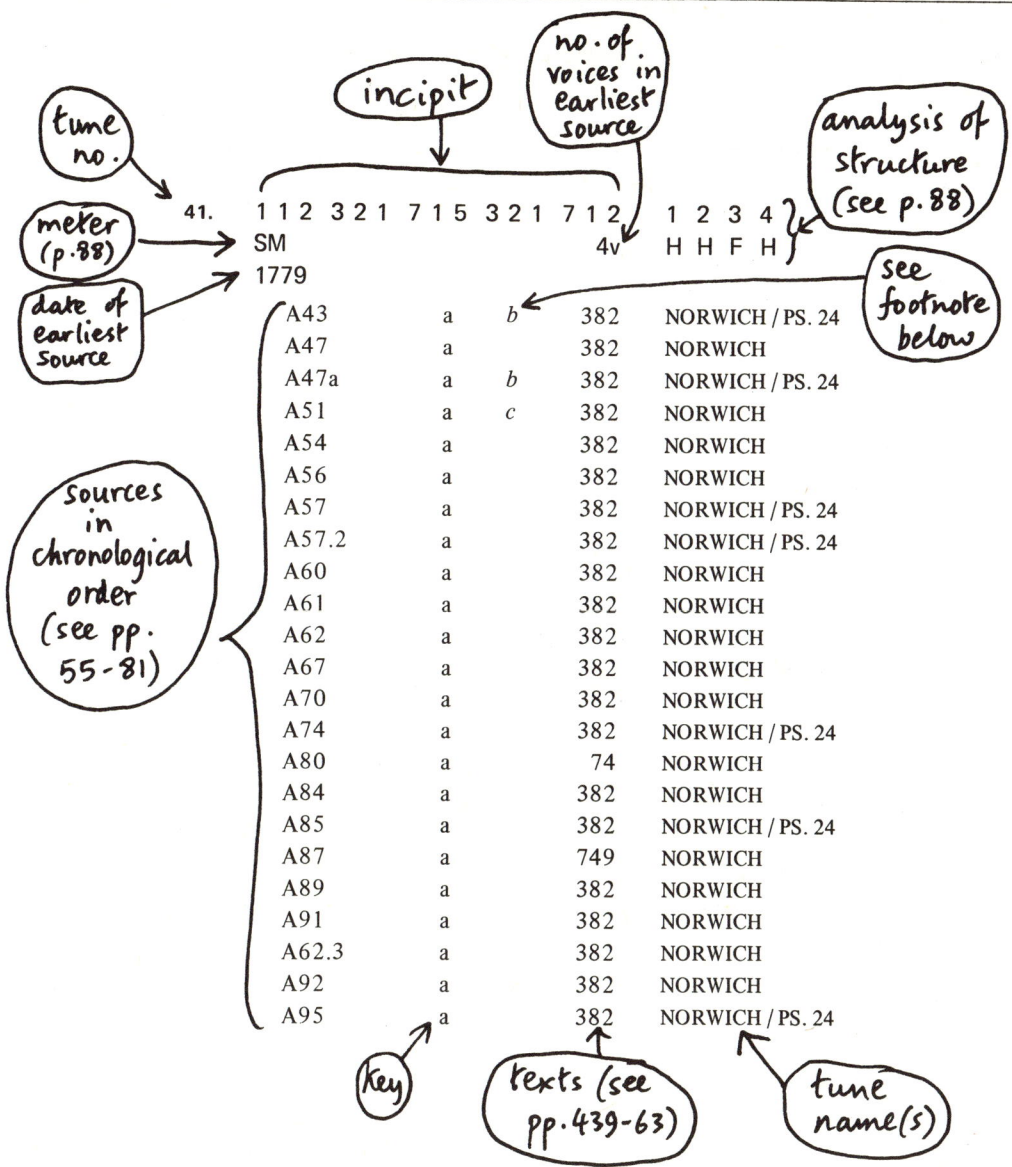

Annotations (handwritten): tune no. · incipit · no. of voices in earliest source · analysis of structure (see p. 88) · meter (p. 88) · date of earliest source · Sources in chronological order (see pp. 55-81) · see footnote below · key · texts (see pp. 439-63) · tune name(s) · composer attributions

41. 1 1 2 3 2 1 7 1 5 3 2 1 7 1 2   1 2 3 4
SM   4v   H H F H
1779

Source	Key	Composer	Text	Tune name(s)
A43	a	b	382	NORWICH / PS. 24
A47	a		382	NORWICH
A47a	a	b	382	NORWICH / PS. 24
A51	a	c	382	NORWICH
A54	a		382	NORWICH
A56	a		382	NORWICH
A57	a		382	NORWICH / PS. 24
A57.2	a		382	NORWICH / PS. 24
A60	a		382	NORWICH
A61	a		382	NORWICH
A62	a		382	NORWICH
A67	a		382	NORWICH
A70	a		382	NORWICH
A74	a		382	NORWICH / PS. 24
A80	a		74	NORWICH
A84	a		382	NORWICH
A85	a		382	NORWICH / PS. 24
A87	a		749	NORWICH
A89	a		382	NORWICH
A91	a		382	NORWICH
A62.3	a		382	NORWICH
A92	a		382	NORWICH
A95	a		382	NORWICH / PS. 24

b Brownson
c Hibbard   composer attributions

Meter. The meter is derived from the tune and text as they appear in the earliest source; incorrect meter designations are ignored. Meter is indicated either by a set of numbers, which tell the number of syllables in each line of text included in a single complete statement of the tune ($X = 10$, $Y = 11$, $Z = 12$); or by letters, which are abbreviations for the standard iambic meters:

CM	=	8686
CMD	=	86868686
CMT	=	868686868686
LM	=	8888
LMD	=	88888888
SM	=	6686
SMD	=	66866686

Number of Voices. This refers to the earliest source.

Structure. The grid of numbers and letters to the right of the tenor incipit represents the structure of the tune. The numbers in the upper row stand for the lines of text (⌢ shows two overlapping lines, M means a mixture of two or more neighboring lines). The letters in the lower row denote the musical treatment of each line of text, as follows:

H   *Plain Homophony.* All the voices that sing the text phrase sing throughout that phrase, without extended melismas, all singing the same syllables together. (If there is only one voice "H" may still be appropriate.)

E   *Extended Homophony.* The texture is homophonic; the phrase is extended beyond its normal length by repetition of a text fragment in all voices, by melismas or long held notes, or by the insertion of internal rests.

A   *Alternating Homophony.* The texture is homophonic, but the number of voices is varied by an alternation between voices or voice pairs or an echo effect.

C   *Cumulative Homophony.* The texture is homophonic, but voices are added in the course of the text phrase, giving a vaguely contrapuntal effect, without text overlap.

O   *Overlap.* This covers phrases which have considerable text *overlap* (i. e., the simultaneous singing of two or more different syllables of the text), but do not have fuging entries preceded by rests.

F   *Fuging.* Two or more voice parts enter non-simultaneously, with rests preceding at least one of the entries, in such a way as to produce text overlap.

Examples of these textures are given on pages ix-xi, *above.*

Date. This is the date of the first printing of the tune. When one source (the first one listed below) is undoubtedly the earliest, the date is the same as the date of this source as given in the List of Sources. Where two or more sources (marked + in the list below the tune description) could be the earliest, the date is based on the dates of all of these. "-1750" means "1750 or earlier."

Composer. The composer (if any) listed with an *a* on the third line is the man who— there is good reason to believe—actually composed the tune, or the music from which the tune was adapted. (Full names and dates are to be found in the Index of Persons.) A composer's name is given here *only* if either:

1. he explicitly claims, in his own book, to have written this tune; or
2. the compiler of the earliest source explicitly attributes the tune to him; or
3. the compiler of an early source, not remote in time or place from the composer's known place of work, attributes the tune to him (in the more doubtful cases a question mark is added).

Less reliable attributions are indicated in footnotes (see *below,* **Footnotes**). They are often merely acknowledgments of an intermediate source.

The Sources of Each Tune

After the three-line description of the tune, there follows, in columns, a table of every known source of the tune, with some details that vary from source to source. Each source has a line to itself.

Source Code. At left is the numbered abbreviation for the source, preceded by one of the letters P, D, S or A. Details of these sources can be found by reference to the List of Sources, pages 55-81. The sources are listed in chronological order, as far as can be determined, according to the dates of publication given in the List of Sources. The following sequence would apply (for example) for dates around 1760:

1759	
-1760	(1760 or before)
1760	
c. 1760	(about 1760)
1760-1	(1760 or 1761)
1760-	(1760 or later)
1761	

For two sources of the same date but in different categories, the sequence is P, D, S, A (since this is the likely direction of influence). It should be kept in mind, however, that many dates, particularly of British sources, are quite approximate, so that the order cannot necessarily be relied on as strictly chronological. Where two or more sources could be the earliest, they are marked +. (Dates of all sources may be found in the List of Sources.)

Key. After the source abbreviation the key of the tune in that source is stated—capital letter for major, lower-case for minor.

Reference Letters and Numbers. There may be:
1. An italic letter, referring to a composer or other source attribution given above or below;
2. A superscript number, referring to a variant given below—either in the tenor incipit, the meter, the number of voices, or the tune structure.

Text Code. The number in the next column refers to the Index of Texts on pages 439-63. It identifies the first line of a text that is either:
1. Underlaid, or
2. Designated as the sole text to be sung with the tune.

When a text is underlaid, other texts designated as alternatives in the same source have not been recorded. When no text is underlaid but two or more alternative texts are designated, this is stated in a footnote.

Tune Name. This is as in the source, except that names such as 20TH PSALM, PSALM 20, have been uniformly given as PS. 20, etc. Small capitals are used for tune names throughout this book.

Footnotes. These give unreliable composer or source attributions (referred to by letter), and variants (referred to by superscript number).

Cross-References

Clear musical resemblances between separately listed tunes, when observed, have been noted. In addition, we have inserted (in their proper sequence) unnumbered incipits with cross-references to numbered tunes. These are of three kinds:
1. The top line of any tune in a British collection of 1780-1800, or of any other tune in which the top line seems to bear the principal part.
2. A variant version of a tenor incipit, as found in one of the later sources.
3. Tunes, numbered **1195-1239**, which are listed out of their proper numerical sequence at the end of the Census.

1.	1 1 1	1 1 1	1 1 1	2 2 7	5 6 4		1 2 3 4
	CM				4v		F H F F
	1791			*a* Handel			
	P291		E	*a*	622		

2.	1 1 1	1 1 1	1 7 7	7 7 1	1 1 7		1 2 3 4 4 4
	LM				3v		F H E E F O
	1791			*a* Handel			
	P291		E	*a*	758		

3.	1 1 1	1 1 1	4 3 4	3 3 3	2 1 1		1 2 3 4 3 4
	CM				3v		H H H H F E
	c.1788			*a* Dalmer			
	P263		E♭	*a*	743		

4.	1 1 1	1 1 1	7 1 2	3 2 3	2 1 3		1 2 3 4
	LM				3v		H F O H
	1794			*a* Atterbury			
	P297		B♭	*a*	150		

5.   1 1 1   1 2 1   2 3 3   4 1 1   6 7 1   1 2 3 4 5 6 5 6 7 8 8
     LMD   3v   C H H H H H H H F H H
     1794   *a* Wight
         P297   G   *a*   397

6.   1 1 1   1 2 1   7 1 1   6 7 5   4 3 5   1 2 3 3 4
     SM   3v   H H F F H
     1786   *a* Harwood
         P259   B♭   *a*   733   BOLTON

7.   1 1 1   1 7 1   6 7 5   2 1 7   6 5 5   1 2 3 4 4
     SM   4v   H H H F H
     c.1800   *a* Harvey
         P321   D   *a*   733   SABBATH

8.   1 1 1   1 7 6   5 6 5   4 3 3   4 5 5   1 2 2 3 4 3 4
     CM   4v   H H E H H H F
     c.1800   *a* Key
         P323   C   *a*   827

     1 1 1   1 7 6   5 6 7   1 3 6   2 5 1:   *soprano of* **17**

     1 1 1   2 1 1   7 1 1   3 3 1   6 5 7:   *soprano of* **729**

     1 1 1   2 1 4   3 2 3   3 3 5   4 3 2:   *soprano of* **711**

9.   1 1 1   2 2 2   1 2 3   1 1 1   2 2 2   1 2 3 3 4 5 6
      888888   4v   F F H O F F F
      1791   *a* S. Arnold
        P291   G   *a*   556

—————

Cf. **10.**

10.   1 1 1   2 2 2   1 2 3   3 3 3   4 4 4   1 2 3 3 4 5 6
      888888   4v   F F H O F F F
      1795   *a* S. Arnold
        A153   G   *a*   556   WASHINGTON

—————

A version of **9.**

     1 1 1   2 2 3   5 6 7   1 7 2   1 3 2:   *soprano of* **1144**

11.   1 1 1   2 3 1   7 1 1   2 1 7   1 7 6   1 2 3 4
      LM   4v   H H F F
      1785   *a* D. Read
        A63   C   *a*   352   ENFIELD
        A63.2   C   *a*   352   ENFIELD
        A80   C   *a*   352   ENFIELD
        A80.4   C   *a*   352   ENFIELD
        A80.5   C   *a*   352   ENFIELD

     1 1 1   2 4 3   2 1 2   3 6 5   4 3 5:   *soprano of* **340**

     1 1 1   3 2 1   7 1 5   1 2 3   6 4 2:   *soprano of* **1100**

12. 1 1 1 3 3 1 1 7 6 5 1 1 2 3 2   1 2 3 4
CM   4v   H F H F
c. 1757
  P166   f   683

13. 1 1 1 4 3 2 1 2 3 3 2 1 1 3 1   1 2 3 4 5̂ 6 5 6
666688   4v   H H H H E F H H
c. 1790-6   *a* Lee

A102	C	174	ZION
A110	C	174	ZION
A164	C *a*	174	ZION
A182	C	174	ZION

14. 1 1 1 5 3 4 3 2 1 5 3 3 7 7 1   1 2 3̂ 4
LM   4v   H H F F
1799   *a* Pilsbury

A189	e	*a*	180	MORNING

15. 1 1 1 5 6 5 5 1 2 3 2 1 1 3 5   1 2 3 4 5̂ 6
666688   4v   H H H H F F
1782   *a* Edson

A47	C	*a*	824	LENOX
A53	C	*a*		LENOX
A60	C	*a*	824	LENOX
A62a	C	*a*		LENOX
A67	C	*a*	325	LENOX
A70	C	*a*	824	LENOX
A74	C		824	LENOX
A80	C	*a*	824	LENOX
A84	C	*a*	824	LENOX
A87	C	*a*	824	LENOX
A89	C		325	LENOX
A91	C	*a*	824	LENOX
A92	C	*a*	325	LENOX
A95	C	*a*		LENOX

A92.3	C	*a*	325	LENOX
A98	C	*a*	824	LENOX
A101	C		824	LENOX
A103	C	*a*	325	LENOX
A106	C	*a*	69	LENOX
A108	C	*a*	824	LENOX
A109	C	*a*	824	LENOX
A106.4	C	*a*	69	LENOX
A113	C	*a*	824	LENOX
A114	C	*a*	824	LENOX
A117	C	*a*	824	LENOX
A119	C	*a*	824	LENOX
A80.4	C	*a*	824	LENOX
A114.B	C	*a*	824	LENOX
A121	C		824	LENOX
A124	C	*a*	824	LENOX
A130	C	*a*	325	LENOX
A131	C	*a*	824	LENOX
A137	C	*a*	824	LENOX
A144[1]	C		824	LENOX
A145	C		824	LENOX
A146	C		824	LENOX
A147	C	*a*	824	LENOX
A148	C	*a*	786	LENOX
A158	C	*a*	824	LENOX
A80.5	C	*a*	824	LENOX
A103.4	C	*a*	325	LENOX
A160	C	*a*	824	LENOX
A163	C	*a*	824	LENOX
A103.5	C	*a*	325	LENOX
A146.5	C		824	LENOX
A168	C	*a*	824	LENOX
A170	C	*a*	824	LENOX
A172	C		824	LENOX
A174	C		824	LENOX
A175	C	*a*	824	LENOX
A181	C	*a*	824	LENOX
A103.6	C	*a*	325	LENOX
A189	C	*a*	325	LENOX

[1] 2v.

15 continued

A190	C	*a*	824	LENOX
A181.5	C	*a*	824	LENOX
A195	C	*a*	824	LENOX
A198	C	*a*	824	LENOX
A200	C	*a*	130	LENOX

16. 1 1 1 6 5 4 3 2 1 7 1 2 1 2 3   1 2 2 3 4 3 4 4 3 4
CM   3v   F F H F F F F F F F
1791   *a* Boyce
   P291   F   *a*   717

1 1 1 6 5 4 3 2 1 7 1 5 4 3 4:   *soprano of* **16**

17. 1 1 1 7 1 1 1 7 1 3 2 2 1 3 2   1 2 3 4 4
CM   4v   F E H O E
1791   *a* S. Arnold
   P291   B♭   *a*   793
   A161   B♭   793   PRUSSIA
   A162   B♭   793   PRUSSIA
   A203   B♭   793   PRUSSIA

1 1 1 7 1 1 1 7 3 2 1 1 4 2 3:   *soprano of* **290**

1 1 1 7 2 3 2 1 7 2 3 2 1 5 1:   *soprano of* **81**

1 1 1 7 3 1 7 6 7 1 7 1 1 4 3:   *soprano of* **192**

1 1 1 7 3 4 3 2 3 2 1 7 1 7 7:   *soprano of* **188**

18. 1 1 1 7 5 6 1 7 2 1 7 1 2 1 7   1 2 3 4
     CM   4v   H F F H
     c.1785   *a* Valentine
        P257   C   *a*   773

     1 1 1 7 6 5 6 7 1 1 7 1 1 7 6:   *soprano of* **692**

19. 1 1 2 1 1 2 5 4 5 3 6 5 4 5 2   1 2 3 4
     LM   4v   H H H F
     c.1776
        P231   G   145

20. 1 1 2 1 3 2 1 2 5 5 3 2 3 6 5   1 1 2 3 4 3 4
     CM   4v   E H F F F H H
     c.1776
        P231   G   649

     1 1 2 1 5 1 2 3 5 3 2 1 2 3 4:   *see* **1207**

21. 1 1 2 1 7 1 2 1 7 1 2 1 1 7 5   1 2 3 4 5 6 7 8
     LMD   3v   F H F F O C F H
     1794   *a* Atterbury
        P297   A   *a*   373

22. 1 1 2 1 7 6 5 2 1 6 5 6 7 1 2   1 2 3 4 5 6 7 8
     CMD   4v   H H H E F F H E
     1794   *a* Belcher
        A135   C   *a*   604

23. 1 1 2 2 5 4 3 2 3 5 6 4 3 1 3   1 2 3 4͡ 4
LM   4v   E F E F F
1754   *a* Everet
   P151   G   196
   P157   G   196
   P266   G   *a*   196

  1 1 2 3 1 1 2 3 3 2 1 7 1 6 5:   *soprano of* **658**

  1 1 2 3 1 1 7 1 1 7 1 2 1 3 2:   *soprano of* **411**

24. 1 1 2 3 1 1 7 1 3 3 2 2 1 7 3   1 2 2 3 4 3 4
LM   4v   H H H H H H F H
c.1800   *a* Harvey
   P321   C   *a*   755   BATH

25. 1 1 2 3 1 2 1 2 5 3 6 4 5 5 5   1 2 2 2 3 4͡ 4
CM   4v   H H H H H F F
c.1776
   P231   G   557

  1 1 2 3 1 2 3 4 3 4 3 2 3 1 6:   *soprano of* **243**

26. 1 1 2 3 1 2 5 4 3 2 2 3 4 3 1   1 2 2 3 3͡ 4͡ 4 4
CM   4v   H H H H E F O H
c.1776
   P231   a   [1]

---

[1] Text given as "This etc. Psalm 22 N[ew] V[ersion]."

27. 1 1 2 3 1 2 7 1 1 1 4 3 2 2 3   1 2 3 4
CM   4v   H E H F
1754

    P151   C   630
    P198   B♭   630

28. 1 1 2 3 1 4 3 2 1 7 7 3 1 2 3   1 2 3 4
LM   4v   H H F H
1800   *a* Newcomb

    A201   a   *a*   142   GARDEN

29. 1 1 2 3 1 4 3 2 2 1 1 7 1 2 5   1 2 3 4 5 6 7 M 8
CMD   4v   H H H H H H F F O
1794   *a* W. Billings

    A136   C   *a*   470   NEW PLYMOUTH

1 1 2 3 1 5 4 3 2 3 3 2 2 3 2:   *see* **31**

30. 1 1 2 3 1 5 4 3 3 4 3 2 5 5 4   1 2 3 4 5 6
668668   2v   F H H F O H
c.1780

    ⁺P242   a   BRIDLINGTON
    ⁺S5[1]   a   371   MESSIAH
    S6[2]   a   218   WIGAN
    S5.2[1]   a   371   MESSIAH

---

[1] 4v, 1 2 3 4 5 6
     F F H F F H

[2] 3v, 1 2 3 4 5 6
     H E H F O ♭

Cf. **31.**

31.   1 1 2 3 1 5 4 3 3 4 3 2 5 5 4   1 2 3 4 4 4
SM   4v   F F H F O E
1784

P253	a	617	WIGAN
P253.2	a	617	WIGAN
A79	a	617	PS. 23
A87	a	617	PS. 23
P266	a	102	WIGAN
P253.4	a	617	WIGAN
A117	a	617	PS. 23
A167[1]	a	617	PS. 23

[1]   1 2 3 4 4 4
     F F H F F F

A version of **30.**

32.   1 1 2 3 1 5 5 5 3 6 6 6 5 1 1   1 2 3 4 5 6 7 8
LMD   4v   H H H H F F O O
1793   *a* Stone

A132	F	*a*	520	NEW BRAINTREE

33.   1 1 2 3 1 5 5 5 5 6 5 6 5 3 2   1 2 3 3 4
CM   4v   H H F F H
1797   *a* Belcher

A168	G	*a*	97	TOPSHAM

1 1 2 3 1 6 1 3 3 1 2 1 7 6 5:   *soprano of* **365**

34.   1 1 2 3 1 7 1 2 7 1 5 1 7 1 2   1 2 3 4
LM   4v   H F H F
c. 1800   *a* Cuzens

D16	C	*a*	421	RINGWOOD

1 1 2 3 1 7 1 2 1 7 1 2 3 3 2:   *soprano of* **1048**

1 1 2 3 2 1 1 2 1 7 1 5 1 1 3:   *soprano of* **374**

1 1 2 3 2 1 1 2 1 7 7 1 2 3 7:   *soprano of* **280**

35.	1 1 2 3 2 1 1 2 3 4 3 2 1 7 5				1 2 3 4 3̂ 4̂ 4
	SM			4v	H H H H F F O
	1785			*a* D. Read	
	A63	a	*a*	353	NORTON
	A63.2	a	*a*	353	NORTON
	A80	a	*a*	353	NORTON
	A80.4	a	*a*	353	NORTON
	A80.5	a	*a*	353	NORTON

36.	1 1 2 3 2 1 1 7 6 5 6 7 1 3 2		1 2 3 4 4
	LM		2v	H H H F H
	c. 1780			
	P242	C		DARBY'S 100

A version of **239**.

37.	1 1 2 3 2 1 1 7 6 7 1 2 7 7 2		1 2 3 4 5 6 7 8 7 8
	LMD		4v	E F H H E H H H H H
	1789			
	P266	C	748	LAINHAM

38.	1 1 2 3 2 1 3 4 5 5 3 1 4 3 2		1 2 3̂ 4
	CM		4v	H H F O
	1800		*a* Huntington	
	A200	a	*a* 235	PS. 40

39. 1 1 2 3 2 1 5 5 4 3 2 1 2 3 2   1 2 3 4
CM   5v   H H F F
1757

    P164   G   13

40. 1 1 2 3 2 1 5 5 5 4 3 4 3 2 1   1 2 3 4̄ 4̄ M̄ 4
CM   4v   H H H O F O F
1778   *a* W. Billings

    A40   F   *a*   165   BENEVOLENCE
    A40.2   F   *a*   .165   BENEVOLENCE
    A40.3   F   *a*   165   BENEVOLENCE
    A40.4   F   *a*   165   BENEVOLENCE

41. 1 1 2 3 2 1 7 1 5 3 2 1 7 1 2   1 2 3 4
SM   4v   H H F H
1779

A43	a	*b*	382	NORWICH / PS. 24
A47	a		382	NORWICH
A47a	a	*b*	382	NORWICH / PS. 24
A51	a	*c*	382	NORWICH
A54	a		382	NORWICH
A56	a		382	NORWICH
A57	a		382	NORWICH / PS. 24
A57.2	a		382	NORWICH / PS. 24
A60	a		382	NORWICH
A61	a		382	NORWICH
A62	a		382	NORWICH
A67	a		382	NORWICH
A70	a		382	NORWICH
A74	a		382	NORWICH / PS. 24
A80	a		74	NORWICH
A84	a		382	NORWICH
A85	a		382	NORWICH / PS. 24
A87	a		749	NORWICH
A89	a		382	NORWICH
A91	a		382	NORWICH
A62.3	a		382	NORWICH

A92	a		382	NORWICH
A95	a		382	NORWICH / PS. 24
A92.3	a		382	NORWICH
A98	a	b	382	NORWICH
A101	a		382	NORWICH
A103	a		382	NORWICH
A106	a		382	NORWICH
A108	a		382	NORWICH
A109	a	b	382	NORWICH
A106.4	a		382	NORWICH
A113	a	e	382	NORWICH
A114	a	b	382	NORWICH
A117	a		749	NORWICH
A119	a		382	NORWICH
A80.4	a		74	NORWICH
A114.B	a	b	382	NORWICH
A130	a	c	382	NORWICH
A131	a		382	NORWICH
A145	a		74	NORWICH
A146	a		382	NORWICH
A147	a		382	NORWICH
A148	a	c	382	NORWICH / PS. 24
A158	a		382	NORWICH
A80.5	a		74	NORWICH
A103.4	a		382	NORWICH
A163	a	b	382	NORWICH
A103.5	a		382	NORWICH
A146.5	a		382	NORWICH
A168	a		382	NORWICH
A170	a	d	74	NORWICH
A172	a		382	NORWICH
A175	a	b	382	NORWICH
A181	a		382	NORWICH
A103.6	a		382	NORWICH
A188	a		382	NORWICH
A189	a		382	NORWICH
A181.5	a	b	382	NORWICH

b Brownson

c Hibbard

d Deaolph

e King

1 1 2 3 2 1 7 5 1 1 1 3 2 1 2:   *soprano of* **373**

42.   1 1 2 3 2 1 7 6 6 2 3 2 1 7 5   1 2 3 4
      LM   4v   H F H H
      1793   *a* Stephenson

A124	C	*a*	115	LORD'S PRAYER
A195	C	*a*	115	LORD'S PRAYER

43.   1 1 2 3 2 2 2 3 2 2 2 1 1 4 4   1 2 3̑ 4 3 4 3 4
      LM   4v   H H F F F O H E
      1794   *a* Belcher

A135	C	*a*	756	NEW SHARON

1 1 2 3 2 2 7 1 2 3 4 3 2 1 7:   *soprano of* **258**

1 1 2 3 2 3 4 5 3 4 5 4 3 2 1:   *see* **126**

44.   1 1 2 3 2 3 4 5 4 5 5 5 5 6 7   1 2 3̑ M 4
      CM   4v   H H F F H
      1790   *a* Nolen

A98	e	*a*	149	BETHFIELD
A109	e	*a*	149	BETHFIELD
A114	e	*a*	149	BETHFIELD
A114.B	e	*a*	149	BETHFIELD

45.   1 1 2 3 2 3 4 5 5 3 2 1 2 3 2   1 2 3 4 3 4̑ M 4̑ 4
      CM   4v   H H H H H F F F O
      1794   *a* W. Billings

A136	a	*a*	276	REVELATION

46. 1 1 2 3 2 5 4 2 1 1 5 6 7 1 7   1 2 3 4 3⌒4
     CM   4v   H H H H F F
     1761
        P183   e   785

47. 1 1 2 3 3 2 1 7 6 7 1 2 3 3 2   1 2 3 4 4
     CM   4v   F O F O H
     1769   *a* Harrott
        P198   G   *a*   249

48. 1 1 2 3 3 3 1 6 6 1 1 2 3 4 6   1 2⌒3 4
     LM   4v   H H F H
     1791   *a* Callcott
        P291   C   *a*   788

49. 1 1 2 3 3 4 4 4 3 3 4 3 2 1 7   1 2 3⌒4 3 4
     CM   3v   H H F O H H
     c.1788   *a* Dalmer
        P263   A   *a*   278

50. 1 1 2 3 3 4 5 1 7 1 6 7 2 1 7   1 2 3 4
     CM   4v   F F F F
     1800   *a* Cole
        A196   E   *a*   736   GENEVA

51. 1 1 2 3 4 2 1 2 2 3 4 5 3 2 3   1 2 3 4 5⌒6 7⌒8 7 8
     66664444   4v   H H H H H O O F H H
     1786   *a* Harrison
        P258   G   *a*   718   CAMBDEN

52. 1 1 2 3 4 3 2 1 1 2 3 4 4 3 4   1 2 3 4 4
     LM   5v   H H F E F
     1798   _a_ Loder
         P310   B♭   _a_   720

53. 1 1 2 3 4 3 2 1 6 5 4 3 5 5 4   1 2 3 4
     LM   3v   H F H H
     1794   _a_ Shield
         P297   F   _a_   707

54. 1 1 2 3 4 3 2 1 7 1 1 6 7 1 2   1 2 3 4
     CM   4v   H H H F
     1759   _a_ French (_E_)
         P170   C   _a_   557

55. 1 1 2 3 4 3 3 2 1 2 1 2 3 2 2   1 2 3 4
     CM   4v   F F H F
     c.1755
         P157   G   599

56. 1 1 2 3 4 3 4 5 5 5 6 5 4 5 1   1 2 3 4͡ 4
     CM   4v   H E H F O
     1750
         P137   G   810
         P157   G   810

57. 1 1 2 3 4 5 1 7 7 1 1 5 5 5 4   1 2 3 4 5 6͡ 6
     888888   4v   H H H H H H F
     1793   _a_ Kimball
         A125   d   _a_   658

58. 1 1 2 3 4 5 2 3 4 5 6 5 4 4 5   1 2 3 4 5 6 6 6
888888   4v   F F F H O F F F
c.1776

  P231   a   146

59. 1 1 2 3 4 5 3 1 1 3 2 1 5 1 1   1 2 3 4
SM   4v   H H F O
1793   *a* Holden

  A124   a   *a*   317   CONTRITION
  A168[1]   a   *b*   317   CONTRITION

_____

[1] 1 1 2 3 4 5 3 1 1 3 2 1 5 1 2

b "Union Harmony"

1 1 2 3 4 5 3 1 1 3 2 1 5 1 2:   *see* **59**

60. 1 1 2 3 4 5 3 4 3 2 1 2 2 3 4   1 2 3 4
CM   4v   H H H F
1750   *a* Costall

  P137   G   *a*   557

61. 1 1 2 3 4 5 3 4 3 2 2 1 3 4 4   1 2 3 M 4
SM   4v   H H F O H
1800   *a* Jenks

  A201   a   *a*   509?   SOMERS

62. 1 1 2 3 4 5 4 3 2 1 1 2 3 4 5   1 2 2 3 4 4
CM   4v   H F H H F E
c.1760

  P182a   G   554
  P212   G   260   KEMPTON
  P228   G   554
  P235   G   260   YOXFORD

63. 1 1 2 3 4 5 4 3 2 1 2 3 5 4 3   1 2 3 4 3 ͡ 4 3 4 4

     SM   4v   H H H O F F H E H

     1781   *a* W. Billings

       A44   a   *a*   365   WAREHAM

64. 1 1 2 3 4 5 4 3 2 1 7 1 3 2 3   1 2 3 4

     LM   4v   H H H F

     1793   *a* Kimball

       A125   a   *a*   117   WOBURN

       A163   a   *a*   117   WOBURN

       A175   a   *a*   117   WOBURN

       A181   a   117   WOBURN

       A188   a   *a*   117   WOBURN

       A181.5   a   *a*   117   WOBURN

65. 1 1 2 3 4 5 4 3 4 3 2 1 3 5 4   1 2 3 4 4

     LM   4v   O F F F H

     c.1776

       P231   G   698

66. 1 1 2 3 4 5 4 3 4 5 4 2 3 3 1   1 2 3 4

     CM   4v   H H F F

     1749   *a* Watts

       P135   G   *a*   714

     1 1 2 3 4 5 4 3 4 6 5 5 3 1 3:   *see* **67**

67. 1 1 2 3 4 5 4 3 4 6 5 5 3 3 3   1 2 3̆ 4 5̆ 6
XXXXYY   4v   H H F F F F
1793   *a* West

    A131   a   *a*   404   JUDGMENT
    A163[1]   a   564   SUNDAY
    A175[1]   a   564   SUNDAY
    A181[1]   a   564   SUNDAY
    A181.5[1] a   564   SUNDAY

[1] 1 1 2 3 4 5 4 3 4 6 5 5 3 1 3

68. 1 1 2 3 4 5 5 4 7 5 5 5 3 7 6   1 2 3̆ M 4
SM   4v   E H F O E
1798   *a* Brooks

    A177   a   *a*   500   HADDAM
    A177.2   a   *a*   500   HADDAM

1 1 2 3 4 5 6 4 2 2 3 4 5 6 4:   *soprano of* **682**

69. 1 1 2 3 4 5 6 7 1 1 7 2 1 7 6   1 2 3 4 4 5̆ 6 7 8 9̆ X̆ M Z
CMT   4v   H H H H H F O H H O F F H
1793   *a* D. Read

    A128   D   *a*   204   ZION
    A172   D   *a*   204   ZION

70. 1 1 2 3 4 6 5 4 3 2 1 7 1 5 3   1 2 3 4̆ 4̆ 4̆ 4
CM   4v   E F F F F F F
1785   *a* D. Read

    A63   a   *a*   211   BARRINGTON
    A63.2   a   *a*   211   BARRINGTON
    A80   a   *a*   211   BARRINGTON
    A80.4   a   *a*   211   BARRINGTON
    A80.5   a   *a*   211   BARRINGTON

71. 1 1 2 3 5 1 7 1 5 6 4 3 2 1 5   1 2 3 3 4ͨ4
CM   3v   H H H H H F
1799
     D6.13   F   GOLDEN GROVE

     1 1 2 3 5 4 3 2 1 7 5 6 7 1 1:   *soprano of* **684**

72. 1 1 2 3 5 4 3 2 2 3 5 4 3 2 1   1 2 3 3 4
CM   4v   H H F H F
1785   *a* D. Read
     A63   a   *a*   388   VIENNA
     A63.2   a   *a*   388   VIENNA
     A80   a   *a*   388   VIENNA
     A80.4   a   *a*   388   VIENNA
     A80.5   a   *a*   388   VIENNA

     1 1 2 3 5 4 3 2 2 5 3 1 6 5 4:   *soprano of* **928**

73. 1 1 2 3 5 5 4 3 2 1 7 1 2 3 4   1 2 3 4ͨ4
CM   4v   H H H F F
c. 1800   *a* Cuzens
     D16   G   *a*   [1]   WINBOURN

-----

[1] Texts 278 and 250 given as alternatives.

74. 1 1 2 3 5 6 5 4 3 2 3 6 6 5 4   1 2 3ͨ4
LM   4v   H H F F
1797   *a* Belknap
     A166   G   *a*   111   BLUE HILL
     A192   G   *a*   111   BLUE HILL

110

75. 1 1 2 3 5 6 5 4 3 4 3 2 1 5 2   1 2 3 4 5͡ 6͡ 7 8
CMD   3v   H H H H F F F H
1800   *a* Babcock
         A192   G   *a*   659   SUNDAY

1 1 2 3 7 1 2 3 4 3 2 1 7 2 3:   *soprano of* **704**

1 1 2 5 5 1 5 5 5 1 1 1 7 7 5:   *soprano of* **1093**

76. 1 1 3 1 2 4 2 3 5 3 4 4 3 1 3   1 2 3͡ 4͡ 3͡ M 4
SM   4v   H H F F F F H
1794   *a* Belcher
         A135   G   *a*   463   HALLOWELL

1 1 3 1 5 5 6 6 5 6 5 4 3 2 3:   *soprano of* **712**

77. 1 1 3 2 1 3 4 3 2 2 7 2 3 2 1   1 2 3 4
CM   4v   F H H O
1754   *a* Everet
         P151   c   *a*   18
         P157   c   *a*   18
         P198[1]   a   18

---

[1] F O O O

1 1 3 2 1 4 3 2 3 3 5 4 3 3 2:   *soprano of* **404**

78. 1 1 3 2 1 5 7 5 4 3 2 1 7̑ 1 3   1 2 3͡ M 4
    SM   4v   H H F O H
    1798   *a* Wetmore
       A177   a   *a*   12   AMERICA
       A177.2   a   *a*   12   AMERICA

79. 1 1 3 2 1 7 6 5 1 2 3 2 1 7 1   1 2 3 3 4 4
    LM   4v   H H E E F O
    c.1766
       P231   C   792

80. 1 1 3 2 3 4 3 2 2 3 4 5 5 5 4   1 2 3 4 3͡ M
    LM   4v   H H H H F F
    1789   *a* French (*A*)
       A93   a   *a*   357   BETHANY

81. 1 1 3 2 7 1 2 3 2 2 1 2 3 2 1   1 2 3 4
    LM   4v   H H F F
    1789
       P266   a   313   BROOK

82. 1 1 3 2 7 5 3 2 1 7 3 3 4 4 5   1 2 3 3 4
    CM   4v   F H F H H
    1798   *a* Kyes
       A177   a   *a*   207   PARADISE
       A177.2   a   *a*   207   PARADISE

83. 1 1 3 3 5 1 1 1 7 1 1 2 1 7 1   1 2 3 4 5͡ 6 7 7 8
    LMD   3v   H H H H F O H H H
    1800
       A196   D   229   UR

1 1 3 3 5 5 4 5 1 1 7 6 5 4 4:   *soprano of* **1121**

1 1 3 4 2 3 3 2 1 7 6 5 4 5 5:   *soprano of* **208**

84.	1 1 3 4 3 2 1 1 3 1 2 1 7 6 5				1 2 3 4 5 6
	668668			4v	H H H F O H
	1790		*a* Edson		
	A96	C	*a*	218	WATERFORD
	A111	C	*a*	218	WATERFORD
	A111.3	C	*a*	218	WATERFORD
	A111.4	C	*a*	218	WATERFORD
	A111.5	C	*a*	218	WATERFORD
	A111.6	C	*a*	218	WATERFORD
	A170	C	*a*	218	WATERFORD
	A200	C	*a*	218	WATERFORD

85.	1 1 3 4 3 2 1 2 3 1 2 1 7 6 5				1 2 3 4 5 6
	668668			4v	H H H F F H
	1800		*a* Jenks		
	A201	C	*a*	217?	

1 1 3 4 5 6 7 1 5 5 4 3 4 5 6:   *soprano of* **900**

86.	1 1 3 5 3 1 2 3 2 3 3 4 3 2 1				1 2 3 4 5 6
	888888			4v	F F H H H H
	1795		*a* French (*A*)		
	A150	A	*a*	85	CASTLE

1 1 3 5 4 3 2 1 3 5 3 2 1 1 3:   *see* **87**

87. 1 1 3 5 4 3 2 2 3 4 5 4 3 2 1   1 2 3 4 4 5 6 6 7 M 8
     SMD   4v   H H H H H H F F F F F H
     1793   *a* Griswold
       [+]A121   A   283   VENUS
       [+]A164[1,2]   A   *a*   283   VENUS
       A174[1]   A   283   CREATION
       A182[1,2]   A   *a*   283   VENUS

     [1] 1 1 3 5 4 3 2 1 3 5 3 2 1 1 3
     [2] 1 2 3 4 5 6 7 8 8
        H H H E F F F F H

     1 1 3 5 4 3 3 2 1 2 1 3 2 1 7:   *see* **88**

88. 1 1 3 5 4 3 3 2 1 2 2 3 2 1 7   1 2 3 4
     LM   4v   H H H F
     c.1746
       P129a   G   443
       P135[1]   G   7
       P145a   G   443

     [1] 1 1 3 5 4 3 3 2 1 2 1 3 2 1 7

     Closely related to **178** and **402**.

89. 1 1 3 5 6 5 4 3 2 1 6 6 1 3 4   1 2 3 4 5 6
     888888   4v   F F H F O H
     1800
       A192   A   606   MEDFIELD

90. 1 1 3 5 6 5 4 3 3 2 2 3 4 3 2   1 2 3 4 4
     SM   4v   H H H F H
     c.1792   *a* Firth
       D12   G   *a*   51   PRICES

91. 1 1 3 6 5 6 7 1 5 1 1 4 3 2 1   1 2 3 4͡ 5͡ M 6
888888   4v   H H H F F F H
1783   *a* Swan

A51	C	*a*	183	MAJESTY
A62	C	*a*	183	MAJESTY
A70	C	*a*	183	MAJESTY
A74	C		183	MAJESTY
A85	C		183	MAJESTY
A91	C	*a*	183	MAJESTY
A62.3	C	*a*	183	MAJESTY

1 1 4 3 1 1 7 1 7 1 1 2 2 2 2:   *soprano of* **688**

92. 1 1 4 3 2 4 3 5 4 3 2 1 7 7 7   1 2 3 4͡ 4
CM   4v   H H H F F
c.1776

P231	g		346

93. 1 1 5 1 1 2 3 3 4 5 4 3 2 1 2   1 2 3 4 5͡ 6͡ 7͡ 8 8 9 X Y Z
CMT   4v   E H H E F F F O H H H H E
1793   *a* Babcock

A132	C	*a*	561	WESTBOROUGH

94. 1 1 5 1 2 3 2 1 3 2 7 1 5 1 2   1 2 3 4
LM   4v   H H H F
1785   *a* D. Read

A63	C	*a*	295	NEW ENGLAND
A63.2	C	*a*	295	NEW ENGLAND
A80	C	*a*	295	NEW ENGLAND
A80.4	C	*a*	295	NEW ENGLAND
A80.5	C	*a*	295	NEW ENGLAND

95. 1 1 5 1 2 3 2 1 7 7 1 2 3 2 3   1 2 3 4 4 4

CM   4v   H C H F F F

c.1785   *a* Valentine

   P257   c   *a*   549

96. 1 1 5 1 2 3 2 3 4 3 2 2 5 4 3   1 2 3 4

CM   4v   F O F E

1785   *a* D. Read

A63	a	*a*	399	CALVARY
A63.2	a	*a*	399	CALVARY
A68	a		399	CALVARY
A70	a	*a*	399	CALVARY
A74	a		399	CALVARY
A80	a	*a*	399	CALVARY
A84	a	*a*	399	CALVARY
A85	a		399	CALVARY
A91	a	*a*	399	CALVARY
A98	a	*a*	399	CALVARY
A108	a	*a*	399	CALVARY
A109	a	*a*	399	CALVARY
A114	a	*a*	399	CALVARY
A119	a	*a*	399	CALVARY
A114.B	a	*a*	399	CALVARY
A121	a		399	CALVARY
A131	a	*a*	399	CALVARY
A145	a	*a*	399	CALVARY
A147	a	*a*	399	CALVARY
A158	a	*a*	399	CALVARY
A80.5	a	*a*	399	CALVARY
A163	a	*a*	399	CALVARY
A168	a	*a*	399	CALVARY
A172	a	*a*	399	CALVARY
A174	a		399	CALVARY
A175	a	*a*	399	CALVARY
A181	a		399	CALVARY
A189[1]	a	*a*	399	CALVARY
A190	a	*a*	399	CALVARY
A181.5	a	*a*	399	CALVARY

---

[1] 1 7 5 1 2 3 2 3 4 3 2 2 5 4 3

97. 115 123 432 132 176   1 2 3 4
CM   4v   H F H F
c. 1760-70

⁺P174	A	593	ST JAMES'
⁺P204	C	563	CANTERBURY
P174.10	A	593	ST JAMES'
P174.11	A	593	ST JAMES'
P174.12	A	593	ST JAMES'

98. 115 123 542 123 143   1 2 3 4̄ 4̄
CM   4v   H H F F F O
1790

A96	C	264	JOYFUL SOUND
A111	C	264	JOYFUL SOUND
A111.3	C	264	JOYFUL SOUND
A111.4	C	264	JOYFUL SOUND
A111.5	C	264	JOYFUL SOUND
A111.6	C	264	JOYFUL SOUND

99. 115 132 153 212 323   1 2 3 4
CM   4v   H H F F
1767

P169.2	A	391	SYSTON

100. 115 132 715 532 213   1 2 3 4
CM   4v   F H E H
1790   *a* Kyes

A96	d	*a*	528	REQUEST
A111	d	*a*	528	REQUEST
A111.3	d	*a*	528	REQUEST
A111.4	d	*a*	528	REQUEST
A111.5	d	*a*	528	REQUEST
A111.6	d	*a*	528	REQUEST

101. 1 1 5 1 4 3 2 1 2 5 3 2 1 5 1   1 2 3͡ M 4
      LM   4v   H H F O H
      1789   *a* Spicer
         A92   a   *a*   101   CARLISLE
         A92.3   a   *a*   101   CARLISLE
         A103   a   *a*   101   CARLISLE
         A103.4   a   *a*   101   CARLISLE
         A103.5   a   *a*   101   CARLISLE
         A174   a   101   CARLISLE
         A103.6   a   *a*   101   CARLISLE
         A189   a   *a*   101   CARLISLE

102. 1 1 5 3 2 7 1 1 5 4 3 2 1 5 3   1 2 3 4 5 6 6
      777777   4v   F H H H H H H
      1789   *a* French (*A*)
         A93   d   *a*   732   ASPIRATION

103. 1 1 5 3 5 6 7 1 1 7 6 1 3 2 4   1 2 3 3 4 4
      CM   4v   H H F F H H
      c.1790   *a* Radiger
         D9   C   *a*   28   NEW CREATION

104. 1 1 5 4 3 2 3 4 5 1 5 6 5 4 3   1 2 3 4 5͡ 6 7 8
      CMD   4v   H H H E F O C H
      1792   *a* W. Read
         A119   E♭   *a*   410   CREATION

      1 1 5 4 3 2 7 1 2 3 4 5 2 3 3:   *soprano of* **105**

105.	1 1 5 4 3 2 7 1 2 3 4 5 5 3 1			1 2 2 3 4	
	CM		4v	F H H H F	
	1759				
	P169	G	249	SILEBY	
	P169.2	G	249	SILEBY	
	P212	G	15	SILEBY	

106.	1 1 5 5 1 2 3 4 3 4 5 4 3 2 2			1 2 3 4 5 6 7 8	
	CMD		4v	H H H F H H H H	
	1722				
	P71.2	A	813		
	P86	A	813		
	P86.4	A	813		
	P107	A	109	**BERWICK**	
	P111a	A	813		
	P123[1,2]	F	813		
	P111a.7	A	813		
	P123.11[1,3]	F	813		
	P111a.8	A	813		
	P180	G	813		
	P111a.9	A	813		
	P117.7	G	806	**BISHOP STORTFORD**	
	P111a.10	A	813		
	P111a.11	A	813		

[1] 1 2 3 4 5 6 7 8
   F F H F F H H H

[2] 1 1 6 5 1 2 1 2 1 2 3 2 2 3 4

[3] 1 1 5 5 1 7 1 2 1 2 3 2 2 3 4

107.	1 1 5 5 1 2 3 4 5 4 3 2 3 5 5			1 2 3 4 5 6 7 8	
	CMD		4v	F H E H H H H H	
	1759				
	P169	a	806	STANFORD	
	P169.2	a	806	STANFORD	
	P212[1]	a	806	STANFORD	

[1] 1 1 5 5 1 2 3 4 5 4 3 2 3 5 6

115 512 345 432 356:   *see* **107**

115 517 121 232 234:   *see* **106**

108.   115 532 555 335 455   1 2 3̑ 4 4
      CM   4v   O H H F H
      1791   *a* Arne
        P291   F   *a*   322

109.   115 534 231 351 765   1 2 3 4 4
      CM   4v   H F F H H
      1791   *a* Callcott
        P291   D   *a*   709

110.   115 537 571 153 542   1 2 3̑ 3 4 5 6 7 8 5̑ 6 7 8
      LMD   4v   H H F F H F H H H F O H H
      1793   *a* Stone
        A132   b   *a*   316   DORCHESTER

111.   115 557 555 555 555   1 2 3 4 5 6 7 8
      CMD   4v   H H H H F H C H
      1791   *a* S. Arnold
        P291   F   *a*   3
        A153   F   *a*   3   FRANCE

112.   115 645 612 131 256   1 2 3 3 4
      LM   4v   H H H F H
      1798   *a* Peck
        A177   D   *a*   784   BLOOMINGGROVE
        A177.2   D   *a*   784   BLOOMINGGROVE

113. 1 1 5 6 5 1 5 6 5 1 5 6 5 3 1   1 2 3͡ M 3 4
CM   4v   H H F F H H
1793   *a* Shumway
    A131   F   *a*   669   WESTMINSTER

114. 1 1 5 6 5 4 3 2 1 5 1 7 1 2 3   1 2 3 4 5͡ 6
666688   4v   H H H E F O
1799   *a* Pilsbury
    A189   e   *a*   50   MOUNT MORIAH

1 1 5 6 7 1 1 7 1 2 1 7 6 5 6:   *see* **115**

1 1 5 6 7 1 1 7 7 2 1 6 5 6 1:   *see* **115**

115. 1 1 5 6 7 1 2 7 7 2 1 6 5 6 1   1 2 3 4 4
CM   4v   H H H H F
c.1746

P129a	C		260	
P144	C		769	BEESLY
P145a	C		260	
A157[1]	C		211	
P144.4	C		769	BEESLY
P198[1]	B		211	
P253[1,2]	C	*b*	280	CARLISLE
P253.2[1,2]	C	*b*	280	CARLISLE
D6.6[3]	C	*b*		CHARLESTOWN
P266[1]	C			NORMANTON
D6.10[3]	C	*b*		CHARLESTOWN

---

[1] 1 1 5 6 7 1 1 7 7 2 1 6 5 6 1

[2] 1 2 3 4 4 4
   H H H H F O

[3] 3v

b Hounsell   *115 continued*

D6.11[3]	C	b		CHARLESTOWN
P253.4[1,2]	C	b	280	CARLISLE
P303[3,4]	C		[5]	CHARLESTOWN
P303.10[3,4]	C		[5]	CHARLESTOWN
D6.12[3]	C	b		CHARLESTOWN
D6.13[3]	C	b		CHARLESTOWN
P303.11[3,4]	C		[5]	CHARLESTOWN

---

[1] 1 1 5 6 7 1 1 7 7 2 1 6 5 6 1

[2] 1 2 3 4 4 4
H H H H F O

[3] 3v

[4] 1 1 5 6 7 1 1 7 1 2 1 7 6 5 6

[5] Assigned text, "Hymn 188 Dr. W[atts]," does not fit tune.

b Hounsell

---

1 1 5 7 2 1 7 5 1 2 1 7 1 1 5: *soprano of* **229**

---

116.   1 1 6 1 3 2 5 3 4 5 6 5 5 6 7   1 2 3 4 5 6 7 8

SMD   4v   H H H H F H H H

1798   *a* Merriman

A177	D	a	203	MINERVA
A177.2	D	a	203	MINERVA

---

117.   1 1 6 4 6 5 3 1 1 5 5 6 7 1 2   1 2 3 4 5 6 5 6 7 8

LMD   4v   H H H H F F F F F F

1799   *a* Pilsbury

A189	E	a	700	NEW HAMPSHIRE

---

1 1 6 5 1 2 1 2 1 2 3 2 2 3 4: *see* **106**

118. 1 1 7 1 1 1 1 1 4 4 4 5 4 3 2   ⌒ ⌒ ⌒
      LM   4v   1 2 3 4 3 4 4 4
      1791   *a* Callcott   H F F F F H H H
          P291   D   *a*   122
          A161   D   164   WARWICK
          A162   D   164   WARWICK
          A203   D   164   WARWICK

119. 1 1 7 1 1 1 2 7 1 1 3 2 3 4 5   1 2 3 4
      LM   3v   H H F H
      1794   *a* B. Cooke
          P297   F   *a*   462

      1 1 7 1 1 1 7 1 1 1 1 1 1 7 1:   *soprano of* **241**

      1 1 7 1 1 1 7 1 1 5 5 5 1 1 7:   *soprano of* **241**

      1 1 7 1 1 2 2 3 4 3 1 5 5 4 5:   *soprano of* **721**

120. 1 1 7 1 1 6 4 5 5 5 3 2 2 2 1   ⌒ ⌒ ⌒
      888888   4v   1 2 3 4 5 6 6
      1791   *a* Callcott   H O F F F F F
          P291   C   *a*   625

      1 1 7 1 1 7 1 2 1 7 7 6 7 6 5:   *soprano of* **1090**

      1 1 7 1 2 1 7 1 2 1 2 3 2 1 5:   *soprano of* **265**

121.   1 1 7 1 2 1 7 6 4 5 4 3 5 1 6   1 2 3 4 5 6 7 8
CMD   4v   H H H H H F F H
1755

    P153   G   562
    P153.2   G   562
    P153.3   G   562

122.   1 1 7 1 2 3 1 4 3 2 3 7 3 1 1   1 2 3 4 5 6 7 7 8 7 7 8
CMD   4v   H H H O F H H H H H H H
c. 1790   *a* M. Cooke

    P274   A   *a*   763

   1 1 7 1 2 3 1 7 7 1 4 5 4 3 2:   *soprano of* **253**

   1 1 7 1 2 3 2 5 4 3 5 5 4 3 2:   *soprano of* **273**

123.   1 1 7 1 2 3 3 2 1 7 6 5 5 1 2   1 2 3 4 5 6 7 8
LMD   4v   H H H H F F O O
1784

    A57   C   820   WASHINGTON
    A57.2   C   820   WASHINGTON
    A70   C   *b*   820   BENNINGTON / WASHINGTON
    A74   C   820   WASHINGTON
    A84   C   820   BENNINGTON
    A85   C   820   BENNINGTON
    A91   C   *b*   820   BENNINGTON / WASHINGTON
    A108   C   *b*   820   BENNINGTON
    A119   C   *b*   820   BENNINGTON

---

b "Massachusetts Harmony"

124. 1 1 7 1 2 3 3 2 2 1 2 3 2 1 7   1 2 3 4̂ M M 3 4
CM   4v   H H F F O O H H
1783   *a* W. Billings

A51	a		504	KETERY
A62	a		504	KETTERY
A65	a	*a*	504	KITTERY
A62.3	a		504	KETTERY
A124	a	*a*	504	KITTERY
A131	a		504	KITTERY
A147	a	*a*	504	KITTERY
A158	a	*a*	504	KITTERY
A160	a	*a*	504	KITTERY
A163	a	*a*	504	KITTERY
A168	a	*a*	504	KITTERY
A190	a	*a*	504	KITTERY

1 1 7 1 2 3 4 3 2 3 3 2 1 1 7:   *see* **125**

125. 1 1 7 1 2 3 4 3 2 3 3 2 1 7 7   1 2 3 4
CM   4v   H F F F
-1749

[+]P135	c	562	
P137	c	678	
P130.2[1]	c	278	OXFORD
P130.3[1]	c	278	OXFORD
[+]P145a	c	278	
P155a	c	278	
P157	c	678	
P174[1]	a	810	WROTHAM
A17	c		PS. 12
A17.2	c		PS. 12
P130.5[1]	c	278	OXFORD
P174.10[1]	a	810	WROTHAM
P235[1]	c	362	WENHASTON
P174.11[1]	a	810	WROTHAM
P174.12[1]	a	810	WROTHAM

---

[1] 1 1 7 1 2 3 4 3 2 3 3 2 1 1 7

126.   1 1 7 1 2 3 4 5 3 4 5 4 3 2 1   1 2 3⌢4
           LM   4v   H H F F
           1785

A62a	g		WILLIAMSTOWN
A67	g	782	WILLIAMSTOWN
A95	g		WILLIAMSTOWN
A113[1]	a	782	WILLIAMSTOWN
A121	g		LESSON III
A131	g	548	WILLIAMSTOWN
A174	g	548	WILLIAMSTOWN
A200	g		WILLIAMSTOWN / LESSON III

[1] 1 1 2 3 2 3 4 5 3 4 5 4 3 2 1

127.   1 1 7 1 2 3 5 4 3 2 1 2 3 2 1   1 2 3 4
           CM   4v   H H F E
           1785   *a* D. Read

A63	g	*a*	644	HUMAN FRAILTY
A63.2	g	*a*	644	HUMAN FRAILTY
A80	g	*a*	644	HUMAN FRAILTY
A80.4	g	*a*	644	HUMAN RRAILTY
A80.5	g	*a*	644	HUMAN FRAILTY

128.   1 1 7 1 2 3 5 4 4 3 1 4 3 2 2   1 2 3 4 5⌢6 5 6
           666688   4v   H H H H O F H H
           1778   *a* W. Billings

A40	G	*a*	524	BOLTON
A40.2	G	*a*	524	BOLTON
A40.3	G	*a*	524	BOLTON
A40.4	G	*a*	524	BOLTON

129.   1 1 7 1 2 4 3 2 1 1 7 6 5 4 5   1 2 3⌢4
           CM   4v   H H F F
           1790   *a* Rogerson

A98	C	84	MARIETTA
A109	C	84	MARIETTA

A114	C		84	MARIETTA
A114.B	C		84	MARIETTA
A124	C		84	MARIETTA
A160	C	a	84	MARIETTA
A177	C		84	MARIETTA
A177.2	C		84	MARIETTA

130. 1 1 7 1 3 2 7 2 4 3 1 5 4 3 1   1 2 3 4 4 M
CM   4v   E H F F O O
1794   a W. Billings
    A136   C   a   89   EGYPT

131. 1 1 7 1 3 6 3 6 5 6 5 4 3 2 2   1 2 3 4
CM   4v   H H F H
c.1785   a Valentine
    P257   G   a   319

132. 1 1 7 1 4 3 2 1 7 1 3 2 5 3 4   1 2 3 4 4
CM   3v   H H H F H
1792-   a Vincent
    D12   A   a   30   FURMAN
    S6   A   FURMAN
    D15   A   a   304   FURMAN

133. 1 1 7 1 4 3 2 3 3 2 1 7 1 2 3   1 2 3 4
LM   4v   H H F F
1793   a Kimball
    A125   C   a   381   CHARLESTOWN

134. 1 1 7 1 5 3 1 5 5 5 6 5 4 3 5   1 2 3 4 3 4
CM   3v   O F H H H H
1797   a R. Merrill
    A171   D   a   438   ALEPPO

135.   1 1 7 1 5 4 2 3 3 6 6 6 4 5 6   1 2 2 3 4 4
CM   4v   H F H H F F
1754
   P151   G   557

1 1 7 1 5 4 3 2 3 2 3 3 2 3 2:   *soprano of* **231**

136.   1 1 7 1 5 4 3 4 3 2 1 2 3 4 5   1 2 3 4 4
LM   4v   H H H O F
1793   *a* Kimball
   A125   E♭   *a*   605   BENNINGTON

1 1 7 1 7 6 5 5 5 1 2 3 4 2 5:   *soprano of* **37**

137.   1 1 7 6 5 4 3 2 1 5 5 6 7 1 2   1 2 3 4 3 4
CM   4v   H H H H F E
1754-5   *a* Tans'ur
   P155   C   *a*   827   COLCHESTER

1 1 7 6 6 5 2 3 4 4 3 3 4 6 1:   *soprano of* **738**

138.   1 1 7 6 7 6 5 1 2 3 2 7 1 7 6   1 2 3 3 4 4
CM   4v   H H F H F H
1760   *a* B. West (*E*)
   P173   C   *a*   789   DAVENTRY

139.   1 2 1 2 3 1 5 5 6 5 4 3 2 1 1   1 2 3 4
       LM   4v   F F F H
       1793

         P293   G   514   DOXOLOGY

140.   1 2 1 3 5 5 6 5 5 3 6 5 4 3 6   1 2 3͡ 4
       CM   4v   H H F F
       1791   *a* Callcott
         P291   E   *a*   624
         A161   E   588   SPAIN
         A162   E   588   SPAIN
         A203[1]   E   588   SPAIN

      [1] 1 2 3 4
         H H F H

       1 2 1 7 1 2 3 2 1 5 4 5 4 3 4:   *see* **141**

141.   1 2 1 7 2 3 2 1 5 4 5 4 3 4 3   1 2 3 4
       LM   4v   E C E F
       c.1746
         P129a   C   480
         P130.2[2]   C   480   MAPHAM
         P130.3[2]   C   480   MAPHAM
         P151[1,2]   C   435
         P157[1,2]   C   435
         P174[2]   A   480   SHOREHAM
         A17[2]   C   PS. 150

      [1] 1 2 1 7 1 2 3 2 1 5 4 5 4 3 4

      [2] 1 2 3 4
         E F E F   *141 continued*

A17.2[2]	C		PS. 150
P130.5[2]	C	480	MAPHAM
P174.10[2]	A	480	SHOREHAM
P235[2]	A	670	ALL SAINTS
A41	C	342	PS. 150
A43	C	342	PS. 150
A47	C	342	PS. 150
A47a	C	342	PS. 150
P174.11[2]	A	480	SHOREHAM
P174.12[2]	A	480	SHOREHAM

[2] 1 2 3 4
     E F E F

142. 1 2 1 7 5 4 2 3 3 3 2 1 2 1 7   1 2 3 4
      CM   4v   H E H F
      1750
           P137   C   391

143. 1 2 1 7 6 7 1 2 3 1 2 2 3 3 2   1 2 3 4
      CM   4v   F H F F
      1750
           P137   C   815
           P198   B♭   815

A version of **948**.

144. 1 2 2 1 1 1 1 6 7 1 7 1 2 2 1   1 2 3 4 5 6 7 8
      LMD   3v   H H F H H F H H
      1794   *a* Dupuis
           P297   F   *a*   800

145. 1 2 2 3 1 1 1 7 4 3 2 1 7 7 1   1 2 3 4 ⌒4
LM   3v   H F H F O
1791
    P292   G   75

146. 1 2 2 3 1 4 3 2 3 3 1 5 4 3 2   1 2 2 3 ⌒4 3 4 4
CM   4v   H H H F F H H H
1788
    A87   A   271   STRATFIELD
    A117   A   271   STRATFIELD

147. 1 2 2 3 1 4 4 2 2 3 3 4 5 2 2   1 2 3 4 5 6 7 8
LMD   4v   H H E F F H H E
1759
    P169   g   758   CHARLEY
    P169.2   g   758   CHARLEY
    A43   a   b   758   CHESHIRE
    A47a   a   b   758   CHESHIRE
    A56   a   758   CHESHIRE
    A84   a   758   CHESHIRE
    P266   g   b   758   ZION
    A106   a   b   758   CHESHIRE
    A106.4   a   b   758   CHESHIRE
    A141   a   758   CHESHIRE
    A203   a   758   CHESHIRE

---

b J. Arnold.

148. 1 2 2 3 1 5 1 2 2 3 4 3 2 2 1   1 2 3 4 4 5 6 7 8
CMD   4v   H H F O H F H F F
c.1790   *a* M. Cooke
    P274   A   *a*   789

1 2 2 3 2 1 7 6 6 7 7 1 5 1 7:   *soprano of* **604**

1 2 2 3 2 3 4 3 2 3 2 3 4 3 2:   *soprano of* **750**

149. 1 2 2 3 5 3 1 5 6 3 1 2 3 4 5   1 2 3 4 3 4
     CM   4v   H H H O F F
     1798   *a* Brooks
       A177   C   *a*   568   HALLELUJAH
       A177.2   C   *a*   568   HALLELUJAH

1 2 2 4 4 3 2 1 7 1 2 3 4 3 2:   *soprano of* **717**

1 2 2 7 5 3 3 2 5 5 1 7 6 5 5:   *soprano of* **752**

150. 1 2 3 1 1 7 6 2 1 7 1 2 1 3 3   1 2 3 4
     LM   3v   H H F H
     1794   *a* Atterbury
       P297   A   *a*   541

151. 1 2 3 1 2 3 4 3 2 1 7 1 2 7 1   1 2 3 4
     LM   3v   H F H H
     1794   *a* S. Arnold
       P297   G   *a*   728

152. 1 2 3 1 2 3 4 5 4 3 2 1 2 5 4   1 2 3 4
     LM   4v   H F H F
     1759   *a* French (*E*)
       P170   a   *a*   518

153.   1 2 3 1 4 2 3 3 2 1 7 1 2 3 1   1 2 3 4 4 4
           SM   4v   H H F H H H
           1789   *a* Dixon
                P266   C   *a*   395   ALBION

           1 2 3 1 5 4 3 4 5 1 7 1 2 7 1:   *soprano of* **154**

154.   1 2 3 1 5 5 5 1 2 3 4 5 5 6 7   1 2 3 4
           CM   4v   F F F O
           1791   *a* S. Arnold
                P291   e   *a*   327

155.   1 2 3 2 1 2 1 7 1 2 3 3 2 1 1   1 2 3 4
           LM   3v   H H F H
           1794   *a* R. Cooke
                P297   E♭   a   460

156.   1 2 3 2 1 3 4 5 3 2 1 2 5 4 3   1 2 3 M 3 4
           7777   4v   H H F F H H
           1793   *a* Shumway
                A131   G   *a*   60   PITTSGROVE

           1 2 3 2 1 3 5 1 7 5 3 1 5 1 7:   *soprano of* **671**

157.   1 2 3 2 1 5 1 7 3 2 3 4 5 4 5   1 2 3 4 5 6
           777777   4v   H H H H H F
           1792-   *a* Firth
                D12   a   *a*   310   FIRTH'S

1 2 3 2 1 5 5 6 5 4 3 2 2 3 2:   *see* **246**

158.   1 2 3 2 1 7 1 5 4 3 1 2 3 4 3   1 2 3 4 3͡ 4
       CM   4v   F F F F F F
       c.1755   *a* Pratt
           P158   B♭   *a*   31

159.   1 2 3 2 1 7 1 7 1 1 7 7 1 2 2   1 2 3 4
       LM   3v   H F H H
       1794   *a* Parsons
           P297   B♭   *a*   455

1 2 3 2 3 1 7 6 7 1 2 1 2 3 2:   *soprano of* **689**

160.   1 2 3 2 3 4 3 4 5 6 5 4 3 2 1   1 2 3 3 4͡ 5 6
       668668   4v   E E F H F F F
       c.1800   *a* Key
           P323   G   *a*   224

161.   1 2 3 2 3 4 5 1 7 6 5 5 6 1 4   1 2 3 4 5͡ 6
       878777   4v   H H H H F O
       1799   *a* Pilsbury
           A189   F   *a*   323   MIDDLESEX

162.   1 2 3 3 2 1 7 1 2 3 4 7 2 2 1   1 2 3͡ 4
       CM   3v   F H F F
       1791   *a* Callcott
           P291   f   *a*   209

163. 1 2 3 3 3 1 1 1 1 1 6 2 1 7 1   1 2 2 3 4 4 5 6 7̂ 8 8
CMD   3v   H H F H H H H H O O H
1794   *a* Stevens
   P297   G   *a*   292

164. 1 2 3 3 3 2 3 4 4 4 4 6 5 4 3   1 2 3 4 4
LM   3v   H H H F H
1794   *a* B. Cooke
   P297   E♭   *a*   642

1 2 3 3 4 5 3 6 1 2 3 4 2 5 7:   *soprano of* **664**

165. 1 2 3 3 4 5 6 7 1 1 2 3 3 4 5   1 2 3 4 5 6 7̂ 8 7 8
LMD   3v   F F F F F F F F H H
1794   *a* B. Cooke
   P297   D   *a*   441

166. 1 2 3 4 2 7 1 2 7 1 3 2 5 3 3   1 2 3 4 5 6 7 8
8⁸ anapests   4v   H H H H H E A F
c.1790   *a* Radiger
   D9   B♭   *a*   660   CONFIDENCE

167. 1 2 3 4 3 2 1 7 1 2 7 3 2 1 7   1 2 3̂ 4 4
CM   3v   H H F F H
1791   *a* Callcott
   P291   C   *a*   825

168. 1 2 3 4 3 2 1 7 7 1 2 3 4 3 2   1 2 2 3 4
CM   5v   H E H O F
c.1755
    P157   B♭   785

169. 1 2 3 4 3 2 2 1 1 5 4 3 2 3 2   1 2 3 4 5 6
666688   4v   H H H H F H
c.1752   *a* Knapp
    P148   G   *a*   711   CANFORD
    P148.2   G   *a*   711   CANFORD
    P148.3   G   *a*   711   CANFORD
    P148.4   G   *a*   711   CANFORD
    P148.5   G   *a*   711   CANFORD

170. 1 2 3 4 3 4 5 6 5 4 3 2 3 5 5   1⌢2 3 4
LM   4v   F F H F
1793   *a* Stephenson
    A124   G   *a*   480   PS. 150
    A195   G   *a*   480   PS. 150

171. 1 2 3 4 3 4 5 6 5 4 3 4 3 3 3   1 2 3 4
CM   4v   H H H F
c.1785   *a* Valentine
    P257   G   *a*   550
    A79   G   550   PS. 11
    A87   G   550   PS. 11
    A117   G   550   PS. 11
    A147   G   *a*   550   PS. 11

    1 2 3 4 3 5 4 3 5 6 5 5 5 1 7:   *see* **172**

172.   1 2 3   4 3 5   4 3 6   7 5 1   5 5 4   1   2   3   4

        CM   4v   H   H   F   F

        c.1776   *a* Bond

          P230   F   *a*   375

         D12[1,2]   F   *a*   FROOME

---

[1]   1 2 3   4 3 5   4 3 5   6 5 5   5 1 7

[2]   1   2   3   4   4

     H   H   F   H   E

173.   1 2 3   4 5 1   1 5 3   4 3 4   6 1 7   1   2   3   4   3   4   4

        CM   4v   F   F   H   H   H   H   H

        1791   *a* Handel

         P291   g   *a*   683

1 2 3   4 5 1   6 5 4   3 4 3   2 1 7:   *soprano of* **722**

174.   1 2 3   4 5 3   4 6 5   4 3 2   1 1 7   1   2   3   4   4

        7778   4v   F   F   H   H   F

        1789   *a* French (*A*)

         A93   G   *a*   78   ATTENTION

         A131   G   *a*   78   ATTENTION

         A150[1]   G   *a*   78   ATTENTION

---

[1]   1   2   3   4   4   4

     F   F   H   H   F   F

175.   1 2 3   4 5 5   4 3 2   3 4 2   3 1 3   1   2   3   4   4

        LM   4v   O   O   F   O   H

        1769   *a* Harrott

         P198   G   *a*   628

1 2 3 4 5 6 1 7 1 2 4 3 2 1 7:   *soprano of* **53**

1 2 3 4 5 6 5 4 3 2 6 5 4 3 1:   *soprano of* **724**

1 2 3 4 5 6 6 5 5 5 1 4 3 7 6:   *soprano of* **173**

176.   1 2 3 4 5 6 7 1 1 3 4 5 6 7 1   1 2 3 4 3 4

       CM   2v   F H H O F H

       c.1785   *a* Tremain

         P256   E   *a*   771

177.   1 2 3 4 5 6 7 1 7 6 5 1 3 2 1   1 2͡ 3͡ 4

       LM   4v   H F O O

       1793   *a* Babcock

         A132   d   *a*   257   ADMIRATION

1 2 4 5 3 4 6 4 2 3 1 6 1 2 2:   *see* **1224**

178.   1 2 3 5 4 3 3 2 1 2 2 3 2 1 7   1 2 3 4

       LM   4v   H H H F

       1750

         P137   G   443

         P157   G   443

         P198   G   443

A version of **402**. Cf. also **88**.

179. 1 2 7   1 2 3   4 2 2   3 4 5   6 5 4   1 2 3 4̂ 4 5 6 7 8 8

LMD   4v   H E H H F H H H E E

1759

P169	g		452	LEICESTER
P169.2	g		452	LEICESTER
P198	g		452	LEICESTER
A43[1]	a	b	452	LEICESTER
A47a[1]	a	b	452	LEICESTER
A56[1]	a		452	LEICESTER
A84[1]	a		452	LEICESTER

[1] 1 2 3 4̂ 4 5 6 7 8 8
    H E H H F H H H A E

b J. Arnold

180. 1 2 7   1 2 3   4 3 2   1 2 3   2 3 4   1 2 3 4 4

CM   4v   H F H F H

c.1783   *a* Barwick

P250	a	*a*	494	WINGHAM

181. 1 2 7   1 7 6   7 5 1   1 1 1   6 7 1   1̂ 2 2̂ 3 4̂ 4

CM   4v   F F H F F O

1791   *a* Callcott

P291	A	*a*	691

182. 1 2 7   3 2 5   4 3 2   1 5 1   7 6 5   1 2 3 4

CM   2v   H H O F

-1783

P249	a		25	CUMBERLAND

A version of **184.**

183.   1 2 7 3 4 5 2 3 2 1 7 1 5 4 3   1 2 3 4
      CM   4v   H H O F
      1789
         P266   a   25   BURINGHAM

A version of **184**.

184.   1 2 7 3 7 3 2 1 7 1 5 4 3 2 7   1 2 3 4
      CM   4v   H H O F
      1754   _a_ Tans'ur
         P130.3   g   300   BIRCHINGTON
         P174   g   300   WENDOVER
         P130.5   g   300   BIRCHINGTON
         P210[1]   g   _a_   300   BIRCHINGTON
         P174.10   g   300   WENDOVER
         P174.11   g   300   WENDOVER
         P174.12   g   300   WENDOVER

[1] 1 3 7 3 7 3 2 1 7 1 5 4 3 2 7

See also **182** and **183**.

185.   1 2 7 5 3 4 3 5 5 1 2 1 7 6 5   1 2 3 4
      CM   4v   H H F H
      1793   _a_ Canfield
         A128   d   _a_   94   SAVOY
         A172   d   _a_   94   SAVOY

      1 2 7 5 7 1 3 2 1 6 7 1 7 3 2:   _see_ **1235**

186.   1 3 1 2 1 2 3 4 5 3 4 5 3 1 2   1 2 3 M 3 4
      SM   4v   H H F O⌃F H
      1793   _a_ Peck
         A128   a   _a_   195   TROY
         A172   a   _a_   195   TROY

187. 1 3 1 2 2 1 7 1 3 2 1 4 3 2 1   1 2 3͡ 4

LM   4v   H H F F

1782   *a* Edson

A47	C	*a*	435	BRIDGEWATER
A51	C	*a*	393	BRIDGEWATER
A56	C		157	BRIDGEWATER
A60[1]	C		157	BRIDGEWATER
A61	C		157	BRIDGEWATER
A62	C	*a*	393	BRIDGEWATER
A62a	C	*a*		BRIDGEWATER
A67	C	*a*	356	BRIDGEWATER
A70	C	*a*	393	BRIDGEWATER
A74	C		393	BRIDGEWATER
A80	C	*a*	315	BRIDGEWATER
A84[1]	C	*a*	157	BRIDGEWATER
A85	C		393	BRIDGEWATER
A87	C	*a*	435	BRIDGEWATER
A89	C		123	BRIDGEWATER
A91	C	*a*	393	BRIDGEWATER
A62.3	C	*a*	393	BRIDGEWATER
A92	C	*a*	123	BRIDGEWATER
A95	C			BRIDGEWATER
A92.3	C	*a*	123	BRIDGEWATER
A98	C	*a*	157	BRIDGEWATER
A101	C		123	BRIDGEWATER
A103	C	*a*	123	BRIDGEWATER
A106	C	*a*	435	BRIDGEWATER
A108	C	*a*	393	BRIDGEWATER
A109	C	*a*	157	BRIDGEWATER
A106.4	C	*a*	435	BRIDGEWATER
A113	C	*a*	852	BRIDGEWATER
A114	C	*a*	157	BRIDGEWATER
A117	C	*a*	435	BRIDGEWATER
A80.4	C	*a*	315	BRIDGEWATER
A114.3	C	*a*	157	BRIDGEWATER
A121[1]	C		393	BRIDGEWATER
A130	C		123	BRIDGEWATER
A131	C	*a*	435	BRIDGEWATER

[1] 1 2 3͡ 4
H H F O

187 continued

A145[1]	C		315	BRIDGEWATER
A146	C		123	BRIDGEWATER
A147	C	*a*	393	BRIDGEWATER
A148[1]	C	*a*	517	BRIDGEWATER
A158[1]	C	*a*	393	BRIDGEWATER
A80.5	C	*a*	315	BRIDGEWATER
A103.4	C	*a*	123	BRIDGEWATER
A163[1]	C	*a*	393	BRIDGEWATER
A103.5	C	*a*	123	BRIDGEWATER
A146.5	C		123	BRIDGEWATER
A167	C	*a*	393	BRIDGEWATER
A170	C	*a*	393	BRIDGEWATER
A172[1]	C		315	BRIDGEWATER
A175[1]	C	*a*	393	BRIDGEWATER
A181[1]	C	*a*	393	BRIDGEWATER
A103.6	C	*a*	123	BRIDGEWATER
A189[1]	C	*a*	393	BRIDGEWATER
A190[1]	C	*a*	157	BRIDGEWATER
A181.5[1]	C	*a*	393	BRIDGEWATER
A200	C	*a*	83	BRIDGEWATER

[1] 1 2 3͡ 4
     H H F O

188. 1 3 1 2 3 2 1 7 3 4 3 2 1 2 2   1 2 3 4 5 6 7 8
CMD   4v   H H F H F F H H
1784

P253	a	552	KINGSTON
A79	a	552	KINGSTON
A87	a	552	KINGSTON
A117	a	552	KINGSTON

189. 1 3 1 2 3 4 5 4 2 3 3 5 5 4 5   1 2 3 4 4
LM   4v   H H H F H
c.1776

P231	a	758

190. 1 3 1 2 4 3 4 3 2 1 7 1 3 1 5   1 2 3̑ 3 4
CM   4v   H H F O F
1793   *a* Kimball
        A125   C   *a*   88   HILLSBOROUGH

1 3 1 2 5 1 7 1 3 2 1 2 3 4 3:   *see* **1201**

191. 1 3 1 2 5 3 1 7 1 2 2 3 3 5 7   1 2 3 4 5̑ 5 6
XXXXYY   4v   H H F H F F E
1796   *a* Ingalls
        A163   a   *a*   590   PENNSYLVANIA
        A175   a   *a*   590   PENNSYLVANIA
        A181   a   590   PENNSYLVANIA
        A188   a   *a*   590   PENNSYLVANIA
        A181.5   a   *a*   590   PENNSYLVANIA

192. 1 3 1 2 5 4 3 2 3 2 3 4 5 3 6   1 2 3 4
CM   4v   H H F H
-1749
        ⁺P135   G   448
        P137   G   489
        P130.2   G   489   CANTERBURY
        P144   G   288   NETTLETON
        ⁺P145a   G   489
        P130.3   G   489   CANTERBURY
        P157   G   489
        P174   G   448   OTFORD
        P182a   G   489
        P144.4   G   288   NETTLETON
        P130.5   G   489   CANTERBURY
        P198   G   489
        P174.10   G   448   OTFORD
        P228   G   489
        P235   G   193   AYLSHAM   *192 continued*

D6[1]	G	b		OTFORD
P242[2,3]	G			CANTERBURY
P246.2[1]	G		448	OTFORD
P253	G	b	588	WORCESTER
P246.4[1]	G		448	OTFORD
P174.11	G		448	OTFORD
P253.2	G	b	588	WORCESTER
D6.6[1]	G	b	568	OTFORD
P266	G	c		NETTLETON
P246.5[1]	G		448	OTFORD
D6.10[1]	G	b	568	OTFORD
D6.11[1]	G	b	568	OTFORD
A116	G			DOMINION
A117	G			DOMINION
S5[1]	G		448	EASSIE
D12	G	b	271	OTFORD
S6[1]	G		448	OTFORD
P174.12	G		448	OTFORD
P253.4	G	b	588	WORCESTER
P303[1]	G		448	OTFORD
P303.10[1]	G		448	OTFORD
D6.12[1]	G	b	568	OTFORD
D6.13[1]	G	b	568	OTFORD
P303.11[1]	G		448	OTFORD

[1] 3v

[2] 2v

[3] 1 2 3 3 4
   H H F O H

b Hayes

c Croft

193.   1 3 1 2 7 1 2 3 3 2 1 6 7 7 6   1 2 3 4 5 6 7 8
       LMD   4v   H H H F H H O H
       1755   *a* J. Smith

         P152   C   *a*   556   WILTON

P220[1,2]   C   *b*   626   ST. MATTHEW'S

[1] 1 2 3 4 3 4 5 6
   H H H F H H O H

[2] Meter = 888888

b Adams

194.   1 3 1   2 7 1   3 2 1   5 4 5   5 4 3   1 2 3 4 5 M 6
        668668   4v   H H H F F O H
        1785   *a* D. Read

          A63   A   *a*   217   AMITY
          A63.2   A   *a*   217   AMITY
          A67   A   *a*   217   AMITY
          A80   A   *a*   217   AMITY
          A85   A   217   AMITY
          A91   A   *a*   217   AMITY
          A101   A   219   AMITY
          A80.4   A   *a*   217   AMITY
          A121   A   217   AMITY
          A131   A   *a*   217   AMITY
          A146   A   219   AMITY
          A150   A   *a*   217   AMITY
          A158   A   *a*   217   AMITY
          A80.5   A   *a*   217   AMITY
          A163   A   *a*   217   AMITY
          A146.5   A   217   AMITY
          A175   A   *a*   217   AMITY
          A181   A   217   AMITY
          A181.5   A   *a*   217   AMITY

195.   1 3 1   3 5 1   1 2 3   4 3 2   1 2 1   1 2 2 3 4 5 6 6
        668668   4v   F F H F F F F F
        1799   *a* Ward

        D15   D   *a*   614   SPALDWICK

196.	1 3 1	3 5 4	3 2 5	6 7 6	5 4 3		1	2	3	4	4	
	CM				4v		H	F	H	F	E	
	1779				*a* Bull							
	A43		G	*a*	637		PS. 21					
	A47a		G	*a*	637		PS. 21					

197.	1 3 1	4 2 3	5 4 2	3 5 1	1 4 2		1	2	2	3	4	4
	LM				4v		H	H	H	H	F	H
	c.1776											
	P231		a		107							

198.	1 3 1	5 2 3	2 1 2	3 3 2	2 5 4		1	2	2	3	4	4
	LM				4v		E	F	F	H	F	F
	c.1776											
	P231		a		685							

199.	1 3 1	5 2 3	4 5 4	3 2 2	1 2 3		1	2	3	4	
	CM				3v		H	F	E	F	
	c.1776										
	P231		a		144						

200.	1 3 1	5 2 3	6 5 4	5 5 6	7 6 5		1	2	2	3	4	4	4
	CM				4v		H	F	F	E	F	F	F
	c.1776												
	P231		a		609								

201.	1 3 1	5 3 1	5 1 7	6 7 1	5 1 5		1	2	3	4	5	6	7	8	7	8
	LMD				4v		H	H	H	H	H	H	H	H	F	H
	1793			*a* Shumway											
	A131		E	*a*	37		SCOTLAND									

202. 1 3 1 5 3 6 5 5 5 4 3 2 5 4 3   1 2 3 4 3 4
LM   4v   H H H H H F
c.1776
   P231   G   [1]

---

[1] Text given as "To God, &c. Psalm 68. New Version."

203. 1 3 1 5 5 3 4 5 5 5 5 4 3 4 3   1 1 2 2 3 4 4 3 4
CM   4v   O F H H H F F H E
c.1776
   P231   a   678

204. 1 3 1 5 5 3 5 1 3 5 5 4 5 6 7   1 2 3 4 M 4
LM   4v   H H F F O O
1787   a D. Read
   A72   f   a   101   CONTEMPLATION
   A119   f   a   101   CONTEMPLATION
   A131   f   a   101   CONTEMPLATION

1 3 1 5 5 6 5 6 7 1 7 1 3 4 6:   *see* **1194**

205. 1 3 1 5 6 5 4 3 2 1 2 3 1 5 1   1 2 3 4 4
CM   4v   F H F O H
1797   a Belcher
   A168   G   a   416   PITTSTON

1 3 1 5 6 5 4 3 2 1 4 2 1 5 5:   *see* **836**

206. 1 3 1 5 6 5 4 3 3 3 6 7 6 5 4 1 2 3 4
CM   4v   F H H F
c.1783
   P250   G   492   MINSTER / SHEPWAY

207. 1 3 1 6 4 3 2 3 6 4 2 5 5 4 3   1 2 3 4 3 M 4 4
SM   4v   H H H H F O H H
1793
   A121   A   281   UNIVERSAL PRAISE

208. 1 3 1 6 7 1 1 2 3 2 1 7 6 5 5   1 2 3 4 4 4
SM   5v   H H F F O H
1786   *a* Harwood
   P259   C   *a*   422   LIVERPOOL

209. 1 3 1 7 2 2 7 5 6 5 1 3 2 7 1   1 2 3 4 5 6 7 8
LMD   4v   H H H H F F F F
1793   *a* Atwell
   A128   C   *a*   519   SALEM
   A172   C   519   SALEM

210. 1 3 1 7 3 2 1 2 3 4 7 3 1 2 3   1 2 3 4 4 5 6 6 7 8 8
CMD   4v   O H O F F F F O F H H
1791   *a* Handel
   P291   B♭   *a*   550

211. 1 3 1 7 5 1 6 2 1 7 1 2 7 1 1   1 2 3 4
CM   4v   F F O F
c.1755
   P157   C   277

212.   1 3 2 1 1 2 3 1 2 7 1 2 3 2 1   1 2 3 4 5 6
        666688   4v   H E H F H O
        c.1746
            P129a   C   802
            P145a   C   802

213.   1 3 2 1 2 1 7 1 3 6 2 7 1 1 7   1 2 3 4 4
        CM   4v   H H H F H
        1786   a Boxwell
            D6   C   JERSEY
            D12   C   a   243   JERSEY

214.   1 3 2 1 2 3 4 5 1 3 2 1 7 1 5   1 2 3 4 5 6
        888888   4v   H H H H F H
        1794   a W. Billings
            A136   a   a   298   COHASSET

215.   1 3 2 1 2 3 4 5 3 4 2 3 1 4 3   1 2 3 4 4
        CM   4v   O O O F O
        1789
            P266   G   470   SPALDFORTH

216.   1 3 2 1 2 3 4 5 3 6 7 1 5 6 7   1 2 3 4 1 2 3 4
        CM   4v   H H H H H H H F
        c.1800   a Key
            P323   F   a   505

149

217. 1 3 2 1 2 3 4 5 4 3 2 1 3 2 1   1 2 3 4 3 4
      CM   4v   H H C H F E
      1754-5   *a* Tans'ur

P155	G	*a*	260	UPMINSTER
P155.2	G	*a*	260	UPMINSTER
P155.3	G	*a*	260	UPMINSTER
A28	G	*a*	260	UPMINSTER
A30	G	*a*	260	UPMINSTER
A31	G	*a*	260	UPMINSTER
A31.6	G	*a*	260	UPMINSTER
A31.7	G	*a*	260	UPMINSTER
A31.8	G	*a*	260	UPMINSTER

218. 1 3 2 1 2 3 4 5 4 3 2 1 7 1 2   1 2 3 3 4 4
      CM   4v   H H F F F H
      1793   *a* Wood

A132	C	*a*	436	MARLBOROUGH

219. 1 3 2 1 2 3 4 5 4 3 2 2 5 4 3   1 2 3 4 4
      CM   4v   H H H F H
      -1749

[+]P135	G		798
P134.2	G		798
P137	G		798
[+]P145a	G		798
P157	G		798
P192	G		798
P198	G		798
P212[1]	G		798

---
[1] 1 3 2 1 2 3 4 5 4 3 4 5 2 2 5

220. 1 3 2 1 2 3 4 5 4 3 2 7 5 1 7   1 2 3 4
      CM   4v   H H F H
      1760   *a* Stephenson

P171	c	*a*	469	
P171.4	c	*a*	469	
A62a	c			PS. 28

221. 1 3 2 1 2 3 4 5 4 3 4 3 2 1 2   1 2 3 4 3 4
CM   4v   H H H H F E
1770   *a* W. Billings
     A33   G   *a*   645   MILTON

Not related to **222.**

222. 1 3 2 1 2 3 4 5 4 3 4 3 2 1 2   1 2 3 4
LM   3v   F H H F
1786   *a* Davis
     D6.6   G   *a*   MILE END
     D6.10   G   *a*   MILE END
     D6.11   G   *a*   MILE END
     P303   G   582   MILE END NEW
     P303.10   G   582   MILE END NEW
     D6.12   G   *a*   MILE END
     D6.13   G   *a*   MILE END
     P303.11   G   582   MILE END NEW

Not related to **221.**

1 3 2 1 2 3 4 5 4 3 4 5 2 2 5:   *see* **219**

223. 1 3 2 1 2 3 4 5 5 1 2 3 1 2 3   1 2 3 4 M 4 4
CM   3v   H H F F F H H
1796   *a* Ingalls
     A163   G   *a*   129   NEW JERUSALEM
     A175   G   *a*   129   NEW JERUSALEM
     A181   G   129   NEW JERUSALEM
     A181.5   G   *a*   129   NEW JERUSALEM
     A195   G   129   NEW JERUSALEM
     A198   G   *a*   129   NEW JERUSALEM

224.   1 3 2   1 2 3   4 5 5   3 4 3   2 1 1   1   2   3   4   3̂   M   4
        LM   4v   H   H   H   H   F   F   H
        1786   *a* W. Billings
           A65   A   *a*   578   BRATTLE STREET

        1 3 2   1 2 3   4 5 5   4 3 2   3 3 2:   *soprano of* **63**

225.   1 3 2   1 2 3   4 5 7   1 1 7   7 6 5   1   2   3̂   4̂   M   4
        LM   4v   H   H   F   F   F   O
        1793
          A121   e   101   MOUNT SION

226.   1 3 2   1 2 5   4 3 2   1 1 3   3 4 5   1   2   3   4
        CM   4v   H   H   F   H
        c.1746
         P129a   201

227.   1 3 2   1 2 5   4 3 2   3 2 1   7 1 2   1   2   3   4   3   4
        CM   3v   H   H   H   F   H   E
        c.1762
         S1   G   NEW HYMN
         S3   G   163   NEW HYMN

        Related to **106.**

228.   1 3 2   1 2 5   4 3 4   3 2 1   7 6 6   1   2   3   3   4
        CM   4v   H   H   F   F   H
        1795   *a* N. Billings
         A150   A   *a*   736   FLYCREEK

229.   1 3 2 1 2 7 1 5 3 5 4 3 2 1 3   1 2 3 4͡ 4
      CM   4v   H H H F F

      c.1783   *a* Barwick

         P250   A   *a*   201   CHATHAM

230.   1 3 2 1 2 7 1 6 5 2 7 1 2 2 3   1 2 3 4
      LM   4v   H F F H

      1759   *a* French (*E*)

         P170   C   *a*   7

231.   1 3 2 1 3 2 1 7 5 4 3 6 4 5 2   1 2 3 4 5 6 7 8
      CMD   4v   H H F H F F H H

      1784

         P253   g   705   MALDEN

         P253.2   g   705   MALDEN

         P253.4   g   705   MALDEN

232.   1 3 2 1 3 2 2 3 5 4 3 2 1 2 3   1 2 3 4 3 4
      SM   4v   H H H H H F

      1793   *a* Kimball

         A125   C   *a*   64   LOUDON

      1 3 2 1 3 2 2 5 4 3 2 1 5 5 5: *see* **1220**

233.   1 3 2 1 3 5 5 6 5 5 6 5 5 1 1   1 2 3 4 5͡ 6͡ 7 M 7 8
      CMD   4v   H H H H F F F F H H

      1793   *a* Stone

         A132   A   *a*   437   POMFRET

234. 1 3 2 1 4 2 2 3 3 2 2 1 1 2 1   1 2 3 4 4
     LM   4v   H H H F F
     c.1755
        P157   C   788

235. 1 3 2 1 4 3 2 1 4 3 2 1 2 3 4   1 2 3 4 5 6 7 8 7 8
     LMD   4v   H H H H F F H H H H
     1794   *a* Belcher
        A135   D   *a*   820   ADMIRATION

236. 1 3 2 1 4 5 4 3 2 1 1 3 3 4 5   1 2 3 4
     CM   4v   H H F H
     c.1752   *a* Knapp
        P148   G   *a*   201   PACKSTON
        P148.2   G   *a*   201   PACKSTON
        P148.3   G   *a*   201   PACKSTON
        P148.4   G   *a*   201   PACKSTON
        P148.5   G   *a*   201   PACKSTON

237. 1 3 2 1 4 5 5 4 3 2 1 1 3 2 1   1 2 3 4
     CM   4v   H H H F
     c.1776
        P231   G   221

1 3 2 1 5 1 7 1 1 2 1 7 6 5 3:   *soprano of* **264**

238.   1 3 2   1 5 1   7 1 2   3 2 1   2 1 7   1   2   3   4   5͡   6

       666688   4v   H   H   F   H   F   F

       1778   a Deaolph

A41	C	*a*	174	PS. 136
A43	C	*a*	174	PS. 136
A47a	C	*a*	174	PS. 136
A54[1]	C		325	PS. 136
A56[1]	C		325	PS. 136
A57[1]	C		325	PS. 136
A57.2[1]	C		325	PS. 136
A60[1]	C		325	PS. 136
A61	C		174	PS. 136
A70	C	*a*	174	PS. 136
A74	C		174	PS. 136
A84	C	*a*	325	PS. 136
A85	C		174	PS. 136
A91	C	*a*	174	PS. 136
A95[1]	C		174	PS. 136
A98	C	*a*	174	PS. 136
A106[1]	C	*a*	174	PS. 136
A108	C	*a*	174	PS. 136
A109	C	*a*	174	PS. 136
A106.4[1]	C	*a*	174	PS. 136
A113[1]	C	*a*	802	PS. 136
A124	C	*a*	174	PS. 136
A131[1]	C	*a*	174	PS. 136
A147	C	*a*	174	PS. 136
A148	C	*a*	174	PS. 136
A158	C	*a*	174	PS. 136
A160	C	*a*	174	PS. 136
A163	C	*a*	174	PS. 136
A168	C	*a*	174	PS. 136
A175	C	*a*	174	PS. 136
A181	C		174	PS. 136
A189[2]	C	*a*	174	PS. 136
A181.5	C	*a*	174	PS. 136

---

[1]   1   2   3   4   5   6

    H   H   F   H   F   H

[2]   1   2   3   4   5͡   6

    H   H   F   H   F   O

239. 1 3 2 1 5 2 7 1 1 1 2 3 2 1 1   1 2 3 4 4
LM   3v   H H H F H
1779

D5	C	578	
S5[1]	C	578	DERBY
D12[1,2]	C	3	DARBY
S6[1]	C		DERBY'S 100
S5.2[1]	C	578	DERBY
S7[1]	C	578	DERBY'S 100
S6.2[1]	C		DERBY'S 100

[1] 1 3 2 1 6 2 7 1 1 1 2 3 2 1 1

[2] 4v

[3] Assigned to text 36 or 578.

---

240. 1 3 2 1 5 3 4 3 2 1 3 2 1 5 3   1 1 2 3 4
CM   4v   H F H H H
1760   *a* Stephenson

P171	g	*a*	272
P171.4	g	*a*	272

---

241. 1 3 2 1 5 4 3 2 1 1 3 3 3 4 5   1 2 3 4 3 4 3 4
LM   4v   H H F O H F H H
1784   *a* Milgrove

P253	A		136	SUNDERLAND
P253.2	A		136	SUNDERLAND
A79	A		136	SUNDERLAND
A87	A		136	SUNDERLAND
P269[1,2]	A	*a*	263	BICESTER
P269.2[1,2]	A	*a*	263	BICESTER
P269.3[1,2]	A	*a*	263	BICESTER
A117	A		136	SUNDERLAND
A153[1,2]	A	*a*	263	BICESTER
P253.4	A		136	SUNDERLAND

[1] 3v

[2] A doxology is set to the last four musical phrases.

242.   1 3 2   1 5 4   3 2 2   5 4 3   2 3 2   1 2 3 4
            LM   3v   H F H F
            -1783

P249	C		435	KINGSTON
A163[1]	C		168	CHRISTMAS HYMN
A175[1]	C		168	CHRISTMAS HYMN
A181[1]	C		168	CHRISTMAS HYMN
A181.5[1]	C		168	CHRISTMAS HYMN

[1] 4v

This is essentially **790** with the opening "Hark, hark" omitted.

243.   1 3 2   1 5 4   3 2 3   1 4 2   1 7 1   1 2 3 4 5 6 7 8 7 8 8 7 8 8
            LMD   4v   H H H H H H H H F F O F F H
            1769   *a* Heighington

P198	G		402	
P253[1,3]	A	*a*	568	DERBY
P253.2[1,3]	A	*a*	568	DERBY
A87[2,3]	A		568	ABINGDON
P266[1,3]	A	*a*	446	ABINGDON
A117[2,3]	A		568	ABINGDON
A137[2,3]	A		568	ABINGTON
P253.4[1,3]	A	*a*	568	DERBY

[1] 1 2 3 4 5 6 7 8 7 8 8
     H H H H H H H H F F H

[2] 1 2 3 4 5 6 7 8 7 8 8 8 7 8 8
     H H H H H H H H F F H F F F H

[3] Metre = CMD

244.   1 3 2   1 5 4   3 4 5   6 5 3   3 2 3   1 2 3 4
            CM   4v   H H H F
            1760   *a* Stephenson

P171	G	*a*	278
P171.4	G	*a*	278

245. 1 3 2 1 5 4 3 6 1 4 3 2 2 3 4   1 2 2 3 4 3 4 4
LM   4v   H A H H H F A H
1789   a Dixon
    P266   C   a   686   EPHESUS

246. 1 3 2 1 5 5 6 5 4 3 2 2 3 2 1   1 2 3 4
CM   4v   H H H F
1757   a J. Arnold

P163	F	a	634	
P117.5	F	a	634	LAINDON
A23	F	a	634	LAINDON
P212	G		645	
P117.6	F	a	634	LAINDON
P117.7	F	a	634	LAINDON
A51	F		634	LAINDON
A54	F		277	KENSINGTON
A56	F		277	KENSINGTON
A62	F		634	LAINDON
A62.3	F		634	LAINDON
A150	G		634	LAINDON

247. 1 3 2 1 5 6 4 5 5 6 5 4 3 4 2   1 2 2 3 4 4
CM   4v   F F H H H F
1759

P169	a	332	SEGRAVE
P169.2	a	332	SEGRAVE
A62a	a		CHARLESTON
A106	a	780	CHARLESTON
A106.4	a	780	CHARLESTON

1 3 2 1 5 6 7 1 3 2 1 7 2 2 1:   *soprano of* **120**

248.   1 3 2   1 5 6   7 1 6   5 4 4   3 1 3   1 2 3 4 5͡6 7 8
LMD   4v   H H H H F F F H H
1796
   A160   C   414   CONTENTMENT

249.   1 3 2   1 6 2   3 4 3   7 1 1   1 3 3   1 2 2 3 4
LM   4v   E H H F F
1754   *a* Everet
   P151   C   *a*   480
   P157   C   *a*   480

1 3 2   1 6 2   7 1 1   1 2 3   2 1 1:   *see* **239**

1 3 2   1 7 1   1 2 3   4 5 1   7 6 1:   *soprano of* **740**

1 3 2   1 7 1   2 1 7   7 1 4   3 2 2:   *soprano of* **853**

1 3 2   1 7 1   2 3 2   2 5 5   4 3 2:   *see* **254**

1 3 2   1 7 1   2 3 3   2 1 7   1 1 2:   *soprano of* **475**

250.   1 3 2   1 7 1   2 3 4   3 3 5   4 3 2   1 2 3 3 4͡4 4͡ 5 6
668668   4v   H H H H F F F H E
1791   *a* Olmstead
   A106   G   *a*   217   PS. 133
   A141 [1]   A   *a*   217   PS. 133
   A203 [1]   A   *a*   217   PS. 133

-----

[1] 1 2 3 3 4 5 4 5 6
   H H H H H H F H E

159

251.   1 3 2 1 7 1 2 3 4 5 5 6 5 4 5   1 2 3 4̑ 5 6
888888   4v   H H H F F H
1786   *a* Harrison
       P258   a   *a*   454   BAKEWELL

252.   1 3 2 1 7 1 2 5 4 3 2 5 3 4 5   1 2 3 4
LM   4v   H H F O
1793   *a* Babcock
       A132   a   *a*   565   WARREN

1 3 2 1 7 1 2 6 5 6 7 1 7 1 7:   *soprano of* **468**

253.   1 3 2 1 7 1 3 2 2 1 2 3 4 5 4   1 2 3 4
LM   4v   H H F H
1789
       P266   a   273   BISHLEY

254.   1 3 2 1 7 1 3 2 2 5 5 4 3 2 2   1 2 3̑ M 4
LM   4v   H H F O H
1786   *a* D. Read
       A72   a   *a*   112   RUSSIA
       A80   a   *a*   112   RUSSIA
       A85   a   112   RUSSIA
       A98   a   112   RUSSIA
       A109   a   112   RUSSIA
       A114   a   112   RUSSIA
       A119   a   *a*   112   RUSSIA
       A80.4   a   *a*   112   RUSSIA
       A114.B   a   112   RUSSIA
       A121[1]   a   112   RUSSIA

---

[1] 1 3 2 1 7 1 2 3 2 2 5 5 4 3 2

A124	a	*a*	112	RUSSIA
A131[2]	a	*a*	112	RUSSIA
A145	a		112	RUSSIA
A147	a	*a*	112	RUSSIA
A148	a	*a*	112	RUSSIA
A158	a	*a*	112	RUSSIA
A80.5	a	*a*	112	RUSSIA
A160	a	*a*	112	RUSSIA
A163	a	*a*	112	RUSSIA
A168	a	*a*	112	RUSSIA
A170	a	*a*	112	RUSSIA
A172	a		112	RUSSIA
A174[2]	a		112	RUSSIA
A175	a	*a*	112	RUSSIA
A181	a		112	RUSSIA
A189	a	*a*	112	RUSSIA
A190	a	*a*	112	RUSSIA
A181.5	a	*a*	112	RUSSIA
A195	a	*a*	112	RUSSIA
A198	a	*a*	112	RUSSIA
A200	a	*a*	112	RUSSIA

[2] 1 3 2 1 7 1 3 2 2 5 5 4 4 2 2

1 3 2 1 7 1 3 2 2 5 5 4 4 2 2:   *see* **254**

1 3 2 1 7 1 3 5 4 3 2 3 3 2 2:   *see* **407**

1 3 2 1 7 1 6 2 1 7 7 5 6 7 1:   *see* **1229**

1 3 2 1 7 1 7 6 2 1 7 1 3 3 2:   *soprano of* **52**

255. 1 3 2 1 7 2 2 2 7 1 2 3 4 5 3   1 2 3 4
CM   4v   H H F H
1799   *a* Hickcock
    A187   a   a   354?   ZION

256. 1 3 2 1 7 5 3 1 7 1 7 5 7 1 2   1 2 3̑ 4 4
CM   4v   E E F F H
1783   *a* Benham

A51	a	a	337	TRUMBULL
A62	a	a	337	TRUMBULL
A70	a	a	337	TRUMBULL
A74	a		337	TRUMBULL
A85	a		337	TRUMBULL
A62.3	a	a	337	TRUMBULL
A96[1]	a		121	TRUMBULL
A103	a	a	337	TRUMBULL
A111[1]	a		121	TRUMBULL
A113	a	a	337	TRUMBULL
A111.3[1]	a		121	TRUMBULL
A111.4[1]	a		121	TRUMBULL
A111.5[1]	a		121	TRUMBULL
A103.4	a	a	337	TRUMBULL
A163	a	b	337	TRUMBULL
A111.6[1]	a		121	TRUMBULL
A103.5	a	a	337	TRUMBULL
A175	a	b	337	TRUMBULL
A103.6	a	a	337	TRUMBULL

[1] 1 3 3 1 7 5 3 1 7 1 7 5 7 1 2

b Strong

257. 1 3 2 1 7 6 5 1 2 3 3 2 1 7 6   1 2 3̑ 4 4
CM   4v   H H F F H
1793   *a* Wood
    A132   C   a   796   FITCHBURGH

258. 1 3 2 1 7 6 5 5 1 7 1 2 1 2 3   1 2 3͡ 4 4
SM   4v   H O H F H
1789   *a* Stevenson
  P266   A   *a*   176   LUDLOW

  1 3 2 3 1 2 3 2 1 2 3 2 1 7 1:   *soprano of* **748**

259. 1 3 2 3 2 1 2 3 4 5 6 5 4 3 1   1 2 3 4
CM   4v   H H F F
c.1760
  P182a   G   278

260. 1 3 2 3 2 1 5 4 3 6 5 4 3 2 1   1 2 3 4 3 4 5 6 7͡ M 7 8
CMD   4v   H H H H H H H H F F H H
1794   *a* W. Billings
  A136   F   *a*   745   CREATION

261. 1 3 2 3 2 3 4 5 6 5 6 5 5 5 5   1 2 3 4 5͡ 6͡ 7͡ M 8
LMD   4v   F H H H F F F O H
1797   *a* Belknap
  A166   G   *a*   166   HANCOCK
  A192   G   *a*   166   HANCOCK

262. 1 3 2 3 3 1 2 7 1 3 4 5 5 5 6   1 2 3 4
CM   4v   H H E F
1760   *a* Stephenson
  P171   G   *a*   447
  P171.4   G   *a*   447

263. 1 3 2 3 4 3 2 1 2 1 2 3 2 3 2   1 2 3 4
        CM   4v   F F O F
        1754   *a* Everet

	P151	B♭	*a*	771	
	P157	B♭	*a*	771	
	P198	G		771	
	P266	B♭	*a*	771	LIVERPOOL

264. 1 3 2 3 4 3 2 4 5 4 2 7 1 2 5   1 2 3 4 3 4 3 4
        CMD   4v   F H H H H H H H
        c.1785   *a* Valentine

| | P257 | g | *a* | 734 |

          1 3 2 3 4 3 4 5 4 3 2 1 3 4 3:   *see* **1237**

265. 1 3 2 3 4 3 2 5 4 3 2 1 7 1 5   1 2 3 4
        CM   4v   H H F H
        c.1783   *a* Barwick

| | P250 | G | *a* | 595 | NEWNHAM |

266. 1 3 2 3 4 3 4 5 4 3 2 1 3 4 5   1̑ 2 2 3 4̑ 4
        CM   4v   F O F F F F
        c.1755

| | P157 | a | | 390 |

267. 1 3 2 3 4 5 3 6 5 4 3 2 3 5 4   1 2 3 4
        CM   4v   H H F O
        1750

	P134.2	a	187	
	P253	a	235	MONMOUTH
	P253.2	a	235	MONMOUTH
	P253.3	a	235	MONMOUTH

268.   1 3 2 3 4 5 4 3 2 1 1 7 5 7 1   1 2 3 4 5 6 7 8
CMD   4v   H H H H H H E F
1786   *a* Wood

A70	b	*a*	457	WALPOLE
A72	b	*b*	457	WALPOLE
A74	b		457	WALPOLE
A84	b	*a*	457	WALPOLE
A85	b		457	WALPOLE
A91	b	*a*	457	WALPOLE
A98	b	*a*	457	WALPOLE
A108	b	*a*	457	WALPOLE
A109	b	*a*	457	WALPOLE
A114	b	*a*	457	WALPOLE
A119	b	*a*	457	WALPOLE
A114.B	b	*a*	457	WALPOLE
A121	b		457	WALPOLE
A124	b	*a*	457	WALPOLE
A130	b	*a*	457	WALPOLE
A131	b	*a*	457	WALPOLE
A132	b	*a*	457	WALPOLE
A147	b	*a*	457	WALPOLE
A148	b	*a*	457	WALPOLE
A158	b	*a*	457	WALPOLE
A160	b	*a*	457	WALPOLE
A163	b	*a*	457	WALPOLE
A168	b	*a*	457	WALPOLE
A170	b	*a*	457	WALPOLE
A174	b		457	WALPOLE
A195	b	*a*	457	WALPOLE
A198	b	*a*	457	WALPOLE

b Thomas

269.   1 3 2 3 4 5 4 3 2 3 2 1 7 1 2   1 2 3 4
CM   4v   E H E F
1760   *a* Stephenson

P171	a	*a*	599
P171.4	a	*a*	599

270. 1 3 2 3 4 5 4 3 2 3 6 4 6 5 3   1 2 3 4
          CM   4v   H H F O
          1795   *a* N. Billings
              A150   e   *a*   388   WEATHERSFIELD

271. [a ghost]

          1 3 2 3 4 5 4 3 3 5 4 5 6 5 4:   *soprano of* **970**

          1 3 2 3 4 5 4 3 4 2 3 1 3 2 5:   *soprano of* **923**

272. 1 3 2 3 4 5 6 4 5 3 3 2 3 5 6   1 2 3 3 4 4
          CM   3v   E F H H F H
          1786
              D6.6   g   HARBRO' NEW
              D6.10   g   HARBRO' NEW
              D6.11   g   HARBRO' NEW
              P303   g   148   HARBRO' NEW
              P303.10   g   148   HARBRO' NEW
              D6.12   g   HARBRO' NEW
              D6.13   g   HARBRO' NEW
              P303.11   g   148   HARBRO' NEW

273. 1 3 2 3 4 5 7 1 4 3 2 3 5 5 4   1 2 3 4
          CM   4v   H F H F
          c.1783   *a* Barwick
              P250   a   *a*   87   CANTERBURY

274. 1 3 2 3 5 4 3 2 1 5 6 5 4 5 5   1 2 3 M 3 4
CM   4v   H H F F F O
1794   *a* W. Billings
         A136   G   *a*   666   ROCKY-NOOK

275. 1 3 2 3 5 4 3 2 2 1 1 2 2 3 4   1 2 3 4
LM   4v   H H O F
1799
         A187   G   364?   PS. 145

276. 1 3 2 3 5 6 5 3 4 3 2 2 3 1 2   1 2 3 4 4 3 4 M 4
SM   4v   H H F F O F F F O
1793   *a* Mitchell
         A132   G   *a*   259   AUSTRIA

277. 1 3 2 4 3 1 2 2 3 2 3 1 3 5 5   1 2 3 4 5 6
888888   4v   H H H F F H
1788   *a* Jocelyn
         A87   A♭   *a*   241   PS. 146
         A189   A♭   *a*   241   PS. 146

278. 1 3 2 5 1 3 2 1 7 1 1 3 1 4 2   1 2 3 4 4
LM   4v   H H H F H
1792
         D10   a   117   MACHPELAH

         1 3 2 5 3 2 1 7 6 7 2 5 6 5 4:   *soprano of* **1120**

         1 3 2 5 4 3 2 1 7 1 2 1 3 1 2:   *see* **279**

279. 1 3 2 5 4 3 2 1 7 1 2 3 3 1 2   1 2 3 4 4
LM   4v   F F O O F
1757   *a* Everet
   P164   G   435
   P198   F   435
   P266[1]   G   *a*   435   EPSOM

---

[1] 1 3 2 5 4 3 2 1 7 1 2 1 3 1 2

280. 1 3 2 5 4 3 3 4 3 2 2 3 4 5 2   1 2 3 4 4
CM   4v   H F H F H
c.1800   *a* Key
   P323   g   *a*   324

281. 1 3 2 5 6 4 3 2 2 3 2 3 4 5 4   1 2 3 4
LM   4v   H H H F
1760   *a* Stephenson
   P171   G   *a*   402
   P171.4   G   *a*   402

1 3 2 5 7 1 4 3 2 1 7 1 1 1 2:   *soprano of* **603**

282. 1 3 2 7 1 7 6 7 5 6 7 1 2 3 2   1 2 3 4
XXYY   4v   H H H F
1760   *a* Stephenson
   P171   C   *a*   484
   P171.4   C   *a*   484

283. 1 3 3 1 1 5 5 3 3 1 1 7 7 1 1   1 2 3ˆ 4
      CM   4v   H H F F
      1786   *a* Stone

         A71   A   *a*   489   PS. 8
         A131[1]   A   *a*   489   PS. 8

      ─────────
      [1] 1 3 3 1 1 5 5 3 4 1 1 7 7 1 1

      1 3 3 1 1 5 5 3 4 1 1 7 7 1 1:   *see* **283**

284. 1 3 3 1 6 5 3 5 1 3 2 1 7 1 2   1 2 3 4 5ˆ 6 7 8
      CMD   3v   H H H H F F H H
      1793   *a* Holden

         A124   C   *a*   379   OMEGA
         A163   C   *a*   379   OMEGA
         A175   C   379   OMEGA
         A175   C   *a*   379   OMEGA
         A181   C   379   OMEGA
         A181.5   C   379   OMEGA

285. 1 3 3 1 7 1 2 3 2 1 3 2 3 1 1   1 2 3ˆ 4
      SM   4v   H H F O
      1790   *a* Edson

         A96   C   *a*   52   ALBANY
         A103[1]   C   *a*   52   ALBANY
         A111   C   *a*   52   ALBANY
         A111.3   C   *a*   52   ALBANY
         A111.4   C   *a*   52   ALBANY
         A111.5   C   *a*   52   ALBANY
         A103.4[1]   C   *a*   52   ALBANY
         A111.6   C   *a*   52   ALBANY
         A103.5[1]   C   *a*   52   ALBANY
         A103.6[1]   C   *a*   52   ALBANY

      ─────────
      [1] 1 2 3 Mˆ 4
           H H F O H

1 3 3   1 7 5   3 1 7   1 7 5   7 1 2:   *see* **256**

286.   1 3 3   2 1 1   2 3 1   2 3 5   4 5 6   1 2 3 4
       CM   4v   H F H F
       1773
          P212   G   494   YARMOUTH

287.   1 3 3   2 1 2   3 4 5   4 3 2   1 5 4   1 2 2 3̑ 4 4
       CM   4v   E H H E F H
       c.1776
          P231   a   211

288.   1 3 3   2 1 2   3 4 5   6 5 4   3 2 1   1 2 3 4 4
       CM   4v   F H H H O
       -1749
          ⁺P135   a   527
          P144   a   527   NEW READING
          ⁺P145a   a   527
          P144.4   a   527   NEW READING

289.   1 3 3   2 1 2   7 1 1   1 7 6   5 5 6   1 2 3 4 5̑ 6̑ M 6
       666688   4v   H H H H F F O H
       1797   *a* Belknap
          A166   C   *a*   274   OUSE

290.   1 3 3   2 1 4   3 2 1   2 3 4   2 1 7   1 2 3 4 4
       CM   4v   H H H F H
       -1789
          ⁺P266   C   221   CAMBRIDGE NEW

[+]D8[1]	C		CAMBRIDGE
[+]P246.5[2,3]	C	531	CAMBRIDGE NEW
P303[2,3]	C	531	CAMBRIDGE NEW
S6[2]	C		CAMBRIDGE NEW
P303.10[2,3]	C	531	CAMBRIDGE NEW
P303.11[2,3]	C	531	CAMBRIDGE NEW

[1] 2v

[2] 3v

[3] 1 2 3 4 4
   H H H H F

291. 1 3 3 2 1 4 3 2 3 2 5 4 3 2 3   1 2 3 4
CM   4v   H F H F
c.1783   *a* Barwick
   P250   G   *a*   562   STURRY

292. 1 3 3 2 1 5 3 6 5 1 5 6 1 7 6   1 2 3̂ 4
LM   4v   H H F F
1789   *a* French (*A*)
   A93   F   *a*   567   OHIO

293. 1 3 3 2 1 5 4 3 4 2 2 1 5 5 4   1 2 3 4 5 6 6
666688   4v   H H E H H E F
1759
   P169   G   130   NOTTINGHAM
   P169.2   G   130   NOTTINGHAM

294. 1 3 3 2 1 5 5 5 5 6 5 4 3 2 1   1 2 3̂ 4 4
CM   4v   H H F F H
1793
   A121   F   349   TOLLAND

295. 1 3 3 2 1 7 1 1 7 7 1 2 3 2 1   1 2 3 4 5 6 7 8
       LMD   3v   H H H H H H F H
       1794   *a* Dupuis
            P297   e-E   *a*   44

       1 3 3 2 2 1 6 5 5 1 1 2 7 1 5:   *see* **1195**

       1 3 3 2 2 1 7 1 2 3 2 1 7 6 6:   *soprano of* **1122**

296. 1 3 3 2 2 2 1 7 5 1 6 7 6 5 5   1 2 3 4
       LM   4v   H H F H
       1793   *a* Howes
            A131   C   *a*   822   CARMEL

297. 1 3 3 2 3 2 1 7 1 3 5 4 3 2 1   1 2 3 4 3 4
       CM   4v   H H H H F E
       1755   *a* Tans'ur
            P155   C   *a*   31   BARBY
            P155.2   C   *a*   31   BARBY
            P155.2   A   *a*   827   BARBY
            A24   A   *a*   BARBY
            P155.3   C   *a*   31   BARBY
            P155.3   A   *a*   827   BARBY
            A28   A   *a*   31   BARBY
            A30   A   *a*   31   BARBY
            A31   A   *a*   31   BARBY
            A31.6   A   *a*   31   BARBY
            A31.7   A   *a*   31   BARBY
            A34   A   31   BARBY
            P210   A   *a*   31   BARBY
            A31.8   A   *a*   31   BARBY
            A39   A   31   BARBY
            A39.2   A   31   BARBY

298. 1 3 3 2 3 4 5 6 5 6 7 1 7 6 7   1 2 3 4 3 4 M 3 4

CM   4v   H H H H F F F H H

1793   *a* Deaolph

    A131   F   *a*   651   MOUNT PLEASANT

299. 1 3 3 2 4 3 1 7 1 5 6 7 1 2 3   1 2 2 3 4 4

CM   4v   O O O O F F

1757

    P164   G   478

    P198   F   .   478

300. 1 3 3 2 4 3 5 4 5 3 4 5 4 2 5   1 2 3 4 4

CM   4v   H H H F F

1797   *a* Swan

    A167   F   *a*   141   DENBIGH

1 3 3 2 5 3 3 2 2 3 4 5 6 7 6:   *soprano of* **1116**

301. 1 3 3 2 5 4 3 2 1 5 3 5 5 6 5   1 2 3 4 5 6

XXXXYY   4v   H H H H F E

1779   *a* Gillet

    A43   A   *a*   619   FREEDOM

    A47a   A   *a*   619   FREEDOM

    A56   A   619   FREEDOM

    A84   A   619   FREEDOM

    A189   A   *a*   619   FREEDOM

1 3 3 2 5 5 4 3 4 1 2 3 2 3 4:   *soprano of* **1163**

1 3 3 2 7 1 2 3 2 1 2 3 1 4 3:   *see* **302**

302.   1 3 3   2 7 1   2 3 2   1 2 3   7 4 3   1 2 3 4 4

CM   4v   H H F O H

1760   *a* Stephenson

P171	C	*a*	678		
A26	C	*a*	678		
A31[1]	C	*a*	678		
A31.6[1]	C	*a*	678		
A31.7[1]	C	*a*	678		
A31.8[1]	C	*a*	678		
A39	C	*a*	678		
P171.4	C	*a*	678		
A41[1]	C	*a*	678	PS. 34	
A43[1]	C	*a*	678	PS. 34	
A39.2	C	*a*	678		
A47[1]	C		678	PS. 34	
A47a[1]	C	*a*	678		
A51[1]	C		678	PS. 34	
A54[1]	C	*a*	678	PS. 34	
P253	C	*a*	823	GUILDFORD	
A56[1]	C	*a*	678	PS. 34	
A57[1]	C		678	PS. 34	
A59[1]	C			PS. 34	
A57.2[1]	C		678	PS. 34	
A60[1]	C		678	PS. 34	
A62[1]	C		678	PS. 34	
P253.2	C	*a*	823	GUILDFORD	
A70[1]	C	*a*	678	PS. 34	
A74[1]	C		678	PS. 34	
A80[1]	C	*a*	568	PS. 34	
A84[1]	C	*a*	678	PS. 34	
A85[1]	C		678	PS. 34	
A87[1]	C		678		
A89[1]	C		678	PS. 34	
A91[1]	C	*a*	678	PS. 34	
A62.3[1]	C		678	PS. 34	
P266[1,2]	C	*a*	678	ST. ANDREW'S	
A92[1]	C	*a*	678	PS. 34	
A95[1]	C			PS. 34	
A92.3[1]	C	*a*	678	PS. 34	
A98[1]	C	*a*	678	PS. 34	
A101[1]	C		678	PS. 34	
A103[1]	C	*a*	678	PS. 34	

A106[1]	C	*a*	678	PS. 34
A108[1]	C	*a*	678	PS. 34
A109[1]	C	*a*	678	PS. 34
A106.4[1]	C	*a*	678	PS. 34
A113[1]	C	*a*	678	PS. 34
A114[1]	C	*a*	678	PS. 34
A117[1]	C		678	
A119[1]	C	*a*	678	PS. 34
D12[1,3]	C	*b*	661	WILTSHIRE
A80.4[1]	C	*a*	568	PS. 34
A114.B[1]	C	*a*	678	PS. 34
A124[1]	C	*a*	678	PS. 34
A130[1]	C	*a*	678	PS. 34
A131[1]	C	*a*	678	PS. 34
A137[1]	C	*a*	678	PS. 34
A144[1,4]	C		678	PS. 34
A145[1]	C		568	PS. 34
A146[1]	C		678	PS. 34
A147[1]	C	*a*	678	PS. 34
A148[1]	C	*a*	678	PS. 34
A158[1]	C	*a*	678	PS. 34
P253.4	C	*a*	823	GUILDFORD
A80.5[1]	C	*a*	568	PS. 34
A103.4[1]	C	*a*	678	PS. 34
A160[1]	C	*a*	678	PS. 34
A163[1]	C	*a*	678	PS. 34
A103.5[1]	C	*a*	678	PS. 34
A146.5[1]	C		678	PS. 34
A168[1]	C	*a*	678	PS. 34
A170[1]	C	*a*	678	PS. 34
A172[1]	C		568	PS. 34
A175[1]	C	*a*	678	PS. 34

[1] 1 3 3 2 7 1 2 3 2 1 2 3 1 4 3

[2] 1 2 3 4 4
     H H F E H

[3] 1 2 3 3 4 4
     H H H H F H

[4] 2v

b "altered from Stevenson"

302 continued

A181[1]	C		678	PS. 34
A103.6[1]	C	*a*	678	PS. 34
A183[1,5,6]	C		678	WILTSHIRE
A189[1]	C	*a*	678	PS. 34
A190[1]	C	*a*	678	PS. 34
A181.5[1]	C	*a*	678	PS. 34
A195[1]	C	*a*	678	PS. 34
A198[1]	C	*a*	678	PS. 34

[1] 1 3 3   2 7 1   2 3 2   1 2 3   1 4 3

[5] 3v

[6] 1 2 3 4 4 4
     H H H E F H

303.   1 3 3   3 1 2   1 7 6   5 5 1   5 6 7   1 2 3 4 5 6 7 7 8
     CMD   4v   H H E H F H F H H
     1790   *a* Morgan

A96	C	*a*	106	MONTGOMERY
A103	C	*a*	106	MONTGOMERY
A106	C	*a*	106	MONTGOMERY
A106.4	C	*a*	106	MONTGOMERY
A111	C	*a*	106	MONTGOMERY
A121	C		106	MONTGOMERY
A124	C	*a*	106	MONTGOMERY
A131	C	*a*	106	MONTGOMERY
A111.3	C	*a*	106	MONTGOMERY
A146	C		106	MONTGOMERY
A111.4	C	*a*	106	MONTGOMERY
A150	C		106	MONTGOMERY
A158	C	*a*	106	MONTGOMERY
A111.5	C	*a*	106	MONTGOMERY
A103.4	C	*a*	106	MONTGOMERY
A160	C	*a*	106	MONTGOMERY
A163	C	*a*	106	MONTGOMERY
A111.6	C	*a*	106	MONTGOMERY
A164	C	*a*	106	MONTGOMERY
A103.5	C	*a*	106	MONTGOMERY
A146.5	C		106	MONTGOMERY
A170	C	*a*	106	MONTGOMERY
A174	C		106	MONTGOMERY

	A175	C	*a*	106	MONTGOMERY
	A181	C		106	MONTGOMERY
	A182	C	*a*	106	MONTGOMERY
	A103.6	C	*a*	106	MONTGOMERY
	A189	C	*a*	106	MONTGOMERY
	A190	C	*a*	106	MONTGOMERY
	A181.5	C	*a*	106	MONTGOMERY
	A200	C	*a*	436	MONTGOMERY

304. 1 3 3 3 1 2 3 4 5 3 4 6 5 4 3   1 2 3 4
LM   4v   H H F H
1799   *a* Wilcockson

	A187	A	*a*	578	PALESTINE

305. 1 3 3 3 1 5 4 3 2 1 3 2 2 1 6   1 2 3 3 4
LM   3v   H H F E H
1797   *a* R. Merrill

	A171	G	*a*	151	

306. 1 3 3 3 2 1 1 6 5 1 3 2 2 1 1   1 2 3 4 5 5̂ 6
666688   4v   H H H H F F O
1785   *a* D. Read

	A63	C	*a*	268	FREETOWN
	A63.2	C	*a*	268	FREETOWN
	A80	C	*a*	268	FREETOWN
	A80.4	C	*a*	268	FREETOWN
	A80.5	C	*a*	268	FREETOWN

307. 1 3 3 3 2 1 2 2 2 3 4 5 1 4 3   1 2 3 4̂ 3̂ 4
CM   4v   H H F F F F
1778   *a* W. Billings

	A40	G	*a*	84	NORTH PROVIDENCE
	A40.2	G	*a*	84	NORTH PROVIDENCE
	A40.3	G	*a*	84	NORTH PROVIDENCE
	A40.4	G	*a*	84	NORTH PROVIDENCE

308. 1 3 3 3 2 1 3 5 5 5 5 6 7 1 7   1 2 3͡ 4 4
CM   4v   F E F F H
1781   *a* W. Billings

A44	A	*a*	416	ASSURANCE
A108	A	*a*	416	ASSURANCE
A119	A	*a*	416	ASSURANCE
A131	A	*a*	416	ASSURANCE

309. 1 3 3 3 2 3 2 1 3 4 6 5 2 3 4   1 2 3 4 3͡ 4͡ M 4 3 4
LM   4v   H H H H F F F H H H
1793   *a* Shumway

A131	A	*a*	576	LEWISBURGH

310. 1 3 3 3 2 3 2 3 4 5 6 7 1 7 6   1 2 3͡ M 3 4
LM   4v   H H F F H H
1800

A192	F	639	CHELMSFORD

311. 1 3 3 3 3 4 5 5 5 6 7 1 1 1 2   1 2 3 4 5 5 6 6
666688   4v   H E H H F F H E
1783   *a* Strong

A51	D	*a*	824	AMERICA
A62	D	*a*	824	AMERICA
A62.3	D	*a*	824	AMERICA

312. 1 3 3 3 4 2 2 2 3 4 5 3 2 1 2   1 2 3͡ 3͡ 4͡ 4
CM   4v   H H F F F F
1783   *a* Lee

A51	G	*a*	84	GEORGIA
A62	G	*a*	84	GEORGIA
A70	G	*a*	84	GEORGIA

A74   G   84   GEORGIA
A85   G   84   GEORGIA
A62.3   G   *a*   84   GEORGIA

Cf. **307.**

313.   1 3 3 3 4 3 2 1 2 3 4 3 4 5 5   1 2 3 4 5 6 7 8 8
        CMD   4v   H H H H H H F H H
        c.1800   *a* Key
           P323   G   *a*   494

314.   1 3 3 3 4 3 2 2 2 3 4 5 3 2 1   1 2 3͜4 4
        CM   4v   H H F F H
        1799   *a* Jenks
           A187   G   *a*   533   VARIETY

315.   1 3 3 3 4 3 2 2 2 5 1 2 3 4 5   1 2 3 4 3͜4
        LM   4v   H H H H F F
        1797   *a* R. Merrill
           A171   G   *a*   639   PLAINFIELD

316.   1 3 3 3 4 3 2 2 5 5 5 3 1 6 4   1 2 3 4 5͜6͜7͜8
        CMD   4v   H H H H F F F O
        1796   *a* W. Smith
           A163   A   *a*   54   PS. 118
           A175   A   *a*   54   PS. 118
           A181   A   54   PS. 118
           A181.5   A   *a*   54   PS. 118

        1 3 3 3 4 3 4 5 1 7 7 5 4 3 1:   *see* **1208**

317. 1 3 3 3 4 5 6 5 3 4 4 4 4 5 2   1 2 3 4 5 6
888888   4v   H O F O O F
c.1776

    P231   G   442

318. 1 3 3 3 5 2 2 2 2 5 5 3 1 2 2   1 2 3 3 4 5 6
888888   4v   H H F F F F H
1796   *a* Ingalls

    A163   G   *a*   275   BALTIMORE
    A175   G   *a*   275   BALTIMORE
    A181   G   275   BALTIMORE
    A181.5   G   *a*   275   BALTIMORE

319. 1 3 3 3 5 3 4 3 2 1 2 2 3 4 4   1 2 3 4
XXYY   4v   F H E H
1800   *a* Hamilton

    A192   A   *a*   484   TRIUMPH

320. 1 3 3 3 5 5 4 5 3 2 3 4 5 6 5   1 2 3 4 4
CM   4v   H H H F O
c.1752   *a* Knapp

    P148   G   *a*   599   SANDWICH NEW
    P148.2   G   *a*   599   SANDWICH NEW
    P148.3   G   *a*   599   SANDWICH NEW
    P155a[1]   G   599
    P148.4   G   *a*   599   SANDWICH NEW
    P148.5   G   *a*   599   SANDWICH NEW
    P220[1]   G   668   SUTTON
    P228   G   445

----

[1] 1 2 3 4 M
   H H H F O

321. 1 3 3 3 5 6 5 4 3 2 2 3 3 4 2   1 2 3 4
CM   4v   F F F F
c.1755
    P157   G   485

1 3 3 3 5 7 2 2 2 7 7 2 6 2 2:   *soprano of* **951**

322. 1 3 3 3 6 5 5 5 1 4 3 2 1 5 3   1 2 3 4 5 6 7 8 7 8 8
CMD   4v   H H H H H H F F F F H
1793   *a* Stone
    A132   F   *a*   185   SPRING

323. 1 3 3 4 3 2 2 3 4 5 4 5 2 3 3   1 2 3 4
SM   4v   H H F F
1793
    ⁺A121   a   733   DAUPHIN
    ⁺A164   a   733   DAUPHIN
    A167   a   733   DAUPHIN
    A174   a   733   DAUPHIN
    A182   a   733   DAUPHIN
    A200   a   833   DAUPHIN

324. 1 3 3 4 3 2 3 2 5 4 3 2 3 5 5   1 2 3 4 5 6 7 8 9 X Y Z
666666667667   4v   H H H F F H H H H H H H
1755
    P153   G   791
    P153.2   G   791
    P153.3   G   791

325. 1 3 3 4 4 3 3 4 4 5 4 5 5 3 4   1 2 3̂ 3 4̂ 5 6
668668   4v   H H F F F F O
c.1760

⁺P174	G	224	CROYDON
⁺P117.5	G	224	CROYDON
P174.10	G	224	CROYDON
P235	G	224	HAVERHILL
P174.11	G	224	CROYDON
P174.12	G	224	CROYDON

1 3 3 4 4 4 3 3 2 3 5 5 6 5 3:   *soprano of* **749**

1 3 3 4 4 5 4 3 3 2 5 3 2 1 2:   *see* **326**

326. 1 3 3 4 4 5 4 3 3 2 5 4 3 2 1   1 2 3 4
CM   4v   H F H F
c.1746

P129a	G	645	
P130[1]	G	645	SEAL
P135	G	645	
P137	G	645	
P130.2[1]	G	645	SEAL
P130.3[1]	G	645	SEAL
P145a	G	645	
P174	G	645	SEAL
P192	G	645	
P130.5[1]	G	645	SEAL
P174.10	G	645	SEAL
P174.11	G	645	SEAL
P174.12	G	645	SEAL

[1] 1 3 3 4 4 5 4 3 3 2 5 3 2 1 2

1 3 3 4 4 6 5 1 7 1 3 2 7 5 7:   *see* **1209**

327.　1 3 3　4 5 1　7 7 7　7 6 5　5 5 4　　1　2　3͡　M　3　4
　　　　LM　　　　　　　　　　　　　　4v　　H　H　F　F　　H　H
　　　　1790　　　　　　　　　*a* Parmeter

A98	e		569	COMPLAINT
A109	e		569	COMPLAINT
A114	e		569	COMPLAINT
A114.B	e		569	COMPLAINT
A121	e		569	REQUEST
A124	e	*a*	569	COMPLAINT
A148	e	*a*	569	COMPLAINT
A158	e	*a*	569	COMPLAINT
A160	e	*a*	569	COMPLAINT
A163	e	*a*	569	COMPLAINT
A175	e	*a*	569	COMPLAINT
A181	e		569	COMPLAINT
A189	e		569	COMPLAINT
A190	e	*a*	569	COMPLAINT
A192	e	*a*	569	COMPLAINT
A181.5	e	*a*	569	COMPLAINT

328.　1 3 3　4 5 4　3 4 3　2 2 3　1 2 1　　1　2　3　3　4
　　　　CM　　　　　　　　　　　　　　4v　　H　H　F　E　H
　　　　1788

A87	a	735	SUNBURY
A117	a	735	SUNBURY

1 3 3　4 5 5　1 7 1　1 5 5　3 3 4:　*see* **1240**

329.　1 3 3　4 5 5　6 7 5　6 4 5　4 3 2　　1　2　3　4　5　6　7͡　8͡　7　8
　　　　SMD　　　　　　　　　　　　　4v　　H　H　H　H　H　H　F　F　F　O
　　　　1793

A121	f	17	DOUGLASS

330. 1 3 3 4 5 6 4 3 2 1 3 5 3 4 5   1 2 3 4 5 6 7 8 8
CMD   4v   H H H H H H F F H
1785   *a* D. Read

A63	A	*a*	647	FIDELITY
A63.2	A	*a*	647	FIDELITY
A80	A	*a*	647	FIDELITY
A80.2	A	*a*	647	FIDELITY
A80.5	A	*a*	647	FIDELITY
A167	A	*a*	647	FIDELITY

331. 1 3 3 5 1 7 6 5 3 1 1 5 7 3 3   1 2 3 4 4 5 6 6
888888   4v   H H H F F H H H
1779   *a* Gillet

A43	f♯	*a*	658	FARMINGTON
A47a	f♯	*a*	658	FARMINGTON
A54	f♯		658	FARMINGTON
A56	f♯		658	FARMINGTON
A60	f♯		658	FARMINGTON
A84	f♯	*a*	658	FARMINGTON
A91	f♯	*a*	658	FARMINGTON
A106	f♯	*a*	658	FARMINGTON
A108	f♯	*a*	658	FARMINGTON
A119	f♯	*a*	658	FARMINGTON
A106.4	f♯	*a*	658	FARMINGTON
A141	f♯	*a*	658	FARMINGTON
A147	f♯	*a*	658	FARMINGTON
A163	f♯	*a*	658	FARMINGTON
A170	f♯	*a*	658	FARMINGTON
A175	f♯	*a*	658	FARMINGTON
A181	f♯		658	FARMINGTON
A189	f♯	*a*	658	FARMINGTON
A181.5[1]	f♯	*a*	658	FARMINGTON
A203	f♯	*a*	658	FARMINGTON

---

[1] 1 3 3 5 5 1 7 6 5 3 1 1 5 7 3

332.　133 537 511 753 453　1 2 3͡ M 4
　　CM　　　　　　　　　　4v　H H F O H
　　1800　　　　　　　*a* Whitney
　　　　A201　　　e　　*a*　　24　　COMPLAINT

333.　133 543 127 123 423　1 2 3͡ 4
　　CM　　　　　　　　　　4v　H H F F
　　1792　　　　　　　*a* Ives
　　　⁺A116　　　a　　*a*　　534　　HAMDEN
　　　⁺A117　　　a　　*a*　　534　　HAMDEN

334.　133 552 233 345 654　1 2 3 4 5 6 7͡ 8͡ 7 M 7 8
　　CMD　　　　　　　　　4v　H H H H H H F F F O H H
　　1793　　　　　　　*a* Shumway
　　　　A131　　　G　　*a*　　621　　JUDGEMENT

335.　133 556 232 121 712　1 2 3 3 4 4
　　CM　　　　　　　　　　4v　E H E H F F
　　c.1776
　　　　P231　　　G　　　　447

336.　133 556 512 321 217　1 2 3͡ 4͡ 4
　　CM　　　　　　　　　　4v　H H F F F
　　1792　　　　　　　*a* Holden
　　　　A119　　　D　　*a*　　417　　NEW SALEM
　　　　A124　　　D　　*a*　　417　　NEW SALEM
　　　　A160　　　D　　　　417　　NEW SALEM
　　　　A163　　　D　　*a*　　417　　NEW SALEM
　　　　A175　　　D　　*a*　　417　　NEW SALEM
　　　　A181　　　D　　　　417　　NEW SALEM
　　　　A181.5　　D　　*a*　　417　　NEW SALEM

337.   1 3 3 5 5 7 1 5 5 6 5 4 3 2 1   1 2 3 4͡ M 6
888888   4v   H H H F F H
1782   *a* Edson

A47	a	*a*	146	GREENFIELD
A51	a	*a*	146	GREENFIELD
A60	a		146	GREENFIELD
A62	a	*a*	146	GREENFIELD
A62a	a	*a*		GREENFIELD
A67	a	*a*	146	GREENFIELD
A70	a	*a*	146	GREENFIELD
A74	a		148	GREENFIELD
A80	a	*a*	658	GREENFIELD
A84	a	*a*	146	GREENFIELD
A85	a		146	GREENFIELD
A87	a	*a*	146	GREENFIELD
A89	a		146	GREENFIELD
A91	a	*a*	146	GREENFIELD
A62.3	a	*a*	146	GREENFIELD
A92	a	*a*	146	GREENFIELD
A95	a			GREENFIELD
A92.3	a	*a*	146	GREENFIELD
A98	a	*a*	146	GREENFIELD
A101	a		146	GREENFIELD
A103	a	*a*	146	GREENFIELD
A106	a	*a*	146	GREENFIELD
A108	a	*a*	146	GREENFIELD
A109	a	*a*	146	GREENFIELD
A106.4	a	*a*	146	GREENFIELD
A113	a	*a*	146	GREENFIELD
A114	a	*a*	146	GREENFIELD
A117	a	*a*	146	GREENFIELD
A119[1]	a	*a*	146	GREENFIELD
A80.4	a	*a*	658	GREENFIELD
A114.B	a	*a*	146	GREENFIELD
A121	a		146	GREENFIELD
A124	a	*a*	146	GREENFIELD
A130	a	*a*	146	GREENFIELD
A131	a	*a*	146	GREENFIELD
A137	a		146	GREENFIELD

---

[1] 3 3 3 5 5 7 1 5 5 6 5 4 3 2 1

A145	a		656	GREENFIELD
A146	a		146	GREENFIELD
A147	a	*a*	146	GREENFIELD
A148	a	*a*	328	GREENFIELD
A158	a	*a*	146	GREENFIELD
A80.5	a	*a*	658	GREENFIELD
A103.4	a	*a*	146	GREENFIELD
A160	a	*a*	146	GREENFIELD
A163	a	*a*	146	GREENFIELD
A103.5	a	*a*	146	GREENFIELD
A146.5	a		146	GREENFIELD
A168	a	*a*	146	GREENFIELD
A170	a	*a*	146	GREENFIELD
A172	a		656	GREENFIELD
A174	a	*a*	146	GREENFIELD
A175	a	*a*	146	GREENFIELD
A181	a		146	GREENFIELD
A103.6	a	*a*	146	GREENFIELD
A189	a	*a*	146	GREENFIELD
A190	a	*a*	146	GREENFIELD
A181.5	a	*a*	146	GREENFIELD
A200	a	*a*	241	GREENFIELD

338. 1 3 3 5 5 7 1 5 5 6 5 4 3 3 2   1 2 3͡ 3 4͡ 4 4
CM   4v   H H F O H F E
1792

[+]A116	E		775	PARADISE
[+]A117	E		775	PARADISE

339. 1 3 3 5 6 5 4 3 2 1 2 3 4 3 2   1 2 3 4
CM   4v   O E H F
c.1783   *a* Barwick

P250	G	*a*	487	BRIDGE

340. 1 3 3 5 6 5 4 3 2 1 3 2 2 1 2   1 2 3 4
       CM   4v   E H H F
       1789

          P266   G   278?   HALIFAX
          D6.11[1]   G   HALIFAX
          D6.12[1]   G   HALIFAX
          D6.13[1]   G   HALIFAX

       ————————

       [1] 3v

341. 1 3 3 5 6 5 4 3 2 1 3 6 2 1 5   1 2 3 4̂ 4 5̂ 5 6̂ 6
       888888   4v   H H H F F O O F F
       c.1776
          P231   G   607

342. 1 3 3 5 6 5 4 3 3 1 4 3 2 1 2   1 2 3 4
       CM   4v   F H H F
       c.1783   *a* Barwick
          P250   G   *a*   594   FOLKSTONE

       1 3 3 5 6 5 4 3 3 4 3 2 3 4 3:   *soprano of* **725**

       1 3 3 6 5 6 7 1 5 6 5 6 5 4 3:   *see* **1210**

       1 3 4 1 7 6 5 4 3 2 2 3 4 5 1:   *see* **395**

343. 1 3 4 2 3 4 5 4 3 2 1 7 5 5 4   1 2̂ 2 3 4 4
       CM   4v   O F F F O O
       1757
          P164   a   253
          P198   g   253

344.   1 3 4 3 1 5 4 3 3 2 1 3 1 2 3   1 2 3 4
SM   4v   H F H F
c.1760   *a* A. Adams (*E*)

P174	G	*a*	226	BARTON
P174.10	G		226	BARTON
P235[1]	G		413	PEASENHALL
P174.11	G		226	BARTON
P174.12	G		226	BARTON

[1] 1 3 4 3 1 5 4 3 4 3 2 3 1 2 3

1 3 4 3 1 5 4 3 4 3 2 3 1 2 3:   *see* **344**

345.   1 3 4 3 1 5 6 5 4 3 4 3 2 3 2   1 2 3 4 3 4
CM   4v   H H H H H F
1747

P130	B♭		789	DARKING
P130.2	B♭		789	DARKING
P130.3	B♭		789	DARKING
P174	G		789	DARKING
A17	G			DARKING
A17.2	G			DARKING
P130.5	B♭		789	DARKING
P212	B♭		789	DARKING
P174.10	G		789	DARKING
P174.11	G		789	DARKING
P266	B♭	*b*	370	DARKING
P174.12	G		789	DARKING

b Knapp

1 3 4 3 1 6 5 3 5 1 7 5 1 7 1:   *soprano of* **745**

346. 1 3 4 3 2 1 1 4 3 4 5 5 4 3 2   1 2 3͡ 4͡ 4
      CM   4v   H H O F O
      1793   a Stone
          A132   F   a   722   BRIMFIELD

      1 3 4 3 2 1 2 1 2 3 2 1 2 2 3:   soprano of **825**

347. 1 3 4 3 2 1 2 3 4 5 3 2 1 7 1   1 2 3͡ 3͡ M 4
      LM   4v   H H F F F H
      1800   a Doolittle
          A201   a   a   408   EXHORTATION

348. 1 3 4 3 2 1 2 3 4 5 6 5 4 3 2   1 2 3 4
      CM   4v   H H F F
      c.1752   a Knapp
          P148   G   a   278   CORFE CASTLE
          P148.2   G   a   278   CORFE CASTLE
          P148.3   G   a   278   CORFE CASTLE
          P182a   G   278
          P183   G   278
          P148.4   G   a   278   CORFE CASTLE
          P148.5   G   a   278   CORFE CASTLE
          P228   G   278

349. 1 3 4 3 2 1 2 5 6 5 4 3 2 2 3   1 2 3 4
      CM   4v   H H F E
      1773   a Mumford?
          P212   G   192
          D6.13[1]   G   a   204   MUMFORD'S

      ———————————
      [1] 3v

1 3 4 3 2 1 5 3 1 7 1 3 4 5 5:   *see* **350**

350.

1 3 4 3 2 1 5 3 1 7 1 5 3 3 6				1 2 3 4 5 6 6	
888888			4v	F H E H H H O	
c.1752		*a* Knapp			
P148	G	*a*	607	KNOWL	
P148	G	*a*	583		
P148.2	G	*a*	607	KNOWL	
P148.2	G	*a*	583		
P148.3	G	*a*	607	KNOWL	
P148.3	G	*a*	583		
P183[1]	G		607		
P148.4	G	*a*	607	KNOWL	
P148.4	G	*a*	583		
P148.5	G	*a*	607	KNOWL	
P148.5	G	*a*	583		
P204[1,2]	G		804	QUEENBOROUGH	
A37[3,4]	G		583		
P220[1,2]	G		607	DARTFORD	
A54[3,4]	G		583		
A56[3,4]	G		583		

---

[1] 5v

[2] 1 3 4 3 2 1 5 3 1 7 1 3 4 5 5

[3] Meter = 8868886

[4] 1 2 3 4 5 6 7
F H E H H H O

351.

1 3 4 3 2 1 5 3 2 1 2 1 2 1 7				1 2 3 4 5 6 7 8	
CMD			4v	H H H H F O F E	
1794		*a* Belcher			
A135	A	*a*	560	WINTHROP	

352.   1 3 4 3 2 1 5 3 7 5 1 3 2 3 4   1 2 3 4
CM   4v   F H F E
1763

P189	G	531	PENBURY
P189.2	G	531	PENBURY
A23	G	531	PENBURY
P189.3	G	531	PENBURY
A31	G	531	PENBURY
P189.4[1]	G	531	PENBURY
A31.6	G	531	PENBURY
A31.7	G	531	PENBURY
A31.8	G	531	PENBURY
A39	G	531	PENBURY
A39.2	G	531	PENBURY
A54	G	531	PENBURY
A56	G	531	PENBURY
A84	G	531	PENBURY

[1] 1 3 4 3 2 1 5 3 7 5 5 5 3 2 3

1 3 4 3 2 1 5 3 7 5 5 5 3 2 3:   *see* **352**

353.   1 3 4 3 2 1 5 6 5 4 3 4 3 2 1   1 2 3 4
CM   3v   H H H F
1795

A153	G	*b*	417	BRENTFORD

b "Williams' Collection"

Based on a non-fuging tune in P189.

354.   1 3 4 3 2 1 6 5 4 3 4 3 2 1 3   1 2 2 3 4 4
CM   3v   F H H F F F
1791   *a* Graun

P291	F	*a*	312

355. 1 3 4 3 2 1 7 1 3 5 4 3 2 3 3   1 2 3 4 5 6
668668   4v   H H F H H F
1774   *a* Bull

A39	G		218	
A41	A	*a*	218	PS. 122
A43	A	*a*	218	PS. 122
A39.2	G		218	
A47a	A	*a*	218	PS. 122
A54	G		218	PS. 122
A56	G		218	PS. 122
A57	A			
A57.2	A			
A60	G		218	PS. 122
A70	G	*a*	218	PS. 122
A74	G			PS. 122
A84	G	*a*	218	PS. 122
A85	G		218	PS. 122
A91	G	*a*	218	PS. 122
A106	G	*a*	218	PS. 122
A108	G	*a*	218	PS. 122
A106.4	G	*a*	218	PS. 122
A113	A	*a*	217	PS. 122
A131	A	*a*	218	PS. 122
A147	A	*a*	218	PS. 122
A152[1,2]	A	*a*	218	ZION
A158	A	*a*	218	PS. 122
A163	A	*a*	218	PS. 122
A189	A	*a*	218	PS. 122

[1] 1 3 2 1 7 1 3 5 4 3 2 3 3 2 2

[2] 1 2 3 4 5 6
     H H H H H F

356. 1 3 4 3 2 1 7 6 7 1 3 1 6 4 3   1 2 3 4 4 5 6
666688   4v   F O O O O F O
1757

P164	B♭	711	
P198	G	711	

193

134 323 432 343 323:   *soprano of* **21**

357.   134 323 453 454 323   1 2 3 4 3 4
SM   4v   H H H H F E
c.1750   *a* Tans'ur
   P142   a   42   NEW MARKET
   P210   a   *a*   702   NEWMARKET

358.   134 333 453 225 543   1 2 3 4
LM   4v   H F H H
1786   *a* Handel
   P258   D   *a*   817   KENSINGTON

359.   134 343 236 713 212   1 2 3 4
CM   4v   H H H F
1754
   P151   C   194
   P157   C   194
   P198   Bb   194

360.   134 343 434 232 343   1 2 3 4
CM   4v   O F F F
1794   *a* W. Billings
   A136   C   *a*   557   ST. ENOCH

361.   134 345 434 565 327   1 2 3 4 4
SM   4v   H H F F F
1786   *a* Stone
   A71   a   *a*   5   DANBURY
   A131   a   *a*   5   DANBURY

362. 1 3 4 3 4 5 5 6 5 6 4 3 2 3 2   1 2 3 4 4
      CM   4v   H H H F H
      c.1800   *a* Cuzens
         D16   G   *a*   [1]   PEMBROKE

[1] Assigned to text 481, 483 or 38.

363. 1 3 4 3 5 6 5 4 3 5 5 1 3 2 2   1 2 3 4
      CM   4v   H H F H
      c.1792   *a* Milgrove
         D12   G   *a*   [1]   BATH CHAPEL

[1] Assigned to text 379 or 655.

      1 3 4 5 1 1 2 3 1 2 3 3 4 5 6:   *see* **690**

      1 3 4 5 1 2 1 7 1 2 3 3 2 1 7:   *soprano of* **651**

364. 1 3 4 5 1 5 4 3 1 2 2 3 3 2 3   1 1 2 3 4
      LM   4v   O H H F H
      1789   *a* French (*A*)
         A93   G   *a*   811   EXHORTATION

365. 1 3 4 5 3 1 3 4 5 4 3 4 3 2 1   1 2 3 4
      LM   6v   F F O F
      c.1755   *a* Everet
         P157   A   261
         P266[1,2]   G   *a*   443   WITTON

[1] 4v

[2] 1 3 4 5 3 1 3 5 5 3 4 3 2 1 7

1 3 4   5 3 1   3 5 5   3 4 3   2 1 7:   *see* **365**

366.   1 3 4   5 3 4   3 2 1   2 3 2   1 2 3   1 2 3 4 4
       LM   4v   F H H F H
       1760   *a* Stephenson
          P171   G   *a*   261
          P182a   G   724
          P171.4   G   *a*   261
          P228   G   724
          P253[1]   G   559   CHESTER
          P253.2[1]   G   559   CHESTER
          A79   G   559   GRATITUDE
          A87   G   559   GRATITUDE
          A117   G   559   GRATITUDE
          P253.4[1]   G   559   CHESTER

       [1] 1 2 3 4
          F H H F

1 3 4   5 3 4   3 2 2   3 4 5   4 3 2:   *see* **1197**

367.   1 3 4   5 3 4   3 2 7   1 1 5   5 3 3   1 2 2 3 4
       LM   4v   H F E H F
       1760   *a* Stephenson
          P171   B♭   *a*   192
          P171.4   B♭   *a*   192

1 3 4   5 3 4   5 6 5   4 3 2   7 1 6:   *see* **1236**

368. 1 3 4 5 3 6 5 4 3 3 2 5 3 6 5   1 2 3 4 4
CM 4v   H H F F H
c.1800

    D17 a 67

369. 1 3 4 5 4 3 2 1 2 3 2 1 5 4 3   1 2 3 4 3̑ 4 M̑ 4
SM 4v   H H H H F O O O
1794 *a* W. Billings

    A136 g *a* 543   WEYMOUTH

370. 1 3 4 5 4 3 2 1 2 7 1 2 3 2 1   1 2 3 4 5 6
666688 4v   H E H F H F
c.1748

    P134 C 802   LONDON NEW
    P137 C 802

371. 1 3 4 5 4 3 2 1 4 3 2 3 2 1 5   1 2 3 4 5 6
886886 3v   H H H F F H
c.1792

    D12 C 19   BROADMEAD

372. 1 3 4 5 4 3 2 5 4 3 4 3 2 1 5   1 2 3 4 5 6
666688 4v   H H H H F H
c.1752 *a* Knapp

    P148 g *a* 374
    P148.2 g *a* 374
    P148.3 g *a* 374
    P148.4 g *a* 374
    P148.5 g *a* 374

373. 1 3 4 5 4 3 2 7 1 3 3 5 4 3 2   1 2 3 4 3 4
CM   4v   A E H E H F
c.1783   *a* Barwick
    P250   B♭   *a*   348   MINSTER

374. 1 3 4 5 4 3 5 4 3 2 1 5 1 1 3   1 2̑ 2 3 4
CM   4v   H F F H F
c.1783   *a* Barwick
    P250   G   *a*   827   WHITSTABLE

375. 1 3 4 5 4 5 4 3 2 1 2 1 2 3 4   1 2 3 4 4
CM   3v   H H H F H
1799
    D15   g   131   LANCASTER

376. 1 3 4 5 4 5 6 7 5 1 7 6 5 4 5   1 2 3̑ 4 3 4
CM   4v   E H F F H H
1786   *a* Wood
    A70   e   *a*   25   PEPPERRELL
    A74   e   25   PEPPERRELL
    A85   e   25   PEPPERRELL
    A98   e   25   PEPPERRELL
    A109   e   25   PEPPERRELL
    A114   e   25   PEPPERRELL
    A114.B   e   25   PEPPERRELL

377. 1 3 4 5 5 3 4 3 2 2 1 2 3 3 4   1 2 3 4 5̑ 6
XXXXYY   4v   H H H E F F
1793
    A121   a   590   WASHINGTON

1 3 4 5 5 5 3 6 4 5 5 3 3 1 1:   *soprano of* **1126**

378.   1 3 4 5 5 5 4 3 2 1 5 5 4 3 1   1 2 2 3 4 3 4
    LM   4v   H H H H F F H F
    1750   *a* Broderip
      P134.2   G   *a*   421

379.   1 3 4 5 5 5 5 6 5 5 1 1 1 6 5   1 2 3 4 4 5 6 7 8 8
    LMD   4v   H H H E E H H H F H
    1793
      A128   F   770   TRIUMPH
      A172   F   770   TRIUMPH

1 3 4 5 5 6 6 5 5 6 5 7 1 2 5:   *soprano of* **1**

380.   1 3 4 5 6 1 7 6 5 3 2 1 5 6 5   1 2 3 4 3 4
    CM   4v   H H F F F O
    1794   *a* Belcher
      A135   F   *a*   84   HARMONY

1 3 4 5 6 5 1 2 3 2 1 6 5 4 3:   *see* **1202**

1 3 4 5 6 5 4 3 1 4 5 3 6 5 4:   *see* **381**

381. 1 3 4 5 6 5 4 3 1 4 5 4 6 5 4   1 2 3 3 4 4
CM   4v   F H E E H H
c.1746

P129a	G	444	
P148	G	444	KNIGHTON
P148[1,2,3]	G	46	
P148.2	G	444	KNIGHTON
P148.2[1,2,3]	G	46	
P148.3	G	444	KNIGHTON
P148.3[1,2,3]	G	46	
P148.4	G	444	KNIGHTON
P148.4[1,2,3]	G	46	
P148.5	G	444	KNIGHTON
P148.5[1,2,3]	G	46	
A39	G	444	KNIGHTON
A47	G	444	KNIGHTON
A54	G	444	KNIGHTON
A56	G	444	KNIGHTON

[1] 1 3 4 5 6 5 4 3 1 4 5 3 6 5 4

[2] Meter = 886886

[3] 1 2 3 4 5 6 6
    F E H E E H H

1 3 4 5 6 5 4 3 2 1 2 3 3 2 2:   *see* **382**

382. 1 3 4 5 6 5 4 3 2 1 2 3 1 2 2   1 2 3 4 4
CM   4v   E E H F H
c.1751

[+]P145a	G	810	
[+]P130.3[1]	G	701	ST. NICHOLAS'
P174	G	701	BORROUGH
P192	G	810	

P130.5[1]	G		701	ST. NICHOLAS'
P174.10	G		701	BORROUGH
P174.11	G		701	BORROUGH
A72	A	b	696	VERNON
P174.12	G		701	BORROUGH
D15[2,3]	G		417	ST. NICHOLAS'

[1] 1 3 4 5 6 5 4 3 2 1 2 7 1 2 2

[2] 1 3 4 5 6 5 4 3 2 1 2 3 3 2 2

[3] 3v

b "from Adams"

1 3 4 5 6 5 4 3 2 1 2 7 1 2 2:   *see* **382**

383. 1 3 4 5 6 5 4 3 2 1 7 2 3 4 5   1 2 3 4 5 6 7 8
      CMD   4v   H H H E F H H E
      1745   *a* Bellamy
          P124   F   *a*   489

1 3 4 5 6 5 4 3 4 3 2 1 5 5 3:   *soprano of* **639**

384. 1 3 4 5 6 5 4 5 3 4 5 4 3 4 3   1 2 3̑ 3̑ M 4
      SM   4v   H H F F O H
      1793
          A121   G   114   WILLINGTON

385. 1 3 5 1 1 7 6 5 4 3 2 2 1 3 2   1 2 3 4̑ 4̑ 4
      CM   4v   H H H F F F
      c.1785   *a* Valentine
          P257   E♭   *a*   468

386.   1 3 5 1 2 1 2 3 2 1 3 3 2 1 2   1 1 2 3 3 4 5 6 6
       666688   3v   F F H H H H F F H
       1799   a I. M. P.
          D6.13   D   a   69   ROTHERHITHE

387.   1 3 5 1 2 1 7 1 1 3 1 2 3 2 1   1 2 2 3 4 4 5 5 6
       888888   4v   H H H F H H H H F
       1783   a Chandler
          A51   C   a   158   PS. 19
          A62   C   a   158   PS. 19
          A62.3   C   a   158   PS. 19
          A148[1]   C   a   158   PS. 19

       _____
       [1] 1 2 2 3 3 4 5 4 5 6
           H H H H H H H H H F

       1 3 5 1 2 3 2 5 7 1 1 2 3 3 1:   soprano of 388

388.   1 3 5 1 2 3 4 5 6 6 3 2 1 7 6   1 2 3 4 3 4
       LM   4v   F H O H F H
       1789   a French (A)
          A93   C   a   262   SUNDERLAND

389.   1 3 5 1 5 1 2 1 5 6 5 4 3 2 5   1 2 3 4 3 4
       CM   4v   H H F O H H
       1795   a Edson
          A148   D   a   84   TROY

390.   1 3 5 1 5 4 3 2 1 1 5 3 2 1 7   1 2 3 4
       LM   4v   H H H F
       1777   a Froud
          P233   F   a   794   STEPNEY

1 3 5 1 5 4 3 2 3 4 3 2 1 7 1:   *soprano of* **687**

391.	1 3 5 1 5 6 5 4 3 2 1 1 3 5 1				1 2 3 4 5 6
	XXXXYY			4v	H H H H F H
	1785		*a* D. Read		
	A63	E	*a*	590	RESURRECTION
	A63.2	E	*a*	590	RESURRECTION
	A80	E	*a*	590	RESURRECTION
	A80.4	E	*a*	590	RESURRECTION
	A150	E	*a*	590	RESURRECTION
	A80.5	E	*a*	590	RESURRECTION

392.	1 3 5 1 5 7 1 6 5 4 3 5 6 6 6				1 2 3 4 4 5 6 7 8
	LMD			3v	F H H H H H H H O
	1795		*a* Babcock		
	A149	E♭	*a*	530	HAMBURG

393.	1 3 5 1 6 1 6 5 4 3 3 2 2 3 4				1 2 3 4 5 6 6 7̑ 8̑ M̑ M
	CMD			4v	H H H H H H H F F O O
	1793		*a* Shumway		
	A131	F	*a*	109	NEW JERSEY

394.	1 3 5 1 7 6 5 1 7 1 2 3 2 1 7				1 2 3 4
	SM			4v	H H H F
	1793		*a* Kimball		
	A125	d	*a*	406	DOVER

395.	1 3 5 1 7 6 5 4 3 2 2 3 4 5 1			1 2 3̑ 4	
	LM 4v			H H F F	
	1783				
	A51	e		389	PITSFIELD
	A62	e		389	PITSFIELD
	A67	e		389	PITSFIELD
	A70	e	b	389	PITSFIELD
	A74	e		389	PITSFIELD
	A85	e		389	PITSFIELD
	A91	e	b	389	PITSFIELD
	A62.3	e		389	PITSFIELD
	A108	e		389	PITSFIELD
	A131[1]	e		389	PITSFIELD

[1] 1 3 4 1 7 6 5 4 3 2 2 3 4 5 1

b "Select Harmony"

396.	1 3 5 1 7 6 5 6 5 4 3 2 1 3 6		1 2 3 4 1 2 3 4
	CM 4v		H H H H H H F F
	c.1800 a Key		
	P323	F	a	40	

397.	1 3 5 3 1 2 2 5 3 2 1 5 6 7 1		1 2 3 4
	SM 4v		H H F H
	1799 a D. Merrill		
	A188	A	a	52	ALFRED

398.	1 3 5 3 1 2 7 1 2 3 2 3 4 5 5		1 2 3̑ M 3 4
	SM 4v		H H F O H H
	1793 a Shumway		
	A131	a	a	617	LAMBERTON

399.   1 3 5 3 1 5 6 7 1 5 1 7 1 2 3   1 2 3 4
        LM   4v   H H F F
        1755
             P153   G   9
             P153.2   G   9
             P153.3   G   9

400.   1 3 5 3 1 5 6 7 1 6 2 2 5 5 6   1 2 3 4 5̂ M 5 6 7 8
        CMD   4v   H H H O F O H H H H
        1793   *a* Caswell
             A128   E   *a*   290   ORDINATION
             A172   E   *a*   290   ORDINATION

        1 3 5 3 3 2 2 4 6 5 4 4 3 3 4:   *see* **1158**

401.   1 3 5 3 3 2 4 4 3 2 3 6 6 5 6   1 2 3̂ M 3 4
        CM   4v   H H F O H H
        1796
             A160   D   741   TRANSITION
             A168   D   *b*   741   TRANSITION

        ———————
        b "Union Harmony"

        1 3 5 3 4 5 3 2 1 2 2 3 2 1 7:   *see* **402**

402.　1 3 5　4 3 1　3 2 1　2 2 3　2 1 2　　1 2　3　4
　　　　LM　　　　　　　　　　　　　　4v　　H H　H　F
　　　　1747

P130	G	421	BRIDGWATER
P117.2[2]	F	680	
P130.2	G	421	BRIDGWATER
P130.3	G	421	BRIDGWATER
P174[1]	G	656	BRIDGWATER
P130.5	G	421	BRIDGWATER
P212	G	73	BRIDGWATER
P174.10[1]	G	656	BRIDGWATER
P235[1]	G	739	BURY
P174.11[1]	G	656	BRIDGWATER
P174.12[1]	G	656	BRIDGWATER

[1] 1 3 5　3 4 5　3 2 1　2 2 3　2 1 7

[2] 1 3 5　4 3 1　3 2 1　2 2 3　2 1 7

Closely related to **88.**

1 3 5　4 3 1　3 2 1　2 2 3　2 1 7:　*see* **402**

403.　1 3 5　4 3 2　1 2 3　4 3 2　3 2 1　　1　2　3︵4　3　4
　　　　LM　　　　　　　　　　　　　　4v　　E　H　F　F　H　H
　　　　1793　　　　　　　　　*a* Kimball
　　　　　A125　　　　A　　*a*　　168　　GEORGIA

1 3 5　4 3 2　1 2 3　4 5 4　3 2 1:　*soprano of* **1123**

404.　1 3 5　4 3 2　1 7 1　1 2 2　3 2 3　　1　2　3　4　5　6　7　8
　　　　8787D　　　　　　　　　　　　4v　　H　F　H　H　H　F　H　H
　　　　c.1800　　　　　　　　　*a* Harvey
　　　　　P321　　　　A　　*a*　　579　　FOUNTAIN

405.   1 3 5 4 3 2 2 3 5 4 3 2 1 1 2   1 2 3 4 3̆ 4̆ M
        SM   4v   H H H H F F F
        1778   *a* W. Billings

A40	a	*a*	16	MARYLAND
A40.2	a	*a*	16	MARYLAND
A40.3	a	*a*	16	MARYLAND
A49	a	*a*	16	MARYLAND
A60	a		16	MARYLAND
A40.4	a	*a*	16	MARYLAND
A67	a	*a*	16	MARYLAND
A70	a	*a*	16	MARYLAND
A74	a		16	MARYLAND
A80	a	*a*	335	MARYLAND
A84	a	*a*	16	MARYLAND
A87	a	*a*	16	MARYLAND
A89	a		16	MARYLAND
A91	a	*a*	16	MARYLAND
A92	a	*a*	16	MARYLAND
A92.3	a	*a*	16	MARYLAND
A101	a		16	MARYLAND
A103	a	*a*	16	MARYLAND
A108	a	*a*	16	MARYLAND
A113	a	*a*	851	MARYLAND
A117	a	*a*	16	MARYLAND
A119	a	*a*	16	MARYLAND
A80.4	a	*a*	335	MARYLAND
A124	a	*a*	16	MARYLAND
A130	a	*a*	16	·MARYLAND
A131	a	*a*	16	MARYLAND
A137	a	*a*	16	MARYLAND
A145	a		335	MARYLAND
A146	a		16	MARYLAND
A147	a	*a*	16	MARYLAND
A158	a	*a*	16	MARYLAND
A80.5	a	*a*	335	MARYLAND
A103.4	a	*a*	16	MARYLAND
A163	a	*a*	16	MARYLAND
A103.5	a	*a*	16	MARYLAND
A146.5	a		16	MARYLAND
A168	a	*a*	16	MARYLAND
A170	a	*a*	16	MARYLAND
A172	a		335	MARYLAND

405 continued

A175	a	a	16	MARYLAND
A181	a		16	MARYLAND
A103.6	a	a	16	MARYLAND
A189	a	a	16	MARYLAND
A190	a		16	MARYLAND
A181.5	a	a	16	MARYLAND

406.   1 3 5 4 3 2 5 3 3 1 1 1 3 2 5   1 2 3 4 5 6 7̂ 8
SMD   4v   H H H E H H F F
c.1798
   A182   A   472   MIDDLESEX

407.   1 3 5 4 3 4 3 2 1 2 3 5 4 2 3   1 2 2 3 4 5 6
888888   4v   H H H H H H F
c.1776
   P231   a   616

   1 3 5 4 3 4 3 2 2 3 5 5 6 5 4:   *soprano of* **1129**

   1 3 5 4 3 4 5 6 2 5 4 5 6 7 1:   *soprano of* **1147**

408.   1 3 5 4 3 5 2 3 2 1 7 3 2 5 4   1 2 3 4
CM   4v   E H O F
1769   *a* Harrott
   P198   G   *a*   766

409.   1 3 5 4 5 3 4 5 4 3 2 1 2 3 5   1 2 3̂ 4̂ M 4
CM   4v   H H F F O H
c.1796   *a* Hibbard
   A164   F   *a*   809   EXHORTATION
   A182   F   *a*   809   EXHORTATION

410. 1 3 5 4 5 4 3 2 2 3 5 3 4 5 5   1 2 3 4̂ M 4̂
CM   4v   H H F F F O
1793   *a* Wood
  ⁺A131   g   503   WILTON
  ⁺A132   g   *a*   503   WILTON

411. 1 3 5 5 3 4 3 2 1 3 2 3 5 4 3   1 2 3 4 5
88887   4v   H H H H F
1755
  P153   G   434
  P153.2   G   434
  P253   G   LYNN
  P153.3   G   434
  P253.2   G   LYNN
  A116   G   343   LYNN
  A117   G   343   LYNN
  P253.4   G   LYNN

412. 1 3 5 5 4 3 2 3 1 5 6 5 4 3 2   1 2 3 4 5 6
666688   4v   H H H H F H
1794   *a* Belcher
  A135   A   *a*   23   PLENITUDE

413. 1 3 5 5 4 5 5 3 2 3 5 4 2 1 3   1 2 3 4̂
SM   4v   H H F F
1783   *a* Brownson
  A51   G   *a*   90   SUTTON
  A62   G   *a*   90   SUTTON
  A62.3   G   *a*   90   SUTTON
  A113   G   *a*   702   SUTTON
  A150   G   *a*   90   SUTTON

414. 1 3 5 5 5 6 5 1 1 5 6 5 4 3 4   1 2 3 4 5 6
888888   4v   H H H F F F
1793   *a* Stone
    A132   E   *a*   241   PETERSHAM

415. 1 3 5 6 1 7 6 6 5 5 1 5 4 3 3   1 2 3 4 5 6
666688   4v   H H H H F H
1792   *a* Ives
    ⁺A116   D   *a*   279   CONNECTICUT
    ⁺A117   D   *a*   279   CONNECTICUT

416. 1 3 5 6 5 1 6 1 7 6 5 1 1 2 3   1 2 3 4 5 6 7 8
LMD   4v   H H H H F F F F
1793   *a* Hall
    ⁺A131   E   *a*   650   CIVIL AMUSEMENT
    ⁺A132   E   *a*   650   CIVIL AMUSEMENT
    A150   E   *a*   650   CIVIL AMUSEMENT

417. 1 3 5 6 5 6 1 5 1 3 5 6 5 4 3   1 2 3 4 5 M 6
668668   4v   H H O F F O H
1799   *a* Temple & D. Merrill
    A188   F   *a*   217   AMITY

418. 1 3 5 6 5 6 7 1 5 1 3 5 4 2 1   1 2 3 M M 4
SM   4v   H H F F F H
1793   *a* West
    ⁺A131   F   *a*   51   VENUS
    ⁺A132[1]   F   51   VENUS
    A174[1]   F   51   VENUS

---
[1] 1 2 3 4 M 4
   H H F F O O

1 3 5 6 7 1 2 3 4 5 3 2 1 7 6:   *soprano of* **657**

419. 1 3 5 6 7 1 3 4 3 2 5 3 1 6 4   1 2 3͡ 4 4
         LM   4v   A F F F F
         1750   *a* Knapp
            P134.2   G   *a*   168
            P157   G   168

420. 1 3 5 6 7 6 5 6 7 1 6 1 7 6 5   1 2 3 4 5͡ 6͡ 7͡ 8͡ 7͡ 8
         LMD   4v   H H H H F F F F F O
         1790
            A96   E   98   SAINT'S REPOSE
            A111   E   98   SAINT'S REPOSE
            A111.3   E   98   SAINT'S REPOSE
            A111.4   E   98   SAINT'S REPOSE
            A111.5   E   98   SAINT'S REPOSE
            A111.6   E   98   SAINT'S REPOSE

1 3 6 4 2 5 4 3 3 2 2 2 3 4 3:   *soprano of* **1127**

421. 1 3 6 5 6 5 4 3 1 4 5 4 3 2 3   1 2 3 4 5͡ 6 7͡ 8
         LMD   4v   H H H H F F F F
         1793   *a* Stone
            A132   F   *a*   799   BROOKFIELD

1 3 7 1 2 3 2 1 2 7 1 7 6 1 2:   *see* **1225**

1 3 7 1 7 6 7 5 1 3 2 5 1 7 6:   *soprano of* **181**

1 3 7 3 7 3 2 1 7 1 5 4 3 2 7:   *see* **184**

422.   1 4 3 4 5 6 7 1 7 6 5 4 3 2 4   1 2 3 4 5 6 6
       868686   4v   F H F E H H H
       1760   *a* B. West (*E*)
           P173   F   *a*   231   EASTHADDON
           P173.2   F   *a*   231   EASTHADDON

1 4 5 6 7 1 1 2 2 1 5 1 1 7 7:   *soprano of* **423**

423.   1 4 5 6 7 1 2 3 3 2 3 4 4 3 5   1 M 2 3 4 5 5 6
       888888   4v   F O O O F F H H
       1786   *a* Purcell
           P258   C   *a*   808   LYME

424.   1 5 1 1 7 1 7 6 5 4 3 6 5 4 3   1 2 3 4 5 6 6
       666688   4v   H H H H H F H
       1793   *a* Kimball
           A125   D   *a*   729   MONMOUTH

425.   1 5 1 2 3 1 2 1 7 1 1 1 3 2 1   1 2 3 4 4
       XXYY   4v   H F F F H
       c.1776
           P231   C   484

426.   1 5 1 2 3 2 1 2 1 7 5 6 1 7 2   1 2 3 4 4
       LM   4v   F F F F F
       -1750
           ⁺P137   C   667
           ⁺P145a   C   667

427.   1 5 1   2 3 2   1 5 4   3 2 1   3 2 1   1 2 3 4
            SM   4v   H H F E
            1785   *a* D. Read

    A63   a   *a*   747   ASIA
    A63.2   a   *a*   747   ASIA
    A80   a   *a*   747   ASIA
    A80.4   a   *a*   747   ASIA
    A80.5   a   *a*   747   ASIA

428.   1 5 1   3 3 1   2 7 2   7 2 4   4 2 3   1 2 3 4 5̂ 6
            878787   4v   H H H H F F
            1794   *a* W. Billings

    A136   B♭   *a*   302   HOPKINTON

    1 5 1   3 4 3   2 1 5   4 5 6   5 4 3:   *soprano of* **342**

429.   1 5 1   3 5 2   1 7 6   5 5 6   7 1 4   1 2 3 4 5 6 7 7 8
            LMD   3v   H H H H F H H H H
            1800

    A196   G   807   DESIRE OF NATIONS

430.   1 5 1   3 5 4   3 2 1   6 2 1   7 6 5   1 2 3̂ 4̂ 3̂ 4
            CM   4v   H H F F F O
            1790   *a* Morgan

    A96   C   *a*   388   PLEASANT VALLEY
    A103   C   *a*   388   PLEASANT VALLEY
    A111   C   *a*   388   PLEASANT VALLEY
    A111.3   C   *a*   388   PLEASANT VALLEY
    A111.4   C   *a*   388   PLEASANT VALLEY
    A111.5   C   *a*   388   PLEASANT VALLEY
    A103.4   C   *a*   388   PLEASANT VALLEY
    A111.6   C   *a*   388   PLEASANT VALLEY
    A103.5   C   *a*   388   PLEASANT VALLEY
    A103.6   C   *a*   388   PLEASANT VALLEY

431. 1 5 1 5 1 7 6 5 4 5 5 5 4 3 1   1 2 3 4 3̂ M 4
CM   4v   H H H H F O O
1770   *a* W. Billings
        A33   F   *a*   296   EUROPE

432. [a ghost]

433. 1 5 1 5 6 5 4 3 2 1 1 4 6 6 5   1 2 3 4 4
CM   4v   H H H E F
1794   *a* Belcher
        A135   F   *a*   763   CAROL

434. 1 5 1 6 1 7 2 1 5 6 7 6 5 6 1   1 2 3 4 5̂ 6̂ 7̂ 8̂ 7̂ 8
CMD   4v   H H H H F F F F F O
1793   *a* Stone
        A132   D   *a*   545   HAMPSHIRE

435. 1 5 1 7 1 2 7 1 3 2 7 5 1 3 3   1 2 3̂ 3̂ 4 5 5 6
668668   4v   H H F F F F H H
1793   *a* West
        A131   D   *a*   218   SHARON

436. 1 5 1 7 1 7 6 5 4 3 4 5 1 7 1   1 2 3 4
CM   4v   H H H F
1784
        P253   d   682   ELY
        P253.2   d   682   ELY
        A79   d   682   GILEAD
        A87   d   682   GILEAD
        A117   d   682   GILEAD
        P253.4   d   682   ELY
        A200   d   682   GILEAD

437.   1 5 1   7 4 5   7 1 2   3 2 1   7 1 3   1   2   M   4
       SM   4v   H   H   F   H
       1797   *a* Belknap

A166	d	*a*	636	RAYNHAM
A192	d	*a*	636	RAYNHAM

438.   1 5 1   7 6 5   4 5 7   5 5 1   2 1 7   1   2   3   4   5͡   6   7   8
       CMD   4v   H   H   H   H   F   H   H   H
       1789   *a* French (*A*)

A93	a	*a*	225	FUNERAL HYMN

       1 5 1   7 6 7   1 6 4   3 4 5   4 3 1:   *soprano of* **109**

439.   1 5 2   3 2 1   2 3 2   1 7 1   1 3 2   1   2   3   4
       CM   4v   E   F   F   H
       c.1755

P157	a		795
P198	g		795

       1 5 2   3 2 1   7 1 2   3 2 3   4 5 6:   *see* **1060**

440.   1 5 2   3 5 4   5 4 3   2 2 1   2 3 4   1   2   2   3   4   4
       CM   4v   H   F   F   E   F   F
       c.1776

P231	a		440

       1 5 2   5 4 3   6 5 3   6 1 4   5 3 4:   *soprano of* **679**

441. 1 5 3 1 2 3 2 1 1 7 6 7 5 6 7   1 2 3 4
CM   4v   H H F H
1789   *a* French (*A*)

| A93 | E | *a* | 104 | DELLY |
| A131 | E | *a* | 104 | DELLY |

442. 1 5 3 1 3 5 6 7 1 1 3 2 1 5 6   1 2 3̑ 4
CM   7(5)v   H H F F
1797   *a* Belknap

| A166 | D | *a* | 651 | SAYBROOK |
| A192 | D | *a* | 651 | SAYBROOK |

1 5 3 2 1 4 3 2 3 2 1 4 3 6 7:   *alto of* **726**

443. 1 5 3 2 1 7 5 4 3 2 2 3 5 4 3   1 2 3 4 5 6
888888   4v   H H H H H F
1760   *a* Stephenson

P171	g	*a*	146	
P171.4	g	*a*	146	
A57	g		146	FAIRFIELD
A57.2	g		146	FAIRFIELD

444. 1 5 3 3 2 7 1 2 3 4 3 2 3 4 5   1 2 3 4
CM   4v   H H H F
1750

| P137 | G | 62 |
| P157 | G | 62 |

445. 1 5 3 4 2 3 2 1 3 2 2 3 4 5 4   1 2̑ 2 2 3̑ 4 3 4
CM   4v   H O F H F F H E
1795   *a* N. Billings

| A150 | a | *a* | 211 | CONVICTION |

446. 1 5 3 4 2 3 4 3 2 1 4 2 2 3 2   1 2 3͡ 3 4͡ 4
LM   4v   F H F F F F
1754   *a* Everet
        P151   G   *a*   623
        P157   G   *a*   623
        P266   G   *a*   623   DUNHAM

447. 1 5 3 4 3 2 1 3 1 3 5 5 5 3 3   1 2 3 4 5 6
666688   4v   H F F H H H
1755
        P153   G   130
        P153.2   G   130
        P153.3   G   130

448. 1 5 3 4 3 2 7 1 2 3 4 5 6 5 4   1 2 3 4 3 4
CM   4v   E H H E H F
1760   *a* Stephenson
        P171   G   *a*   341
        P182a   G   385
        P171.4   G   *a*   341
        P228   G   385

449. 1 5 3 4 5 3 1 2 3 4 3 2 1 7 3   1 2 3 4 4
CM   4v   F F F H F
1754   *a* Everet
        P151   a   *a*   221
        P157   a   *a*   221
        P198   B♭   221

        1 5 3 4 5 3 2 1 3 2 7 1 2 3 4:   *see* **1203**

450. 1 5 3 4 7 1 2 3 5 5 3 7 5 3 5   1 2 $\overset{\frown}{3}$ 4
LM   4v   H H F O
1798   *a* Weeks
   A177   a   *a*   396   SEVERIA
   A177.2   a   *a*   396   SEVERIA

451. 1 5 3 5 4 3 2 1 7 1 2 3 2 2 4   1 2 3 4
LM   4v   E F E E
-1750
   [+]P137   G   435
   [+]P145a[1]   G   435

---

[1] 1 5 1 5 4 3 2 1 7 1 2 3 2 3 5

1 5 3 6 4 2 5 3 2 3 5 4 3 3 2:   *soprano of* **656**

1 5 3 6 4 3 2 1 5 1 2 3 2 1 6:   *see* **1211**

452. 1 5 3 6 5 4 3 2 1 3 4 5 6 5 4   1 2 3 4 5 6 7 8
CMD   4v   H H F E H E H H
1760   *a* Stephenson
   P171   G   *a*   109
   P171.4   G   *a*   109

453. 1 5 3 6 5 6 7 1 2 3 2 4 3 2 1   1 2 3 $\overset{\frown}{4}$ $\overset{\frown}{5}$ M 6
886886   4v   H E H F F F H
1793
   [+]A131   E   *b*   536   HARMONY
   [+]A132   E   *c*   536   HARMONY

---

b West

c Hall

153 671 456 325 351:   *soprano of* **713**

454.   154 317 123 215 321   1 2 3 4 4
       LM   4v   H H F H H
       1793   *a* Coan
           A128   a   *a*   340   CORINTH
           A172   a   *a*   340   CORINTH

455.   154 321 123 223 127   1 2 3 4 5 6 7 8
       CMD   4v   H H H H F H F H
       1759   *a* French (*E*)
           P170   D   *a*   709
           P266   D   *a*   91   MARLOW

456.   154 321 212 314 555   1 2 3 4 3 3 4
       SM   4v   H H H H F H E
       -1755   *a* Tans'ur
          ⁺P142   a   *a*   456   GUILFORD
          ⁺P155   a   *a*   456   GUILFORD
           P155.2   a   *a*   456   GUILFORD
           P155.3   a   *a*   456   GUILFORD
           A28   a   *a*   456   GUILFORD
           A30   a   *a*   456   GUILFORD
           A31   a   *a*   456   GUILFORD
           A31.6   a   *a*   456   GUILFORD
           A31.7   a   *a*   456   GUILFORD
           A34   a   456   GUILFORD
           P210   a   *a*   456   GUILFORD
           A31.8   a   456   GUILFORD

457.   154 321 217 134 542   1 2 3 4
       CM   4v   F H F F
       c.1755
           P157   a   673

154 321 231 323 456:   *see* **458**

458.   154 321 232 323 456   1 2 2 3͡ 4 3͡ 4
LM   3v   H H H O F O F
-1789   *a* Broderip

[+]P269	G	*a*	578	BROMLEY
P269.2	G	*a*	578	BROMLEY
[+]P246.5[1,2]	G		37	BROMLEY
P269.3	G	*a*	578	BROMLEY
D6.11[1]	G	*a*	37	BROMLEY
D12[3]	G	*a*	37	BROMLEY
P303[1,2]	G		37	BROMLEY
A153[3,4]	G	*a*	37	BROMLEY
S6[4]	G	*a*		BROMLEY
P303.10[1,2]	G		37	BROMLEY
D6.12[1]	G	*a*	37	BROMLEY
P309[3,4]	G	*a*	421	BROMLEY
A183	G		578	BROMLEY
D6.13[1]	G	*a*	37	BROMLEY
A195[3]	G	*a*	37	BROMLEY
A198[3]	G	*a*	37	BROMLEY
P303.11[1,2]	G		37	BROMLEY

[1] 154 321 231 323 456

[2] 1 2 2 3͡ 4
H H H O F

[3] 4v

[4] 1 2 2 3͡ 4 3 4
H H H O F H F

459.   154 321 234 325 532   1 2 2 3 4
CM   4v   F H H O F
1754   *a* Costall

P151	a	*a*	201
P157	a	*a*	201
P198	g		201

Related to **733**.

---

460.   1 5 4   3 2 1   2 3 4   5 5 3   2 1 4   1   2   3   4   5   6   7   8   9   X   Y   Z
     CMT   4v   H   H   H   H   H   H   H   H   H   H   F   H
     1795
       A152   G   67   RESURRECTION

---

461.   1 5 4   3 2 1   2 3 6   5 4 3   2 5 3   1   2   3   4   4
     CM   4v   F   O   O   F   O
     1769   *a* Harrott
       P198   g   *a*   467

---

462.   1 5 4   3 2 1   3 4 3   2 1 3   1 6 2   1   2   3   3   4
     LM   4v   H   H   F   H   H
     1798   *a* Kyes
       A177   C   *a*   359   RESURRECTION
       A177.2   C   *a*   359   RESURRECTION

---

463.   1 5 4   3 2 1   4 3 2   3 2 1   5 3 2   1   2   3   4   5   6
     886886   3v   H   H   H   F   F   H
     1750
       P137   C   19

---

464.   1 5 4   3 2 1   4 5 1   7 5 4   4 3 1   1   2   3   4   5   6   5   6
     666688   4v   H   H   H   H   F   F   H   H
     1798   *a* Coan
       A177   e   *a*   401   DELIGHT
       A177.2   e   *a*   401   DELIGHT

---

465.   1 5 4   3 2 1   7 1 1   2 2 5   5 3 4   1   2   3   4
     LM   4v   H   H   H   F
     1750
       P134.2   G   518

466. 1 5 4 3 2 1 7 1 2 3 4 2 5 2 5   1 2 3 4 5 6 7 8
      CMD   4v   F F F F H H H H
      c.1752   *a* Knapp

P148	G	*a*	563	WINBORNE
P148.2	G	*a*	563	WINBORNE
P148.3	G	*a*	563	WINBORNE
P148.4	G	*a*	563	WINBORNE
P148.5	G	*a*	563	WINBORNE

467. 1 5 4 3 2 1 7 1 2 3 4 5 3 4 5   1 2 3 4 4
      CM   3v   F H H H H
      1789

P269	F	204	SOUTHWARK
P269.2	F	204	SOUTHWARK
P269.3	F	204	SOUTHWARK
D12[1]	F		SOUTHWARK NEW

---

[1] 4v

A variant of **1132.**

468. 1 5 4 3 2 1 7 1 5 4 3 2 2 3 2   1 2 3 4 3 4
      LM   4v   H F H H H H
      1786   *a* Harwood

P259	B♭	*a*	578	LICHFIELD

    1 5 4 3 2 3 1 2 1 1 7 1 2 3 1:   *soprano of* **472**

469. 1 5 4 3 2 3 2 1 2 3 4 5 5 4 3   1 2 3 4 5 6
      888888   4v   H H H H F F
      1789   *a* French (*A*)

A93	a	*a*	376	PREPARATION

470. 1 5 4 3 2 3 2 1 7 1 2 3 1 5 4   1 2 3 4 5 6 7 8
CMD   4v   H H H H H H H F
1750

    P137   G   812
    P157   G   812

471. 1 5 4 3 2 3 3 2 3 1 1 5 6 7 1   1 2 3 3 4
SM   4v   H H F H H
1793   *a* Coan

    A128   a   *a*   291   RESOLUTION
    A172   a   *a*   291   RESOLUTION

472. 1 5 4 3 2 3 3 3 2 1 7 1 3 4 3   1 2 2 3 4 4 4
CM   4v   F H F F H H F
1789   *a* Dixon

    P266   g   *a*   201   ROCHESTER

473. 1 5 4 3 2 3 4 2 1 2 3 4 6 6 4   1 2 3 4
CM   4v   H H H F
c.1746

    P129a   G   62
    P145a   G   62

    1 5 4 3 2 3 4 3 5 1 4 3 2 1 1:   *see* **1239**

474. 1 5 4 3 2 3 4 5 3 5 4 3 2 2 3   1 2 3 4 3̂ 4 3 4
CM   4v   H H H H F F H H
1786   *a* W. Billings

    A65   a   *a*   753   WHEELERS POINT
    A131   a   *a*   753   DARTMOUTH

1 5 4 3 2 3 4 5 5 3 4 2 3 4 4:   *see* **475**

475.   1 5 4 3 2 3 4 5 5 3 4 2 3 5 4   1 2 3 4

LM   4v   H H H F

c.1770-5

[+]P204	g	77	GREENWICH
[+]P220	g	77	ST. THOMAS'S
P266[1]	a	191	NORTHWOOD
P269[2,3]	a	72	BANBURY
P269.2[2,3]	a	72	BANBURY
D8[3]	a	684	CAMBRIDGE
P269.3[2,3]	a	72	BANBURY
D6.13[3,4]	a		HOLY LAND

---

[1]   1 5 4 3 2 3 4 5 5 4 3 2 3 5 4

[2]   1 2 3 4 4
    H H H F H

[3]   3v

[4]   1 5 4 3 2 3 4 5 5 4 3 2 3 4 4

1 5 4 3 2 3 4 5 5 4 3 2 3 5 4:   *see* **475**

476.   1 5 4 3 2 3 4 5 6 5 5 3 1 7 1   1 2 3 3 4

LM   4v   H H F H H

1793   *a* Coan

A128	a	*a*	378	PANTON
A172	a	*a*	378	PANTON

477.   1 5 4 3 2 3 5 4 2 1 7 1 2 3 4   1 2 3 4

CM   4v   H H H F

1759   *a* French (*E*)

P170	A	*a*	216	
P266	A	*a*	447	EGHAM

1 5 4   3 3 2   1 7 1   2 3 4   3 2 1:   *soprano of* **466**

478.   1 5 4   3 4 5   4 3 3   3 1 2   3 5 5   1 2 3 4
       SM   4v   H H F H
       1800   *a* Wilcockson
          A201   a   *a*   NEW FIELD

479.   1 5 4   3 4 5   4 3 4   5 1 6   1 5 7   1 2 3͡ 4
       SM   4v   H H F F
       1800   *a* Kimball
          A202   E   *a*   406   BRENTWOOD

480.   1 5 4   3 4 5   5 6 5   4 3 2   3 2 1   1 2 3 4 3 4
       CM   4v   H H H H F E
       1754-5   *a* Tans'ur
          P155   G   *a*   277   DORCHESTER
          P155.2¹   G   *a*   277   DORCHESTER
          A28¹   G   *a*   277   DORCHESTER
          A30¹   G   *a*   277   DORCHESTER
          A31¹   G   *a*   277   DORCHESTER
          A31.6¹   G   *a*   277   DORCHESTER
          A31.7¹   G   *a*   277   DORCHESTER
          A31.8¹   G   *a*   277   DORCHESTER
          A39¹   G   277   DORCHESTER
          A39.2¹   G   277   DORCHESTER

¹ 1 5 4   3 4 5   5 6 5   4 3 2   3 2 3

1 5 4   3 4 5   5 6 5   4 3 2   3 2 3:   *see* **480**

481.   1 5 4 3 4 5 6 7 7 5 4 3 4 5 5   1 2 3 4 3͡ 4
       LM   4v   H H H H F F
       1787   a W. Billings
            A77   f   a   357   CRUCIFIXION

482.   1 5 4 3 4 5 7 6 5 4 3 4 5 7 5   1 2 3 4 M 3 4
       CM   4v   H H H H F H H
       1778   a W. Billings
            A40   f♯   a   787   DUNSTABLE
            A40.2   f♯   a   787   DUNSTABLE
            A40.3   f♯   a   787   DUNSTABLE
            A40.4   f♯   a   787   DUNSTABLE

       1 5 4 3 4 6 5 4 3 2 3 5 3 6 5:   see **1204**

       1 5 4 3 5 1 3 2 2 3 3 2 1 2 1:   see **1196**

483.   1 5 4 3 5 1 7 1 3 3 2 1 6 2 1   1 2 3 4 5 6 7 8 5͡ 6͡ 7 8
       LMD   4v   H H H E H O H H F F O H
       1790   a Swan
            A96   C   a   748   CANTON
            A111   C   a   748   CANTON
            A132   C   a   748   CANTON
            A111.3   C   a   748   CANTON
            A111.4   C   a   748   CANTON
            A150   C   a   748   CANTON
            A111.5   C   a   748   CANTON
            A111.6   C   a   748   CANTON
            A167   C   a   748   CANTON
            A174   C   748   CANTON

484.   1 5 4   3 5 4   3 2 2   3 4 5   1 4 3   1 2 3 4
LM   4v   H H F H
1793
          A121   Eb   641   LONDON

485.   1 5 4   3 5 4   6 5 6   7 7 1   1 7 6   1 2 3 4 4 5 6 7 8
CMD   4v   H H H F H H H H F
c.1760
          P175   e   [1]   IPPLEPEN
          P175.2   e   [1]   IPPLEPEN
          P175.3   e   [1]   IPPLEPEN
          P175.4   e   [1]   IPPLEPEN
          P235   e   776   NORTHWALSHAM

[1] Text 652 or 776 indicated.

486.   1 5 4   3 6 5   1 5 4   3 2 1   5 3 3   1 2 3͡ 4
SM   4v   H H F O
1797   *a* Slater
          A167   G   *a*   9   HADLEY

1 5 4   4 3 5   6 3 4   5 4 3   5 3 1:   *soprano of* **673**

487.   1 5 4   4 3 5   6 4 3   3 2 2   7 5 1   1 2 3 4 4
CM   3v   H F H H H
c.1790   *a* Radiger
          D9   Eb   *a*   682   PROCLAMATION

488. 1 5 4 5 1 3 2 1 5 6 4 3 2 1 2   1 2 3 4 4
CM   4v   H E F F E
1760   *a* Stephenson

P171	G	*a*	277
P171.4	G	*a*	277

Cf. **489.**

489. 1 5 4 5 1 3 2 1 5 6 4 3 2 1 2   1 2 3 3 4 5 6 6
886886   4v   H H E H F H F E
1760   *a* Stephenson

P171	G	*a*	46
P171.4	G	*a*	46

Similar to **488** with solos added.

490. 1 5 4 5 2 3 4 5 3 2 7 3 4 5 4   1 2 3̂ M 4
CM   4v   H H F O H
1786   *a* Stone

A70	g	*a*	587	HADLEY
A74	g		587	HADLEY
A85	g		587	HADLEY
A131	g	*a*	584	HADLEY
A132	g	*a*	587	HADLEY
A163	g		584	HADLEY
A181	g		584	HADLEY

491. 1 5 4 5 2 3 4 5 5 4 5 3 1 2 3   1 2 3 3̂ 4 4
SM   4v   H H F F F H
1799   *a* Jenks

A187	a	*a*	182	WILTON

492.   1 5 4   5 3 3   1 2 3   1 2 3   4 3 2   1 2 3 4 4
       CM   4v   F E H F E
       1760   *a* Stephenson

P171	G	*a*	489	
P183	G		489	
P171.4	G	*a*	489	
P235	G		489	ST. EDMUND'S
A57	G		489	HANOVER
A57.2	G		489	HANOVER

493.   1 5 4   5 4 3   2 3 4   3 2 2   3 4 5   1 2 3 4 3 4
       CM   4v   H H H H F E
       1770   *a* W. Billings

A33	a	*a*	25	TAUNTON

494.   1 5 4   5 6 5   4 7 6   5 1 2   3 2 1   1 2 3 4 4
       LM   4v   E H F F H
       1793

A128	e	493	SUPPLICATION
A172	e	493	SUPPLICATION

495.   1 5 5   1 1 2   3 4 5   1 2 3   4 5 4   1 2 3 M
       LM   4v   H H F F
       1793   *a* Stone

A132	b	*a*	767	ABINGTON

496.   1 5 5   1 1 3   2 3 3   2 2 3   3 1 7   1 1 2 3 4 3 4
       LM   4v   F F H F F F H
       1794   *a* Belcher

A135	A	*a*	86	FARMINGTON

497. 1 5 5 1 1 7 1 5 5 3 4 5 1 3 3   1 2 3 4
SM   3v   H H F H
1800

A195	d		103	COMPASSION
A196	d		103	COMPASSION
A198	d		103	COMPASSION

498. 1 5 5 1 1 7 6 5 5 1 1 5 5 4 3   1 2 3 4
LM   4v   H H F H
1799   *a* Jenks

A187	e	*a*	230	CANAAN

499. | 1 5 5 1 1 7 6 5 5 6 5 4 3 2 3   1͡ 2 2 3 4 4 5͡ 6 7 8 8
CMD   4v   H F H F F H H F E H H
1759

P169	d		211	LOUGHBOROUGH
P169.2	d		211	LOUGHBOROUGH
A41	e	*b*	211	LOUGHBOROUGH
A43	e	*b*	211	LOUGHBOROUGH
A47a	e	*b*	211	LOUGHBOROUGH
A56	e		211	LOUGHBOROUGH
A84	e		211	LOUGHBOROUGH
A106	e	*b*	211	LOUGHBOROUGH

b J. Arnold

500. 1 5 5 1 2 1 2 2 3 2 1 1 2 1 7   1 2 3 4 5 6 7 8 7 8
CMD   4v   H H H H H H H H F H
1793

A121	F		2	VENGEANCE

501. 1 5 5 1 2 1 2 3 2 1 2 3 4 5 4   1 2 3 4 5 6 7 8 9 X Y Z Z
     LMT   4v   H H H H H H H H H F F F F H
     1800   *a* Doolittle
       A201   A   *a*   242   JEFFERSON

502. 1 5 5 1 2 3 4 5 4 3 2 2 5 4 3   1 2 3 4 4
     CM   4v   H H H F F
     c. 1800   *a* Cuzens
       D16   B♭   *a*   [1]   CHESTERFIELD

----
[1] Assigned to text 277, 525 or 815.

503. 1 5 5 1 3 2 2 2 2 3 4 3 1 4 2   1 2 1 2 3 3 4 4
     CM   3v   H H F F H F H H
     1799   *a* I. M. P.
       D6.13   C   *a*   284   CUMBERLAND STREET

504. 1 5 5 1 3 2 2 3 2 1 7 1 2 3 1   1 2 3 4 5 6 7 8
     LMD   4v   F H F F F F H H
     1796   *a* W. Smith
       A163   C   *a*   61   PEMBROKE
       A175   C   *a*   61   PEMBROKE
       A181   C   61   PEMBROKE
       A181.5   C   *a*   61   PEMBROKE

505. 1 5 5 1 3 2 3 1 1 2 3 2 1 7 6   1 1 2 2 3 3 3 4 5 5 6 6
     666688   4v   H H F H H F H H F F F F
     c. 1776
       P231   C   802

506.   1 5 5   1 4 3   2 1 7   1 5 1   2 3 2   1 2 3 4 3͡ 4

        CM   4v   H H E H F F

        1794   *a* W. Billings

          A136   C   *a*   47   ST. ANDREW'S

507.   1 5 5   1 5 1   2 3 2   1 6 5   5 6 5   1 2 3͡ 4 4

        CM   4v   H H F F E

        1795   *a* Storm

          A148   D   *a*   270   SOUNDING JOY

508.   1 5 5   1 5 6   5 4 3   2 2 1   2 3 2   1 2 3 4

        CM   3v   H F H F

        1799

          D15   F   488   BERWICK

Variant of **12.**

509.   1 5 5   1 7 1   2 1 7   6 5 5   1 7 1   1 2 2 3͡ 3 4 4

        XXXX   4v   H H H F F H H

        1792   *a* Hawley

         ⁺A116   d   *a*   10   BABEL

         ⁺A117   d   *a*   10   BABEL

510.   1 5 5   1 7 1   2 3 1   2 3 1   1 7 6   1 2 3 4

        LM   4v   H H F H

        1795   *a* N. Billings

          A150   C   *a*   61   OAKSCREEK

511. 1 5 5 1 7 1 3 2 2 1 2 3 1 2 5   1 2 3 4 5 6
XXXXYY   4v   H H H H F H
1799   *a* D. Merrill
  A188   C   *a*   223   VERMONT

512. 1 5 5 1 7 1 7 6 5 4 3 4 5 5 1   1 2 3 4 5 6 7 8 7 8
8866D   4v   H H H H F F F O H H
1793   *a* Shumway
  A131   f♯   *a*   361   BURLINGTON

513. 1 5 5 1 7 5 1 7 1 2 3 1 7 1 1   1 2 3 4
SM   4v   H H H F
1782   *a* Brownson

A47	d	*a*	5	NORFOLK
A51	d	*a*	16	NORFOLK
A62	d	*a*	16	NORFOLK
A67	d	*a*	5	NORFOLK
A80	d	*a*	5	NORFOLK
A62.3	d	*a*	16	NORFOLK
A114	d	*a*	16	NORFOLK
A80.4	d	*a*	5	NORFOLK
A114.B	d	*a*	16	NORFOLK
A131	d	*a*	5	NORFOLK
A145	d		5	NORFOLK
A148	d	*a*	16	NORFOLK
A150	d	*a*	16	NORFOLK
A80.5	d	*a*	5	NORFOLK
A167	d	*a*	16	NORFOLK
A172	d		5	NORFOLK
A200	d		16	NORFOLK

514.   1 5 5 1 7 6 5 4 3 5 4 3 2 2 3   1 2 3 4 3̑ 4
CM   4v   E E H H F F
1786   *a* French (*A*)

A71	f♯	*a*	570	BERWICK
A72	f♯	*b*	570	BERWICK
A131	f♯	*a*	570	BERWICK

b "Taken from Thomas" [i. e. from A71]

515.   1 5 5 2 3 4 5 4 3 2 1 2 2 1 2   1 2 3 4
LM   4v   H H H F
c.1776

P231	a	720

516.   1 5 5 3 1 1 7 6 7 5 6 7 1 7 1   1̑ 2 1̑ 2̑ 3 4̑ 4
CM   3v   F F F F H O F
1791   *a* Steffani

P291	G	*a*	20

517.   1 5 5 3 1 2 7 1 5 5 4 3 2 1 2   1 2 3 4
CM   4v   H E F F
1759

P169	G	798	WOODHOUSE
A17	G		PS. 15
A17.2	G		PS. 15
P212	G	473	WOODHOUSE
A37	G		
A39	G		
A39.2	G		
A53	G		PS. 15
A54	G		PS. 15
A56	G		PS. 15
A57	G		PS. 15
A57.2	G		PS. 15
A74	G		PS. 15

518.   1 5 5 3 1 3 4 5 5 1 7 6 5 4 5   1 2 3 4̂ 5̂ 6
888888   4v   H H H F F O
1786

    A68   e   658   HENSDALE

519.   1 5 5 3 1 3 5 4 3 2 3 2 1 2 4   1 2 3̂ 4
LM   4v   H H F F
1783   *a* Brownson

    A51   a   *a*   725   LITCHFIELD
    A62   a   *a*   725   LITCHFIELD
    A70   a   *a*   725   LITCHFIELD
    A74   a   725   LITCHFIELD
    A85   a   725   LITCHFIELD
    A87   a   725   LITCHFIELD
    A62.3   a   *a*   725   LITCHFIELD
    A92   a   *a*   725   LITCHFIELD
    A92.3   a   *a*   725   LITCHFIELD
    A101   a   725   LITCHFIELD
    A103   a   *a*   725   LITCHFIELD
    A113   a   *a*   435   LITCHFIELD
    A117   a   725   LITCHFIELD
    A146   a   725   LITCHFIELD
    A103.4   a   *a*   725   LITCHFIELD
    A103.5   a   *a*   725   LITCHFIELD
    A146.5   a   725   LITCHFIELD
    A167   a   *a*   725   LITCHFIELD
    A103.6   a   *a*   725   LITCHFIELD

520.   1 5 5 3 1 4 3 2 1 5 6 6 6 5 4   1 2 3 4̂ 5̂ 6
888888   4v   H H H F F O
1799   *a* Jenks

    A187   G   *a*   275?   CURIOSITY

235

521. 1 5 5 3 1 4 3 4 3 2 1 3 2 3 1   1 2 3 4
CM   4v   H H H F
1760   a Stephenson

P171	G	a	211
P182a	G		227
P228	G		227
P171.4	G	a	211

1 5 5 3 1 5 4 3 4 2 3 4 5 4 5:   *soprano of* **516**

522. 1 5 5 3 1 6 5 4 6 5 5 1 7 6 1   1 2 3 4 4 5 6 7 M 8
LMD   4v   H H H H O F F F F H
c.1796

A164	F		548	CYPRUS
A182	F		548	CYPRUS

523. 1 5 5 3 2 1 7 1 1 5 6 5 4 3 4   1 2 3 4 5 6 7 8 7 8 8
SMD   4v   H H H O F F F O H E H
1799   a Pilsbury

A189	b	a	282	MASSACHUSETTS

1 5 5 3 3 1 1 2 2 5 5 5 6 5 3:   *soprano of* **1005**

524. 1 5 5 3 3 7 7 5 5 3 5 6 4 5 5   1 2 3 4 5 6 7 8
CMD   4v   H H F F F H H H
1793   a Stone

A132	f♯	a	247	WARD

525. 155 345 543 213 543   1 2 3̂ M 3 4
      CM   4v   H H F F H H
      1794   *a* W. Billings
         A136   g   *a*   694   BROAD COVE

526. 155 351 712 321 764   1 2 3 4 3 4 4
      CM   4v   E H H H H F F
      c.1783   *a* Barwick
         P250   C   *a*   701   ST. DUNSTAN'S

527. 155 356 712 321 767   1 2 2 3̂ 4 5̂ 6 7 8̂ 8 8 8
      CMD   4v   H H H F F F F F F F F H
      1759
         P169   D   678   QUORNDON
         P169.2   D   678   QUORNDON
         P198   C   678   QUORNDON

528. 155 423 122 317 715   1 2 3̂ M 4
      CM   4v   H H F O E
      1786   *a* Canfield
         A72   a   *a*   508   DANBURY
         A85[1]   a   508   DANBURY
         A131[2]   a   *a*   508   DANBURY
         A158[1]   a   *b*   508   DANBURY
         A163[1]   a   *b*   508   DANBURY
         A164   a   508   DANBURY
         A174[2]   a   508   DANBURY
         A175[1]   a   *b*   508   DANBURY
         A181[1]   a   508   DANBURY
         A182   a   508   DANBURY
         A195[1]   a   *b*   508   DANBURY
         A198[1]   a   *b*   508   DANBURY
         A181.5[1]   a   *b*   508   DANBURY

[1] 155 423 122 321 771
[2] 155 423 322 317 715
b Read

529. 1 5 5 4 3 1 3 5 6 7 1 5 3 3 4   1 2 3̂ M̂ 3̂ 4
CM   4v   H H F F F F
1800   *a* Belknap
    A192   G   *a*   602   EAST NEEDHAM

530. [a ghost]

1 5 5 4 3 2 1 4 3 2 3 2 1 5 3:   *see* **1238**

531. 1 5 5 4 3 2 1 5 4 3 2 1 2 1 7   1 2 3 4
CM   4v   H H H F
c.1746
    P129a   G   233

532. 1 5 5 4 3 2 1 6 7 1 1 5 6 5 4   1 2 3̂ 4̂ 3̂ M̂
CM   4v   H H F F F F
1800   *a* Belknap
    A192   G   *a*   417   CARLISLE

533. 1 5 5 4 3 2 3 4 5 6 7 1 1 1 7   1 2 3 4̂ 5̂ 6
668668   4v   H H H F F O
1800
    A192   G   218   NEW HAVEN

1 5 5 4 3 2 7 5 5 4 3 2 1 3 5:   *see* **1221**

534.   155 435 321 233 212   1 2 3 4 5 6 7 8 7 8
       LMD   4v   H H H H H H F F F H
       1793   *a* Shumway
          A131   g   *a*   752   PENNSYLVANIA

535.   155 436 515 654 321   1 2 M 4
       SM   4v   H H F E
       1797   *a* Belknap
          A166   G   *a*   828   HOLLISTON
          A192   G   *a*   828   HOLLISTON

536.   155 511 711 765 654   1 2 3 4 5 M 6
       888888   4v   H H H F F O H
       1793   *a* Shumway
          A131   F   *a*   158   CRANBURY

537.   155 514 321 143 456   1 2 2 3 4 3 4 4
       CM   4v   H H H H H H F H
       c.1790   *a* Radiger
          D9   E   *a*   189   ATTENTION

538.   155 517 177 651 321   1 2 3 4 5 6 7 8
       LMD   4v   H H H H F F F O
       1797   *a* Belknap
          A166   e   *a*   437   NO. FOUR

       155 531 234 332 225:   *soprano of* **1188**

239

539. 1 5 5 5 3 1 2 3 5 6 5 5 5 5 3   1 2 3 4 5 6 6
888888   4v   H H E F H H H
c.1790-6

A102	F		244	SMYRNA
A110	F		244	SMYRNA

540. 1 5 5 5 3 2 1 7 1 2 3 4 5 5 3   1 2 3͡ 3 4
LM   4v   F F F F F
1782-3   *a* D. Read

A49	a	*a*	834	STRATFORD
A70	a	*a*	834	STRATFORD
A74	a		834	STRATFORD
A80	a	*a*	607	STRATFORD
A84	a		834	STRATFORD
A85	a		834	STRATFORD
A87	a	*a*	834	STRATFORD
A117	a	*a*	834	STRATFORD
A80.4	a	*a*	607	STRATFORD
A145	a		607	STRATFORD
A80.5	a	*a*	607	STRATFORD
A172	a		607	STRATFORD
A189	a	*a*	834	STRATFORD

1 5 5 5 3 2 2 2 3 4 2 3 5 4 3: *soprano of* **540**

541. 1 5 5 5 3 4 3 2 1 2 1 3 4 5 4   1 2 3͡ 4 4
CM   4v   H E O F H
1783   *a* Brownson

A51	f♯	*a*	453	NEWPORT
A62	f♯	*a*	453	NEWPORT
A62.3	f♯	*a*	453	NEWPORT

542.   1 5 5 5 4 2 1 7 2 5 6 5 4 5 4   1 2 3⌒4 3⌒4 M 4
      LM   4v   H H F F F F F H
      1793   *a* Stone
        A132   *a*   *a*   498   GARDINER

543.   1 5 5 5 4 3 2 2 3 3 4 4 5 5 5   1 2 3 4 4
      CM   4v   H H F F H
      c. 1800
        D17   *a*   190   PRINCES ST.

544.   1 5 5 5 4 3 5 1 5 6 4 5 1 7 6   1 2 3 4 5⌒6
      666688   3v   H H E H F F
      1793   *a* Russ
        A124   E♭   *a*   174   NEW HAMPSHIRE

545.   1 5 5 5 4 3 7 7 1 1 3 2 3 7 7   1 2 3⌒4 3⌒4
      SM   4v   H H F F O O
      1794   *a* Belcher
        A135   *g*   *a*   16   ST. MARK'S

546.   1 5 5 5 5 3 2 1 5 5 6 7 1 7 1   1 2 3 4 3⌒4 4 4
      CM   4v   H H H E F F F E
      1778   *a* W. Billings
        A40   G   *a*   558   MEDWAY
        A40.2   G   *a*   558   MEDWAY
        A40.3   G   *a*   558   MEDWAY
        A40.4   G   *a*   558   MEDWAY

547. 1 5 5 5 5 4 3 2 1 2 3 4 5 5 6   1 2 3 4 5͡ M 6 6 7͡ 8
CMD   4v   H H H H F O H H F F
1793

    A128   F   318   MORNING
    A172   F   318   MORNING

548. 1 5 5 5 5 4 3 2 1 3 5 5 7 6 5   1 2 3͡ 4 4
LM   4v   H H F F H
1793

    A128   e   378   REFUGE
    A172   e   378   REFUGE

549. 1 5 5 5 5 4 3 3 3 2 1 1 1 1 2   1 2 3͡ 4 3 4
CM   4v   H H F F H H
1793   *a* Wood

    A132   G   *a*   126   STILL RIVER

550. 1 5 5 5 5 6 7 5 4 3 4 5 5 6 7   1 2 3 4 5͡ 6 7 8
LMD   4v   H H H H F F H H
1800   *a* Howd

    A201   e   *a*   760   WHITES TOWN

551. 1 5 5 5 6 7 6 7 5 1 1 7 6 6 5   1 2 3 4 3͡ 4 4
LM   4v   H H H H F F H
1793   *a* Babcock

    A132   F   *a*   844   WRENTHAM

552. 1 5 5 6 4 3 2 3 2 1 5 6 7 1 1   1 2 3 4
CM   4v   H H F E
1791   *a* Holyoke

A105	G	*a*	674	HINSDALE
A163	G	*a*	674	HINSDALE
A175	G	*a*	674	HINSDALE
A175	G		674	HINSDALE
A181	G		674	HINSDALE
A190	G	*a*	674	HINSDALE
A181.5	G	*a*	674	HINSDALE
A195	G	*a*	674	HINSDALE
A198	G	*a*	674	HINSDALE

553. 1 5 5 6 4 5 6 5 4 3 4 5 5 1 7   1 2 3 4 5̑ 6 7 8
CMD   4v   H H H H F F H H
1793   *a* Kimball

A125	e	*a*	407	LEICESTER

1 5 5 6 5 3 3 2 2 3 4 5 1 7 6:   *soprano of* **295**

554. 1 5 5 6 5 4 3 2 1 2 3 5 4 3 4   1 2 3͡ M 3͡ M 3͡ 4
CM   4v   H H F F F O F O
1793   *a* Shumway

A131	g	*a*	610	LANCASTER

555. 1 5 5 6 5 4 3 4 3 2 2 3 5 3 2   1 2 3 4
CM   4v   H H F F
1760   *a* Stephenson

P171	G	*a*	594	
P182a	G		595	
P228	G		595	
P171.4	G	*a*	595	

556. 1 5 5 6 5 4 4 5 5 4 2 3 3 2 1   1 2 3 4
          LM   4v   H H H F
          c.1792
              D12   a   289   LEWTON

557. 1 5 5 6 5 6 7 1 1 1 5 6 5 4 3   1 2 3 4 3̂ 4
          LM   4v   H H H H F H
          1785   a D. Read
              A63   F   a   710   DOXOLOGY
              A63.2   F   a   710   DOXOLOGY
              A80   F   a   710   DOXOLOGY
              A80.4   F   a   710   DOXOLOGY
              A80.5   F   a   710   DOXOLOGY

558. 1 5 5 6 5 6 7 1 1 6 2 1 7 6 7   1 2 3 4̂ 4 4
          7787   3v   H H H F F H
          c.1800   a Harvey
              P321   D   a   HEAD OF THE CHURCH

559. 1 5 5 6 5 6 7 1 5 6 7 1 5 4 3   1 2 3 4 M 6
          666688   4v   H H H H F H
          1800   a Belknap
              A192   G   a   615   BERLIN

560. 1 5 5 6 6 1 7 1 5 6 5 4 3 2 5   1 2 3̂ 4 4
          CM   4v   H H F F E
          1795   a Edson
              A148   F   a   735   BOSTON

561. 1 5 5   6 6 7   7 1 7   6 5 4   3 2 1   1 2 3 4 4 3̑ M 3 4
CM   4v   H H H H H F O H H
1794   *a* W. Billings
   A136   F   *a*   417   WASHINGTON-STREET

   1 5 5   6 7 1   5 3 1   6 5 4   3 5 5:   *see* **1198**

562. 1 5 5   7 5 1   7 1 2   3 7 5   3 6 5   1 2 3 4 5̑ 6 5 6 7 8
SMD   4v   H H H H F F F H H H
1795   *a* N. Billings
   A150   c   *a*   749   SUPPLICATION

563. 1 5 5   7 5 3   2 2 1   2 3 1   2 1 7   1 2 3̑ 3 4 4
CM   4v   H H F F E H
1795   *a* Gillet
   A148   c   *a*   735   GRATITUDE
   A200   c   *a*   735   GRATITUDE

564. 1 5 5   7 5 6   5 4 3   2 2 3   3 5 4   1 2 2 3 4 4 5 6 7 8 8
CMD   4v   H H H E H H H H F H H
1759
   P169   G   753   THRUSSINGTON
   P169.2   G   753   THRUSSINGTON

565. 1 5 5   7 7 5   5 5 3   4 4 5   3 2 7   1 2 3̑ 4 4
LM   4v   H H F F H
1799   *a* D. Merrill
   A188   f♯   *a*   108   MOUNT VERNON

566. 1 5 5 7 7 5 5 5 5 5 5 5 1 7 6   1 1 2 3 4
LM   4v   H H H F F
1793   *a* Stone
    A132   f   *a*   359   STURBRIDGE

567. 1 5 6 3 4 5 4 3 2 4 3 2 1 3 4   1 2 3 4
8X8X   2v   F H H H
c. 1745   *a* Alcock
    P126   c   *a*   132
    P237[1,2]   d   *a*   132
    P269[3]   d   *a*   516   ELY
    P269.2[3]   d   *a*   516   ELY
    P269.3[3]   d   *a*   516   ELY

---

[1] 1 2 3 4 5 6 7 8
   F H H H H H H H

[2] 4v

[3] 3v

568. 1 5 6 4 2 3 2 5 5 1 6 7 5 3 7   1 1 2 3 M
CM   4v   F F O F F
c. 1775
    P228   G   6

569. 1 5 6 4 5 3 2 3 4 2 3 2 1 3 2   1 2 3 4 5 6 5 6
888888   4v   H H F F F F F F
1779   *a* Alcock
    P237   G   *a*   626   PS. 112 PROPER

Based on a non-fuging tune in P126.

570. 1 5 6 5 3 1 2 1 5 6 7 1 2 7 5   1 2 3 4 5 6 5̂ 6 7̂ 8 8
76767776   4v   E H C H H H F F H O H
1793   *a* Hall
      A132   F   *a*   118   DEVOTION

571. 1 5 6 5 3 1 5 3 1 6 5 6 7 1 5   1 2 3 4 5̂ 6̂ 7 8
LMD   4v   H H H H F F F H
1783   *a* Swan
      A51   F   *a*   603   BRISTOL
      A62   F   *a*   603   BRISTOL
      A62a   F   *a*   BRISTOL
      A67   F   *a*   578   BRISTOL
      A71   F   *a*   603   BRISTOL
      A80   F   *a*   342   BRISTOL
      A85   F   603   BRISTOL
      A87   F   603   BRISTOL
      A89   F   578   BRISTOL
      A91   F   *a*   603   BRISTOL
      A62.3   F   *a*   603   BRISTOL
      A92   F   *a*   603   BRISTOL
      A92.3   F   *a*   603   BRISTOL
      A98   F   *a*   603   BRISTOL
      A101   F   578   BRISTOL
      A103   F   *a*   603   BRISTOL
      A106   F   *a*   356   BRISTOL
      A108   F   *a*   603   BRISTOL
      A109   F   *a*   603   BRISTOL
      A106.4   F   *a*   356   BRISTOL
      A113   F   *a*   603   BRISTOL
      A114   F   *a*   603   BRISTOL
      A117   F   603   BRISTOL
      A119   F   *a*   603   BRISTOL
      A80.4   F   *a*   342   BRISTOL
      A114.B   F   *a*   603   BRISTOL
      A121   F   578   BRISTOL
      A124   F   *a*   603   BRISTOL
      A131   F   *a*   603   BRISTOL
      A132   F   *a*   603   BRISTOL
      A137   F   603   BRISTOL
      A145   F   342   BRISTOL   *571 continued*

A146	F		578	BRISTOL
A147	F	*a*	603	BRISTOL
A80.5	F	*a*	342	BRISTOL
A103.4	F	*a*	603	BRISTOL
A160	F	*a*	603	BRISTOL
A163	F	*a*	603	BRISTOL
A103.5	F	*a*	603	BRISTOL
A146.5	F		578	BRISTOL
A168	F	*a*	603	BRISTOL
A170	F	*a*	603	BRISTOL
A172	F		342	BRISTOL
A175	F	*a*	603	BRISTOL
A181	F		603	BRISTOL
A103.6	F	*a*	603	BRISTOL
A189	F	*a*	603	BRISTOL
A190	F	*a*	603	BRISTOL
A181.5	F	*a*	603	BRISTOL
A198	F	*a*	603	BRISTOL
A200	F	*a*	603	BRISTOL

572. 1 5 6 5 3 4 5 4 3 2 1 2 3 1 7   1 2 3 4
CM   4v   H O F F
1754

     P151   G   753

573. 1 5 6 5 3 6 5 6 1 5 6 5 1 5 5   1 2 2 3 4 5 6 6 7 8
LMD   4v   H H H H H F F H H E
1793   *a* Stone

     A132   F   *a*   45   WESTMINSTER

574. 1 5 6 5 3 6 5 6 1 7 6 5 6 7 1   1 2 3 4 5 6 7 M 7 8 7 8
CMD   4v   H H E H F F F F F F E H
1793   *a* Stone

     A131   F   *a*   741   MONMOUTH

156 536 715 356 555:   *see* **1212**

575.   156 536 765 121 565   1 2 3̂ 4̂ 4
       CM   4v   H H F F O
       1797
          A167   F   501   BRIDPORT

156 543 176 565 435:   *soprano of* **354**

576.   156 543 231 212 345   1 2 3 4
       CM   4v   H H F O
       1794   *a* Belcher
          A135   F   *a*   510   UNION

577.   156 543 335 566 771   1̂ 2 3 4 5 6 7 8
       LMD   4v   F O E H H H H H
       1789   *a* French (*A*)
          A93   F   *a*   185   ANNAPOLIS

578.   156 543 456 543 245   1 2 3̂ 4̂ M 3 4
       CM   4v   H H F F F H H
       1793   *a* Baird
          A132   a   *a*   765   WALTHAM

579.   156 543 456 545 534   1 2 3 4 5̂ 6̂ 7 8
       CM   4v   H H H H F F F H
       1793   *a* Stone
          A132   A   *a*   41   WATERTOWN

249

580.   1 5 6 5 7 7 1 7 5 7 2 7 5 1 7   1 2 3 3 4
       CM   4v   H H F H H
       c. 1790-6
          A102   d   750   DAMASCUS
          A110   d   750   DAMASCUS

       1 5 6 7 1 2 1 2 3 2 1 7 5 1 2:   *see* **629**

581.   1 5 6 7 1 2 3 2 1 4 3 5 1 2 3   1 2 3 4 5̑ 6 7̑ 8
       CMD   4v   H H H H F F E O
       1794   *a* Belcher
          A135   C   *a*   277   LINCOLN
       _____

       First note of tenor misprinted 2.

       1 5 6 7 1 2 3 2 2 3 4 3 3 2 1:   *soprano of* **629**

582.   1 5 6 7 1 3 1 1 5 1 2 7 5 1 1   1 2 3 4 3 4 5 6 7 8 7 8
       LMD   4v   H H H H H E F H H O E H
       c. 1790-6
          A102   C   476   REPROOF / PS. 141

583.   1 5 6 7 1 5 3 1 5 1 3 2 1 1 7   1 2 3 4 5 6 7 8
       CMD   4v   H H H H E H F H
       c. 1796   *a* Langdon
          A164   d   *a*   528   GROTON
          A182   d   *a*   528   GROTON

584.   1 5 6   7 1 5   4 3 2   3 3 4   3 2 2   1 2 3 4 5 6 7 8
SMD   4v   H H H E F F F F
1793   *a* Atwell
   A128   G   *a*   51   FRANKLIN
   A172   G   *a*   51   FRANKLIN

1 5 6   7 5 1   2 1 7   1 2 1   2 3 4:   *soprano of* **643**

585.   1 5 7   1 2 3   2 1 3   2 3 4   3 2 5   1 2 3 4
CM   4v   H H F O
1794   *a* Belcher
   A135   C   *a*   741   CONVERSION

586.   1 5 7   1 3 2   7 1 2   2 3 2   1 1 7   1 M 3 4 4 4
LM   4v   H O H F O H
c. 1776
   P231   C   239

587.   1 5 7   1 7 6   5 4 3   4 7 7   1 5 4   1 2 3 4 4
LM   4v   H H F O H
1800   *a* Hamilton
   A192   e   *a*   663   BURLINGTON

588.   1 5 7   5 3 5   4 3 5   5 5 7   1 5 1   1 2 3 4
SM   4v   H H H F
1783   *a* Brownson
   A51   e   *a*   353   WESTFIELD
   A62   e   *a*   353   WESTFIELD
   A62.3   e   *a*   353   WESTFIELD
   A98   e   *a*   353   WESTFIELD
   A109   e   *a*   353   WESTFIELD
   A114   e   *a*   353   WESTFIELD
   A114.B   e   *a*   353   WESTFIELD

157 666 543 243 456:   *soprano of* **710**

162 751 456 544 355:   *soprano of* **589**

589.   162 751 457 125 562   1 2 2 3 3 4 4
LM   4v   F H H H H F H
1791   *a* Callcott
   P291   C   687

590.   165 112 556 513 212   1 2 3 3 4
CM   3v   H H H C F
1789-   *a* Mason
   D8   C   *a*   553   GUILFORD

591.   165 123 321 432 511   1 2 3͡ 4
SM   4v   H H F F
1785   *a* D. Read
   A63   B♭   *a*   733   LISBON
   A63.2   B♭   *a*   733   LISBON
   A68   B♭   733   LISBON
   A80   B♭   *a*   733   LISBON
   A113   B♭   *a*   733   LISBON
   A119   B♭   *a*   733   LISBON
   A80.4   B♭   *a*   733   LISBON
   A121   B♭   733   LISBON
   A124   B♭   *a*   733   LISBON
   A145   B♭   733   LISBON
   A147   B♭   *a*   733   LISBON
   A158   B♭   *a*   733   LISBON
   A80.5   B♭   *a*   733   LISBON
   A160   B♭   *a*   733   LISBON
   A163   B♭   *a*   733   LISBON
   A168   B♭   *a*   733   LISBON

A170	B♭	*a*	733	LISBON
A172	B♭	*a*	733	LISBON
A174	B♭		733	LISBON
A175	B♭	*a*	733	LISBON
A181	B♭		733	LISBON
A190	B♭	*a*	733	LISBON
A195	B♭	*a*	733	LISBON
A198	B♭	*a*	733	LISBON
A181.5	B♭	*a*	733	LISBON

592. 1 6 5 1 2 3 4 3 2 3 3 2 3 1 7   1 2 3 4
LM   4v   H H H F
1760   *a* Stephenson

P171	C	*a*	720	
P171	C	*a*	720	
A57	C		720	HATFIELD
A57.2	C		720	HATFIELD

593. 1 6 5 3 1 2 2 1 7 6 1 7 5 1 1   1 2 3 4 5 6 M 6
666688   4v   H H H H F F O H
1793   *a* Stone

| A132 | C | *a* | 826 | CHARLTON |

594. 1 7 1 1 3 1 2 2 1 2 3 2 1 7 2   1 2 3 4 3 4 5 6
878787   4v   H H H H H H F H
1793

| A131 | a | 173 | ASHFIELD |
| A174 | a | 173 | ASHFIELD |

595. 1 7 1 2 1 2 2 3 4 3 1 2 3 5 3   1 2 3 4 3 4
LM   4v   E H H H F O
1794   *a* Belcher

| A135 | A | *a* | 29 | THE DAWN |

596.	1 7 1 2 3 1 5 7 1 1 1 7 1 3 5			1 2 3 4 5 6 7 8 7 8
	SMD			4v	H H H H H O F F H H
	c.1790-6				

	A102	a		353	PRUSSIA
	A110	a		353	PRUSSIA
	A164	a		353	LANGDON
	A174	a		353	PRUSSIA
	A182	a		353	LANGDON

597.	1 7 1 2 3 4 5 4 3 2 2 5 7 1 2				1 2 3 4 4 4
	CM			4v	H F F H E H
	1731-		*a* Bedford	

	P104	g	*a*	502
	P104.2	g	*a*	502
	P129a	g		502
	P145a	g		502

598.	1 7 1 3 2 1 2 1 7 1 1 1 5 6 5				1 2 3 4 M 6
	888888			4v	H H H F F H
	1786		*a* Ashton	

	P258	c	*a*	658	ORMSKIRK

599.	1 7 1 3 4 5 3 1 1 7 6 5 7 7 1			1 2 3 4 4
	CM		4v	H H F H E
	c.1790-6			

	A102	a	299	KINGSTON
	A110	a	299	KINGSTON

600.	1 7 1 5 5 5 6 5 6 3 3 3 4 3 4				1 2 3 3 4 3 4 4 5 6 7 8
	CMD			3v	H H H H H H H F H H H E
	1789		*a* T. Williams	

	P269	F	*a*	418	GEORGIA
	P269.2	F	*a*	418	GEORGIA
	P269.3	F	*a*	418	GEORGIA
	A183	F		835	GEORGIA

601. 1 7 1 5 7 1 2 3 3 2 3 2 3 1 1   1 2 3 4 5 6 7 8 8
LMD   4v   H H C H H F A H
1793   *a* Kimball

    A125   C   *a*   137   GLOUCESTER
    A181   C   137   GLOUCESTER
    A181.5   C   *a*   137   GLOUCESTER

1 7 1 6 4 3 2 5 3 1 4 5 6 7 1:   *soprano of* **1050**

602. 1 7 1 7 6 5 4 3 2 1 2 3 7 6 5   1 2 3 4 5 6
888888   4v   H H E H F E
c.1790-6

    A102   d   101   PALESTINE
    A110   d   101   PALESTINE

1 7 2 3 2 1 2 1 7 1 5 1 7 1 2:   *soprano of* **180**

603. 1 7 2 3 2 1 2 3 4 3 2 1 1 3 4   1 2 3 4
CM   4v   E F F E
c.1783   *a* Barwick

    P250   g   *a*   638   NEWINGTON

1 7 3 2 3 5 4 3 2 1 1 7 1 2 3:   *soprano of* **183**

604. 1 7 5 1 2 3 2 1 7 6 6 5 2 3 1   1 2 3 4 3͡ 4
LM   4v   H E F H F O
1754   *a* Everet

    P151   C   402
    P157   C   402
    P266[1]   C   *a*   402   ARABIA

---

[1] 1 2 3 4 3͡ 4
   H O F H F O

175 123 234 322 543:   *see* **96**

605.   175 123 543 271 171   1 2 3 4
        CM   4v   H H F E
        1793   *a* Wood
            A132   a   *a*   411   SOUTHBOROUGH

606.   175 123 617 117 275   1 2 3̂ 4̂ 4
        CM   3v   H H F F F
        1791   *a* Callcott
            P291   C   *a*   144

607.   175 131 271 321 712   1 2 3 4 3 4
        LM   4v   H H H H F H
        1789   *a* French (*A*)
            A93   a   *a*   641   MINDEN

608.   175 165 525 145 511   1̂ 2 3̂ 4̂ 5 6
        668668   4v   F O H O F H
        1792   *a* Cook
            A111   C   *a*   217   FRIENDSHIP
            A111.3   C   *a*   217   FRIENDSHIP
            A111.4   C   *a*   217   FRIENDSHIP
            A111.5   C   *a*   217   FRIENDSHIP
            A111.6   C   *a*   217   FRIENDSHIP

609.   175 171 711 713 221   1 2 3 4
        8886   3v   F F F H
        1765   *a* Stanley
            P191   F   *a*   523   PS. 33

610.	1 7 5 3 3 4 3 4 5 5 7 7 7 5 1			1 2 3͡ 4͡ 3 4
	LM		4v	H H F F F H
	1798		*a* Coan	
	A177	e	*a*	117	RECOVERY
	A177.2	e	*a*	117	RECOVERY

611.	1 7 5 5 2 3 4 3 2 1 1 3 4 5 3			1 2͡ 3 4 5 6 7 8 9 X Y͡ Z Y Z
	LMT		4v	E O O H H H H F H E F O H E
	1795		*a* D. Read	
	A157	a	*a*	181	HAMPSHIRE
	A172	a	*a*	181	HAMPSHIRE

612.	1 7 5 5 4 7 7 7 5 3 3 1 5 7 1			1 2 3͡ 4͡ 3͡ 4
	CM		4v	H H F F F O
	1793		*a* Stone	
	A132	c	*a*	252	SHOREHAM

613.	1 7 5 5 7 5 7 1 1 5 5 5 3 4 6			1 2 3͡ 4
	LM		4v	H H F F
	1785		*a* D. Read	
	A63	d	*a*	542	NAPLES
	A63.2	d	*a*	542	NAPLES
	A70	d	*a*	542	NAPLES
	A74	d		542	NAPLES
	A80	d	*a*	542	NAPLES
	A84	d	*a*	542	NAPLES
	A85	d		542	NAPLES
	A91	d	*a*	542	NAPLES
	A98	d	*a*	542	NAPLES
	A108	d	*a*	542	NAPLES
	A109	d	*a*	542	NAPLES
	A114	d	*a*	542	NAPLES
	A119	d	*a*	542	NAPLES
	A80.4	d	*a*	542	NAPLES
	A114.B	d	*a*	542	NAPLES

613 continued

A121	d		542	NAPLES
A124	d	a	542	NAPLES
A145	d		542	NAPLES
A147	d	a	542	NAPLES
A160	d	a	542	NAPLES
A80.5	d	a	542	NAPLES
A167	d	a	542	NAPLES
A168	d	a	330	NAPLES / PS. 139
A170	d	a	542	NAPLES
A172	d		542	NAPLES
A189	d	a	542	NAPLES
A190	d	a	542	NAPLES

614. 1 7 5 6 5 1 7 6 5 5 6 7 5 1 7   1 2 3 4 5 6 7 8 8 8
          7777D   4v   H H H H H H H F H H
          1785   *a* D. Read

A63	D	a	836	BARNSTABLE
A63.2	D	a	836	BARNSTABLE
A80	D	a	836	BARNSTABLE
A80.4	D	a	836	BARNSTABLE
A80.5	D	a	836	BARNSTABLE

1 7 5 6 5 4 5 6 7 5 1 7 6 7 6:   *see* **1231**

1 7 5 6 7 1 6 4 6 5 1 2 7 1 6:   *see* **1234**

1 7 5 7 1 2 5 5 1 2 3 2 1 7 1:   *soprano of* **646**

1 7 6 4 3 2 1 2 3 3 6 7 1 2 1:   *see* **1200**

615. 1 7 6 5 1 2 2 2 1 7 1 2 2 3 1 │ 1 2 3 4 5 6
      XXXXYY   4v   H H H H F H
      1793   *a* Wood
         A132   d   *a*   590   CANDIA

616. 1 7 6 5 1 2 3 4 5 5 5 4 2 3 2 │ 1 2 3 4
      CM   4v   F E H F
      1755
         P153   G   216
         P153.2   G   216
         P153.3   G   216

1 7 6 5 1 7 7 1 5 1 1 1 7 6 6: *alto of* **970**

617. 1 7 6 5 3 4 3 2 1 1 3 4 5 1 7 │ 1 2 3 4 4
      LM   4v   H H H F H
      1799   *a* FFitch
         P313   F   *a*   686   CHIGWELL

618. 1 7 6 5 3 4 5 6 5 5 3 5 1 1 7 │ 1͡ 2 3 4 3 4
      LM   4v   F F H H H F
      c.1800   *a* Cuzens
         D16   E♭   *a*   [1]   CUMBERLAND

---

[1] Assigned to text 159 or 234.

619. 1 7 6 5 3 5 6 5 4 3 4 5 3 4 3 │ 1 2 3 4
      CM   4v   F F H F
      1755
         P153   G   81
         P153.2   G   81
         P153.3   G   81

620. 1 7 6 5 4 3 2 1 2 3 3 4 5 6 5   1 2 3̑ M 3 4
      LM   4v   H H F F H H
      1793   *a* French (*A*)
         A121   d   *a*   56   TYOT

621. 1 7 6 5 4 3 4 5 3 2 3 2 5 4 5   1 2 3 4
      CM   4v   H E F H
      1760   *a* B. West (*E*)
         P173   C   *a*   821   TEMSFORD
         P173.2   C   *a*   821   TEMSFORD

      1 7 6 5 4 3 4 5 4 5 6 5 5 5 5:   *soprano of* **636**

622. 1 7 6 5 4 3 5 1 2 3 2 7 1 7 6   1 2 3 4 5 6 7 8
      LMD   4v   F H H H H H H H
      1759
         P169   C   480   BURTON
         P169.2   C   480   BURTON
         P198   B♭   480
         P212   C   480
         A41   C   *b*   480   BURTON
         A43   C   *b*   480   BURTON
         A47   C   480   BURTON
         A47a   C   *b*   480   BURTON
         A56   C   480   BURTON
         A84   C   480   BURTON
         A106   C   *b*   480   BURTON

      b Arnold

623. 1 7 6 5 4 3 5 1 2 5 5 4 3 6 6   1 2 3 4
      LM   4v   F F F F
      c.1775   *a* Senior
         P226   D   *a*   585

624. 1 7 6 5 4 3 5 6 5 5 5 6 7 1 2   1 2 3 4 4 5 6 7 8 8 8
  CMD   4v   F F H F F H H H H F F
  1759
      P169   C   595   SHEPSHEAD
      P169.2   C   595   SHEPSHEAD

625. 1 7 6 5 4 4 3 4 5 6 5 4 3 2 1   1 2 2 3 4 4
  LM   4v   F H H F A H
  1789   *a* Dixon
      P266   D   *a*   127   EMSWORTH

  1 7 6 5 5 6 5 4 3 2 7 1 5 5 5:   *alto of* **696**

626. 1 7 6 5 6 5 6 7 5 1 7 2 5 5 6   1 2 3 3 4
  CM   4v   F H F F F
  1794   *a* Belcher
      A135   D   *a*   566   ECSTACY

627. 1 7 6 5 7 1 2 3 1 4 3 2 5 3 4   1 2 3 4 4
  CM   4v   H H F H H
  1760   *a* B. West (*E*)
      P173   a   *a*   627   LONGBUCKLY
      P173.2   a   *a*   627   LONGBUCKLY

628. 1 7 6 7 1 1 1 1 4 3 3 3 3 2 1   1 2 2 2 3 4 4
  CM   3v   H F F O F H H
  1791   *a* Callcott
      P291   E♭   *a*   721

629.   1 7 6 7 1 2 1 2 3 2 1 7 5 1 2   1 2 2 3 4 4
       CM   4v   F O O O O O
       1757   *a* Everet
           P164   B♭   838
           P266[1]   B♭   *a*   838   STOCKWITH

---

   [1] 1 5 6 7 1 2 1 2 3 2 1 7 5 1 2

630.   1 7 7 1 1 7 1 2 7 1 2 3 1 7 5   1 2 3 4
       CM   4v   F F H F
       c.1775   *a* Senior
           P226   B♭   *a*   764

631.   1 7 7 1 2 3 1 7 6 5 7 1 2 3 4   1 2 3 4̂ 4
       LM   4v   H H H F F
       c.1800   *a* Cuzens
           D16   B♭   *a*   [1]   FALMOUTH

---

   [1] Assigned to "Ps. 87 (O.V., N.V. or Watts)," but the tune
   fits only N.V. (text 152) or Watts (text 143).

632.   1 7 7 1 2 3 3 4 3 2 2 3 3 4 2   1 2 3 4 5 6
       XXXXYY   4v   H H F H H H
       1790   *a* D. Read
           A96   a   *a*   564   ADMONITION
           A111   a   *a*   564   ADMONITION
           A111.3   a   *a*   564   ADMONITION
           A145   a   564   ADMONITION
           A111.4   a   *a*   564   ADMONITION
           A111.5   a   *a*   564   ADMONITION
           A111.6   a   *a*   564   ADMONITION
           A167   a   *a*   564   ADMONITION
           A172   a   564   ADMONITION
           A189   a   *a*   564   ADMONITION

1 7 7 1 2 3 3 4 4 5 5 5 4 3 4:   *soprano of* **1060**

1 7 7 1 2 3 4 3 2 1 7 1 2 3 6:   *soprano of* **526**

1 7 7 1 3 2 2 7 7 1 1 2 1 7 7:   *soprano of* **147**

633.	1 7 7 3 1 2 2 5 4 3 2 1 3 1 1			1 2 3 4
	SM		4v	H H F H
	1799		*a* Jenks	
	A187	a	*a*	90?	FAIR HAVEN

634.	1 7 7 3 4 3 4 5 4 5 3 1 7 5 7			1 2 3 4 4
	SM		4v	H H F H E
	1792		*a* Kyes	
	A111	a	*a*	509	MORTALITY
	A111.3	a	*a*	509	MORTALITY
	A111.4	a	*a*	509	MORTALITY
	A111.5	a	*a*	509	MORTALITY
	A111.6	a	*a*	509	MORTALITY
	A188	a		509	MORTALITY

635.	2 1 1 7 1 6 5 4 3 3 4 3 2 1 1			1 2 3 4
	LM		3v	H H F H
	1794		*a* Dupuis	
	P297	G	*a*	116	

2 1 7 1 2 3 3 2 1 7 7 1 2 3 4:   *soprano of* **848**

2 1 7 2 1 7 3 3 3 2 5 5 4 3 3:   *soprano of* **685**

636.   2 1 7 6 5 4 3 4 5 6 7 1 5 2 2   1 1 2 2 3 4 4 4
    CM   4v   F F F E F F F H
    1789
      P266   D   478   GIRTON

2 1 7 6 7 1 2 5 1 1 1 1 7 7 7:   *soprano of* **1040**

637.   2 2 2 3 2 3 4 3 2 1 2 5 1 1 1   1 2 3 4 4
    LM   4v   H H F F F
    1789   *a* French (*A*)
      A93   G   730   BEAUTY
      A121   G   730   BEAUTY
      A131   G   *a*   730   BEAUTY

638.   2 3 4 2 3 2 1 7 2 3 3 3 3 5 5   1 2 2 3 4
    CM   4v   H H H H F
    c.1775   *a* Senior
      P226   C   *a*   165

639.   2 3 4 2 4 3 4 5 3 5 6 4 5 3 3   1 2 3 4
    CM   4v   H F O O
    1754   *a* Everet
      P151   G   *a*   761
      P157   G   *a*   761
      P198   F   761
      P212   G   613
      P266[1]   G   703   DONCASTER

[1] 1 2 2 3 4 4
    H F F H O O

2 3 5 4 3 2 4 3 5 7 1 2 7 1 2:   *soprano of* **950**

640.   2 5 4 3 2 1 1 1 7 1 1 2 3 4 5   1 2 3 4 3 4
      LM   3v   H H H H O F
      1794   *a* R. Cooke
        P297   F   *a*   803

641.   2 5 4 3 2 1 2 1 3 2 1 7 3 4 5   1 2 3 4
      CM   4v   F H F H
      1759   *a* French (*E*)
        P170   G   *a*   838

642.   2 5 4 3 2 1 7 1 3 2 3 4 3 2 1   1 2 3 4
      CM   4v   F H H H
      1759
        P169   G   646   RUDDINGTON
        P169.2   G   646   RUDDINGTON

643.   2 5 5 4 3 5 5 6 5 6 5 6 5 4 3   1 2 3 4
      CM   4v   F H F H
      c.1775   *a* Senior
        P226   D   *a*   557

644.   2 5 5 5 4 4 4 4 3 3 3 3 2 7 7   1 2 3 4 5 6 6
      888888   4v   O F F F F F H
      1791   *a* Handel
        P291   f♯   *a*   676

645. 2 5 5 5 5 4 3 5 5 5 5 4 3 5 1   1 2 3 4 5 5 6 7 8
CMD   4v   H H H H C C H F H
c.1790   *a* M. Cooke
   P274   F   *a*   613

   2 5 6 7 1 2 3 2 1 4 3 5 1 2 3:   *see* **581**

646. 2 7 5 7 2 1 5 5 6 5 5 5 5 5 5   1 2 3 4 4
CM   4v   F H F F F
c. 1775   *a* Senior
   P226   D   *a*   785

647. 3 1 1 5 5 3 2 1 7 1 2 5 5 3 4   1 2 3 4
CM   4v   H H F F
1800   *a* Kimball
   A202   G   *a*   597   GORHAM

648. 3 1 1 5 6 5 6 5 4 3 4 3 2 1 3   1 2 3 4
CM   4v   F F H F
1750
   P137   G   681
   P253[1]   G   250   GAINSBOROUGH
   P253.2[1]   G   250   GAINSBOROUGH
   A79[1]   G   250   GAINSBOROUGH
   A87[1]   G   250   GAINSBOROUGH
   A117[1]   G   250   GAINSBOROUGH
   P253.4[1]   G   250   GAINSBOROUGH

---

[1] 1 2 2 3 4 4
   F F H H F F

Related to **662**.

3 1 1 6 3 3 3 2 3 4 3 2 7 6 5:   *soprano of* **115**

3 1 1 7 1 1 7 1 7 1 2 3 1 4 3:   *soprano of* **192**

649. 3 1 1 7 1 2 3 2 1 7 1 1 3 1 6   ‧1 2 M͡ 3͡ 4͡ 4
CM   4v   F O F F O O
1791   *a* Steffani
   P291   Bb   *a*   82

650. 3 1 2 3 1 1 7 1 3 4 4 3 3 3 2   1 2 3 4 5 6 7͡ 8
LMD   3v   H F F F H H H O
1794   *a* Atterbury
   P297   G   *a*   329

651. 3 1 2 3 3 4 3 2 3 5 5 5 5 5 5   1 2 3 4
LM   3v   H F H H
1794   *a* Atterbury
   P297   Eb   *a*   303

3 1 2 3 4 5 2 1 7 1 1 7 1 3 1:   *soprano of* **215**

652. 3 1 2 3 6 5 4 3 1 2 3 3 2 1 7   1 2 3 4 5 6 7 8 8
LMD   3v   H H H F H H H H H
1794   *a* Stevens
   P297   G   *a*   68

653. 3 1 3 1 1 1 7 1 7 6 5 6 6 6 3   1 2 3 4 4
          CM   4v   H H F H H
          1733   *a* Bedford
              D1   Bb   *a*   238

654. 3 1 3 3 2 3 2 1 7 2 2 1 1 2 3   1 2 2 3͡4 4͡3 4͡4 4 4
          CM   3v   F H H F O O O F F H H
          1791   *a* Hasse
              P291   F   *a*   479

655. 3 1 3 3 3 1 5 5 3 2 1 1 3 3 5   1 2 3 4 5 6
          XXXXYY   3v   H H H H F H
          1800   *a* Adams (*A*)
              A201   A   *a*   590   OLD 50TH

          3 1 3 4 6 7 1 6 3 5 2 1 7 2 3:   *soprano of* **966**

656. 3 1 4 1 1 1 7 1 3 4 3 4 5 4 3   1 1 2 2 3 4 4 5 6 7 8
          CMD   4v   H H H H E H H H H F H
          c.1790   *a* M. Cooke
              P274   Bb   *a*   612

          3 1 4 3 2 1 5 2 3 5 5 4 3 2 1:   *soprano of* **477**

          3 1 5 5 4 3 2 1 7 1 2 5 4 3 2:   *soprano of* **291**

657. 3 1 5 6 1 7 6 5 6 7 1 2 7 1 5   1 2 3 4 5 6 7 8 9 X X Y Z Z
    LMT   3v   H O O F F H H F H F F H H H
    1794   *a* R. Cooke
      P297   B♭   *a*   125

    3 1 7 1 2 1 7 6 5 6 7 1 7 3 2:   *soprano of* **263**

    3 1 7 1 2 3 1 2 3 4 3 2 3 3 7:   *soprano of* **251**

658. 3 1 7 1 3 1 7 1 1 2 2 2 2 1 7   1 2 3 4 5 6 7 8 8
    CMD   4v   H H F H H H F H H
    1791   *a* S. Arnold
      P291   C   *a*   664
      A156   C   840   FRANKLIN
      A162   C   840   FRANKLIN
      A203   C   840   FRANKLIN

659. 3 1 7 1 4 3 2 1 5 4 5 4 5 3 1   1 2 3 4 4
    SM   4v   H H F F O
    1793
      A128   a   368   RELIGION
      A172   a   368   RELIGION

    3 1 7 1 7 1 7 1 7 1 5 1 1 2 1:   *soprano of* **458**

660. 3 1 7 6 7 1 2 3 2 1 1 2 3 2 3   1 2 3 4 4
    CM   6v   F F O F F
    1757
      P164   B♭   793

661. 3 2 1 1 1 7 7 6 2 1 7 7 2 2 1   1 2 3 4 4 4
CM   3v   H H H F F O
1791   *a* Callcott

    P291   F   *a*   253
    A142   F   560   CUMBERLAND
    A162   F   560   CUMBERLAND
    A203   F   560   CUMBERLAND

3 2 1 1 2 1 7 1 3 2 2 1 7 6 5:   *soprano of* **1152**

662. 3 2 1 1 5 6 5 6 5 4 3 4 3 2 1   1 2 3 4 4
CM   4v   F F H F E
c.1755
    P157   G   681

See also **648**.

3 2 1 1 7 1 6 5 5 1 1 2 3 2 1:   *soprano of* **598**

3 2 1 2 1 1 7 1 5 3 2 1 3 2 2:   *soprano of* **617**

3 2 1 2 3 4 3 4 5 6 5 6 7 1 5:   *soprano of* **628**

663. 3 2 1 2 3 4 5 4 3 2 3 1 1 2 3   1 2 2 3 4 4
CM   4v   H H F F F H
1759
    P169   G   449   NORMANTON
    P169.2   G   449   NORMANTON
    P212[1]   G   449   NORMANTON

----

[1] 3 2 1 2 5 6 5 4 3 2 3 1 1 2 3

3 2 1 2 3 5 1 5 4 3 3 2 6 5 7:   *see* **1205**

3 2 1 2 5 4 3 4 3 2 1 7 1 1 1:   *soprano of* **171**

3 2 1 2 5 6 5 4 3 2 3 1 1 2 3:   *see* **663**

664. 3 2 1 3 2 1 6 6 5 4 3 2 1 5 5   1 2 3 3 4
    CM   4v   F O F F O
    1791   *a* Callcott
      P291   F   *a*   489

665. 3 2 1 4 3 2 3 2 3 4 3 2 1 7 1   1 2 3 4 4 4
    LM   4v   H F H H O H
    1789   *a* French (*A*)
      A93   A   *a*   71   BAGGADUCE
      A131[1]   A   *a*   71   BAGGADUCE

_____

[1] 3 2 1 4 3 2 3 2 3 4 3 2 1 7 7

3 2 1 4 3 2 3 2 3 4 3 2 1 7 7:   *see* **665**

666. 3 2 1 5 1 2 3 4 5 5 1 2 3 4 2   1 2 3 4 4
    7787   4v   H H F F F
    1799   *a* Pilsbury
      A189   A   *a*   188   CANAAN

667. 3 2 1 5 1 5 4 3 2 1 3 4 3 4 2   1 2 2 3 3 4 4
CM   3v   H H H H H F F
1799   *a* Hawes
    D15   F   *a*   284   LITTLEPORT

668. 3 2 1 5 5 4 3 2 3 5 6 5 6 5 4   1 2 3 4 3 4
CM   4v   H F E H H H
1760   *a* B. West (*E*)
    P173   F   *a*   494   CARRINGTON
    P173.2   F   *a*   494   CARRINGTON

669. 3 2 1 6 7 1 2 1 2 3 2 1 3 2 1   1 2 3 4 5 6
888888   3v   O F O H A H
1794   *a* Atterbury
    P297   G   *a*   139

    3 2 1 7 1 2 1 2 3 4 3 2 1 2 3:   *soprano of* **160**

670. 3 2 1 7 1 2 3 4 3 2 3 4 5 5 5   1 2 3 4 5 6
888888   2v   H H H H F F
1701   *a* R. King
    P51   F   *a*   350
    P51.2   F   *a*   350
    P51.3   F   *a*   350
    P51.4   F   *a*   350
    P80   F   *a*   607
    P89   F   529
    P135   F   556
    P134.2[1]   F   804
    P143[1]   F   *a*   350
    P144   F   *a*   350
    P182a   F   *a*   350

A22[1]	G		607	PS. 50
A22.2[1]	G		607	PS. 50
P144.4	F	*a*	350	
A22.3[1]	G		607	PS. 50
P266[2]	F	*b*	350	GAINSBOROUGH
P267[3]	F		350	

[1] 3v

[2] 4v

[3]
```
1 2 3 4 5 6
H H H H H F
```

b Top 2v are by Dixon.

3 2 1 7 1 5 5 5 4 4 3 3 3 2 2: *see* **1052**

3 2 1 7 5 3 6 4 5 1 7 1 2 3 3: *soprano of* **894**

671. 3 2 1 7 5 4 3 2 5 2 5 1 7 6 5   1 2 3 4 5̂ 6
     878747   4v   H F F H F F
     1792-

| | D12 | Eb | | 495 | KENTUCKY |

672. 3 2 1 7 6 2 1 7 3 2 1 1 3 3 3   1 2 2̂ 3 3 4
     LM   3v   H O H O H F
     1791   *a* Handel

| | P291 | | F | *a* | 720 |

3 2 1 7 6 5 4 3 4 5 6 7 1 2 3: *soprano of* **638**

673.   3 2 2 1 1 6 7 2 1 6 3 4 2 5 2   1 2 3 4 5 6 7 8 7 8
       CMD   4v   H H H H H H H H F H
       c.1790   *a* M. Cooke
         P274   G   *a*   160

674.   3 2 2 3 1 7 3 2 5 5 4 5 2 7 1   1 1 2 3 4 3 3 3 4
       CM   3v   C C H F O O H F H
       1791   *a* Handel
         P291   E♭   *a*   483

675.   3 2 2 3 4 3 2 1 3 4 5 6 5 4 2   1 2 3 4
       SM   4v   H H F F
       c.1746

P129a	a	706	
P148	a	706	STUDLAND
P148.2	a	706	STUDLAND
P148.3	a	706	STUDLAND
P148.4	a	706	STUDLAND
P148.5	a	706	STUDLAND

       3 2 2 3 4 5 4 3 2 1 1 5 3 4 2:   *soprano of* **649**

       3 2 3 1 6 7 1 5 4 3 4 3 5 1 1:   *soprano of* **1193**

676.   3 2 3 4 5 1 2 1 7 2 1 3 2 1 7   1 2 3 4 5 6 7 8 9 X Y Z
       LMT   3v   H H H H H H F F F F H H
       1794   *a* Shield
         P297   E♭   *a*   675

677.   3 2 3 4 5 4 3 2 7 1 2 3 4 3 2   1 2 3 4͡ 4

         CM   4v   H E F F F

         1754   *a* Everet

           P151   G   *a*   245

           P157   G   *a*   245

           P198[1]   F   245

---

     [1] 1 2 3 4

         H O F F

      3 2 3 4 5 6 1 7 1 2 1 5 4 3 4:   *soprano of* **1051**

      3 2 3 4 6 5 4 3 2 1 5 5 4 3 2:   *soprano of* **144**

678.   3 2 5 1 2 3 6 5 4 3 2 1 1 7 2   1 2 3 4 5 6 7 8

         CMD   4v   H E H H E H F H

         1760   *a* B. West (*E*)

           P173   F   *a*   445   LEICESTER

           P173.2   F   *a*   445   LEICESTER

      3 2 5 5 4 3 2 3 4 3 2 1 3 2 5:   *soprano of* **606**

      3 2 5 5 6 7 1 7 7 7 1 1 7 6 5:   *soprano of* **1060**

      3 2 7 1 2 3 4 5 5 5 4 3 4 3 2:   *soprano of* **1060**

      3 2 7 1 5 3 4 3 2 5 5 5 4 3 2:   *soprano of* **1112**

3 2 7 1 5 3 5 6 4 5 7 3 7 1 2: *tenor of* **1060** *in* P292

679. 3 2 7 3 2 5 4 3 3 1 5 5 6 5 3   1 2 3 4 5 5 6 7 8 8
      CMD   4v   H H F H H H H F H H
      c. 1790   *a* M. Cooke
         P274   G   *a*   133

680. 3 3 1 1 1 6 4 3 2 3 1 1 7 7 2   1 2 2 3 4 3 4
      LM   3v   H H H C H F H
      c. 1788   *a* Dalmer
         P263   A   *a*   363

681. 3 3 1 2 2 1 5 5 4 3 4 1 2 3 5   1 1 2 3 4 5 6 6 7 8 9 X Y Z
      LMT   4v   E F F H H F H H E H E E O F
      c. 1775   *a* Senior
         P226   B♭   *a*   146

3 3 2 1 1 2 7 1 3 2 1 7 6 5 1: *soprano of* **1083**

682. 3 3 2 1 1 7 7 1 2 3 4 2 1 7 1   1 2 3 4 4 3 4 4
      SM   4v   H H H H H F H H
      1798   *a* Loder
         P310   B♭   *a*   702

683. 3 3 2 1 1 7 7 1 2 5 1 1 1 1 1   1 2 2 3 4 4 4
      LM   4v   H H F F O O O
      1791   *a* Handel
         P291   G   *a*   273

684.   3 3 2   1 2 1   1 2 7   1 2 3   3 3 1   1   2   2   3   4   4   5   6   6   7   8   8   7   8
      CMD   4v   H   F   H   H   C   F   E   F   H   H   H   H   F   H
      c.1785   *a* Tremain
        P256   A   *a*   277

      3 3 2   1 2 5   1 2 7   2 5 6   7 2 5:   *soprano of* **1192**

685.   3 3 2   1 3 2   1 4 4   4 3 4   4 5 4   1   2   3   4   4   4   4
      LM   4v   F   F   F   F   O   F   F
      1791   *a* Graun
        P291   G   *a*   496

686.   3 3 2   1 5 4   3 2 3   3 2 3   4 5 3   1   2   3   4   4
      LM   3v   H   H   H   F   H
      1794   *a* Haydn
        P297   E♭   *a*   65

      3 3 2   1 5 6   5 4 3   5 1 7   6 5 6:   *soprano of* **119**

      3 3 2   1 7 1   2 3 1   1 1 7   1 1 4:   *soprano of* **475**

      3 3 2   3 1 7   7 1 2   3 4 5   5 4 5:   *soprano of* **600**

687.   3 3 2   3 3 2   1 7 3   2 1 7   6 7 1   1   2   3   4   4   5   6   7   7   8
      LMD   4v   H   H   H   F   H   H   H   C   O   E
      1798   *a* Cantelo
        P310   F   *a*   739

688. 3 3 2 3 4 3 2 1 2 3 6 5 4 5 5   1 2 3 4
CM   3v   H H F H
-1784   *a* Milgrove

    ⁺P242   A   HUNTINGDON
    ⁺P253¹   A   *a*   769   BATH CHAPEL
    P253.2¹   A   *a*   769   BATH CHAPEL
    P266¹   G   444   BATH CHAPEL
    P253.4¹   A   *a*   769   BATH CHAPEL

¹ 4v

3 3 2 3 4 5 4 3 2 1 7 1 7 1 1:   *soprano of* **921**

3 3 2 5 6 4 3 7 7 1 2 4 5 5 5:   *soprano of* **51**

3 3 2 7 3 2 1 7 1 3 2 2 5 3 1:   *soprano of* **23**

689. 3 3 3 1 2 3 2 1 7 2 3 4 3 2 1   1 2 2 3 4
CM   4v   H H H H F
1773
    P212   C   815
    P235   C   447   CHEDISTON

690. 3 3 3 2 1 1 2 3 1 2 3 5 4 5 6   1 2 3 4
CM   4v   H F H F
-1749
    ⁺P135   G   372
    P137¹   G   444
    P130.2   G   444   YARMOUTH
    ⁺P145a   G   444
    P152   G   *b*   444   DOVER

P155a	G	444	
P157[1]	G	444	
P174	G	445	YARMOUTH
P174.10	G	445	YARMOUTH
P220	G	827	YARMOUTH
P235	G	444	DOVER
P174.11	G	445	YARMOUTH
P174.12	G	445	YARMOUTH
D15[2,3]	G	506	BATHFIELD

[1] 1 3 4 5 1 1 2 3 1 2 3 5 4 5 6

[2] 1 2 2 3 4
   H F H H F

[3] 3v

b "From A. Adams"

691.   3 3 3 2 1 2 3 3 5 5 4 3 2 3 2   1 2 3 4 5 6 6
       6 6 6 6 8 8   3v   H H H H F H H
       1800   *a* Kimball
          A202   D   *a*   618   NEW YEAR

692.   3 3 3 2 1 7 1 2 3 4 3 2 3 7 1   1 2 3 4 4
       LM   4v   H F H F H
       1786   *a* Ashton
          P258   B♭   *a*   159   MOSLEY STREET

693.   3 3 3 2 1 7 1 7 6 5 6 7 1 3 2   1 2 3 4 5 6 7 8 9 X
       8 8 8 8 8 D   3v   F H H H H H H H H H
       1794   *a* Dupuis
          P297   G   *a*   212

694.   3 3 3 2 2 2 2 3 3 7 1 2 3 4 3   1 2 3 4
       LM   3v   F F F F
       1791   *a* Pergolesi
          P291   E♭   *a*   499

3 3 3 2 2 3 3 2 3 4 2 3 4 5 3:   *soprano of* **630**

3 3 3 2 3 4 5 3 3 2 1 4 3 2 2:   *soprano of* **1128**

695.   3 3 3 3 1 7 1 3 4 5 4 3 2 1 7   1 2 3 4 3 4
    LM   4v   O H H H F E
    c.1755
      P157   C   628

3 3 3 3 2 1 7 6 6 7 1 7 6 1 7:   *soprano of* **210**

3 3 3 3 2 7 3 2 1 2 3 4 3 3 3:   *soprano of* **131**

3 3 3 3 3 3 3 3 1 2 2 2 2 2 5:   *soprano of* **2**

3 3 3 3 4 3 2 1 2 3 4 3 4 5 5:   *soprano of* **313**

3 3 3 3 5 2 3 4 3 3 5 3 5 2 3:   *soprano of* **4**

3 3 3 4 2 3 3 3 2 3 2 3 2 2 7:   *soprano of* **558**

696.   3 3 3 4 4 1 4 3 2 1 7 2 5 3 3   1 2 2 3 4 4
    CM   3v   O O F O F F
    1791   *a* Handel
      P291   Bb   *a*   308

697.   3 3 3   4 4 2   2 3 5   5 4 4   3 3 2   1 2 3 4 5 6 7 8
       LMD   3v   H O F F F H H H
       1794   *a* Webbe
          P297   f   *a*   759

       3 3 3   4 4 4   3 4 5   5 1 7   1 5 3:   *soprano of* **9**

       3 3 3   4 5 6   4 4 5   5 3 3   3 4 5:   *soprano of* **914**

       3 3 3   5 5 7   1 5 5   6 5 4   3 2 1:   *see* **337**

698.   3 3 4   2 3 3   3 6 5   4 3 2   3 5 1   1 2 3 4 5 6 7 8 8 8
       LMD   3v   H H H H H H H H F H
       1800   *a* Kimball
          A202   D   *a*   360   SHIRLEY

699.   3 3 4   3 1 2   1 2 1   7 1 7   1 2 2   1 2 3 4
       LM   3v   H H F H
       1794   *a* Wight
          P297   E   *a*   25

700.   3 3 4   3 2 1   1 7 1   2 1 3   2 1 2   1 2 3 4
       LM   3v   H H O F
       1794   *a* Haydn
          P297   E♭   *a*   307

701. 3 3 4 3 2 3 2 1 2 2 3 4 5 6 5   1 2 3 4
CM   3v   H F C H
1794   *a* J. S. Smith[1]
    P297   C   *a*   448

---

[1] "The style from Morley"

702. 3 3 4 3 3 2 1 7 1 2 1 5 1 2 3   1 1 2 3 3 4 5 6 6
888888   3v   H H F F H F H H F
1791   *a* Handel
    P291   e   *a*   248

3 3 4 3 4 5 6 5 3 4 6 5 3 2 3:   *soprano of* **1124**

3 3 4 3 6 5 4 3 3 5 4 3 2 1 7:   *soprano of* **1114**

3 3 4 3 6 7 6 5 4 5 6 4 3 6 1:   *soprano of* **1146**

703. 3 3 4 5 3 4 3 2 1 1 2 3 5 4 3   1 2 3 4 3 4
CM   3v   H H H H H F
1763   *a* Hopkinson?
    A18   G   *a*   474   PS. 4

704. 3 3 4 5 4 3 2 1 1 7 1 3 4 5 3   1 2 3 4 3 4 4
CM   4v   H H H H F F F
c.1790   *a* Collins
    P273   a   *a*   319

705. 3 3 4 5 4 3 2 3 4 2 5 3 2 1 7   1 2 3 4 5 6 7 8 9 X Y Z Y Z
      LMT   3v   H H H H H H H F H H H H O H
      1793   *a* Handel
        A130   G   *a*   342   PS. 148

      Cf. **979.**

      3 3 4 5 4 3 2 7 1 7 1 2 3 4 5:   *soprano of* **846**

706. 3 3 4 5 5 1 7 1 5 5 5 5 2 3 6   1 2 3 4 4
      LM   3v   H F F O H
      1794   *a* Atterbury
        P297   E♭   *a*   672

707. 3 3 4 5 5 4 3 4 3 3 2 5 1 7 1   1 2 3 4 3 4 4
      LM   4v   H F H H H H H
      c. 1785
        P255   A   794

      3 3 4 5 5 5 6 7 7 5 5 5 7 1 5:   *soprano of* **861**

      3 3 4 5 5 6 6 6 5 5 6 5 4 3 2:   *soprano of* **49**

708. 3 3 4 5 6 5 5 5 4 5 7 6 5 5 4   1 2 2 3 3 4
      LM   4v   H H H F H H
      1798   *a* Loder
        P310   E♭   *a*   273

334 571 761 555 323:   *soprano of* **1086**

709.   335 112 342 155 567   1 2 3 4 3 4 5 5 6 7 8 8 8
      LMD   4v   H H F F H H H H H F H H E
      1794   *a* Olmsted

A141	C	*a*	136	WETHERSFIELD
A203	C	*a*	136	WETHERSFIELD

335 432 321 237 155:   *soprano of* **886**

710.   335 444 321 721 234   1 2 3 4 5 6
      888888   3v   H H F F H H
      1794   *a* Webbe

P297	E	*a*	643

711.   335 543 235 555 245   1 2 3 4 5 6 7 8
      LMD   4v   H H F H H H H H
      c.1785   *a* Tremain

P256	G	*a*	719

712.   335 554 435 555 553   1 2 3 4 5 6 7 8
      CMD   4v   H H H H H H E F
      c.1785   *a* Tremain

P256	G	*a*	609

713.   335 645 651 553 364   1 2 3 4 5 6
      XXXXXX   4v   H F F F H F
      c.1790   *a* M. Cooke

P274	F	*a*	830

3 3 6 5 5 6 7 1 6 5 5 5 4 3 3:   *soprano of* **3**

714. 3 3 7 5 4 3 6 3 2 3 5 4 4 5 7   1 2 3 4
      LM   3v   H H F F
      1790
          P270   A   119   ACTON

715. 3 4 2 1 7 1 1 2 4 3 2 3 3 4 2   1 2 3 4 5 6 7 8
      SMD   4v   F F F F H H O F
      1794   *a* Belcher
          A135   F   *a*   200   ST. PAUL'S

3 4 2 3 1 2 7 1 4 3 5 4 3 2 1:   *see* **1226**

3 4 2 3 4 5 4 5 3 4 5 6 5 5 4:   *soprano of* **1113**

716. 3 4 3 2 1 7 1 3 2 1 7 1 5 5 5   1 2 2 3 3 4 5 6 6 6
      888888   4v   F O C H H C C H H C
      1791   *a* S. Arnold
          P291   G   *a*   114
          A153   G   *a*   114   SOUTHWARK

717. 3 4 4 2 2 1 2 4 2 1 7 1 5 5 5   1 2 3 4
      CM   4v   H H F F
      1791   *a* Buononcini
          P291   c   *a*   390

285

3 4 4 3 5 1 1 7 1 5 5 4 5 2 5:   *soprano of* **1169**

3 4 5 1 2 3 4 5 4 3 5 1 7 6 5:   *soprano of* **5**

718.	3 4 5 1 2 3 6 4 3 2 1 7 2 1 1			1 2 3 4 4
	CM		4v	H H F H H
	c.1790		*a* Radiger	
	D9	C *a*	366	ONLY PORTION

3 4 5 1 6 7 1 2 3 3 4 5 1 6 7:   *soprano of* **165**

3 4 5 1 7 6 5 4 3 5 6 1 4 3 3:   *soprano of* **1118**

3 4 5 1 7 6 5 4 5 6 5 4 4 3 3:   *soprano of* **912**

719.	3 4 5 3 4 5 4 5 2 5 5 5 2 1 1			1 2 3 4 3 4
	CM		4v	H H H E F E
	-1755		*a* Tans'ur	
	⁺P142	G *a*	515	UPPINGHAM
	⁺P155	G *a*	515	UPPINGHAM
	P155.2	G *a*	515	UPPINGHAM
	P155.3	G *a*	515	UPPINGHAM
	A28	G *a*	515	UPPINGHAM
	A30	G *a*	515	UPPINGHAM
	A31	G *a*	515	UPPINGHAM
	A31.6	G *a*	515	UPPINGHAM
	A31.7	G *a*	515	UPPINGHAM
	P210	G *a*	515	UPPINGHAM
	A31.8	G *a*	515	UPPINGHAM

345 345 654 323 453:   *soprano of* **151**

345 432 123 433 245:   *soprano of* **888**

720. 345 432 172 345 432   1 2 3 4 5 6
666666   4v   H H H F F H
1755
    P153   a   254
    P153.2   a   254
    P182a   a   254
    P228   a   254
    P153.3   a   254

345 432 323 322 344:   *soprano of* **159**

721. 345 435 171 322 173   1̑ 2 3 4 5 6̑ 7 8
LMD   3v   F F H F H O F H
1794   *a* Webbe
    P297   B♭   *a*   708

722. 345 435 413 655 654   1 2 2 3 4
LM   4v   H H F H H
1791   *a* Handel
    P291   G   *a*   358

345 516 251 123 451:   *soprano of* **155**

345 543 234 565 443:   *soprano of* **162**

723. 3 4 5 5 5 3 7 1 3 2 3 4 5 2 1   1 2 3 4
CM   4v   H E F H
1793   *a* Coan
A128   a   *a*   251   BETHEL
A172   a   *a*   251   BETHEL

3 4 5 5 5 4 3 6 6 6 7 1 7 6 5:   *soprano of* **164**

3 4 5 5 5 6 6 5 5 3 4 4 3 2 3:   *soprano of* **163**

724. 3 4 5 6 3 4 1 6 2 4 3 2 3 1 7   1 2 3 4 5 6 6
888888   4v   H H F F F F O
1791   *a* Callcott
P291   G   *a*   442

3 4 5 6 5 1 2 3 4 3 2 2 3 4 5:   *soprano of* **172**

3 4 5 6 5 4 3 2 3 4 2 5 4 3 2:   *soprano of* **167**

3 4 5 6 5 4 3 2 3 4 3 5 5 5 5:   *soprano of* **150**

3 4 5 6 5 4 3 4 3 2 3 3 4 5 5:   *soprano of* **1041**

3 4 5 7 1 4 3 4 3 2 1 3 6 5 5:   *soprano of* **986**

3 5 1 2 3 3 7 1 2 1 5 3 1 2 5:   *soprano of* **670**

725. 3 5 1 3 2 3 4 5 5 3 1 6 4 2 5   1 2 2 3 4 ⌢4
      CM   4v   H F O O F F
      1754   *a* Everet
         P151   G   *a*   622
         P157   G   *a*   622
         P198   F   622
         P266   G   *a*   622   OWSTON

726. 3 5 1 7 1 6 7 1 7 1 7 5 7 1 2   1 2 3 4 4
      LM   3v   H H H F H
      1791   *a* Handel
         P291   E♭ *a*   387

3 5 1 7 6 5 4 3 5 5 4 5 5 5 4:   *soprano of* **1011**

727. 3 5 2 3 2 1 7 1 5 1 1 2 1 4 3   1 2 2 3 4
      CM   4v   F F H F F
      c.1755
         P157   a   213
         P198[1]   g   213

      ───────────
      [1] 3 5 2 3 2 1 7 1 5 1 1 2 1 5 3

3 5 2 3 2 1 7 1 5 1 1 2 1 5 3:   *see* **727**

289

728. 3 5 3 1 3 5 5 5 3 1 3 2 4 3 2   1 2 3 4 5 6 7 7 8 7 8
CMD   3v   H H H H H H F H H H H
1800
   A195   G   1   MANTUA
   A196   G   1   MANTUA
   A198   G   1   MANTUA

729. 3 5 3 2 3 4 3 2 3 5 6 5 6 7 1   1 2 3 4
CM   4v   H H H F
c.1800   *a* Harvey
   P321   G   *a*   447   NEWBURY

730. 3 5 3 4 2 3 4 5 5 5 4 3 2 2 5   1 2 3 4 4
LM   3v   F E F H H
1794   *a* M. Cooke
   P297   e   *a*   405

   3 5 3 5 6 5 4 3 2 1 5 4 3 5 3:   *soprano of* **339**

731. 3 5 3 5 6 5 4 3 2 1 7 1 3 4 5   1 2 3 4 4 5 6
888888   4v   H F O F F F O
1757
   P164   G   591
   P198   F   591

732. 3 5 4 3 2 1 2 3 4 5 4 3 2 3 5   1 2 3 4 5 6 7 8 7 8
CMD   4v   F F F H H H H H H H
1795
   A152   G   271   MESSIAH

733. 3 5 4 3 2 1 3 5 5 4 3 2 3 2 1   1 2 3 4 3 4
CM   4v   F H H H H F
1759

P169	A	201	WOODTHORPE
P169.2	A	201	WOODTHORPE

Related to **459.**

3 5 4 3 2 1 7 1 4 3 2 1 7 1 5:   *soprano of* **279**

734. 3 5 4 3 2 3 2 1 7 1 3 2 3 4 3   1 2 3 4 4
CM   4v   H H F H H
c.1752   *a* Knapp

P148	g	*a*	624	LONG FLEET
P148.2	g	*a*	624	LONG FLEET
P148.3	g	*a*	624	LONG FLEET
P148.4	g	*a*	624	LONG FLEET
P148.5	g	*a*	624	LONG FLEET
A39	g		624	LONG FLEET
A39.2	g		624	LONG FLEET
A54	g		624	LONG FLEET
A56	g		624	LONG FLEET

735. 3 5 4 3 2 3 4 5 4 5 5 3 2 1 5   1 2 3 4 3 4 4
LM   4v   F E F H H O O
1754   *a* Everet

P151	G	*a*	794	
P157	G	*a*	794	
P198	F		794	
P266	G	*a*	794	HUNGERFORD

736.	3 5 4	3 2 3	5 4 3	1 7 6	3 2 1		1	2	3	4	3	4		
	CM				4v		C	H	C	H	F	E		
	1754-5			*a* Tans'ur										
	P155	G	*a*	40		WESTERHAM								
	P155.2	G	*a*	40		WESTERHAM								
	P155.3	G	*a*	40		WESTERHAM								
	A28	G	*a*	40		WESTERHAM								
	A30	G	*a*	40		WESTERHAM								
	A31	G	*a*	40		WESTERHAM								
	A31.6	G	*a*	40		WESTERHAM								
	A31.7	G	*a*	40		WESTERHAM								
	P210	G	*a*	40		WESTERHAM								
	A31.8	G	*a*	40		WESTERHAM								

3 5 4 3 5 1 7 5 6 5 4 3 3 5 7:   *soprano of* **1025**

737.	3 5 4	3 5 3	7 1 2	1 2 3	2 3 4		1	2	2	2	3	4
	CM				4v		H	H	H	H	H	F
	c.1775			*a* Senior								
	P226	C	*a*	135								

738.	3 5 4	4 3 1	7 1 1	1 6 1	5 4 3		1	2	3	4	5	6	7	8
	LMD				3v		H	H	F	H	H	H	H	H
	1794			*a* Stevens										
	P297	E♭	*a*	512										

739.	3 5 4	4 3 3	4 2 3	3 2 3	4 5 4		1	2	3	4	3	4
	LM				4v		F	F	F	F	H	H
	1750												
	P137		a	720									
	P157		a	720									

3 5 4 5 6 7 1 7 1 7 6 5 5 4 3:   *soprano of* **997**

3 5 5 1 3 6 5 4 4 3 4 5 1 6 5:   *soprano of* **1137**

3 5 5 1 6 5 4 3 3 2 5 4 3 2 3:   *soprano of* **145**

3 5 5 3 1 5 5 5 5 4 3 2 3 6 5:   *soprano of* **1117**

3 5 5 3 4 5 6 2 5 5 3 6 5 4 4:   *soprano of* **148**

3 5 5 4 3 4 5 3 2 1 2 3 4 3 2:   *see* **1223**

3 5 5 4 3 4 5 6 5 5 5 2 3 4 5:   *soprano of* **869**

740. 3 5 5 5 4 2 3 3 5 5 5 3 4 4 4   1 2 3 4 5 6 7 8
66664444   4v   H H H H H F F O
c.1785
    P256   G   802

741. 3 5 5 5 5 4 3 2 1 2 5 4 3 4 3   1 2 3 4
CM   4v   H F F F
1769   *a* Harrott
    P198   G   *a*   326

3 5 5 5 5 5 4 3 2 3 1 1 7 2 2:   *counter of* **776**

3 5 5 5 5 5 5 1 1 1 2 1 7 1 1:   *soprano of* **772**

742.	3 5 5 6 6 7 2 1 1 1 2 3 2 1 1			1 2 3̂ 4 4
CM			3v	H H F F H
1794		*a* Callcott		
P297	G	*a*	338	

3 5 5 6 7 3 7 1 7 5 4 3 4 3 5:   *see* **743**

743.	3 5 5 6 7 3 7 1 7 6 5 3 4 3 5			1 2 3 4 5̂ 6̂ 7̂ M
LMD			4v	H H H H F F F O
1791		*a* Hall		
A108	c	*a*	456	ALL SAINTS NEW
A111	c	*a*	456	ALL SAINTS
A119	c	*a*	456	ALL SAINTS NEW
A121[1]	c		456	ALL SAINTS NEW
A130[2]	c	*a*	456	ALL SAINTS NEW
A131[2]	c	*a*	456	ALL SAINTS NEW
A132	c	*a*	456	ALL SAINTS NEW
A111.3	c	*a*	456	ALL SAINTS
A145	c		456	ALL SAINTS
A147	c	*a*	456	ALL SAINTS NEW
A111.4	c	*a*	456	ALL SAINTS
A158	c	*a*	456	ALL SAINTS NEW
A111.5	c	*a*	456	ALL SAINTS
A163	c	*a*	456	ALL SAINTS NEW
A111.6	c	*a*	456	ALL SAINTS
A164[1]	c	*a*	456	ALL SAINTS NEW
A170	c	*a*	456	ALL SAINTS NEW
A172	c		456	ALL SAINTS

A175[2]	c	a	456	ALL SAINTS NEW
A181[2]	c		456	ALL SAINTS NEW
A182[1]	c	a	456	ALL SAINTS NEW
A189	c	a	456	ALL SAINTS NEW
A181.5[2]	c	a	456	ALL SAINTS NEW
A200[3]	c	a	456	ALL SAINTS NEW

---

[1] 5 5 5 6 7 3 7 1 7 5 4 3 4 3 5

[2] 3 5 5 6 7 3 7 1 7 5 4 3 4 3 5

[3] 5 5 5 6 7 3 7 1 7 6 5 3 4 3 5

744. 3 5 6 4 5 3 4 2 3 1 2 3 4 5 4   1 2 3 3 4 4
CM   4v   F F H F F H
1769   *a* Harrott
   P198   G   *a*   599

745. 3 5 6 5 3 4 5 1 5 5 6 5 5 4 5   1 2 3 4 4 4
CM   4v   H F O F F F
1791   *a* Handel
   P291   F   *a*   771

746. 3 5 6 5 3 4 5 6 5 3 6 5 4 2 3   1 2 3 4 5 6 7 8
CMD   4v   H H H H F F H H
c.1757
   P166   C   27

747. 3 5 6 5 4 3 1 4 2 3 2 1 3 4 2   1 2 3 4
CM   4v   O F O F
1754   *a* Everet
   P151   G   *a*   838
   P198   F   838

748.　3 5 6　5 4 5　5 4 3　2 1 7　1 5 5　　1　2　3　4　3　4
　　　CM　　　　　　　　　　　　　　4v　　H　H　H　E　H　F
　　　c.1783　　　　　　　　　　*a* Barwick
　　　　　P250　　　　　G　　*a*　　133　　MONGHAM

749.　3 5 6　6 6 6　5 5 6　5 5 2　3 1 3　　1　2　3　4̂ 4̂ 4
　　　LM　　　　　　　　　　　　　　3v　　H　H　H　O　F　F
　　　1793　　　　　　　　　　　*a* Kimball
　　　　　A125　　　　　G　　*a*　　601　　BOXFORD
　　　　　A147　　　　　G　　*a*　　601　　BOXFORD

750.　3 5 7　1 7 1　2 1 7　1 7 1　2 1 7　　1　2　3̂ 4̂ 4
　　　LM　　　　　　　　　　　　　　4v　　O　F　F　F　F
　　　1791　　　　　　　　　　　*a* Graun
　　　　　P291　　　　　b　　*a*　　533
　　　　　A161[1]　　　b　　　　533　　FRANCE
　　　　　A162[1]　　　b　　　　533　　FRANCE
　　　　　A203　　　　　b　　　　533　　FRANCE

────────────

[1]　3 5 7　1 7 2　2 1 7　1 7 1　2 1 7

3 5 7　1 7 2　2 1 7　1 7 1　2 1 7:　*see* **750**

3 6 5　4 5 6　1 5 5　5 5 3　2 2 2:　*soprano of* **467**

751.　3 7 1　2 7 1　1 1 2　3 5 5　1 7 5　　1　2　2　3̂ 4　5　6　7　8
　　　CMD　　　　　　　　　　　　　4v　　F　F　H　F　O　H　F　F　E
　　　c.1775　　　　　　　　　　*a* Senior
　　　　　P226　　　　　a　　*a*　　469

752.   3 7 7   2 5 5   5 5 5   5 4 3   2 1 1   1 2 3 4 4

      CM   4v   H F F H H

      c.1775   *a* Senior

         P226   g   *a*   450

753.   4 2 5   5 5 6   6 5 6   7 1 2   5 1 7   1 2 3 3 4 4

      CM   4v   F F F F H H

      1791   *a* Callcott

         P291   B♭   *a*   474

754.   5 1 1   1 1 2   7 1 1   5 5 5   4 3 4   1 2 3 4 5 6 7 8

      CMD   4v   H H H H F F O O

      1793   *a* R. Munson

         A128   d   *a*   571   ETERNITY

         A172   d   *a*   571   ETERNITY

      5 1 1   1 1 3   3 2 2   5 5 5   5 6 7:   *see* **755**

755.   5 1 1   1 1 3   3 2 3   5 5 5   5 6 7   1 1 2 3 3 4 5 5 6 7 7 8 8

      CMD   4v   H H H H H H F H H H H H H

      1779   *a* Gillet

         A43   a   *a*   584   JUDGMENT

         A56   a   *a*   584   JUDGMENT

         A84[1]   a   584   JUDGMENT

---

[1]   5 1 1   1 1 3   3 2 2   5 5 5   5 6 7

756.	5 1 1	1 1 3	3 3 3	5 5 3	1 4 3	1 2 3 4 4
	LM				4v	H H F F H
	1778			*a* W. Billings		
	A40	C	*a*		35	HEATH
	A40.2	C	*a*		35	HEATH
	A40.3	C	*a*		35	HEATH
	A40.4	C	*a*		35	HEATH

5 1 1   1 1 3   3 4 4   4 3 2   5 3 5:   *soprano of* **768**

757.	5 1 1	1 1 7	1 1 3	3 3 2	1 1 3	1 2 3 M 4
	SM				4v	H H F F H
	1789			*a* Wood		
	A94	D	*a*		55	DOOMS DAY
	A130	D	*a*		55	DOOMS DAY
	A147	D	*a*		55	DOOMS DAY
	A167	D	*a*		55	DOOMS DAY
	A168[1]	D	*a*		55	DOOMS DAY
	A170	D	*a*		55	DOOMS DAY
	A200	D	*a*		55	DOOMS DAY

[1] 5 1 1   1 7 1   1 1 3   3 3 2   1 1 3

758.	5 1 1	1 2 1	7 1 2	3 3 1	2 3 2	1 2 3 4
	SM				4v	H H F H
	1800					
	A195	C			57	BETHSAIDA
	A196	C			57	BETHSAIDA
	A198	C			57	BETHSAIDA

759. 5 1 1 1 2 3 1 7 6 5 5 1 1 1 3   1 2 3 4 3 4 4

LM   4v   H H H H F F H

1794   *a* W. Billings

    A136   C   *a*   344   INVOCATION

760. 5 1 1 1 2 3 1 2 1 1 1 2 2 3 5   1 2 3 4 4 4

CM   4v   H H F F E H

1783   *a* Swan

A51	C	*a*	696	RAINBOW
A60	C		696	RAINBOW
A62	C	*a*	696	RAINBOW
A62a	C	*a*		RAINBOW
A67	C	*a*	696	RAINBOW
A70	C	*a*	696	RAINBOW
A74	C		696	RAINBOW
A85	C		696	RAINBOW
A89	C		696	RAINBOW
A91	C	*a*	696	RAINBOW
A62.3	C	*a*	696	RAINBOW
A92	C	*a*	696	RAINBOW
A95	C		696	RAINBOW
A92.3	C	*a*	696	RAINBOW
A98	C	*a*	696	RAINBOW
A101	C		696	RAINBOW
A103	C	*a*	696	RAINBOW
A106	C	*a*	696	RAINBOW
A108	C	*a*	696	RAINBOW
A109	C	*a*	696	RAINBOW
A106.4	C	*a*	696	RAINBOW
A113	C	*a*	696	RAINBOW
A114	C	*a*	696	RAINBOW
A119	C	*a*	696	RAINBOW
A114.B	C	*a*	696	RAINBOW
A124	C	*a*	696	RAINBOW
A131	C		696	RAINBOW
A146	C		696	RAINBOW
A147	C	*a*	696	RAINBOW
A103.4	C	*a*	696	RAINBOW
A160	C	*a*	696	RAINBOW

A103.5	C	*a*	696	RAINBOW
A146.5	C		696	RAINBOW
A168	C	*a*	696	RAINBOW
A170	C	*a*	696	RAINBOW
A103.6	C	*a*	696	RAINBOW
A190	C	*a*	696	RAINBOW
A198	C	*a*	696	RAINBOW

761. 5 1 1 1 2 3 2 1 5 6 2 1 7 1 3   1 2 3 4
CM   4v   H H F H
1800

A196	B♭		632	REVIVING HOPE

762. 5 1 1 1 2 3 2 3 4 3 2 5 5 5 6   1 2 3 3 4
CM   4v   F F H H F
c. 1800   *a* Key

P323	G	*a*	586	

5 1 1 1 2 3 2 3 4 3 5 5 5 5 6:   *soprano of* **762**

763. 5 1 1 1 2 3 3 1 6 2 3 1 7 7 1   1 2 3 4 5 6
668668   4v   H H H F F F
1794   *a* D. Read

A145	C	*a*	301	HAMILTON
A172	C	*a*	301	HAMILTON

764. 5 1 1 1 2 3 3 3 3 2 1 3 4 3 2   1 2 3 4
CM   4v   H H F F
1800

A192	C		179	GOSHEN

300

765. 5 1 1 1 2 3 4 3 2 2 3 3 4 4 5   1 2 3 4 3 4 4
      CM   4v   H H F H F H O
      1786/7   *a* Harris
          A72   a   *a*   351   CRUCIFIXION
          A98   a   *a*   351   CRUCIFIXION
          A109   a   *a*   351   CRUCIFIXION
          A114   a   *a*   351   CRUCIFIXION
          A119   a   *a*   351   CRUCIFIXION
          A114.B   a   *a*   351   CRUCIFIXION
          A158   a   *b*   351   CRUCIFIXION
          A163   a   *b*   351   CRUCIFIXION
          A175   a   *b*   351   CRUCIFIXION
          A181   a   351   CRUCIFIXION
          A181.5   a   *b*   351   CRUCIFIXION

      b D. Read

766. 5 1 1 1 2 3 4 4 4 5 4 3 2 4 3   1 2 3 4 3 4
      CM   4v   H H F F F F
      1794   *a* W. Billings
          A136   C   *a*   531   GILEAD

767. 5 1 1 1 2 3 4 5 5 6 5 4 3 2 5   1 2 3 4 3 4
      CM   4v   H H F F H H
      1793   *a* West
          A131   e   *a*   99   MORPHEUS

768. 5 1 1 1 3 1 1 1 1 2 5 1 1 7 1   1 2 3 4 5 6 7 8 8
      CMD   4v   H H F H H H F H H
      c.1790   *a* M. Cooke
          P274   B♭   *a*   138

301

769. 5 1 1 1 3 1 7 6 5 4 5 5 1 1 5   1 2 2 3 4 4
LM   4v   H E E F H H
c.1790-6   *a* Lee

	A102	d		731	SCOTLAND
	A110	d		731	SCOTLAND
	A167	c	*a*	731	SCOTLAND

770. 5 1 1 1 3 2 2 2 3 2 1 1 2 1 7   1 2 3 4 3 4
CM   4v   H H F F H H
1800   *a* Jenks

| | A201 | C | *a* | 271? | POUNDRIDGE |

771. 5 1 1 1 6 5 5 5 7 1 2 3 2 1 7   1 2 3 4 3 M 4
CM   4v   H H F F F O H
1793   *a* Stone

| | A132 | C | *a* | 172 | OXFORD |

5 1 1 1 7 1 1 1 3 3 3 2 1 1 3:   *see* **757**

772. 5 1 1 1 7 1 2 1 2 3 3 3 4 3 2   1 2 3 4 5 6 7 8
SMD   4v   H H H H F F H H
1786   *a* Corelli

| | P258 | C | *a* | 64 | LONSDALE |

773. 5 1 1 1 7 1 2 3 3 2 7 5 7 1 1   1 2 3 4 5 6
666688   4v   H H H H F F
1783   *a* O. King

	A51	C	*a*	633	HEBRON
	A62	C	*a*	633	HEBRON
	A62.3	C	*a*	633	HEBRON

A124	C	*a*	633	HEBRON
A148	C	*a*	633	HEBRON
A150	C	*a*	633	HEBRON
A160	C	*a*	633	HEBRON

774. 5 1 1 1 7 1 5 6 5 4 3 4 5 6 5   1 2 3 3 4
 SM   4v   H H F F H
 1788

A85	E	90	STODDARD
A189[1]	E	90	MOUNT CARMEL

---

[1] 1 2 3 M M 4
   H H F F O H

775. 5 1 1 1 7 1 7 1 5 5 4 4 3 3 4   1 2 2 3 4 4
 LM   3v   H H H F H H
 1794   *a* Haydn
   P297   C   *a*   620

776. 5 1 1 1 7 5 4 4 4 3 1 7 7 7 7   1 2 2 3 4 4 3 4 4 4
 CM   3v   F F H F F F H H H H
 1791   *a* Handel
   P291   D   *a*   761

777. 5 1 1 2 1 4 3 2 2 1 7 1 2 1 7   1 2 3 4 5 6 7 M 8
 LMD   4v   H H H H F F F F H
 1786   *a* Carpenter
   A67   C   *a*   364   PS. 145

778.   5 1 1   2 1 7   6 5 3   4 3 2   1 5 5   1 2 3 4 3 4 4 4 5 6 7 8 7 8
CMD   4v   H H H H F F F F F O A H H H
1789   *a* French (*A*)
  A93   E   *a*   420   BABEL

779.   5 1 1   2 1 7   6 5 5   1 5 6   6 6 5   1 2 3 4 5 6 7 8
CMD   4v   H H H H F O H E
1794   *a* Belcher
  A135   D   *a*   398   BLISS

5 1 1   2 2 3   2 1 7   6 6 5   5 1 7:   *soprano of* **775**

780.   5 1 1   2 3 2   1 5 4   5 4 3   2 3 2   1 2 3 3 4 4
CM   4v   E H F H H H
1795   *a* N. Billings
  A150   D   *a*   552   BOYLSTON

781.   5 1 1   2 3 2   1 7 1   1 7 7   5 5 5   1 2 3 4
CM   4v   H H F H
1793   *a* Canfield
  A128   e   *a*   694   WILMINGTON
  A172   e   *a*   694   WILMINGTON

782.   5 1 1   2 3 3   4 5 4   3 3 2   1 1 7   1 2 3 4
CM   4v   H F F F
c.1790   *a* Radiger
  D9   B♭   *a*   652   PROSPECT

783. 5 1 1 2 3 3 4 5 6 5 4 3 5 6 5   1 2 3 4 5 6 7 8 5 6 7 8
      66664444   4v   F H H H H H H H H H H H
      1795

       A152   G   729   PROTECTION

784. 5 1 1 2 7 1 2 3 1 2 3 2 1 7 6   1 2 3 4͡
      LM   4v   H H F F
      1786   *a* D. Read

       A72   C   *a*   576   DEVOTION
       A85   C   576   DEVOTION
       A124   C   *a*   576   DEVOTION
       A158   C   *a*   576   DEVOTION
       A160   C   *a*   576   DEVOTION
       A163   C   *a*   576   DEVOTION
       A175   C   *a*   576   DEVOTION
       A180   C   576   DEVOTION
       A181   C   576   DEVOTION
       A190   C   *a*   576   DEVOTION
       A181.5   C   *a*   576   DEVOTION
       A195   C   *a*   576   DEVOTION
       A198   C   *a*   576   DEVOTION

785. 5 1 1 2 7 5 7 1 3 6 7 1 7 6 5   1 2 3 4 3 4
      CM   5v   H H H H F H
      c.1755

       P157   D   709

786. 5 1 1 2 7 6 5 1 3 2 2 3 3 2 1   1 2 3 4͡ 5 6
      888888   4v   H H H F F H
      1798   *a* Brooks

       A177   d   *a*   658   ENTREATY
       A177.2   d   *a*   658   ENTREATY

787. 5 1 1 3 1 2 5 3 2 1 7 1 1 3 3   1 2 M 4 5 6 7 8 7 8
          SMD   4v   H H F H H H H H H H
          1799   *a* Jenks
               A187   C   *a*   283?   SALEM

788. 5 1 1 3 1 6 2 3 2 1 3 4 3 2 1   1 2 3̑ M 4
          CM   4v   H H F O H
          1793
               A128   B♭   331   VESPERS
               A172   B♭   331   VESPERS

789. 5 1 1 3 2 1 2 4 3 2 1 7 1 1 3   1 2 3 3 4
          SM   4v   H H F H H
          1793   *a* Holden
               A124   C   *a*   596   CONCORD
               A160   C   596   CONCORD
               A168   C   596   CONCORD
               A170   C   *a*   596   CONCORD
               A177   C   *a*   596   CONCORD
               A177.2   C   *a*   596   CONCORD
               A189   C   596   CONCORD
               A190   C   *a*   596   CONCORD
               A195   C   596   CONCORD
               A198   C   596   CONCORD

790. 5 1 1 3 2 1 5 4 3 2 2 5 4 3 2   1 2 3 4
          LM   3v   E F H F
          1760   *a* Stephenson
               P171   C   *a*   168   CHRISTMAS HYMN
               A31   C   168   CHRISTMAS HYMN
               A31.6   C   168   CHRISTMAS HYMN
               A31.7   C   168   CHRISTMAS HYMN
               A34   C   168   CHRISTMAS HYMN
               A31.8   C   168   CHRISTMAS HYMN

A39	C		168	CHRISTMAS HYMN
P171.4	C	*a*	168	CHRISTMAS HYMN
A39.2	C		168	CHRISTMAS HYMN
A54	C		168	CHRISTMAS HYMN
A56	C		168	CHRISTMAS HYMN
A57[1]	C		168	CHRISTMAS HYMN
A57.2[1]	C		168	CHRISTMAS HYMN
A84[1]	C		168	CHRISTMAS HYMN

[1] 4v

Cf. **242.**

791. 5 1 1 3 2 1 7 1 1 1 3 2 1 7 1   1 2 3 4 3 4 5 6 7 8 M 8
CMD   4v   H H F F F F F F F O H
1793   *a* Stone

A132	C	*a*	266	GRAFTON
A167	C	*a*	266	GRAFTON

792. 5 1 1 3 2 1 7 1 5 6 5 4 3 4 7   1 2 3 M 3 4
CM   4v   H E F F H E
1797   *a* Belknap

A166	d	*a*	415	MALDEN

793. 5 1 1 3 2 1 7 6 5 2 7 1 7 1 5   1 2 3 4 5 6
888866   4v   O F F F F F
c.1775

P228	D		572	

794. 5 1 1 3 3 3 3 4 5 6 5 4 3 4 3   1 2 3 4 5 6
XXXXXY   3v   F H F E E F
1760   *a* Stephenson

P171	C	*a*	256	
P171.4	C	*a*	256	

795. 5 1 1 3 4 2 2 3 5 4 4 3 2 1 5   1 2 3 4 5 6
888888   4v   H H H F H H
1793   *a* Coan

A128	C	*a*	228	GUILFORD
A172	C	*a*	228	GUILFORD

796. 5 1 1 3 7 1 1 7 5 1 3 2 7 1 2   1 2 3 4 4
XXXX   4v   F H E H H
1785   *a* Gillet

A62a	c	*a*	10	BABYLON
A106	c	*a*	10	BABYLON
A200	c	*a*	10	BABYLON

5 1 1 4 3 2 5 5 6 7 1 1 1 1 1:   *soprano of* **1162**

797. 5 1 1 5 3 1 1 1 7 1 5 1 1 1 2   1 2 3 4 5 6
XXXXYY   4v   H H H H O F
1793   *a* Caswell

A128	E♭	*a*	590	MOUNT SINAI
A172	E♭	*a*	590	MOUNT SINAI

798. 5 1 1 5 3 6 6 5 3 2 1 5 1 1 1   1 2 3 4 5 6 6
886886   4v   E H H H H F H
1786   *a* Carpenter

A72	E♭	*a*	697	SOUTHWELL
A131	E♭	*a*	697	SOUTHWELL

799. 5 1 1 5 6 7 1 1 5 3 6 5 4 3 2   1 2 3͡ M 3 4
SM   4v   H H F O F H
1793   *a* Kimball

A125	E	*a*	392	YARMOUTH

A175	E	*a*	392	YARMOUTH
A181	E		392	YARMOUTH
A188	E	*a*	392	YARMOUTH
A181.5	E	*a*	392	YARMOUTH
A195	E	*a*	392	YARMOUTH
A198	E	*a*	392	YARMOUTH

5 1 1 6 3 3 3 2 3 4 3 2 7 6 5:   *soprano of* **115**

800. 5 1 1 6 5 1 2 3 2 1 3 4 3 2 1   1 2 3 4
CM   4v   H H F H
1793   *a* Hibbard
   A121   C   318   BETHEL
   A201   C   *a*   318   BETHEL

801. 5 1 1 6 5 4 3 5 5 3 1 1 5 6 7   1 2 2 3 4 3 4
SM   4v   H H H F H H H
c.1790-6
   A102   D   203   MOUNT VERNON
   A110   D   203   MOUNT VERNON

802. 5 1 1 6 6 1 2 3 2 4 3 1 1 3 5   1 2 3̂ 4 M 4̂ 4
LM   4v   H H F F F F F
1793   *a* Washburn
   A131   C   *a*   635   VOICE OF NATURE

803. 5 1 1 7 1 2 2 3 2 1 7 1 5 1 1   1 2 3 4
SM   4v   H H F C
1793
   A121   d   617   CONTENTMENT

804. 5 1 1 7 1 2 3 2 1 7 5 4 4 5 6   1 2 3 $\overparen{4}$ $\overparen{4}$

LM   4v   H H F F F O

1787   *a* D. Read

A80	a	*a*	101	PROVIDENCE
A87	a		101	PROVIDENCE
A96	a	*a*	101	PROVIDENCE
A111	a	*a*	101	PROVIDENCE
A117	a		101	PROVIDENCE
A80.4	a	*a*	101	PROVIDENCE
A111.3	a	*a*	101	PROVIDENCE
A145	a		101	PROVIDENCE
A111.4	a	*a*	101	PROVIDENCE
A111.5	a	*a*	101	PROVIDENCE
A80.5	a	*a*	101	PROVIDENCE
A111.6	a	*a*	101	PROVIDENCE
A172	a		101	PROVIDENCE

5 1 1 7 1 6 7 1 5 5 5 4 6 7 7:   *alto of* **867**

805. 5 1 1 7 5 1 2 1 7 1 1 2 3 2 1   1 2 3 $\overparen{4}$ $\overparen{M}$ $\overparen{4}$

LM   4v   H H F F F F

1796   *a* D. Read

A163	E	*a*	409	DEANFIELD
A175	E	*a*	409	DEANFIELD
A181	E		409	DEANFIELD
A189	E		409	DEANFIELD
A181.5	E	*a*	409	DEANFIELD

806. 5 1 1 7 5 1 7 1 1 1 1 2 1 7 6   1 2 3 $\overparen{4}$ $\overparen{5}$ $\overparen{6}$ $\overparen{6}$ $\overparen{M}$ $\overparen{M}$

886886   4v   H H H F F F O F O

1774   *a* W. Billings

A39	F	53	LANESBOROUGH
A39.2	F	53	LANESBOROUGH
A54	F	53	LANEBOROUGH
A56	F	53	LANEBOROUGH

A65	F	*a*	53	NORTHBOROUGH
A131	F		536	NORTHBOROUGH
A189[1]	F		53	LANEBOROUGH

---

[1] 1 2 3 4 5 6 6 6 6
   H H H O F O O E O

5 1 1   7 5 1   7 1 7   1 7 1   3 2 1:   *soprano of* **302**

807.   5 1 1   7 5 3   2 1 2   2 3 2   1 2 7   1 2 3 4 5 6 7 7 8
        LMD   3v   H H H H F F O H H
        1783   *a* Swan

A54	d		820	MONTAGUE
A56	d		820	MONTAGUE
A62a[1]	d			MONTAGUE
A67[1]	d	*a*	123	MONTAGUE
A70[1]	d	*b*	820	MONTAGUE
A74[1]	d	*a*	820	MONTAGUE
A80[1]	d	*a*	175	MONTAGUE
A85[1]	d	*a*	820	MONTAGUE
A91[1]	d	*b*	820	MONTAGUE
A92[1]	d	*a*	412	MONTAGUE
A95[1]	d		820	MONTAGUE
A92.3[1]	d	*a*	412	MONTAGUE
A98[1]	d	*a*	820	MONTAGUE
A101[1]	d		412	MONTAGUE
A103[1]	d	*a*	412	MONTAGUE
A106[1]	d	*a*	123	MONTAGUE
A108[1]	d	*a*	820	MONTAGUE
A109[1]	d	*a*	820	MONTAGUE
A106.4[1]	d	*a*	123	MONTAGUE
A113[1]	d	*a*	820	MONTAGUE
A114[1]	d	*a*	820	MONTAGUE

---

[1] 4v: 1 2 3 4 5 6 7 8
       H H H H F F O H

b Edson   *807 continued*

A119[1]	d	*a*	820	MONTAGUE
A80.4[1]	d	*a*	175	MONTAGUE
A114.B[1]	d	*a*	820	MONTAGUE
A124[1]	d	*a*	820	MONTAGUE
A131[1]	d	*a*	412	MONTAGUE
A145[1]	d		175	MONTAGUE
A146[1]	d	*a*	412	MONTAGUE
A147[1]	d	*a*	820	MONTAGUE
A80.5[1]	d	*a*	175	MONTAGUE
A103.4[1]	d	*a*	412	MONTAGUE
A160[1]	d	*a*	820	MONTAGUE
A163[1]	d	*a*	820	MONTAGUE
A103.5[1]	d	*a*	412	MONTAGUE
A146.5[1]	d	*a*	412	MONTAGUE
A168[1]	d	*a*	820	MONTAGUE
A170[1]	d	*a*	820	MONTAGUE
A172[1]	d		175	MONTAGUE
A175[1]	d	*a*	820	MONTAGUE
A181[1]	d		820	MONTAGUE
A103.6[1]	d	*a*	412	MONTAGUE
A189[1]	d	*a*	412	MONTAGUE
A190[1]	d	*a*	820	MONTAGUE
A181.5[1]	d	*a*	820	MONTAGUE
A200[1]	d	*a*	820	MONTAGUE

[1] 4v: 1 2 3 4 5 6 7 8
       H H H H F F O H

808.	5 1 1 7 5 3 4 5 5 3 3 5 1 7 3		1 2 3 M 3 4	
	CM	4v	H H F F H H	
	1788	*a* Holden		
	A85	d	383	HOLLIS
	A98	d	383	HOLLIS
	A109	d	383	HOLLIS
	A114	d	383	HOLLIS
	A119	d	*a*	383	HOLLIS
	A114.B	d	383	HOLLIS
	A124	d	*a*	383	HOLLIS
	A158	d	*a*	383	HOLLIS

A160	d		383	HOLLIS
A163	d	*a*	383	HOLLIS
A168	d	*b*	383	HOLLIS
A175	d	*a*	383	HOLLIS
A181	d		383	HOLLIS
A190	d	*a*	383	HOLLIS
A181.5	d	*a*	383	HOLLIS
A195	d		383	HOLLIS
A198	d		383	HOLLIS

b "Union Harmony"

5 1 1   7 5 3   4 5 6   5 5 1   1 7 7:   *see* **809**

809. 5 1 1   7 5 3   4 5 6   5 7 1   1 7 7   1 2 3 4 4

LM   4v   H H F F H

1786   *a* Goff

A71	f♯	*a*	679	STRATFIELD
A98	f♯	*a*	679	STRATFIELD
A109	f♯	*a*	679	STRATFIELD
A114	f♯	*a*	679	STRATFIELD
A114.B	f♯	*a*	679	STRATFIELD
A124	f♯	*a*	679	STRATFIELD
A131[1]	f♯	*a*	71	STRATFIELD
A148	f♯	*a*	679	STRATFIELD
A150	f♯	*a*	679	STRATFIELD
A158	f♯	*a*	679	STRATFIELD
A160	f♯	*a*	679	STRATFIELD
A163	f♯	*a*	679	STRATFIELD
A174[1]	f♯		71	STRATFIELD
A175	f♯	*a*	679	STRATFIELD
A181	f♯	*a*	679	STRATFIELD
A189	f♯	*a*	720	STRATFIELD
A190	f♯	*a*	679	STRATFIELD
A181.5	f♯	*a*	679	STRATFIELD

[1] 5 1 1   7 5 3   4 5 6   5 5 1   1 7 7

810.   5 1 1 7 5 3 5 4 3 2 3 4 5 5 6   1 2 3 4 M 6 7 8 8

      CMD   4v   H H H H F H F H H

      c.1796   *a* Rollo

A164	f♯	*a*	457	REPENTANCE
A174	f♯		457	REPENTANCE
A182	f♯	*a*	457	REPENTANCE
A188[1]	f♯		457	REPENTANCE

[1] 5 1 1 7 6 5 4 3 5 4 3 2 3 4 5

811.   5 1 1 7 5 4 3 4 5 1 7 6 5 7 1   1 2 3 4 5̑ 6̑ 7 8

      CMD   4v   H H H H F F O H

      1797   *a* Belknap

A166	e	*a*	211	ROWLEY

812.   5 1 1 7 5 6 4 5 7 7 7 7 7 5 3   1 2̑ 2̑ 2 3 4 5 6 7 8 8

      CMD   4v   H O F F F H H H H F H

      1759

P169	c		795	HATHORNE
P169.2	c		795	HATHORNE

813.   5 1 1 7 5 6 6 5 5 3 5 6 7 1 5   1 2 3 4̑ M 4̑

      CM   4v   H H F F O O

      1790   *a* Morgan

A96	E	*a*	90	SOUNDING JOY
A111	E	*a*	90	SOUNDING JOY
A111.3	E	*a*	90	SOUNDING JOY
A111.4	E	*a*	90	SOUNDING JOY
A111.5	E	*a*	90	SOUNDING JOY
A111.6	E	*a*	90	SOUNDING JOY
A167	E	*a*	90	SOUNDING JOY

814. 5 1 1 7 5 6 7 1 3 3 2 1 7 1 3   1 2 3͡ 4
       LM   4v   H E F F
       1793   *a* Kimball

A125	C	*a*	689	STONEHAM
A181	C		689	STONEHAM
A181.5	C	*a*	689	STONEHAM

815. 5 1 1 7 6 5 3 5 6 5 4 3 2 5 1   1 2 3͡ 4 3 4
       SM   4v   H H F F H H
       1795   *a* Chandler

A148	F	*a*	90	WESTPOINT

816. 5 1 1 7 6 5 4 3 3 4 5 5 5 4 5   1 2 3 4͡ 4
       CM   4v   H H H F F
       c.1752   *a* Knapp

P148	D	*a*	703	LONG-HAM
P148.2	D	*a*	703	LONG-HAM
P148.3	D	*a*	703	LONG-HAM
P148.4	D	*a*	703	LONG-HAM
P148.5	D	*a*	703	LONG-HAM
P204[1]	D		380	GRAVESEND
P220[1]	D		380	GRAVESEND

---

[1] 5 1 1 7 6 5 5 4 3 3 4 5 5 5 4

Clearly derived from **818** in P129a.

817.   [a ghost]

5 1 1 7 6 5 4 3 5 4 3 2 3 4 5:   *see* **810**

5 1 1 7 6 5 5 4 3 3 4 5 5 5 4:   *see* **816**

818. 5 1 1 7 6 5 5 5 3 4 5 6 7 7 5   1 2 3 4͡ 4
      CM   4v   H H H F F
      c. 1746
          P129a   E♯   703
          A145a   E♯   703
          P157¹   E♯   790
          A198¹   D   790

      ¹ 5 1 1 7 6 5 5 5 5 6 5 4 3 5 1

      See **816.**

      5 1 1 7 6 5 5 5 5 6 5 4 3 5 1:   *see* **818**

819. 5 1 1 7 7 1 1 2 1 7 1 7 6 5 3   1 2 3 4 3͡ 4
      LM   4v   H E H H F F
      1789   *a* French (*A*)
          A93   d   *a*   458   CAROLINA

820. 5 1 1 7 7 2 2 1 1 2 2 1 7 6 5   1 2 3 4 5͡ 6 7 8 7 8
      CMD   4v   H H H H F F H H H H
      1796
          A160   C   204   CANTON
          A168   C   *b*   204   CANTON
          A195   C   204   CANTON
          A198   C   204   CANTON

      b "Union Harmony"

821. 5 1 1 7 7 6 6 5 4 3 1 4 4 3 2   1 2 3͡ 4 4
      LM   4v   H H F F H
      1793
          A121   F   *a*   590   DISSOLUTION

822. 5 1 2 1 2 3 1 4 3 2 2 7 1 7 6   1 2 3͡ 4
SM   4v   H H F O
1791   *a* Davis

A103	A	*a*	52	NORRISTOWN
A103.4	A	*a*	52	NORRISTOWN
A103.5	A	*a*	52	NORRISTOWN
A103.6	A	*a*	52	NORRISTOWN

5 1 2 1 2 3 2 1 7 1 6 5 5 1 2:   *bass of* **170**

823. 5 1 2 1 2 3 2 3 2 3 4 3 2 1 2   1 2 3 4
CM   2v   F H H H
c.1757

P166	G		22

824. 5 1 2 1 2 3 2 3 4 3 3 4 5 6 5   1 2 3 3 4͡ 4 5 6 7 8
CMD   4v   E E H H F F H H H F
c.1800   *a* Key

P323	G	*a*	806

825. 5 1 2 1 2 3 4 3 4 5 5 3 4 5 7   1 2 3 4 M M͡ M͡ M͡
SM   4v   H H H H F   F   F   F
1781   *a* W. Billings

A44	a	*a*	544	FRAMINGHAM
A49	a	*a*	544	FRAMINGHAM
A51	a	*a*	544	FRAMINGHAM
A62	a	*a*	544	FRAMINGHAM
A70	a	*a*	544	FRAMINGHAM
A74	a		544	FRAMINGHAM
A91	a	*a*	544	FRAMINGHAM
A62.3	a	*a*	544	FRAMINGHAM
A131	a	*a*	544	FRAMINGHAM

826. 5 1 2 1 2 3 4 3 6 5 4 3 2 3 4   1 1 2 3 4
      SM   4v   F F F H H
      c. 1755
            P157   G   702

827. 5 1 2 1 2 3 4 5 4 3 2 1 3 2 2   1 2 3 4 3 4
      LM   4v   H H H H F F
      1794   *a* W. Billings
            A136   C   *a*   526   DEDHAM

828. 5 1 2 1 2 3 4 5 5 5 6 5 4 3 2   1 2 3 4 5 6 7 8
      CMD   4v   F E H H H H H H
      1744
            P123   F   482
            P123.11   F   482
            P180[1]   G   482

      ――――――――――
      [1] 3v

829. 5 1 2 1 2 3 6 4 3 2 1 7 6 7 1   1 2 3 4 4
      SM   4v   H H F F H
      1792-   *a* Walker
            D12   B♭   *a*   762   FINSBURY

830. 5 1 2 1 3 2 1 7 2 3 4 5 6 4 3   1 2 3 4 3 4
      CM   3v   H H F F H H
      1800   *a* Rogerson
            A196   C   *a*   49   REHOBOTH

831. 5 1 2 1 3 4 5 6 7 1 1 7 5 6 7   1 2 3 4 5 6 7 8
      LMD   4v   H H F F F F F F
      1792   *a* Atwell
      [+]A116   E   *a*   742   CREATION
      [+]A117   E   *a*   742   CREATION

      5 1 2 1 4 3 4 3 2 1 3 2 1 2 3:   *soprano of* **345**

      5 1 2 1 6 1 2 3 1 2 1 7 6 5 5:   *see* **1213**

832. 5 1 2 1 6 6 7 1 5 4 5 3 4 5 3   1 2 3 4 5 6 6
      888888   4v   F O O F H H O
      1757
         P164   D   816
         P198[1]   C   816

      ───────────
      [1] 5 1 2 1 6 6 7 1 5 4 5 3 4 5 4

      5 1 2 1 6 6 7 1 5 4 5 3 4 5 4:   *see* **832**

833. 5 1 2 1 7 1 1 7 1 3 2 3 4 5 5   1 2 3 4
      XXYY   4v   E H F E
      1790
         A96   C   484   WALLING (S) FORD
         A111   C   484   WALLING (S) FORD
         A111.3   C   484   WALLING (S) FORD
         A111.4   C   484   WALLING (S) FORD
         A111.5   C   484   WALLING (S) FORD
         A111.6   C   484   WALLING (S) FORD   *833 continued*

A174[1]	C	484	WALLINGSFORD
A177	C	484	WALLINGFORD
A177.2	C	484	WALLINGFORD

[1]
1	2	3	4
O	H	F	E

834.
5 1 2 1 7 6 4 5 1 7 2 3 1 2 1   1 2 3 4 5̂ 6
668668   4v   H H H F F O
1785   *a* Strong

A62	D	*a*	614	ROYALSTON
A70	D	*a*	614	ROYALSTON
A74	D		614	ROYALSTON
A85	D		614	ROYALSTON
A91	D	*a*	614	ROYALSTON
A62.3	D	*a*	614	ROYALSTON
A108	D	*a*	614	ROYALSTON

835.
5 1 2 1 7 6 5 6 5 3 1 5 4 3 2   1 2 3 4 5 6
666688   4v   H H H H F H
1790   *a* Morgan

A96	F	*a*	824	WETHERSFIELD
A103[1]	F	*a*	824	WETHERSFIELD
A111	F	*a*	824	WETHERSFIELD
A111.3	F	*a*	824	WETHERSFIELD
A111.4	F	*a*	824	WETHERSFIELD
A111.5	F	*a*	824	WETHERSFIELD
A103.4[1]	F	*a*	824	WETHERSFIELD
A111.6	F	*a*	824	WETHERSFIELD
A103.5[1]	F	*a*	824	WETHERSFIELD
A103.6[1]	F	*a*	824	WETHERSFIELD

[1]
1	2	3	4	M	6
H	H	H	H	F	H

836.   5 1 2 1 7 6 7 6 7 1 7 1 2 3 2   1 2 3 4
      CM   4v   F F H F
      c.1757
          P166   G   485

      5 1 2 3 1 2 2 5 3 6 5 4 3 2 1:   *soprano of* **751**

837.   5 1 2 3 1 2 3 2 1 6 5 2 5 3 3   1 2 3 4 5 6
      666688   4v   H H H H F F
      c.1796   *a* Griswold
          A164   C   *a*   824   SCOTLAND
          A182   C   *a*   824   SCOTLAND

838.   5 1 2 3 1 2 3 4 4 3 2 1 5 5 5   1 2 3 4 5 6
      888884   4v   H H F F F H
      1799
          A189   A   170   VERMONT

839.   5 1 2 3 1 2 7 1 3 5 4 3 4 3 2   1 2 3 4 3 4
      LM   4v   H F H F H F
      1778
          P235   G   400   EAST DEREHAM

840.   5 1 2 3 1 4 3 2 2 5 6 7 1 7 6   1 2 3 4
      SM   4v   H H F F
      1793   *a* Stone
          A132   f   *a*   636   FUNERAL HYMN

      5 1 2 3 1 5 2 3 2 1 7 1 2 3 4:   *see* **846**

841. 5 1 2 3 1 5 2 3 4 3 2 1 3 6 7   1 2 3 4 5 6 7̑ 8
CMD   4v   H H H H H H F F
1795   *a* N. Billings
   A150   C   *a*   154   BLESSING OF THE SPRING

842. 5 1 2 3 1 5 5 3 1 5 3 2 1 7 2   1 2 3 4 5̑ 6 7 8
LMD   4v   H H H H F F H E
1790   *a* Morgan

A96	A	*a*	336	HUNTINGTON
A103	A	*a*	336	HUNTINGTON
A111	A	*a*	336	HUNTINGTON
A121[1]	A		342	HARMONY
A131	A	*a*	215	HUNTINGTON
A111.3	A	*a*	336	HUNTINGTON
A111.4	A	*a*	336	HUNTINGTON
A148	A	*a*	600	HUNTINGTON
A111.5	A	*a*	336	HUNTINGTON
A103.4	A	*a*	336	HUNTINGTON
A111.6	A	*a*	336	HUNTINGTON
A164	A	*a*	342	HUNTINGTON
A103.5	A	*a*	336	HUNTINGTON
A170	A	*a*	578	HUNTINGTON
A174	A		342	HUNTINGTON
A182	A	*a*	342	HUNTINGTON
A103.6	A	*a*	336	HUNTINGTON
A200	C	*a*	606	HARMONY

[1] 5 1 2 3 1 5 5 4 3 1 5 3 2 1 7

5 1 2 3 1 5 5 4 3 1 5 3 2 1 7:   *see* **842**

5 1 2 3 1 7 1 5 5 6 7 1 1 2 1:   *soprano of* **243**

5 1 2 3 1 6 6 1 2 3 4 3 5 4 3:   *see* **1230**

5 1 2 3 2 1 2 3 4 5 4 3 3 2 3:   *soprano of* **1039**

843.   5 1 2 3 2 1 2 3 4 5 5 3 3 1 1   1 2 3̂ 3 4̂ 4
        CM   4v   F H F F F F
        c.1758   *a* Stephenson

P168	g	a	309	
P212	g		465	
A36	a	a	309	PS. 3
A37	g		309	
A39	a	a	309	
P220[1]	g		227	DERBY
P227	g	a	309	
A41	a	a	796	PS. 3
A43	a	a	796	PS. 3
A39.2	a	a	309	
A47	a	a	796	PS. 3
A47a	a	a	796	PS. 3
A54	a	a	309	PS. 3
P253[2]	g		546	ASHTON
A56	a	a	309	PS. 3
A57	a		796	PS. 3
A60	a		309	PS. 3
P253.2[2]	g		546	ASHTON
A70	a	a	796	PS. 3
A74	a		796	PS. 3
A80	a	a	796	PS. 3
A85	a		796	PS. 3
A87	a	a	796	PS. 3
A91	a	a	796	PS. 3
P266	g		213	LINCOLN
A98	a	a	796	PS. 3
A108	a	a	796	PS. 3
A109	a	a	796	PS. 3
A114	a	a	796	PS. 3

---

[1] 1 2 3 4̂ 4
     F H F F F

[2] 1 2 3 3 4̂ 4
     F H F H F F

843 continued

A117	a	*a*	796	PS. 3
A119	a	*a*	796	PS. 3
A80.4	a	*a*	796	PS. 3
A114.B	a	*a*	796	PS. 3
A131[2]	a	*a*	796	PS. 3
A145	a		796	PS. 3
A147	a	*a*	796	PS. 3
A158	a	*a*	796	PS. 3
P253.4[2]	a		546	ASHTON
A80.5	a	*a*	796	PS. 3
A163	a	*a*	796	PS. 3
A168	a	*a*	796	PS. 3
A172	a		796	PS. 3
A175	a	*a*	796	PS. 3
A181	a		796	PS. 3
A189	a	*a*	796	PS. 3
A181.5	a	*a*	796	PS. 3

[2] 1 2 3 3 4 4
    F H F H F F

844. 5 1 2 3 2 1 4 2 7 1 2 3 3 1 1   1 1 2 3 4 5 6
666688   4v   F F H H H F F
1794   *a* Belcher

    A135   C   *a*   69   JUBILANT

845. 5 1 2 3 2 1 4 3 2 1 5 3 2 3 4   1 2 3 4
SM   4v   H H F E
1782   *a* D. Read

    A47   A   *a*   538   STAFFORD
    A60   A   538   STAFFORD
    A62a   A   STAFFORD
    A63   A   *a*   538   STAFFORD
    A63.2 A   *a*   538   STAFFORD
    A67   A   *a*   538   STAFFORD
    A70   A   *a*   538   STAFFORD
    A74   A   538   STAFFORD

A80	A	*a*	538	STAFFORD
A85	A		538	STAFFORD
A87	A	*a*	538	STAFFORD
A89	A		538	STAFFORD
A91	A	*a*	538	STAFFORD
A92	A	*a*	538	STAFFORD
A95	A			STAFFORD
A92.3	A	*a*	538	STAFFORD
A98	A	*a*	538	STAFFORD
A101	A		538	STAFFORD
A103	A	*a*	538	STAFFORD
A108	A	*a*	538	STAFFORD
A109	A	*a*	538	STAFFORD
A113	A	*a*	538	STAFFORD
A114	A	*a*	538	STAFFORD
A117	A	*a*	538	STAFFORD
A119	A	*a*	538	STAFFORD
A80.4	A	*a*	538	STAFFORD
A114.B	A	*a*	538	STAFFORD
A121	A		538	STAFFORD
A124	A	*a*	538	STAFFORD
A130	A	*a*	538	STAFFORD
A131	A	*a*	538	STAFFORD
A137	A	*a*	538	STAFFORD
A145[1]	A		538	STAFFORD
A146	A		538	STAFFORD
A147	A	*a*	538	STAFFORD
A148	A	*a*	538	STAFFORD
A158	A	*a*	538	STAFFORD
A80.5	A	*a*	538	STAFFORD
A103.4	A	*a*	538	STAFFORD
A160	A	*a*	538	STAFFORD
A163	A	*a*	538	STAFFORD
A103.5	A	*a*	538	STAFFORD
A146.5	A	*a*	538	STAFFORD
A168	A	*a*	538	STAFFORD
A170	A	*a*	538	STAFFORD
A172[1]	A		538	STAFFORD
A175	A	*a*	538	STAFFORD
A181	A		538	STAFFORD

[1] 5 1 2 3 2 1 4 3 3 1 5 3 2 3 4

845 continued

A103.6	A	*a*	538	STAFFORD
A189	A	*a*	538	STAFFORD
A190	A	*a*	538	STAFFORD
A181.5	A	*a*	538	STAFFORD
A198	A	*a*	538	STAFFORD

5 1 2 3 2 1 4 3 3 1 5 3 2 3 4:   *see* **845**

846. 5 1 2 3 2 1 5 2 3 2 1 7 1 2 3   1 2 3 4
CM   2v   H H F O
1763

P189	G	501	DOWN
P189.2	G	501	DOWN
P189.3	G	501	DOWN
A31	G	501	DOWN
P189.4	G	501	DOWN
A31.6	G	501	DOWN
A31.7	G	501	DOWN
A31.8	G	501	DOWN
A39	G	501	DOWN
A39.2	G	501	DOWN
A54	G	501	DOWN
A56	G	501	DOWN
P269[1]	G	501	DOWN
P269.2[1]	G	501	DOWN
P269.3[1]	G	501	DOWN
D6.11[1,2]	G	501	FOUNTAIN
D12[1]	G	501	FOUNTAIN
D6.12[1,2]	G	501	FOUNTAIN

[1] 3v

[2] 5 1 2 3 1 5 2 3 2 1 7 1 2 3 4

A non-fuging form of this tune is in P242.

847. 5 1 2 3 2 1 5 3 1 2 7 5 1 7 1   1 2 3 4 4 5 6 7 8 8 8
LMD   4v   H H H H H H H H A F E
1795   *a* N. Billings
   A150   d   *a*   43   OTSEGO

848. 5 1 2 3 2 1 5 7 1 2 3 2 2 3 4   1 2 3 4
CM   4v   H H H F
c.1785   *a* Valentine
   P257   a   *a*   624
   A79   a   624   PS. 20
   A87   a   624   PS. 20
   A117   a   624   PS. 20

849. 5 1 2 3 2 1 7 1 2 3 5 4 3 2 5   1 2 3 4 3̂ 4
LM   4v   H H H H F F
1794   *a* W. Billings
   A136   a   *a*   818   GREAT PLAIN

850. 5 1 2 3 2 1 7 1 2 5 5 3 1 3 5   1 2 3 4 5 6
888888   4v   H H F H H F
1786
   A67   d   658   PS. 89
   A201   d   658   PS. 89

851. 5 1 2 3 2 1 7 1 3 2 1 7 1 7 7   1 2 3̂ 4
LM   4v   F H F F
1795   *a* N. Billings
   A150   d   *a*   369   RECOVERY

852. 5 1 2 3 2 1 7 5 3 4 2 7 5 3 4   1 2 3 M M 4
      CM   4v   H E F O F O
      1798   *a* Kyes
           A177   d   *a*   507   SURPRISE
           A177.2   d   *a*   507   SURPRISE

853. 5 1 2 3 2 1 7 6 6 5 2 3 2 1 1   1 2 3 4 4
      CM   4v   H H H F H
      1789   *a* Stevenson
           P266   c   *a*   721   LITCHFIELD

      5 1 2 3 2 3 2 3 4 5 5 3 3 1 1:   *soprano of* **843**

854. 5 1 2 3 2 3 4 3 2 1 7 6 5 1 7   1 2 3 4 5 6 7 8 8
      7676D   4v   H H F O H F H O F
      1792-   *a* Walker
           D12   C   *a*   466   CULMSTOCK
           A189   C   *a*   466   DEVONSHIRE

855. 5 1 2 3 2 3 4 3 2 2 1 7 1 3 2   1 2 3 4
      CM   4v   H H F H
      1797   *a* R. Merrill
           A171   d   *a*   92   SANDWICH

856. 5 1 2 3 2 3 4 3 4 5 1 7 6 7 1   1 2 2 3 4 4
      LM   2v   F F F F F F
      1778   *a* Burney
           P235   F   *a*   443   SIBTON

328

5 1 2 3 2 3 4 5 3 2 1 7 2 3 6: *soprano of* **863**

857.	5 1 2 3 2 3 4 5 4 3 2 2 3 4 5			1 2 3 4 5 6 7 8
	CMD		4v	H H H F H H H H
	1733			
	P88.3	F	806	
	P118	G	806	HOOKENNORTON
	P120	G	b	485	BUCKINGHAM
	P118.2	G	806	HOOKENNORTON
	P88.4	F	806	
	P88.5	F	806	

b Holdroyd

See **858**; also related to **106, 107.**

858.	5 1 2 3 2 3 4 5 4 3 2 2 3 4 5			1 2 3 4
	CM		4v	H H H F
	1741			
	P117	F	806	
	P117.2[1]	F	806	
	P117.3[1]	F	806	
	P117.4[1]	F	806	
	P155a[1]	F	806	

[1] 5 1 2 3 2 3 4 5 4 3 2 5 5 4 3

Similar to **857**; also related to **106, 107.**

5 1 2 3 2 3 4 5 4 3 2 5 5 4 3: *see* **858**

859.	5 1 2 3 2 5 4 3 4 5 3 2 1 1 7			1 2 3 4 3 4 4
	CM		4v	H H C H F H E
	1760		*a* Tans'ur	
	P155.2	g	*a*	494	RYHALL

859 continued

P155.3	g	*a*	494	RYHALL
A28	g	*a*	494	RYALL
A30	g	*a*	494	RYALL
A31	g	*a*	494	RYALL
A31.6	g	*a*	494	RYALL
A31.7	g	*a*	494	RYALL
A31.8	g	*a*	494	RYALL
A39	a		494	RYALL
A39.2	a		494	RYALL

860. 5 1 2 3 2 7 1 3 4 5 6 5 4 3 4   1 2 3 4 5 6 7 8
          66664444   4v   H H H E H H H F
          1733

P88.3	F		130	
P107	A		802	LONDON NEW
P120	G	*b*	802	CANTERBURY
P88.4	F		130	
P129a	G		713	
P134.2	A		802	
P145a	G		713	
P88.5	F		831	
P157	A		802	
P174	G		130	EYNSFORD
P174.10	G		130	EYNSFORD
P235	G		802	CHELMSFORD
P174.11	G		130	EYNSFORD
P174.12	G		130	EYNSFORD

b Holdroyd

5 1 2 3 3 2 1 7 1 5 6 6 5 1 4:   *soprano of* **1191**

861. 5 1 2 3 3 2 3 4 4 3 4 5 1 1 7   1 2 3 4 5 6 7 8
          LMD   4v   H H H H F H H F
          c.1785   *a* Valentine

P257	D	*a*	575	

862. 5 1 2 3 3 2 7 1 3 6 1 7 1 7 6   1 2 3̂ 4̂ 3̂ 4
     LM   4v   H H F F F F
     1800   *a* Adams
        A201   C   *a*   ASHBY

863. 5 1 2 3 3 3 4 5 3 2 2 6 6 5 4   1 2 3 4
     CM   4v   C H F E
     1791   *a* S. Arnold
        P291   G   *a*   594

864. 5 1 2 3 3 4 5 4 3 2 1 7 1 3 2   1 2 3 4 3 4
     CM   4v   E H E F E E
     c. 1788   *a* Dalmer
        P263   A   *a*   433

865. 5 1 2 3 3 5 3 2 1 3 2 5 1 3 2   1 2 3 4 5̂ 6̂ 7̂ 8̂ 7 7 8
     SMD   3v   H H H H F F F F O H H
     1792   *a* Brown
        A119   C   *a*   596   MOUNT SION
        A158   C   *a*   596   MOUNT SION
        A175   C   *a*   596   MOUNT SION
        A181[1]   C   596   MOUNT SION

---

   [1] 4v

     5 1 2 3 4 3 2 1 3 2 1 7 6 5 7:   *see* **1228**

866. 5 1 2 3 4 3 2 2 6 1 2 3 2 3 1   1 2 3̂ 4
     CM   4v   H H F F
     1794   *a* Belcher
        A135   C   *a*   47   MAJESTY

867.   5 1 2   3 4 3   4 3 4   5 5 6   5 4 3   1   2   3   4   5   5   6

668668   3v   F   H   H   H   F   F   F

1786

D6.6	G	218	SOUTHWARK
D6.10	G	218	SOUTHWARK
D6.11	G	218	SOUTHWARK
P303	G	218	SOUTHWARK
P303.10	G	218	SOUTHWARK
D6.12	G	218	SOUTHWARK
D6.13	G	218	SOUTHWARK
P303.11	G	218	SOUTHWARK

868.   5 1 2   3 4 5   3 2 1   7 1 2   3 2 3   1   2   3   4   4

CM   4v   F   O   F   F   F

1754   *a* Everet

P151	a	*a*	311	
P157	a	*a*	311	
P198	g		311	

869.   5 1 2   3 4 5   4 3 2   1 2 2   5 3 2   1   2   3   3   4   4   4

CM   3v   H   H   H   H   H   H   F

c.1790

P246.5	C	652	HEPHZIBAH
P303	C	652	HEPHZIBAH
P303.11	C	652	HEPHZIBAH
P303.12	C	652	HEPHZIBAH

870.   5 1 2   3 4 5   4 3 2   1 2 3   5 4 3   1   2   3   4

LM   4v   H   H   F   H

1789   *a* French (*A*)

A93	a	*a*	654	FAIRHAVEN

5 1 2 3 4 5 4 3 2 1 3 2 1 7 1 :   *soprano of* **6**

871.   5 1 2 3 4 5 4 3 4 3 2 3 3 2 3   1 2 3 4 5 6
        886886   4v   H H H F F H
        1755

> | P153 | G | 19 |
> | P153.2 | G | 19 |
> | P153.3 | G | 19 |

872.   5 1 2 3 4 5 4 5 4 3 2 1 4 3 2   1 2 3͡ 4 5 6 7 8
        CMD   4v   H H O F H H H H
        1794   *a* W. Billings

> | A136 | B♭ | *a* | 722 | VICTORY |

5 1 2 3 4 5 5 1 7 1 3 2 1 1 7 :   *soprano of* **1133**

873.   5 1 2 3 4 5 5 4 3 2 1 7 2 1 7   1 2 3 4͡ 4
        LM   4v   H H H O F
        1783   *a* Brownson

> | A51 | a | *a* | 101 | CAMBRIDGE |
> | A62 | a | *a* | 101 | CAMBRIDGE |
> | A62.3 | a | *a* | 101 | CAMBRIDGE |

874.   5 1 2 3 4 5 5 4 3 2 3 4 3 2 1   1 2 3 4 3 4
        LM   4v   O O F O O F
        1757

> | P164 | a | 486 |
> | P198 | g | 486 |

5 1 2 3 4 5 5 6 2 1 7 1 2 3 4 :   *soprano of* **122**

875. 5 1 2 3 4 5 6 4 3 2 5 7 7 7 5   1 2 3 4 5 6 7 7
8868886   4v   H H H H H F H H
1783   *a* Brownson

A51	e	a	583	BUCKLAND
A62	e	a	583	BUCKLAND
A62.3	e	a	583	BUCKLAND
A130	e	a	583	BUCKLAND
A131	e	a	583	BUCKLAND

876. 5 1 2 3 4 5 6 5 4 3 2 1 1 2 3   1 2 3 4
LM   4v   F H F H
c.1752   *a* Knapp

P148	G	a	496	KEYNSON
P148.2	G	a	496	KEYNSON
P148.3	G	a	496	KEYNSON
P182a	G		169	
P148.4	G	a	496	KEYNSON
P148.5	G	a	496	KEYNSON
A37	G		496	KRYNSON
P228	G		169	

5 1 2 3 5 3 1 2 1 7 1 1 1 2 1:   *see* **1214**

877. 5 1 2 3 5 3 4 3 5 3 1 4 3 2 1   1 2 3̑ 4 3 4
SM   4v   H H F F E H
1795   *a* N. Billings

A150	bb	a	706	GARDNER

878. 5 1 2 3 5 4 3 2 1 2 3 2 5 4 3   1 2 3 4
CM   3v   H H E F
c.1790   *a* Radiger

D9	A	a	115	EXCELLENCY

5 1 2 3 5 4 3 2 1 5 4 3 1 7 6:   *see* **1215**

879.	5 1 2 3 5 4 3 2 2 3 1 3 5 1 7			1 2 3 4 5 6	
	888866		4v	H F F H F F	
	1755				
	P153	G	572		
	P153.2	G	572		
	P153.3	G	572		

880.	5 1 2 3 5 4 3 2 2 4 5 3 2 1 7			1 2 3 ⌢4	
	6666		4v	H H F F	
	1799		*a* Pilsbury		
	A189	a	*a* 208	MADDISON	

881.	5 1 2 3 5 4 3 2 5 5 4 3 6 5 4			1 2 3 4 4	
	CM		4v	H F H O H	
	1755				
	P153	G	63		
	P153.2	G	63		
	P153.3	G	63		

882.	5 1 2 3 5 7 1 3 2 1 7 1 5 7 1			1 2 3 4 5 6 7 8	
	LMD		4v	H H H H F H H H	
	c.1790-6				
	A102	d	393	CARMEL	
	A110	d	393	CARMEL	

5 1 2 3 6 5 4 3 2 1 2 3 2 3 1:   *soprano of* **969**

5 1 2 5 1 2 3 4 4 4 3 4 2 5 5:   *soprano of* **1153**

883.   5 1 3   1 3 2   2 3 1   4 2 1   1 3 3   1   2   3 3   M   3   4

      SM   4v   H   H   F   F   F   H   H

      1793   *a* West

         A131   C   *a*   640   PRECEPT

884.   5 1 3   1 7 6   2 3 4   3 2 2   1 2 3   1   2   3   4   5   6

      666688   4v   H   H   H   H   F   H

      1796

         A160   B♭   325   VERONA

         A168   B♭   *b*   325   VERONA

         A195   B♭   325   VERONA

         A198   B♭   325   VERONA

b "Union Harmony"

885.   5 1 3   2 1 3   5 1 7   6 5 4   3 2 3   1   2   3   4   5   6   5   6

      666688   4v   H   H   H   H   C   H   O   F

      1779   *a* B. West (*A*)

         A43   G   *a*   524   PROVIDENT

         A47a   G   *a*   524   PROVIDENT

         A89   G   524   PROVIDENCE

         A101   G   524   PROVIDENCE

         A106   G   *a*   524   PROVIDENCE

         A106.4   G   *a*   524   PROVIDENCE

         A146   G   524   PROVIDENCE

         A146.5   G   524   PROVIDENCE

886.   5 1 3   2 1 7   1 5 3   5 1 2   3 3 2   1   2   3   4   5   6   7   7   8   8

      SMD   3v   E   H   H   H   H   H   F   F   O   H

      1789   *a* Taylor

         P269   C   *a*   171   STEPNEY

         P269.2   C   *a*   171   STEPNEY

         P269.3   C   *a*   171   STEPNEY

         A183   C   171   STEPNEY

887.   5 1 3   2 1 7   1 7 6   5 6 7   1 7 6   1 2 3̑ 4 3 4
       CM   4v   H H F F H O
       1794   *a* W. Billings
          A136   C   *a*   501.   MORNING HYMN

888.   5 1 3   2 1 7   5 1 7   1 5 5   1 7 1   1 2 3 4
       LM   3v   O H F H
       1794   *a* Dupuis
          P297   A   *a*   757

889.   5 1 3   2 4 3   2 1 1   2 1 7   7 1 1   1 2 3 4 5̑ M 6 7 8
       SMD   4v   H H H H F O H H H
       1793   *a* J. Munson
          A128   A   *a*   617   PRINCETON
          A172   A   *a*   617   PRINCETON

890.   5 1 3   2 7 1   2 3 2   1 2 3   1 4 3   1 2 3 4 4
       CM   4v   H H F E H
       1795   *a* A. King
          A148   a   *a*   210   HILLSBOROUGH

       5 1 3   2 7 1   5 5 5   3 6 4   3 2 2:   *soprano of* **1069**

       5 1 3   5 1 7   1 2 3   1 7 1   1 2 3:   *see* **891**

891. 5 1 3 5 1 7 1 2 3 1 7 1 1 3 3   1 2 3 4 5 6 6 7̂ 8
         LMD   4v   H H H H O H H F F
         1788   *a* Belcher

⁺A85	C		639	APPEARANCE
⁺A91	C		639	APPEARANCE
A131	C		639	APPEARANCE
A135[1]	C	*a*	639	APPEARANCE

[1] 5 1 3 5 1 7 1 2 3 1 7 1 1 2 3

892. 5 1 3 5 3 1 4 3 2 2 1 7 6 5 1   1 2 3̂ M 5̂ 6 7̂ 8̂ 8
         LMD   4v   H H F F F F F F O
         1789   *a* French (*A*)

A93	C	*a*	32	DEVOTION
A131	C		32	DEVOTION

5 1 3 5 3 4 2 1 7 1 3 3 2 2 4:   *soprano of* **680**

893. 5 1 3 5 4 3 2 1 2 .3 2 1 7 1 7   1 2 3 4 3̂ M
         SM   4v   H H H H F F
         1778   *a* W. Billings

A40	C	*a*	33	AURORA
A40.2	C	*a*	33	AURORA
A40.3	C	*a*	33	AURORA
A49	C	*a*	33	AURORA
A51	C	*a*	33	AURORA
A62	C	*a*	33	AURORA
A40.4	C	*a*	33	AURORA
A70	C	*a*	33	AURORA
A74	C		33	AURORA
A84	C	*a*	33	AURORA
A91	C	*a*	33	AURORA
A62.3	C	*a*	33	AURORA
A189	C	*a*	33	AURORA
A190	C	*a*	33	AURORA

894.   5 1 4 3 6 5 1 7 1 2 4 3 6 5 4   1 2 3 4 3 4 4
       CM   4v   H H H H F O H
       1791   *a* Callcott
           P291   G   *a*   277

       5 1 5 1 1 2 3 4 5 6 5 4 3 2 1:   *soprano of* **694**

895.   5 1 5 1 3 3 2 1 7 1 3 3 3 3 3   1 1 2 2 3 4
       LM   3v   H H H H F H
       c. 1788   *a* Dalmer
           P263   A   *a*   37

       5 1 5 1 3 3 2 1 7 1 7 1 2 3 5:   *soprano of* **895**

896.   5 1 5 3 1 2 6 5 5 3 4 3 2 1 3   1 2 3 4 5 6 7 8
       CMD   4v   H H H H F F O E
       1793
           A128   G   772   ADAMS
           A172   G   772   ADAMS

897.   5 1 5 3 1 5 4 3 2 3 6 7 1 2 3   1 2 3 3 4 5 6 6 7 8 9 9 7 8 9 9
       886T   4v   H H H H F H H H F F E F F F H F
       -1750   *a* Broderip
           P136   C   *a*   19

898. 5 1 5 3 4 5 1 7 7 5 3 4 6 5 3   1 2 3 4 4 3 4
CM   4v   H H F F F F F
1796   *a* W. Smith

A163	e	*a*	778	CANTERBURY NEW
A167[1]	e	*b*	571	MORTALITY
A175	e	*a*	778	CANTERBURY NEW
A177	e	*b*	571	MORTALITY
A180[1]	e		1100	MORTALITY
A181	e		778	CANTERBURY NEW
A177.2	e	*b*	571	MORTALITY
A187[1]	e	*b*	571	MORTALITY
A181.5	e	*b*	778	MORTALITY
A201[1]	e	*b*	571	MORTALITY

b Weeks

[1] 1 2 3 4 4 M 4
     H H F F F F O

899. 5 1 5 3 5 4 3 2 1 5 7 2 1 7 6   1 2 3 3 4
CM   4v   H H F H H
1799   *a* I. M. P.

D15	F	*a*	147	BATTERSEA

900. 5 1 5 3 5 6 5 6 7 1 7 1 2 3 3   1 2 3 4
SM   4v   F E F H
1793

P293	D	265	SWANINGTON

5 1 5 4 3 2 1 2 1 7 1 5 6 7 1:   *soprano of* **714**

901. 5 1 5 4 3 2 1 5 6 5 4 3 2 5 7   1 2 3 4 3̂ 4
       SM   4v   H H H E F F
       1800   *a* Baird
          A192   e   *a*   509   MILTON

       5 1 5 4 3 4 5 1 2 3 2 1 7 1 7:   *soprano of* **691**

902. 5 1 5 4 6 5 4 3 1 2 3 5 5 4 2   1 2 3 4̂ 5 6
       668668   4v   H H H F O H
       1798   *a* Kyes
          A177   F   *a*   217   HARMONY
          A177.2   F   *a*   217   HARMONY

903. 5 1 5 5 3 4 5 3 1 2 3 2 1 1 3   1 2 3 4 5 6 7 8 8
       LMD   4v   H H H H H H F H H
       1800   *a* Kimball
          A202   e   *a*   490   JAMESTON

904. 5 1 5 5 4 3 2 1 5 1 2 3 2 1 1   1 2 3 4 3 4
       CM   4v   H H H F H H
       c.1783   *a* Barwick
          P250   B♭   *a*   815   BOUGHTON

       5 1 5 5 4 4 4 2 5 4 3 5 6 7 1:   *soprano of* **742**

905. 5 1 5 5 5 4 3 5 1 3 2 1 7 1 2   1 2 3 4 5 6 6
       666688   4v   H H H H F H H
       1800   *a* Kimball
          A202   C   *a*   21   PEMBROKE

906. 5 1 5 5 6 5 4 3 2 1 1 5 4 3 4   1 2 3 4 5 6 7 8 7 8
      LMD   4v   H H H H F H H H H H
      1800   a Kimball
           A202   e   a   320   INCONSTANCY

907. 5 1 5 5 6 5 5 4 3 3 3 2 1 5 4   1 2 3 4 5 6
      886886   3v   H F H H H H
      1765   a Nares
           P191   E   a   198   PS. 147

      5 1 5 6 5 3 4 3 4 3 2 1 2 3 4:   soprano of **699**

908. 5 1 5 6 5 6 7 1 5 1 7 1 5 4 3   1 2 3 4 3 4 M
      LM   4v   H H H H F F O
      1784   a Kimball
           A56   D   86   INVITATION
           A84   D   86   INVITATION
           A109   D   a   86   INVITATION
           A114   D   a   86   INVITATION
           A114.B   D   a   86   INVITATION
           A121   D   86   INVITATION
           A124   D   a   86   INVITATION
           A125   D   a   86   INVITATION
           A137   D   a   86   INVITATION
           A147   D   a   86   INVITATION
           A148   D   a   86   INVITATION
           A160[1]   D   a   86   INVITATION
           A163   D   a   86   INVITATION
           A168   D   a   86   INVITATION
           A189   D   86   INVITATION
           A195[1]   D   a   86   INVITATION
           A198[1]   D   a   86   INVITATION

[1] "Corrected from the Rural Harmony" [i.e. A125].

909.   5 1 5   6 5 7   5 5 5   1 7 6   2 5 7   1   2   3   4   5   6
      666688   4v   H H H H H F
      c.1757

        P166   G   711

910.   5 1 5   6 7 1   2 3 4   3 2 1   5 1 7   1   2 3   4
      LM   4v   H O F   F
      1793

        A121   C   686   DECLARATION

911.   5 1 5   6 7 1   2 7 1   1 5 2   4 5 1   1   2   3   4   5   6   7   8
      CMD   4v   H H H H H H H F
      1741   *a* Chetham
        P120   C   *a*   419   YARMOUTH
        P152   C   *a*   419   YARMOUTH

912.   5 1 5   7 1 2   3 2 5   5 1 5   5 7 5   1   2   2   3   4   4
      CM   4v   H H H F F H
      1791   *a* Callcott
        P291   E   *a*   394

      5 1 6   2 2 1   5 4 2   1 7 1   1 5 5:   *soprano of* **608**

913.   5 1 6   5 5 3   1 5 1   6 4 3   3 4 3   1   2   3   4   5   6   5   6
      888888   4v   H H F F O F F F
      1798

        A177   F   158   MOUNT VERNON
        A177.2   F   158   MOUNT VERNON

5 1 6 7 5 6 7 1 1 3 1 2 7 5 5:   *see* **1233**

5 1 7 1 1 4 3 2 1 7 7 1 5 6 5:   *soprano of* **467**

914.   5 1 7 1 2 1 2 3 2 3 4 3 6 5 4   1 2 3 4 3 3 4
        CM   4v   H H H H H H F
        c. 1800   *a* Key
          P323   F   *a*   216

915.   5 1 7 1 2 1 5 3 5 1 2 3 4 5 4   1 2 3 4 5 6 7̑ 8 7̑ 8
        LMD   4v   H H H H H C H H F F
        1793   *a* Kimball
         A125   D   *a*   578   READING

5 1 7 1 2 1 7 6 5 4 3 5 4 3 2:   *see* **916**

916.   5 1 7 1 2 1 7 6 5 5 6 5 4 3 2   1 2 3̑ 4
        CM   4v   H H F F
        1794   *a* Rogerson
         A147   d   *a*   355   SARATOGA
         A153[1]   d   *a*   355   SARATOGA
         A168   d   *a*   355   SARATOGA

---

[1] 5 1 7 1 2 1 7 6 5 4 3 5 4 3 2

917. 5 1 7 1 2 3 1 7 1 2 3 2 1 7 1   1 2 3͡ 4
CM   4v   H E F F
1783   *a* Wood

A54	c		377	ANDOVER
A56	c		377	ANDOVER
A70	c	*a*	377	ANDOVER
A72	c	*b*	377	ANDOVER
A74	c		377	ANDOVER
A85	c		377	ANDOVER
A91	c	*a*	377	ANDOVER
A98	c	*a*	377	ANDOVER
A108	c	*a*	377	ANDOVER
A109	c	*a*	377	ANDOVER
A114	c	*a*	377	ANDOVER
A119	c	*a*	377	ANDOVER
A114.B	c	*a*	377	ANDOVER
A158	c	*a*	377	ANDOVER
A163	c	*a*	377	ANDOVER
A175	c	*a*	377	ANDOVER
A181	c		377	ANDOVER
A181.5	c	*a*	377	ANDOVER

b "Taken from Thomas" [i. e. from A70].

918. 5 1 7 1 2 3 1 7 1 2 3 4 3 2 1   1 2 3 4 3 4
CM   4v   H H H H F H
c.1783   *a* Barwick

P250	B♭	*a*	812	CHILLHAM

919. 5 1 7 1 2 3 1 7 5 6 7 1 3 7 2   1 2 3͡ M 4
CM   4v   H H F O H
1792

A111	e	837	CRUCIFICTION
A111.3	e	837	CRUCIFICTION
A111.4	e	837	CRUCIFICTION
A111.5	e	837	CRUCIFICTION
A111.6	e	837	CRUCIFICTION

920. 5 1 7 1 2 3 2 1 2 3 4 3 2 1 3   1 2 3⌢4⌢4
CM   4v   H H F F F
1789   *a* French (*A*)
   A93   C   *a*   483   CHINA

921. 5 1 7 1 2 3 2 1 2 3 4 3 2 1 6   1 2 3⌢4⌢5 5 6
888888   4v   H H F F O H H
1786   *a* Harrison
   P258   A   *a*   241   WORKSOP

922. 5 1 7 1 2 3 2 1 2 3 4 5 4 3 2   1 2 2 3 4 4
SM   4v   F H H H F C
1789   *a* Dixon
   P266   a   *a*   706   GOSPORT MEETING

5 1 7 1 2 3 2 1 2 5 7 1 2 3 4:   *soprano of* **1024**

923. 5 1 7 1 2 3 2 1 2 7 1 5 5 5 1   1 2 3 4
CM   4v   H H H F
c.1775   *a* Senior
   P226   F   *a*   187

5 1 7 1 2 3 2 1 3 2 1 1 7 7 1:   *soprano of* **730**

924. 5 1 7 1 2 3 2 1 6 7 1 6 5 4 3   1 2 3 4 5 6 4 5 6
      886886   4v   H H H H H F H H F
      c.1792   *a* Walker
         D12   D   *a*   598   BALTIMORE
         A153   D   *b*   598   BALTIMORE

      _____

      b J. Walker

925. 5 1 7 1 2 3 4 3 2 3 4 5 4 3 2   1 1 2 3 4
      LM   3v   H H H F H
      1794   *a* Webbe
         P297   A   *a*   11

926. 5 1 7 1 2 3 5 6 4 5 5 1 2 3 2   1 2 3 M 3 4
      CM   4v   H H F F O H
      1793   *a* Kimball
         A125   d   *a*   255   MARBLEHEAD

927. 5 1 7 1 3 2 1 7 1 1 1 7 1 2 7   1 2 3 4 5 6 7 8
      CMD   4v   H H F H H H H F
      1793   *a* Mitchell
         A132   C   *a*   629   SACRAMENT

928. 5 1 7 1 3 2 1 7 2 3 4 3 2 3 5   1 2 3 4
      CM   3v   H F F F
      1791   *a* Callcott
         P291   a   *a*   777

929. 5 1 7 1 3 2 2 1 3 2 7 1 1 1 1   1 2 3͡ 4
      SM   4v   H H F F
      1799
          A186   C   246   GOSPEL

930. 5 1 7 1 3 2 4 3 2 1 7 1 1 6 6   1 2 3 4 5͡ M 6 7 8
      CMD   4v   H H H H F O H H E
      1786   a Bunnel
          A72   C   a   204   NEW MILFORD

931. 5 1 7 1 5 4 3 4 5 5 7 1 7 6 5   1 2 M͡ 3 4
      CM   4v   H H F O H
      1797   a R. Merrill
          A171   d   a   775   WILMINGTON

932. 5 1 7 1 5 6 7 1 2 1 7 6 6 5 5   1 2 3 4 4
      CM   4v   H H H H F
      1759
          P169   C   502   GREAT LEAK
          P169.2   C   502   GREAT LEAK
          P212   C   502   GREAT LEAK
          A62a   C   MORRISTOWN
          A85   C   84   MORRISTOWN
          A91   C   84   MORRISTOWN
          A106   C   774   MORRISTOWN
          A106.4   C   774   MORRISTOWN

      5 1 7 1 6 5 4 3 2 1 3 1 5 5 6:   *soprano of* **1135**

      5 1 7 1 6 5 4 3 3 2 1 2 2 3 2:   *soprano of* **995**

933.   5 1 7   1 6 5   4 3 6   5 2 5   1 7 6   1   2   3   3   4
     CM   4v   H   H   H   H   F
     c. 1800   *a* Harvey
        P321   E♭   *a*   482   TROWBRIDGE

     5 1 7   1 7 1   1 6 1   7 3 4   5 4 3:   *soprano of* **245**

     5 1 7   1 7 1   7 1 7   1 5 1   1 7 1:   *counter of* **458**

934.   5 1 7   1 7 6   5 1 7   2 1 7   1 7 6   1   2   3̑   M
     CM   4v   H   H   F   F
     1785   *a* D. Read

A63	D	*a*	741	CHARLESTOWN
A63.2	D	*a*	741	CHARLESTOWN
A70	D	*a*	741	CHARLESTOWN
A74	D		741	CHARLESTOWN
A80	D	*a*	741	CHARLESTOWN
A85	D		741	CHARLESTOWN
A91	D	*a*	741	CHARLESTOWN
A108	D	*a*	741	CHARLESTOWN
A119	D	*a*	741	CHARLESTOWN
A80.4	D	*a*	741	CHARLESTOWN
A131	D	*a*	741	CHARLESTOWN
A147	D	*a*	741	CHARLESTOWN
A80.5	D	*a*	741	CHARLESTOWN
A168	D	*a*	741	CHARLESTOWN
A175	D	*a*	741	CHARLESTOWN
A181	D		741	CHARLESTOWN
A190	D	*b*	741	CHARLESTON
A181.5	D	*a*	741	CHARLESTOWN

b Frothingham

935.   5 1 7 1 7 6 5 4 3 4 3 2 1 5 5   1 2 3 4 3̑ 4̑ M 4
            CM   4v   H H H H F F F E
            1778   *a* W. Billings

A40	E	*a*	763	BETHLEHEM
A40.2	E	*a*	763	BETHLEHEM
A43	E	*a*	763	BETHLEHEM
A40.3	E	*a*	763	BETHLEHEM
A47	E	*a*	763	BETHLEHEM
A47a	E	*a*	763	BETHLEHEM
A54	E		763	BETHLEHEM
A56	E		763	BETHLEHEM
A57	E		763	BETHLEHEM
A57.2	E		763	BETHLEHEM
A60	E		763	BETHLEHEM
A40.4	E	*a*	763	BETHLEHEM
A70	E	*a*	763	BETHLEHEM
A74	E		763	BETHLEHEM
A84	E	*a*	763	BETHLEHEM
A85	E		763	BETHLEHEM
A87	E	*a*	763	BETHLEHEM
A89	E		763	BETHLEHEM
A91	E	*a*	763	BETHLEHEM
A101	E		763	BETHLEHEM
A103	E	*a*	763	BETHLEHEM
A108	E	*a*	763	BETHLEHEM
A117	E	*a*	763	BETHLEHEM
A119	E	*a*	763	BETHLEHEM
A131	E	*a*	763	BETHLEHEM
A146	E		763	BETHLEHEM
A147	E	*a*	763	BETHLEHEM
A103.4	E	*a*	763	BETHLEHEM
A103.5	E	*a*	763	BETHLEHEM
A146.5	E		763	BETHLEHEM
A168	E	*a*	763	BETHLEHEM
A103.6	E	*a*	763	BETHLEHEM

936.   5 1 7 1 7 6 5 4 3 4 5 5 1 7 6   1 2 3̑ 4̑ M̑ 4̑
            CM   4v   H H F F F O
            1785   *a* D. Read

A63	C	*a*	38	ANNAPOLIS

A63.2	C	*a*	38	ANNAPOLIS
A70	C	*a*	38	ANNAPOLIS
A74	C		38	ANNAPOLIS
A80	C	*a*	38	ANNAPOLIS
A85	C		38	ANNAPOLIS
A91	C	*a*	38	ANNAPOLIS
A108	C	*a*	38	ANNAPOLIS
A119	C	*a*	38	ANNAPOLIS
A80.4	C	*a*	38	ANNAPOLIS
A131	C	*a*	38	ANNAPOLIS
A147	C	*a*	38	ANNAPOLIS
A158	C	*a*	38	ANNAPOLIS
A80.5	C	*a*	38	ANNAPOLIS
A163	C	*a*	38	ANNAPOLIS
A168	C	*a*	38	ANNAPOLIS
A175	C	*a*	38	ANNAPOLIS
A181	C		38	ANNAPOLIS
A181.5	C	*a*	38	ANNAPOLIS

937. 5 1 7 1 7 6 7 1 4 3 2 1 5 1 2   1 2 3 4
CM   4v   H E F H
c.1783   *a* Barwick

      P250   C   *a*   260   RAINHAM

      5 1 7 6 5 1 2 3 4 3 3 3 3 2 1:   *soprano of* **706**

      5 1 7 6 5 1 7 1 2 1 7 1 3 2 1:   *see* **938**

938. 5 1 7 6 5 1 7 1 2 1 7 1 3 2 2   1 2 3 4 5 6
668668   4v   H H E F F H
1788   *a* Holden

      A85   D   614   NEW CANAAN   *938 continued*

A119[1]	D	*a*	614	NEW CANAAN
A121[2]	D		614	NEW CANAAN
A124[1]	D	*a*	614	NEW CANAAN
A148[1]	D	*a*	614	NEW CANAAN
A160[1]	D		614	NEW CANAAN
A163[1]	D	*a*	614	NEW CANAAN
A168[1]	D	*b*	614	NEW CANAAN
A175[1]	D	*a*	614	NEW CANAAN
A181[1]	D		614	NEW CANAAN
A190[1]	D	*a*	614	NEW CANAAN
A181.5[1]	D	*a*	614	NEW CANAAN
A195[1]	D		614	NEW CANAAN
A198[1]	D		614	NEW CANAAN

[1] 5 1 7 6 5 1 7 1 2 1 7 1 3 2 1

[2] 1 2 3 4 5 6
   H H E F F O

b "Union Harmony"

939. 5 1 7 6 5 2 6 7 7 1 7 6 5 4 3   1 2 3 4 5 6 7 8
CMD   4v   H H H H F H F H
1795
    A152   D   47   FLORENCE

5 1 7 6 5 3 3 2 2 1 1 7 5 1 7:   *soprano of* **753**

5 1 7 6 5 4 3 2 3 4 3 5 1 7 6:   *soprano of* **700**

5 1 7 6 5 4 3 2 3 4 5 6 7 6 5:   *see* **735**

940.   5 1 7 6 5 5 3 6 5 4 4 3 2 5 4   1 2 3 4 5͡ 6
      666688   4v   H H H H F F
      1800   *a* Kimball
        A202   D   *a*   713   NORTHFIELD

      5 1 7 6 5 6 1 5 1 4 3 2 3 2 3:   *soprano of* **941**

      5 1 7 6 5 6 5 4 4 3 5 6 1 4 3:   *soprano of* **1082**

      5 1 7 6 5 6 5 5 1 1 1 7 6 7 1:   *see* **941**

941.   5 1 7 6 5 6 5 5 1 1 7 6 7 1 3   1 2 3͡ 3 4͡ 4
      CM   5v   F O O O F F
      c. 1755
        P157   D   205
        P198   C   205
        P220[1]   D   611   CRAYFORD
        P266[1,2,3,4]   D   *b*   421   WINTERINGHAM

---

[1] 5 1 7 6 5 6 5 5 1 1 1 7 6 7 1

[2] 4v

[3] 1 2 3 3 4 4
   F O O O F H

[4] Meter = LM

b "adapted by Dixon"

942.   5 1 7 6 5 6 7 1 5 1 6 5 4 3 2   1 2 3 4
      CM   4v   F A F A
      1789   *a* Dixon
        P266   E♭   *a*   220   REDBOURN

5 1 7 6 5 6 7 1 7 1 1 1 6 5 4:   *soprano of* **942**

943.   5 1 7 6 5 6 7 1 7 1 5 6 1 2 1   1 2 3 4 5 6
      888888   4v   H H F H H H
      1783   *a* Chandler

A51	D	*a*	606	PS. 46
A62	D	*a*	606	PS. 46
A70	D	*a*	606	PS. 46
A91	D	*a*	606	PS. 46
A62.3	D	*a*	606	PS. 46
A98	D	*a*	606	PS. 46
A108	D	*a*	606	PS. 46
A109	D	*a*	606	PS. 46
A114	D	*a*	606	PS. 46
A119	D	*a*	606	PS. 46
A114.B	D	*a*	606	PS. 46
A121[1]	D		606	PS. 46
A124	D		606	PS. 46
A131	D	*a*	606	PS. 46
A147	D	*a*	606	PS. 46
A148	D	*a*	606	PS. 46
A158	D	*a*	606	PS. 46
A160	D	*a*	606	PS. 46
A163	D	*a*	606	PS. 46
A168	D	*a*	606	PS. 46
A170	D	*a*	606	PS. 46
A175	D	*a*	606	PS. 46
A181	D		606	PS. 46
A190	D	*a*	606	PS. 46
A181.5	D	*a*	606	PS. 46
A198	D	*a*	606	PS. 46

[1] 5 1 7 6 5 6 7 1 7 1 5 6 7 1 2

5 1 7 6 5 6 7 1 7 1 5 6 7 1 2:   *see* **943**

5 1 7 6 6 6 6 7 1 1 1 1 1 1 1:   *soprano of* **1138**

944.	5 1 7 6 7 1 2 1 7 1 2 3 4 3 7			1 2 3 3 4 4 4		
	CM		3v	F H H H H H H		
	1791		*a* Callcott			
	P291	B♭ *a*	557			

945.	5 1 7 6 7 5 6 5 4 3 3 4 5 5 5			1 2 3 4		
	CM		4v	H H F E		
	1786/7		*a* D. Read			
	⁺A72	D *a*	560	WINSOR		
	⁺A80	D *a*	560	WINSOR		
	A80.4	D *a*	560	WINSOR		
	A145	D	560	WINSOR		
	A80.5	D *a*	560	WINSOR		
	A172	D	560	WINSOR		

946.	5 1 7 6 7 6 5 4 3 2 3 4 4 3 5			1 2 3 4 3 4 4		
	CM		4v	H H F H F H H		
	1789		*a* Dixon			
	P266	D *a*	192			

947.	5 1 7 6 7 6 5 6 5 1 7 1 2 3 2			1 2 3 4 3 3 3 4 5 6 7 8		
	SMD		4v	H H H H H H H H F H F H		
	1792		*a* Holden			
	A115	D *a*	48	CHRISTMAS		

948.   5 2 1 7 6 7 1 2 3 1 2 7 1 3 2   1 2 3 4
       CM   4v   F H F F
       c.1746

P129a	C	494	
P130	C	611	CRANLEY
P117.2	C	562	CRANLEY
P130.2	C	611	CRANLEY
P145a	C	494	
P117.3	C	562	CRANLEY
P130.3	C	611	CRANLEY
P117.4	C	562	CRANLEY
P174	A	611	CRANLEY
P117.5	C	562	CRANLEY
A17	C		CRANLEY
A17.2	C		CRANLEY
P117.6	C	562	CRANLEY
P130.5	C	611	CRANLEY
P174.10	A	611	CRANLEY
P117.7	C	562	CRANLEY
P174.11	A	611	CRANLEY
P174.12	A	611	CRANLEY

Cf. **143.**

949.   5 2 2 2 3 1 1 7 5 5 4 4 5 3 2   1 2 3 4 4
       CM   4v   F H H H H
       1795   *a* D. Read

A157	a	*a*	167	CYPRESS
A172	a	*a*	167	CYPRESS

950.   5 2 3 5 4 3 2 1 7 1 2 1 7 1 2   1͡ 2 2 3 3 4
       LM   4v   F F H F H H
       1791   *a* Callcott

P291	B♭	*a*	286

951. 5 3 1 1 1 1 2 7 5 5 5 2 2 7 2   1 2 3̂ 4 5 6 7 8
CM   4v   H H F F H H H H
c.1785   *a* Valentine
    P257   B♭   *a*   716

952. 5 3 1 1 1 7 7 6 5 4 3 2 1 5 4   1 2 3 4 4 5 5 6 6 5 6 6
777777   4v   F F F F H F H H H H H H
c.1792   *a* Haweis
    D11   D   128   CANONE
    D6.13[1]   D   *a*   128   ALDWINKLE

---

[1] 2v

    5 3 1 1 3 6 5 4 3 5 5 5 6 5 4:   *alto of* **1187**

953. 5 3 1 1 7 6 5 4 3 2 1 5 6 4 2   1 2 3 4̂ 4
CM   2v   H F H O O
c.1757
    P166   D   785

954. 5 3 1 2 3 1 3 4 5 4 3 2 3 2 1   1 2 3 4
LM   4v   F H H E
c.1755
    P157   a   758

    5 3 1 2 3 3 4 3 2 1 7 1 2 5 3:   *see* **1232**

955.   5 3 1 2 3 4 5 4 3 2 3 2 1 7 1   1 2 3 4͡ 4

       LM   4v   F F H O O

       1757

P164	g	58	
P198	g	58	

       5 3 1 2 7 1 2 3 4 3 2 1 7 2 1:   *soprano of* **446**

956.   5 3 1 3 2 1 3 5 5 1 1 1 7 1 5   1 2 3 4 4

       CM   4v   F H H H H

       1796   *a* Holden

A160	d		388	PS. 119
A168	d	*b*	388	PS. 119
A190	d	*a*	388	PS. 119

       b "Union Harmony"

957.   5 3 1 3 5 6 5 1 1 7 6 5 4 3 4   1 2 3 4͡ 5 6

       888888   4v   H H H F F H

       1794   *a* Belcher

A135	D	*a*	241	ST. DAVID'S NEW

958.   5 3 1 3 5 6 5 1 7 6 5 6 7 1 4   1 2 3 4͡ 5͡ 6 M 8

       6684D   4v   H H H O F F F H

       1793   *a* Shumway

A131	F	*a*	589	FREEHOLD

959. 5 3 1 4 2 3 2 3 6 5 4 5 5 6 5   1 2 3 4 5 M̑ M̑ M̑
66664444   4v   H H H H F O O O
1784

    A57   E   802   PARIA

    A57.2   E   802   PARIA

960. 5 3 1 4 3 2 1 2 2 3 4 5 4 5 5   1 2 3 4 5 6̑ 7 8
CMD   4v   H H H H F F F H
1797   *a* R. Merrill

    A171   F   *a*   751   MAJORCA

961. 5 3 1 4 3 2 3 5 6 5 1 3 6 5 7   1 2 3 4 5 6 7 8 7 8
SMD   3v   H H F H H H H H H H
1796

    A160   D   662   LORD'S DAY

    A168   D   *b*   662   LORD'S DAY

    A190   D   662   LORD'S DAY

    A195   D   662   LORD'S DAY

    A198   D   662   LORD'S DAY

_____

b "Union Harmony"

    5 3 1 5 4 3 2 3 2 5 4 4 3 3 6: *soprano of* **609**

962. 5 3 1 5 5 4 4 7 7 3 4 5 3 7 7   1 2 3 4 5̑ 6 6
888888   4v   H H H F F H H
1794   *a* Belcher

    A135   e   *a*   146   PROTECTION

963. 5 3 1 5 5 6 7 5 1 1 5 1 7 7 6   1 2 3̆ M 4
      CM   4v   H H F F H
      1800   *a* Jenks
          A201   e   *a*   WASHINGTON

      5 3 1 5 5 7 7 7 5 1 5 4 3 4 5:   *see* **964**

964. 5 3 1 5 5 7 7 7 7 1 5 4 3 4 5   1 2 3̆ 4̆ 4̆ 3̆ 4
      CM   4v   H H F F F F F
      -1793   *a* W. Smith
          ⁺A121   e   388   PS. 119
          A158¹   e   *a*   162   PS. 119
          A163¹   e   *a*   162   PS. 119
          ⁺A164¹   e   692   PS. 119
          A174¹   e   692   PS. 119
          A175¹   e   *a*   162   PS. 119
          A181¹   e   388   PS. 119
          A182¹   e   692   PS. 119
          A189¹   e   162   PS. 119
          A181.5¹   e   *a*   162   PS. 119
          A195¹   e   162   PS. 119
          A198¹   e   *a*   162   PS. 119
          A201¹   e   162   PS. 119

      ¹ 5 3 1 5 5 7 7 7 5 1 5 4 3 4 5

965. 5 3 1 6 1 6 5 3 5 4 3 4 3 4 5   1 2 3 3 4
      CM   4v   E H F H H
      1800   *a* Stone
          A192   F   *a*   531   GREENSBURG

966. 5 3 1 6 4 5 3 4 3 3 2 1 1 7 6   1 2 3 4 5 6 7 8
CMD   4v   H C H C H F E H
c.1785   *a* Valentine
   P257   A   *a*   448
   A116   A   306   URANIA
   A117   A   306   URANIA

967. 5 3 1 6 6 5 7 1 1 1 1 1 1 1 1   1 2̑ 3 4
LM   3v   F F F H
1794   *a* Webbe
   P297   a   *a*   461

968. 5 3 1 6 6 6 5 6 1 5 3 1 4 3 2   1 2 3 4 4 3 4
CM   4v   H H F F F F F
1783   *a* D. Read
   A51   D   *a*   677   SHERBURNE
   A62a[1]   D   SHERBURNE
   A63   D   *a*   763   SHERBURNE
   A63.2   D   *a*   763   SHERBURNE
   A70   D   *a*   763   SHERBURNE
   A74   D   763   SHERBURNE
   A80   D   *a*   763   SHERBURNE
   A85   D   763   SHERBURNE
   A91   D   *a*   763   SHERBURNE
   A92   D   *a*   568   SHERBURNE
   A95[2]   D   SHERBURNE
   A92.3   D   *a*   568   SHERBURNE
   A98   D   *a*   763   SHERBURNE
   A101   D   568   SHERBURNE
   A103   D   *a*   568   SHERBURNE
   A106   D   *a*   531   SHERBURNE
   A108   D   *a*   763   SHERBURNE
   A109   D   *a*   763   SHERBURNE

---

[1] 5 3 2 6 6 6 5 6 1 5 3 1 4 3 2

[2] 5 3 2 6 6 6 5 6 1 5 3 2 4 3 2

968 continued

A113	D	*a*	763	SHERBURNE
A119	D	*a*	763	SHERBURNE
A80.4	D	*a*	763	SHERBURNE
A121	D		763	SHERBURNE
A130	D	*a*	763	SHERBURNE
A131	D	*a*	763	SHERBURNE
A145	D		763	SHERBURNE
A146	D		568	SHERBURNE
A147	D	*a*	763	SHERBURNE
A148	D	*a*	531	SHERBURNE
A158	D	*a*	763	SHERBURNE
A80.5	D	*a*	763	SHERBURNE
A103.4	D	*a*	568	SHERBURNE
A160	D	*a*	763	SHERBURNE
A163	D	*a*	763	SHERBURNE
A103.5	D	*a*	568	SHERBURNE
A146.5	D		568	SHERBURNE
A168	D	*a*	763	SHERBURNE
A172	D	*a*	763	SHERBURNE
A175	D	*a*	763	SHERBURNE
A181	D		763	SHERBURNE
A103.6	D	*a*	568	SHERBURNE
A189	D	*a*	568	SHERBURNE
A190	D	*a*	763	SHERBURNE
A181.5	D	*a*	763	SHERBURNE
A195	D	*a*	763	SHERBURNE
A198	D	*a*	763	SHERBURNE
A200	D	*a*	547	SHERBURN

969.   5 3 1 7 1 2 1 4 3 2 1 7 1 5 3   1 2 3 4
       LM   3v   F F F F
       1794   *a* Webbe
          P297   G   *a*   671

       5 3 1 7 5 4 3 2 1 2 3 2 3 4 5:   *soprano of* **1063**

970. 5 3 2　1 1 5　3 4 5　3 2 1　1 5 5　　1 2 3 4
　　　CM　　　　　　　　　　　　　3v　　F F F F
　　　c.1746

P129a	G			
P148	G		372	UPTON
P148.2	G		372	UPTON
P148.3	G		372	UPTON
P148.4	G		372	UPTON
P148.5	G		372	UPTON

971. 5 3 2　1 1 6　5 5 4　3 3 2　5 5 6　　1 2 3 4
　　　CM　　　　　　　　　　　　　4v　　H H H F
　　　c.1783　　　　　　　　*a* Barwick

P250	E	*a*	440	HEARNE

972. 5 3 2　1 1 7　6 5 7　1 2 3　4 3 2　　1 2 3 4 M⌢3 4
　　　CM　　　　　　　　　　　　　4v　　H H H H F F H
　　　1786　　　　　　　　　*a* Mann

A70	a	*a*	497	SOLITUDE
A74	a		497	SOLITUDE
A85	a		497	SOLITUDE
A91	a	*a*	497	SOLITUDE
A108	a	*a*	497	SOLITUDE
A163	a		24	SOLITUDE
A175	a		24	SOLITUDE

973. 5 3 2　1 2 1　7 1 6　4 2 1　7 1 3　　1 2 3 4
　　　CM　　　　　　　　　　　　　3v　　H H F E
　　　c.1790　　　　　　　　*a* Radiger

D9	A	*a*	334	HUMILIATION

974. 5 3 2 1 2 3 4 3 4 5 5 6 7 1 6   1 2 3 4 3 4 5 6 7 8 7 8
CMD   3v   H H F H F H F H F H F H
1774

D4	D	379	
D6	D	715	BRABROOK
D6.6	D	715	BRABROOK
D6.10	D	715	BRABROOK
D6.11	D	715	BRABROOK
P303	D	379	BRABROOK
P303.10	D	379	BRABROOK
D6.12	D	715	BRABROOK
D6.13	D	715	BRABROOK
P303.11	D	379	BRABROOK

975. 5 3 2 1 2 3 4 5 2 3 4 5 3 2 5   1 2 3 3 4 5 6 7 7 8 7 8
CMD   4v   H H F F H C H H H H C H
1798

A181	a	378	SOLITUDE NEW
A188	a	378	SOLITUDE NEW
A181.5	a	378	SOLITUDE NEW

5 3 2 1 2 3 4 5 3 1 3 2 1 2 3:   *soprano of* **976**

976. 5 3 2 1 2 3 4 5 3 1 3 2 2 2 3   1 2 3 4 5 4 5 6
888888   4v   F C H H H F H H
1789   *a* Dixon

P266	G	*a*	676	CONSTANTINOPLE

977. 5 3 2 1 2 3 4 5 3 7 6 5 4 3 2   1 2 3 4 4 5 6 6 7 8
CMD   4v   H H H H H F O O H H
1789   *a* French (*A*)

A93	a	*a*	503	PATUXET
A121	a	*a*	503	PATUXET
A131	a	*a*	503	PATUXET

978.   5 3 2 1 2 3 4 5 6 4 3 1 2 3 2   1 2 3 2 3 4 4 5͡ 6 7͡ 8
      LMD   3v   F F H H H H E F O F O
      1791   *a* Cooper

A108	b	*a*	181	CRUCIFIXION
A119	b	*a*	181	CRUCIFIXION

The LMD is rearranged so that it appears to be 885Y8888.
See also **982**, of which this tune is a variant.

979.   5 3 2 1 2 3 4 5 6 5 5 5 4 5 1   1 2 3 4 3 4 5 6 7 8 9 X Y Z
      LMT   4v   H H H H H H H F H H H H O H
      c.1791-6   *a* Handel

A110	G		342	PS. 148
A167	G	*a*	342	PS. 148
A200[1]	G	*a*	342	PS. 148

[1] 5 3 2 1 7 1 6 5 5 4 3 4 2 5 1

This is arranged from **705** by the addition of a tenor part.
There is some alteration in text underlay.

980.   5 3 2 1 2 3 4 5 7 1 1 7 5 4 3   1 2 3͡ 4 5 6 7 8
      CMD   4v   H H F F H H H H
      1799   *a* Jenks

A187	e	*a*	740	MAJESTY

981.   5 3 2 1 2 3 5 7 1 2 3 1 5 6 7   1 2 3͡ M 4
      CM   4v   H H F F H
      1793   *a* Allin

A124	d	*a*	156	GRANBY
A160	d	*a*	156	GRANBY

982. 5 3 2 1 3 4 5 4 4 2 2 3 1 2 3   1 2 3 4 5 6 7̑ 8
LMD   3v   F F H H F H F F
1790   *a* Cooper

A98	b	*a*	181	CRUCIFIXION
A109	b	*a*	181	CRUCIFIXION
A114	b	*a*	181	CRUCIFIXION
A114.2	b	*a*	181	CRUCIFIXION
A190	b	*a*	181	CRUCIFICTION

See also **978.**

983. 5 3 2 1 3 5 4 5 5 3 2 1 3 2 1   1 2 3 4
LM   4v   F F F H
1791   *a* Callcott

P291	G	*a*	435

5 3 2 1 3 5 4 5 7 1 4 3 5 5 1:   *soprano of* **983**

984. 5 3 2 1 4 3 2 1 7 1 5 5 7 1 2   1 2 3 4 5̑ 6 7 8 5 6 7 8
CMD   4v   H F H H F F H H H F F H
1795   *a* Hering

D13	B♭	*a*	723

985. 5 3 2 1 4 5 1 7 3 4 6 5 1 7 6   1 2 2 3 4 4 4 4
SM   4v   H E H F F F H H
1783   *a* Strong

A51	e	*a*	335	PS. 90
A62	e	*a*	335	PS. 90
A70	e	*a*	335	PS. 90
A74	e		335	PS. 90
A85	e		335	PS. 90

A91	e	*a*	335	PS. 90
A62.3	e	*a*	335	PS. 90
A98	e	*a*	335	PS. 90
A108	e	*a*	335	PS. 90
A109	e	*a*	335	PS. 90
A114	e	*a*	335	PS. 90
A114.B	e	*a*	335	PS. 90

986.   5 3 2 1 5 4 1 6 5 1 7 1 1 1 2   1 2 3 4 5 6 7 8
LMD   3v   H H F H F O F H
1794   *a* Dupuis

P297	a	*a*	258	

987.   5 3 2 1 5 5 1 2 3 2 1 7 1 1 5   1 2 3 4 5 5
86458   4v   H H H H F H
1799   *a* Pilsbury

A189	e	*a*	459	EDSON

988.   5 3 2 1 5 6 5 4 3 5 5 1 5 4 3   1 2 3 4 4
LM   4v   H H H F H
1792-

D12	E	330	HORSLEY
D15[1]	E	330	

---

[1] 3v

989.   5 3 2 1 5 7 1 7 3 2 1 5 4 3 5   1 2 3 4 5 6 5 6
XXXXYY   4v   H H H H F F F H
c. 1790-6

A102	d	590	RANDOLPH
A110	d	590	RANDOLPH

990.   5 3 2   1 5 7   6 5 6   7 3 4   5 1 1   1   2   3   4
        CM   4v   F   H   F   H
        1760   *a* B. West (*E*)

P173	e♭	*a*	211	WATFORD
P173.2	e♭	*a*	211	WATFORD

991.   5 3 2   1 6 5   4 3 1   7 6 5   4 3 2   1   2   3   4   4
        CM   4v   H   E   F   E   H
        1760   *a* B. West (*E*)

P173	G	*a*	502	WILLIAMSTED
P173.2	G	*a*	502	WILLIAMSTED

        5 3 2   1 7 1   2 3 2   1 5 1   7 1 2:   *soprano of* **992**

992.   5 3 2   1 7 1   2 3 2   1 5 4   3 3 5   1   2   3   4   3   4   4
        CM   4v   F   H   F   H   F   F   H
        1789   *a* Dixon

P266	G	277	MARNHAM

993.   5 3 2   1 7 1   2 3 4   3 2 1   4 5 2   1   2   3   4   5   6   7   8
        LMD   4v   F   F   F   F   H   H   H   H
        1745   *a* Broderip

P125	G	*a*	443	
P137[1]	G		686	
P149	G	*a*	443	WELLS
P156	G	*a*	443	WELLS

---

[1] The last four phrases are newly composed.

5 3 2   1 7 1   6 5 5   4 3 4   2 5 1:   *see* **979**

5 3 2   1 7 6   5 6 7   1 2 5   4 3 2:   *see* **1216**

5 3 2   1 7 6   6 5 1   2 3 4   5 4 3:   *soprano of* **994**

994.   5 3 2   1 7 6   6 5 4   5 6 7   1 7 3   1 2 3 4
        CM   4v   F F F F
        1791   *a* Steffani
          P291   G   *a*   703

5 3 2   1 7 7   1 1 5   3 4 5   5 1 1:   *see* **1217**

5 3 2   3 1 1   7 1 7   1 2 3   4 5 4:   *soprano of* **366**

995.   5 3 2   3 1 1   7 1 7   6 5 1   6 2 2   1 2 3 4
        LM   3v   H F F F
        1791   *a* Callcott
          P291   C   *a*   475

996.   5 3 2   3 1 2   3 2 5   3 1 2   2 1 5   1 2 3 4 4
        CM   4v   F F F H F
        1759
          P169   a   737   LONG WHATTON
          P169.2   a   737   LONG WHATTON
          P235   a   737   BECCLES

997. 5 3 2 3 4 5 5 6 7 1 7 1 1 3 1   1 2 3 4
      CM   4v   H H H F
      c.1783   *a* Barwick
          P250   D   *a*   444   DOVER

998. 5 3 2 3 5 5 4 3 5 5 5 5 4 5 5   1 2 3͡ 4 5 6 7 8
      CMD   4v   F H F O H H E H
      1761   *a* Catchpole
          P183   G   *a*   25

999. 5 3 2 5 2 3 2 3 1 7 1 2 4 2 3   1 2 2 3 4 5 6 7 8
      CMD   4v   F H H H C F H H O
      1759
          P169   a   394   HOETON
          P169.2   a   394   HOETON

      5 3 2 6 6 6 5 6 1 5 3 1 4 3 2: *see* **968**

      5 3 2 6 6 6 5 6 1 5 3 2 4 3 2: *see* **968**

1000. 5 3 3 1 1 5 1 3 2 1 3 3 4 5 4   1 2 3 4 4
       CM   4v   H E H F H
       c.1776
           P231   G   489

1001. 5 3 3 1 1 7 1 2 3 3 5 3 5 5 4   1 2 3 4
       LM   4v   F H H F
       1760   *a* Stephenson
           P171   G   *a*   234
           P171.4   G   *a*   234

1002. 5 3 3   1 2 1   2 3 4   5 5 1   1 3 3   1 2 3 4̂ 4

CM   4v   F H F F F

1760   *a* Stephenson

P171	A	*a*	238	
P182a	A		238	
P171.4	A	*a*	238	
P228	A		238	
A43	A	*a*	238	MILFORD
A47a	A	*a*	238	MILFORD
P249[1,2]	G		678	WARWICK
P253	A	*a*	250	APPLEBY
A56	A		238	MILFORD
A57	A		238	MILFORD
A57.2	A		238	MILFORD
A60	A		238	MILFORD
A62a	A	*a*		MILFORD
P253.2	A	*a*	250	APPLEBY
A70	A	*a*	238	MILFORD
A74	A		238	MILFORD
A80	A	*a*	197	MILFORD
A84	A	*a*	238	MILFORD
A85	A		238	MILFORD
A87	A		797	MILFORD
A91	A	*a*	238	MILFORD
A95	A			MILFORD
A98	A	*a*	238	MILFORD
A106	A	*a*	238	MILFORD
A108	A	*a*	238	MILFORD
A109	A	*a*	238	MILFORD
A106.4	A	*a*	238	MILFORD
A113	A	*a*	238	MILFORD
A114	A	*a*	238	MILFORD
A117	A		797	MILFORD
A119	A	*a*	238	MILFORD
A80.4	A	*a*	197	MILFORD
A114.B	A	*a*	238	MILFORD

[1] 3v

[2] 1̂ 1 2 3 4̂ 4
   F F H F F F

1002 continued

A124	A		238	MILFORD
A130	A	a	531	MILFORD
A131	A	a	238	MILFORD
A141	A		238	MILFORD
A145	A		197	MILFORD
A147	A	a	238	MILFORD
A148	A	a	238	MILFORD
A158	A	a	238	MILFORD
P253.4	A	a	250	APPLEBY
A80.5	A	a	197	MILFORD
A160	A	a	238	MILFORD
A163	A	a	238	MILFORD
A168	A	a	238	MILFORD
A172	A		197	MILFORD
A175	A	a	238	MILFORD
A181	A		238	MILFORD
A189	A	a	238	MILFORD
A190	A	a	238	MILFORD
A181.5	A	a	238	MILFORD
A195	A	a	238	MILFORD
A198	A	a	238	MILFORD
A200	A	a	238	MILFORD
A203	A		238	MILFORD

5 3 3   1 2 1   2 3 4   5 5 2   2 3 3:   *soprano of* **1002**

1003.   5 3 3   1 2 3   4 2 1   3 6 5   4 3 4   1 2 3 4 5 6 6
888888   4v   H H H F F F H
1791   *a* Holyoke

A105	A	a	241	OHIO
A164	A	b	241	OHIO
A170	A	a	241	OHIO
A182	A	b	241	OHIO

b Edson

5 3 3 1 4 5 3 2 5 6 6 5 4 3 3: *alto of* **115**

5 3 3 2 1 4 3 2 5 3 1 7 6 5 4: *soprano of* **1055**

1004. 5 3 3 2 1 7 1 2 3 3 5 5 2 3 4   1 2 3 4 3 4
LM   4v   H H H H F H
1793   *a* Holden
   A124   G   *a*   532   LANESFIELD

5 3 3 2 3 1 1 5 6 7 1 7 1 3 2: *soprano of* **648**

1005. 5 3 3 3 3 5 5 5 5 7 7 1 4 3 5   1 1 2 3 4͡ 4
CM   4v   H H F O F F
c.1775   *a* Senior
   P226   a   *a*   233

1006. 5 3 3 4 5 1 7 6 5 7 1 5 4 3 4   1 2 3͡ 4
CM   4v   H H F O
1797   *a* R. Merrill
   A171   e   *a*   153   SILESIA

1007. 5 3 3 5 5 1 1 1 3 2 1 7 6 5 5   1 2 3͡ M 4
CM   4v   H H F F H
1788   *a* Holden
   A85   D   545   ALSTEAD
   A98   D   *a*   545   ALSTEAD
   A109   D   *a*   545   ALSTEAD
   A114   D   *a*   545   ALSTEAD
   A119   D   *a*   545   ALSTEAD
   A114.B   D   *a*   545   ALSTEAD

1008.   5 3 3 6 5 4 3 4 3 2 2 3 5 4 2   1 2 1 2 3 4 3 4 3 4

CM   4v   H F F O H F F E H H

1770

    P200   F   34

    5 3 4 2 3 6 7 1 5 6 7 1 2 3 7:   *soprano of* **1150**

1009.   5 3 4 3 2 1 5 5 1 7 6 5 5 1 5   1 2 3 4 5 6

886886   4v   H H E F H F

1785   *a* D. Read

A63	e	*a*	726	COMPLAINT
A63.2	e	*a*	726	COMPLAINT
A70	e	*a*	726	COMPLAINT
A74	e		726	COMPLAINT
A80	e	*a*	726	COMPLAINT
A85	e		726	COMPLAINT
A80.4	e	*a*	726	COMPLAINT
A80.5	e	*a*	726	COMPLAINT

1010.   5 3 4 3 4 3 4 5 1 7 1 7 1 7 1   1 2 3 3 4

CM   4v   F F F F F

c.1775

⁺P174.10	D		537	DERBY
⁺P220	D		537	SHOREHAM
P174.11	D		537	DERBY
P174.12	D		537	DERBY

1011.   5 3 4 3 4 5 6 5 6 7 1 6 5 5 1   1 2 3 4 M M

LM   4v   H H H H F F

1781   *a* W. Billings

A44	D	*a*	710	ADORATION

1012.   5 3 4   3 5 1   2 3 4   3 2 3   2 1 2   1   2   3   4
        CM   2v   F   F   H   H
        c.1757
            P166   C   59

1013.   5 3 4   5 1 6   2 1 7   1 2 2   2 3 5   1   2   3   4   5   6   6   6
        886886   3v   H   H   H   H   H   H   F   H
        c.1790   *a* Radiger
            D9   E♭   *a*   704   PRAISE

1014.   5 3 4   5 1 7   1 5 1   7 1 5   4 3 4   1   2   3   4̑   4
        SM   4v   H   H   F   F   H
        1793   *a* West
            A131   d   *a*   5   HAVERHILL

        5 3 4   5 1 7   6 5 3   4 5 1   7 6 5:   *soprano of* **652**

1015.   5 3 4   5 3 1   2 1 7   6 7 6   6 5 5   1   2   3̑   4   3̑   3   4
        LM   4v   H   H   F   F   F   F   E
        1795   *a* N. Billings
            A150   E   *a*   297   COOPERSTOWN

1016.   5 3 4   5 4 3   1 4 2   4 3 1   2 3 2   1   1   2   3   4   4
        CM   4v   F   H   O   F   H   H
        1789   *a* French (*A*)
            A93   F   *a*   556   FARNUM
            A131 [1]   F   *a*   556   FARNUM

------

[1] 1   1   2   3   4
     F   H   O   F   E

1017. 5 3 4 5 4 3 2 1 7 7 1 2 3 2 3   1 2 3 4͡ 4
LM   4v   F O O O O
1769   _a_ Harrott
    P198   g   _a_   496

1018. 5 3 4 5 4 3 2 3 4 5 5 5 4 3 4   1 2 3 4
CM   4v   H H F H
1759
    P169   a   222   REMPSTONE
    P169.2   a   222   REMPSTONE

In A43 and later American editions this tune is non-fuging due
to a different text underlay.

    5 3 4 5 6 2 2 2 5 3 2 1 3 4 3:   _soprano of_ **735**

    5 3 4 5 6 2 3 4 3 5 6 6 5 5 5:   _soprano of_ **650**

1019. 5 3 4 5 6 5 1 7 6 5 4 2 3 4 5   1 2 3 4 5 6 7 8 8
CMD   4v   H H H H H H F H H
1793   _a_ Kimball
    A125   E♭   _a_   305   TOPSFIELD
    A163   E♭   _a_   305   TOPSFIELD
    A175   E♭   _a_   305   TOPSFIELD
    A181   E♭   305   TOPSFIELD
    A181.5   E♭   _a_   305   TOPSFIELD

1020. 5 3 4 5 6 5 4 3 2 1 5 6 7 1 7   1 2 3 4 5 6
886886   3v   H H H F H F
c.1792
    D11   F   269

1021. 5 3 4 5 6 5 6 7 1 5 3 5 6 5 4   1 2 3 4
       CM   4v   H H F H
      1797   *a* Belknap

A166	F	*a*	185	SPRING
A192	F	*a*	185	SPRING

1022. 5 3 4 5 6 7 1 2 1 7 1 1 5 1 2   1 2 3 4 M 4
       CM   4v   H H H H F H
      1799

A186	D	738	ALBANY

1023. 5 3 4 5 6 7 1 6 5 3 5 3 4 5 6   1 2 3 4 5 6 7 M 8
       CMD   4v   H O F F F F F F H
      1797   *a* West

A167	F	*a*	797	EDAM
A181[1]	F		797	EDAM
A188[1]	F		797	EDOM
A181.5[1]	F		797	EDOM
A195[1]	F		797	EDAM
A198[1]	F	*b*	797	EDAM

[1] 1 2 3 4 5 6 M 7 8 8
    H O F F F F F   F F H

b "Village Harmony"

1024. 5 3 4 5 7 1 2 3 4 5 5 5 5 5 5   1 2 3 4
       CM   4v   H H F F
      c.1757

P166	a	678	

      5 3 4 5 7 1 5 6 5 4 3 3 2 5 6: *soprano of* **1190**

1025. 5 3 5 1 1 7 6 7 1 2 1 7 1 1 3   1 2 3 4
CM   4v   H H H F
c.1783   *a* Barwick
     P250   A   *a*   688   LEEDS

5 3 5 1 2 1 1 3 1 3 2 1 7 6 5:   *see* **1199**

1026. 5 3 5 1 3 4 6 5 3 4 3 2 1 2 1   1 2 3 4
CM   4v   F O F F
1789   *a* French (*A*)
     A93   G   *a*   375   RUSSEL
     A121   A   *a*   375   RUSSELL

1027. 5 3 5 1 3 6 7 1 1 2 3 2 5 5 6   1 2 3 4
LM   4v   F H F H
1789
     P266   C   814   CORINTH

5 3 5 1 3 6 7 1 7 7 1 2 1 2 4:   *soprano of* **1027**

1028. 5 3 5 1 6 5 4 3 2 1 1 4 5 6 1   1 2 3 4 5 6
XXXXYY   4v   E F H H F F
c.1796   *a* Griswold
     A164   E   *a*   590   PS. 50
     A174   E   590   CUMBERLAND
     A182   E   *a*   590   PS. 50

5 3 5 1 6 5 6 5 4 3 2 1 1 3 3:   *see* **1218**

1029. 5 3 5 4 2 4 3 1 2 3 5 2 3 2 1   1 2 3 4 5̂ 6̂ 7̂ M 8
         SMD   4v   H H H H F F F F H
         1797   *a* Swan
              A167   C   *a*   801   ORANGE

         5 3 5 4 3 6 5 1 1 7 7 1 4 5 3:   *soprano of* **645**

1030. 5 3 5 7 1 7 2 1 7 1 5 7 1 7 6   1 2 3̂ 4̂ 4
         CM   4v   H H F F F
         1794   *a* Belcher
              A135   d   *a*   692   OCEAN

         5 3 6 5 1 1 7 1 5 6 6 7 4 5 6:   *soprano of* **674**

         5 3 6 5 4 3 5 1 4 3 2 1 5 6 7:   *soprano of* **1172**

1031. 5 4 2 1 5 4 3 2 7 1 2 3 3 2 1   1 2 3 4̂ 4
         LM   3v   H H H O F
         1794   *a* Callcott
              P297   F   *a*   491

         5 4 2 3 2 1 3 2 3 1 7 7 5 3 3:   *soprano of* **1032**

1032. 5 4 2 3 2 1 5 6 6 5 5 5 3 4 5   1 2 3 4 4
         SM   4v   F H H F H
         1789
              P266   g   702   HARPSWELL

379

5 4 3 1 7 6 5 4 3 1 5 6 4 2 5:   *soprano of* **669**

1033. 5 4 3 2 1 1 2 3 4 5 3 2 1 1 7   1 2 2 3 4 4
CM   4v   F H H F H H
c.1746

P129a	a	550	
P148	a	550	CREEKMOOR
P148.2	a	550	CREEKMOOR
P148.3	a	550	CREEKMOOR
P182a	a	550	
P148.4	a	550	CREEKMOOR
P148.5	a	550	CREEKMOOR
P220	a	321	NORTHFLEET
P228	a	550	

5 4 3 2 1 1 7 6 5 5 6 5 4 3 5:   *soprano of* **635**

1034. 5 4 3 2 1 2 3 2 1 5 2 1 2 3 2   1 2 3 4
CM   4v   F H F F
1754

P130.3	G	563	MINSTER
P130.5	G	563	MINSTER

5 4 3 2 1 2 3 4 5 6 6 6 5 5 5:   *see* **1052**

1035. 5 4 3 2 1 2 5 4 3 2 1 2 3 4 5   1 2 3 4
CM   4v   F H H H
1797   *a* Hamilton

A170	f♯	*a*	513	LANESBOROUGH

1036.　5 4 3　2 1 2　7 1 6　5 4 3　4 2 1　　1　2　3　4　4
　　　　　LM　　　　　　　　　　　　　　　3v　　H　H　H　F　H
　　　　　1799
　　　　　　　D15　　　　　　G　　*b*　　514　　MARYLAND

　　　　　―――――――

　　　　　b "Italian"

1037.　5 4 3　2 1 3　2 1 7　1 6 5　4 3 5　　1　2　3　4　5　6　5　6
　　　　　666688　　　　　　　　　　　　4v　　H　H　H　H　F　F　F　F
　　　　　1795　　　　　　　　　　*a* Hering
　　　　　　　D13　　　　　　g　　*a*　　477

　　　　　5 4 3　2 1 4　3 2 5　4 3 6　6 6 6:　*soprano of* **672**

　　　　　5 4 3　2 1 4　3 3 2　1 2 7　1 1 5:　*soprano of* **683**

1038.　5 4 3　2 1 5　1 6 4　3 2 1　5 1 6　　1　2　2　3　3　3　4
　　　　　CM　　　　　　　　　　　　　　　4v　　F　H　H　H　H　H　H
　　　　　1792　　　　　　　　　*a* J. T. & A. B.
　　　　　　　S5　　　　　　C　　*a*　　445　　FORFAR
　　　　　　　S5.2　　　　　C　　*a*　　445　　FORFAR

　　　　　5 4 3　2 1 5　3 6 7　1 1 7　6 5 4:　*soprano of* **216**

1039.　5 4 3　2 1 5　6 5 4　3 2 1　1 1 7　　1　2　3　4
　　　　　LM　　　　　　　　　　　　　　　4v　　O　H　F　C
　　　　　1791　　　　　　　　　*a* S. Arnold
　　　　　　　P291　　　　　　A　　*a*　　458

1040.   5 4 3 2 1 7 6 2 5 1 7 1 3 3 3   1 2 3 4 5 6 7 8
       CMD   4v   H H H H O H F E
       c.1785   *a* Valentine
          P257   B♭   *a*   451

       5 4 3 2 3 1 3 2 2 3 2 3 1 2 3:   *soprano of* **308**

1041.   5 4 3 2 3 1 6 5 5 5 6 5 7 1 7   1 2͡ 3 4 3 4
       CM   4v   H H F F H H
       1791   *a* S. Arnold
          P291   G   *a*   214

       5 4 3 2 3 2 1 7 1 2 3 2 7 1 2:   *see* **1042**

1042.   5 4 3 2 3 2 1 7 1 3 2 7 1 2 3   1 2 3 4
       CM   4v   F E F E
       c.1746

P129a	. a	314	
P148	a	314	HAM-PRESTON
P148.2	a	314	HAM-PRESTON
P148.3	a	314	HAM-PRESTON
P182a	a	314	
P148.4	a	314	HAM-PRESTON
P148.5	a	314	HAM-PRESTON
P204	g	80	ASHFORD
P174.10[1]	g	449	YORK
P220	g	80	SWANSCOMBE
P228	a	314	
P174.11[1]	g	449	YORK
P174.12[1]	g	449	YORK

----

[1] 5 4 3 2 3 2 1 7 1 2 3 2 7 1 2

5 4 3　2 3 4　3 2 1　5 1 2　3 4 5:　*soprano of* **396**

5 4 3　2 3 4　3 4 3　2 3 3　2 2 4:　*soprano of* **1130**

1043.	5 4 3　2 3 4　5 4 3　2 2 3　4 5 1			1 2 3 3 4
	CM		4v	H H F H E
	1796		*a* Holden	
	A160	f♯	511	PHILIPPI
	A190	f♯　*a*	511	PHILIPPI

1044.	5 4 3　2 3 4　5 4 5　3 4 5　6 5 6			1 2 3 4
	CM		4v	H F H F
	1754			
	P151	F	594	

5 4 3　2 3 4　6 5 4　3 4 5　6 5 4:　*alto of* **944**

1045.	5 4 3　2 5 3　4 5 4　5 2 3　1 2 2			1 2 3 4 3 4 4
	CM		4v	H E H H F F E
	1765		*a* Tans'ur	
	P155.3	F　*a*	646	LONDON

1046.	5 4 3　3 4 3　2 1 2　3 1 1　4 3 4			1 2 3 4 5 6 7 8 8
	8⁸ anapaests		3v	H H H H F H F E H
	c.1790		*a* Radiger	
	D9	A　*a*	4	FUNERAL HYMN

1047. 5 4 3 4 2 7 1 4 3 4 3 2 2 5 3   1 2 3 4 5 6
      888888   3v   H H H H F F
      c.1790   *a* Radiger
        D9   A   *a*   63   THE BLESSED

      5 4 3 4 3 2 1 4 3 2 1 2 5 4 3:   *soprano of* **1189**

      5 4 3 4 3 2 3 2 1 5 1 2 3 2 1:   *soprano of* **918**

1048. 5 4 3 4 5 1 2 3 4 3 2 1 7 1 1   1 2 3 4 5 6 5 5 6
      666688   4v   H C H H H F O H H
      1789   *a* Dixon
        P266   C   *a*   711   DAMASCUS

      5 4 3 5 1 7 1 1 7 6 5 6 7 1 6:   *soprano of* **153**

      5 4 3 5 4 3 2 7 1 1 7 5 6 7 1:   *soprano of* **623**

1049. 5 4 3 5 5 3 2 1 1 2 3 4 3 2 1   1 2 3 4 3 4
      CM   4v   H H H H F H
      1795
        A152   F   379   REDEMPTION

1050. 5 4 3 6 2 1 7 1 1 4 3 4 5 5 6   1 2 3 4 5 6 7 8
      LMD   3v   H H H H F F H H
      1794   *a* R. Cooke
        P297   D   *a*   140

5 4 3 6 2 5 1 4 3 2 2 5 7 3 5:   *soprano of* **661**

1051. 5 4 3 6 5 4 3 2 3 4 3 3 4 5 6   1 2 3 4 5 6
           XXXXYY   4v   H H H H H F
           1789   *a* Dixon
               P266   F   *a*   590   JEHOSHAPHAT'S VALLEY

5 4 3 6 7 1 3 2 1 3 5 1 7 1 2:   *see* **1206**

5 4 4 3 1 1 5 6 5 4 3 6 5 4 2:   *soprano of* **108**

1052. 5 5 1 1 1 1 1 5 5 5 5 5 5 6 5   1 2 3 4 5 6 7 7 8 9 X X Y Y Z Z
           LMT   4v   F H F F F F H H H H H O F H O H
           1791   *a* Callcott
               P291   C   *a*   840
               A161[1]   C   840   DARTMOUTH
               A162[1]   C   840   DARTMOUTH
               A203[1]   C   840   DARTMOUTH

           _____

           [1] 5 4 3 2 1 2 3 4 5 6 6 6 5 5 5

           Law rearranged the voices.

1053. 5 5 1 1 2 3 2 2 3 5 5 1 4 4 3   1 2 3 3 4 3 4 5 6
           878747   4v   H H F F F F O H H
           1793   *a* Shumway
               A131   C   *a*   95   NIXINGTON

5 5 1 1 7 5 4 5 6 5 4 4 3 3 4:   *soprano of* **654**

1054.   5 5 1   2 3 4   3 2 1   7 1 2   3 2 5   1 2 3 4 3̑ M
        CM   4v   H H H H F F
        1789   a French (A)
            A93   C   a   240   RESOLUTION

        5 5 1   4 3 4   4 2 5   3 2 1   4 5 5:   soprano of **644**

1055.   5 5 1   7 1 1   1 7 2   5 5 1   6 7 1   1 2 3 4 5 6 7 8 8
        CMD   4v   H H F H A H A H E
        c.1790   a M. Cooke
            P274   C   a   446

1056.   5 5 1   7 1 5   4 5 5   6 7 1   5 4 7   1 2 3̑ 4̑ M 4
        LM   4v   H H F F O H
        1793
            A121   d   408   SANBORNTOWN
            A150[1]   d   408   SANBORNTOWN

        _____
        [1] 1 2 3̑ 4 3 4
             H H F F H H

1057.   5 5 1   7 5 1   7 1 2   1 1 7   1 7 6   1 2 3 4 5̑ 6̑ 7̑ 8
        LMD   4v   H H H H F F O O
        1785   a D. Read
            A62a   e   GREENWICH
            A72   e   a   336   GREENWICH
            A80   e   a   336   GREENWICH
            A91   e   a   336   GREENWICH
            A92   e   336   GREENWICH

A92.3	e		336	GREENWICH
A98	e	*a*	336	GREENWICH
A101	e		336	GREENWICH
A103	e		336	GREENWICH
A109	e	*a*	336	GREENWICH
A114	e	*a*	336	GREENWICH
A119	e	*a*	336	GREENWICH
A80.4	e	*a*	336	GREENWICH
A114.B	e	*a*	336	GREENWICH
A121	e		336	GREENWICH
A124	e	*a*	336	GREENWICH
A130	e	*a*	336	GREENWICH
A131	e	*a*	336	GREENWICH
A137	e	*a*	336	GREENWICH
A145	e	*a*	336	GREENWICH
A146	e		336	GREENWICH
A147	e	*a*	336	GREENWICH
A148	e	*a* ·	336	GREENWICH
A158	e	*a*	336	GREENWICH
A80.5	e	*a*	336	GREENWICH
A103.4	e		336	GREENWICH
A160	e	*a*	336	GREENWICH
A163	e	*a*	336	GREENWICH
A164	e		336	GREENWICH
A103.5	e		336	GREENWICH
A146.5	e		336	GREENWICH
A168	e	*a*	336	GREENWICH
A170	e	*a*	336	GREENWICH
A172	e	*a*	336	GREENWICH
A174	e		336	GREENWICH
A175	e	*a*	336	GREENWICH
A181	e		336	GREENWICH
A182	e		336	GREENWICH
A103.6	e		336	GREENWICH
A189	e	*a*	336	GREENWICH
A190	e	*a*	336	GREENWICH
A181.5	e	*a*	336	GREENWICH
A195	e	*a*	336	GREENWICH
A198	e	*a*	336	GREENWICH
A200	e	*a*	336	GREENWICH

1058. 5 5 1 7 5 4 3 5 4 3 2 3 4 5 7   1 2 3̑ 4 3 4
CM   4v   H H F F H H
1798   *a* Wetmore

    A177   d   *a*   692   GRANVILLE
    A177.2   d   *a*   692   GRANVILLE

1059. 5 5 1 7 6 5 4 5 5 3 4 5 1 7 7   1 2 3̑ 4 5 6
666666   4v   H H H F F H
1799   *a* Pilsbury

    A189   e   *a*   521   DARTMOUTH

    5 5 1 7 6 5 5 4 3 3 2 5 5 4 3:   *soprano of* **1134**

    5 5 2 1 7 7 1 6 7 7 2 2 3 2 5:   *soprano of* **567**

1060. 5 5 2 3 2 1 7 1 2 3 2 3 4 5 6   1 2 3 4
CM   4v   H E H F
-1749

    [+]P135   a   237
    P137[1]   a   236
    P130.2   a   236   STROUD
    P144   a   199   NEW NEWBERY
    [+]P145a   a   236
    P130.3   a   236   STROUD
    P152   g   *b*   253   HATFIELD
    P155a   a   236
    P157[1]   a   236
    P174   g   236   CUDHAM
    P175   a   STROUD
    A17   g   PS. 5
    P189   g   199   NEWBERY
    P189.2   g   199   NEWBERY

A23	g		199	NEWBURY
P189.3	g		199	NEWBERY
P144.4	a		199	NEW NEWBERY
A17.2	g			PS. 5
A28	g	c	199	NEWBURY
A30	g	c	199	NEWBURY
P130.5	a		236	STROUD
P198[1]	g		236	
A31	g	c	199	NEWBURY
A31.6	g	c	199	NEWBURY
A31.7	g	c	199	NEWBURY
A31.8	g	c	199	NEWBURY
A39	g	c	199	NEWBURY
P174.10	g		236	CUDHAM
P235	g		253	WRENTHAM
A41	a	c	199	NEWBURY
P117.7[2]	g		832	CUDHAM
A43	a	c	199	NEWBURY
A39.2	g		199	NEWBURY
P242[1,2,5]	a			STROUD
P246[3]	a		199	NEWBURY
A45	a			NEWBURY
A47	a		199	NEWBURY
P246.2[3]	a		199	NEWBURY
P249[1,2,5]	a		124	SEAFORTH
P253	g		577	STROUD
A57	a		199	NEWBURY
P246.4[3]	a		199	NEWBURY
A59	a			NEWBURY
P174.11	g		236	CUDHAM
A57.2	a		199	NEWBURY
P253.2	g		577	STROUD

[1] 1 5 2 3 2 1 7 1 2 3 2 3 4 5 6

[2] 2v

[3] 3v

[5] 1 2 3 4 4
    H E H F H

b "From A. Adams"

c "Williams"

1060 continued

A70	a		199	NEWBURY
A74	a		199	NEWBURY
A84	a		199	NEWBURY
A87	a		577	NEWBURY
A89	g		318	PS. 5
A91	a		199	NEWBURY
P266[1]	a		236	NEWBURY
A92	a		318	NEWBURY
A92.3	a		318	NEWBURY
A101	g		318	PS. 5
P246.5[3]	a		199	NEWBURY
P292[3,4,5]	a		555	
A103	a		318	NEWBURY
A106	a			NEWBURY
A106.4	a			NEWBURY
A117	a		577	NEWBURY
D12[1,6]	a		842	NEWBURY
S6[1,3]	a			STROUD
A131	a	*c*	577	
A146	g		318	PS. 5
P174.12	g		236	CUDHAM
P253.4	g		577	STROUD
P303[3,5]	a		199	NEWBURY
A103.4	a		318	NEWBURY
P303.10[3,5]	a		199	NEWBURY
A103.5	a		318	NEWBURY
A146.5	g		318	PS. 5
A167	g		199	NEWBURY
A103.6	a		318	NEWBURY
A189	a	*c*	644	
A200	a		318	
P303.11[3,5]	a		199	NEWBURY

[1] 1 5 2 3 2 1 7 1 2 3 2 3 4 5 6

[3] 3v

[4] Tune in soprano

[5] 1 2 3 4 4
H E H F H

[6] 1 2 3 4 4
H F H F F

c "Williams"

1061. 5 5 3 1 5 6 5 1 3 3 2 1 1 3 4   1 2 3 4 5 6 7 8
      LMD   4v   H H H E F H H H
      c. 1790-6

        A102   D   572   MONTVILLE
        A110   D   572   MONTVILLE

      5 5 3 2 1 4 3 3 3 4 5 6 5 4 3:   *soprano of* **681**

1062. 5 5 3 2 3 1 7 1 5 6 7 3 4 2 1   1 2 3 4
      CM   4v   H H H F
      1798   *a* Kyes

        A177   a   *a*   511   DESPAIR
        A177.2   a   *a*   511   DESPAIR

1063. 5 5 3 3 3 1 7 1 4 5 4 5 6 7 3   1 2 2 2 3 4̑ 4
      CM   4v   H H H H F H O
      1791   *a* Callcott

        P291   g   *a*   93

      5 5 3 3 3 4 2 2 2 1 2 3 4 3 2:   *soprano of* **111**

1064. 5 5 3 4 3 2 3 4 4 3 5 1 1 7 1   1 2 3 4 5 6 5 6 5 6
      886886   4v   H H F H H H H H H F
      1797   *a* Dixon

        P651   E♭   *a*   267   RESURRECTION

      5 5 3 4 5 6 5 5 6 5 6 7 1 6 5:   *soprano of* **1089**

1065. 5 5 3 5 1 7 1 2 3 4 3 1 7 6 2   1 2 3 4 3 4 5 6 5 6
      666688   4v   H H H H F H H H H H
      1794   *a* Olmsted

A141	C	*a*	325	PS. 84
A203	C	*a*	325	PS. 84

1066. 5 5 3 5 6 7 1 1 6 6 5 4 3 2 5   1 2 3 4 3 4
      SM   4v   H H F F H H
      1800   *a* Jenks

A201	E	*a*	283	SUNDERLAND

1067. 5 5 3 5 6 7 5 3 5 4 3 4 4 5 7   1 2 3 4 4
      SM   4v   H H F H H
      1798   *a* Brooks

A177	e	*a*	509	BRIMFIELD

1068. 5 5 3 6 1 7 7 1 7 1 2 7 5 1 6   1 2 3 4 5 M M
      668668   4v   H H H E F F O
      1783   *a* Benham

A51	E	*a*	218	CHATHAM
A62	E	*a*	218	CHATHAM
A62.3	E	*a*	218	CHATHAM
A167	E	*a*	218	CHATHAM

1069. 5 5 4 2 3 3 1 4 2 1 7 7 7 1 2   1 2 3 4 5 6 6
      886886   3v   H H H F F C H
      1791

P292	E♭	202	

1070.   5 5 4   3 1 3   4 5 1   3 2 1   3 4 2   1 2 3 4 3 4
LM   5v   F F F F H H
1759   *a* French (*E*)
    P170   G   *a*   435

1071.   5 5 4   3 1 5   6 5 3   1 2 3   4 5 1   1 2 3 4 5 6 7̑ 8
CMD   4v   H H H H F F O O
1799   *a* D. Merrill
    A188   F   *a*   79   UNITY

    5 5 4   3 2 1   2 2 2   5 1 1   7 1 6:   *soprano of* **708**

1072.   5 5 4   3 2 1   2 3 2   1 2 3   4 5 5   1 2 3 3 4 3 4
CM   4v   H H F F F H H
1770   *a* Parker?[1]
    P200   F   *a*   445

---

[1] "by Mr. Parker" entered in MS. on British Library Copy

1073.   5 5 4   3 2 1   2 3 2   1 3 4   5 4 3   1 2 3̑ 4 4 5 6 7 8
CMD   4v   F H F F H H H H H
1750
    P137   A   609
    P157   A   609

1074.   5 5 4   3 2 1   2 3 2   3 2 1   3 4 5   1 2 3 4
SM   4v   F H F H
1795
    A152   G   51   PORTLAND

1075. 554 321 356 554 323   1 2 3 4 4
LM   3v   F H F F H
1778
     P235   D   8   NORWICH NEW

1076. 554 321 543 515 654   1 2 3 4͡ 4
LM   4v   H H H F F
c.1800   *a* Cuzens
     D16   E♭   [1]   AMERTON

[1] Assigned to PS. 32 (OV, NV or Watts); only 66 and 191 fit the tune.

1077. 554 321 571 234 555   1 2 2 3 4 4
LM   4v   H O H H H F
1792-   *a* Handel
     D12   A   *a*   744   MANNING
     A153   A   *a*   744   MANNING

1078. 554 323 432 121 234   1 2 3 3 4 4
CM   4v   F F H H F H
c.1800   *a* Key
     P323   G   *a*   372

     554 323 456 543 231:   *soprano of* **1125**

1079. 554 323 645 354 365   1 2 3 4 3 4
CM   4v   H H H F H H
1755
     P153   G   812
     P153.2   G   812
     P153.3   G   812

5 5 4 3 4 3 2 1 1 2 1 1 7 1 5:   *soprano of* **1078**

1080. 5 5 4 3 4 3 2 1 1 3 5 5 6 5 4   1 2 3 4 5 6
668668   4v   H H H H H F
1800   *a* Kimball
   A202   G   *a*   218   ROYALSTON

1081. 5 5 4 3 4 3 2 1 7 1 2 3 5 6 6   1 2 2 3 4
CM   4v   F H H H F
1759
   P169   G   236   DISHLEY
   P169.2   G   236   DISHLEY

1082. 5 5 4 3 4 5 5 5 5 6 5 4 5 5 5   1 2 3 4 4 5 6 7 8
CMD   4v   H H A H H H H F H
c.1790   *a* M. Cooke
   P274   E   *a*   812

1083. 5 5 4 3 5 4 2 3 5 5 3 2 2 2 5   1 2 3 4 4
CM   4v   H H F H H
c.1775   *a* Senior
   P226   C   *a*   440

1084. 5 5 4 3 5 5 7 1 1 7 5 4 7 2 1   1 2 3 4 5 6 7 8 7 8
LMD   4v   H H F H H H H H H H
1800
   A196   d   540   TEMPLE

1085.   5 5 4   3 5 6   1 7 2   1 7 6   6 5 5   1 2 3 3 4 5 5 6 6
        886886   3v   H H H H H H F F H
        1799   *a* Woodhead
            D15   D   *a*   70   ELY

1086.   5 5 4   3 5 6   7 1 6   5 4 3   2 3 1   1 2 3 4 4
        SM   4v   F C F H H
        1789   *a* Dixon
            P266   E♭   *a*   206   ROME

1087.   5 5 4   3 6 5   4 5 5   7 5 5   3 4 5   1 2 3͡ M 3 4
        CM   4v   H H F F H H
        1783   *a* Mitchell
            A132   d   *a*   105   CHOCKSET

1088.   5 5 4   3 6 5   7 1 1   6 5 4   3 6 5   1 2 3 4 3͡ 3 4
        LM   4v   H H H H F O E
        1794   *a* Belcher
            A135   E   *a*   648   RAPTURE

1089.   5 5 4   4 3 2   3 2 3   4 5 6   6 5 6   1 2 3 3 4
        SM   4v   H F H H H
        1786   *a* Grimshaw
            P258   F   *a*   113   ST. JOHN'S

1090.   5 5 4   5 4 3   1 2 1   7 1 5   5 6 7   1 2 3 4 4
        CM   4v   H H A F E
        c.1785   *a* Valentine
            P257   d   *a*   211

554 556 555 516 717:   *soprano of* **192**

554 556 765 432 556:   *soprano of* **436**

1091.   554 777 176 545 544   1 2 3͡ 4
       YYY5   4v   H H F F
       1794   *a* Belcher
         A135   e   *a*   779   HEROISM

555 111 366 614 321:   *soprano of* **48**

1092.   555 112 234 217 122   1 2 3 4 5 6 7 8 5 6 7 8
       CMD   4v   F F H H H F H H H H H H
       1750
         P137   A   494

1093.   555 116 543 346 255   1 2 3 4 4
       CM   4v   H H F H H
       c.1785   *a* Valentine
         P257   D   *a*   790
         A79   D   386   TEMPLETON
         A87   D   386   TEMPLETON
         A117   D   386   TEMPLETON

555 117 711 553 346:   *see* **1222**

1094. 5 5 5 1 2 1 2 3 3 6 2 7 5 1 7   1 2 3̑ M 4
       LM   4v   H H F O E
       1793   *a* Kimball

          ⁺A124   D   *a*   631   ROWLEY
          ⁺A125   D   *a*   631   ROWLEY

1095. 5 5 5 1 2 1 7 6 4 5 5 3 5 1 2   1̑ 2 2 3 4 4
       CM   4v   F F E F H F
       1759

          P169   D   232   SWEEDLAND
          P169.2   D   232   SWEEDLAND
          A43   D   *b*   232   KEEN

       b Arnold

1096. 5 5 5 1 2 1 7 6 5 4 3 5 1 5 3   1̑ 2 3 4
       CM   3v   F F H H
       1800

          A196   D   186   EXULTATION

1097. 5 5 5 1 2 3 4 3 2 7 1 3 4 3 2   1 2 3 4 4 5 6 7 8̑ 8
       CM   4v   H H H F E H E H F F
       1759

          P169   C   277   BARROW UPON SOARE
          P169.2   C   277   BARROW UPON SOARE

       5 5 5 1 3 2 1 7 1 6 6 5 1 1 7:   *soprano of* **686**

       5 5 5 1 4 3 6 2 5 1 2 3 4 3 2:   *soprano of* **140**

1098. 5 5 5 1 4 6 5 3 4 2 1 5 1 7 6   1 2 3 4 4
LM   3v   H H H H F
c. 1790   *a* Radiger
　　D9   D   *a*   333   CONFESSION

1099. 5 5 5 1 6 5 3 3 1 2 3 5 1 7 2   1 2 3 3 4 4
CM   4v   H H F F F H
1800   *a* Jenks
　　A201   F♯   *a*   403   LIBERTY

1100. 5 5 5 1 6 5 5 5 1 7 1 1 2 2 3   1 2 3 4
CM   4v   H F H F
c. 1775   *a* Senior
　　P226   D   *a*   821

1101. 5 5 5 1 7 1 1 5 4 3 6 5 4 5 5   1 2 3 4 3 4
SM   4v   H H H H F O
1778   *a* W. Billings
　　A40   D   *a*   282   PHILADELPHIA
　　A40.2   D   *a*   282   PHILADELPHIA
　　A40.3   D   *a*   282   PHILADELPHIA
　　A47   D   *a*   282   PHILADELPHIA
　　A51   D   *a*   282   PHILADELPHIA
　　A54   D   282   PHILADELPHIA
　　A56   D   282   PHILADELPHIA
　　A57   D   282   PHILADELPHIA
　　A57.2   D   282   PHILADELPHIA
　　A62   D   *a*   282   PHILADELPHIA
　　A40.4   D   *a*   282   PHILADELPHIA
　　A70   D   *a*   282   PHILADELPHIA
　　A74   D   282   PHILADELPHIA
　　A84   D   *a*   282   PHILADELPHIA   *1101 continued*

A85	D		282	PHILADELPHIA
A87	D	*a*	282	PHILADELPHIA
A89	D		282	PHILADELPHIA
A91	D	*a*	282	PHILADELPHIA
A62.3	D	*a*	282	PHILADELPHIA
A101	D		282	PHILADELPHIA
A108	D	*a*	282	PHILADELPHIA
A117	D	*a*	282	PHILADELPHIA
A119	D	*a*	282	PHILADELPHIA
A130	D	*a*	282	PHILADELPHIA
A146	D		282	PHILADELPHIA
A147	D	*a*	282	PHILADELPHIA
A146.2	D		282	PHILADELPHIA

1102. 5 5 5 1 7 1 2 3 2 1 7 6 5 1 2   1 2 2 3 4 M M 4

LM   4v   H H H F F F F H

1778   *a* W. Billings

A40	E	*a*	339	WASHINGTON
A40.2	E	*a*	339	WASHINGTON
A40.3	E	*a*	339	WASHINGTON
A47	E	*a*	339	WASHINGTON
A51	E	*a*	339	WASHINGTON
A62	E	*a*	339	WASHINGTON
A62a	E	*a*		WASHINGTON
A40.4	E	*a*	339	WASHINGTON
A70	E	*a*	339	WASHINGTON
A74	E		339	WASHINGTON
A84	E	*a*	339	WASHINGTON
A85	E		339	WASHINGTON
A87	E	*a*	339	WASHINGTON
A89	E		339	WASHINGTON
A91	E	*a*	339	WASHINGTON
A92	E	*a*	339	WASHINGTON
A62.3	E	*a*	339	WASHINGTON
A92.3	E	*a*	339	WASHINGTON
A101	E		339	WASHINGTON
A103	E	*a*	339	WASHINGTON
A108	E	*a*	339	WASHINGTON
A117	E	*a*	339	WASHINGTON

A119	E	*a*	339	WASHINGTON
A130	E	*a*	339	WASHINGTON
A131	E	*a*	339	WASHINGTON
A146	E		339	WASHINGTON
A103.5	E	*a*	339	WASHINGTON
A146.5	E		339	WASHINGTON
A189	E	*a*	339	WASHINGTON
A103.6	E	*a*	339	WASHINGTON

1103. 5 5 5 1 7 1 3 2 2 3 1 7 5 1 2   1 2 3 4 5 6 7 7 8
LMD   4v   H H H H F F F F F
1794

A145	e	663	SMITHFIELD
A172	e	663	SMITHFIELD

1104. 5 5 5 1 7 1 3 2 3 5 3 1 4 3 2   1 2 3 4 4
LM   4v   H H F F H
1800   *a* Jenks

A201	C	*a*	578?	FRANKLIN

1105. 5 5 5 1 7 1 3 2 7 1 3 2 1 7 1   1 2 3 4 3 4 M 4
CM   4v   H H H H F F O O
1794   *a* Chandler

A141	d	*a*	580	AMENIA
A203	d	*a*	580	AMENIA

5 5 5 1 7 1 6 5 4 3 5 5 4 5 3:   *soprano of* **676**

1106. 5 5 5 1 7 3 1 2 1 7 6 5 4 7 6   1 2 3 4 4
CM   4v   H H F F H
1797   *a* R. Merrill
     A171   d   *a*   551   PETITION

1107. 5 5 5 3 1 2 1 7 6 5 1 1 1 3 4   1 2 3 4 4 3 4
CM   4v   H H F F F F F
1792   *a* Gillet
     A106.4   D   *a*   531   SHELBURNE
     A150   D   *a*   531   SHELBURNE

     5 5 5 3 1 5 6 7 1 5 1 3 2 4 3:   *soprano of* **1108**

1108. 5 5 5 3 1 5 6 7 1 5 5 1 2 7 1   1 1 2 3 3 4
CM   3v   H F H H O H
1794   *a* Webbe
     P297   F   *a*   781

1109. 5 5 5 3 1 5 7 1 1 5 4 3 7 6 5   1 2 3 4 3 4
CM   4v   H H F F F H
1799   *a* Jenks
     A187   e   *a*   383   NORTH SALEM

1110. 5 5 5 3 4 1 7 6 5 3 5 5 7 5 4   1 2 3 4
CM   4v   H H F H
1790
     A96   a   167   ATTENTION
     A111   a   167   ATTENTION
     A111.3   a   167   ATTENTION
     A111.4   a   167   ATTENTION
     A111.5   a   167   ATTENTION
     A111.6   a   167   ATTENTION

1111. 5 5 5 3 4 6 5 5 7 7 5 4 5 3 5   1 2 3̂ 4 3 4
SM   3v   H H F F H H
1797   *a* R. Merrill

    A171   e   *a*   368   LIBERTY

1112. 5 5 5 4 3 2 1 3 2 1 7 2 3 2 3   1 2 3̂ 4
LM   4v   H H O F
c.1746

P129a	g		657	
P148	g		657	POOLE NEW
P148.2	g		657	POOLE NEW
P148.3	g		657	POOLE NEW
P182a	g		657	
P148.4	g		657	POOLE NEW
P148.5	g		657	POOLE NEW
A36	g		657	POOL
A39	g		657	POOL
P228	g		657	
A41	g	*b*	657	POOL
A43	g	*b*	657	POOL
A39.2	g		657	POOL
A47	g		657	POOL
A47a	g	*b*	657	POOL
A54	g		657	POOL
A56	g		657	POOL
A57	g		657	POOLE
A57.2	g		657	POOLE
A61	g		657	POOL
A70	g	*b*	657	POOL
A74	g		657	POOLE
A84	g	*b*	657	POOL
A85	g		657	POOLE
A91	g	*b*	657	POOL
P266	g	*b*	657	POOLE
A98	g	*b*	657	POOL

---

b Knapp

1112 continued

A106	g	b	657	POOL
A108	g	b	657	POOL
A109	g	b	657	POOL
A114	g	b	657	POOL
A119	g	b	657	POOL
A114.B	g	b	657	POOL
A131	g	b	657	POOL
A137	g	b	657	POOL

b Knapp

1113. 5 5 5 5 1 1 7 1 2 3 1 2 1 1 3   1 2 3 4 5 6 7 8
CMD   4v   A H F O F H H H
1791   *a* S. Arnold
   P291   G   *a*   272

1114. 5 5 5 5 1 5 5 5 5 1 5 5 1 2 5   1 2 3 3 4 4 4 4 3 4
CM   4v   H H F F H H H H H E
1791   *a* Callcott
   P291   F   *a*   768
   A161   F   727   PIKE
   A162   F   727   PIKE
   A203   F   727   PIKE

  5 5 5 5 1 7 1 3 4 5 4 3 2 1 7:   *see* **695**

1115. 5 5 5 5 1 7 6 5 5 3 3 4 5 5 1   1 2 3 4 5 6 7 8 7 8
LMD   4v   H H H H H H F F H H
1795   *a* Babcock
   A149   E   *a*   367   DORCHESTER
   A192   E   *a*   367   DORCHESTER

1116.   5 5 5 5 2 3 5 5 5 5 5 3 2 2 2   1 2 3 4
         CM   4v   H O H F
         c.1775   *a* Senior
              P226   G   *a*   653

1117.   5 5 5 5 3 2 7 1 6 5 5 2 1 7 2   1 2 2 3 4 4
         CM   4v   O F E F F F
         c.1775   *a* Senior
              P226   A   *a*   205

1118.   5 5 5 5 3 4 5 5 3 4 3 2 5 5 7   1 2 3 4 4 5 6 7 8 8
         CMD   4v   O H F O H H H O O H
         1791   *a* Callcott
              P291   D   *a*   609

         5 5 5 5 4 3 2 1 3 5 5 5 4 5 1:   *soprano of* **933**

         5 5 5 5 4 3 4 5 6 7 1 7 6 5 5:   *soprano of* **118**

         5 5 5 5 4 6 5 4 3 5 5 1 3 2 2:   *soprano of* **701**

1119.   5 5 5 5 5 1 7 1 2 3 3 1 1 6 5   1 2 3 4 3 3 4
         LM   4v   H H H H F H H
         1793   *a* Holden
              A124   C   *a*   578   RAPTURE
              A195   C   578   RAPTURE

1120.	5 5 5　5 5 2　2 2 1　7 1 2　3 4 5	1　2　2　3　4　4
	CM　　　　　　　　　　　　　　4v	H　F　E　H　F　H
	c.1775　　　　　　　　　　*a* Senior	
	P226　　　　　B♭　　*a*　　447	

1121.	5 5 5　5 5 3　1 7 7　7 6 5　4 3 2	1　2　3　4
	LM　　　　　　　　　　　　　　4v	H　F　O　F
	c.1775　　　　　　　　　　*a* Senior	
	P226　　　　　a　　*a*　　687	

1122.	5 5 5　5 5 3　3 3 2　5 5 4　5 5 4	1　2　3　4　4
	CM　　　　　　　　　　　　　　4v	H　O　F　O　O
	c.1775　　　　　　　　　　*a* Senior	
	P226　　　　　C　　*a*　　815	

1123.	5 5 5　5 5 5　4 3 1　2 2 3　2 1 1	1　2　3　4
	CM　　　　　　　　　　　　　　4v	H　E　F　F
	c.1775　　　　　　　　　　*a* Senior	
	P226　　　　　g　　*a*　　522	

1124.	5 5 5　5 5 5　4 3 5　4 4 3　4 5 5	1　2　3　4
	CM　　　　　　　　　　　　　　4v	H　H　F　H
	c.1785　　　　　　　　　*a* Tremain	
	P256　　　　　F　　*a*　　703	

1125.	5 5 5　5 5 5　4 5 6　5 4 3　5 4 4	1　2　3　4
	CM　　　　　　　　　　　　　　4v	F　H　H　F
	c.1755　　　　　　　　　　*a* Senior	
	P226　　　　　a　　*a*　　311	

1126. 5 5 5 5 5 5 5 1 6 7 3 5 5 1 1   1 2 3 4
      XXXX   3v   H F H F
      c.1775   *a* Stephenson
          P227   G   *a*   26

      5 5 5 5 5 5 5 5 5 7 6 5 4 5 1:   *soprano of* **7**

1127. 5 5 5 5 5 5 6 2 3 2 2 2 5 4 4   1 2 2 3 4 4 5 6 6 7 8
      CMD   4v   F H F E H H F H H O O
      1791   *a* S. Arnold
          P291   G   *a*   492

      5 5 5 5 5 5 6 7 1 5 4 4 3 3 6:   *soprano of* **385**

1128. 5 5 5 5 5 6 5 5 5 4 5 5 4 5 5   1 2 3 3 4 4 5 6 7 8 8
      CMD   4v   H H A A F H H F A H F
      1791   *a* S. Arnold
          P291   G   *a*   795

1129. 5 5 5 5 5 6 5 5 5 5 1 7 7 1 6   1 2 3 4 4
      LM   4v   H H F E E
      c.1775   *a* Senior
          P226   a   *a*   464

1130. 5 5 5 5 5 6 5 5 5 5 5 6 7 1 6   1 2 3 4
      CM   4v   H H H F
      c.1775   *a* Senior
          P226   A   *a*   76

5 5 5   5 5 6   5 5 5   6 5 4   3 4 5:   *soprano of* **242**

5 5 5   5 6 2   1 7 1   7 1 3   1 7 6:   *soprano of* **688**

1131.	5 5 5 5 6 7 1 2 3 2 1 1 1 7 6			1 2 3̑ 4 4	
	CM		4v	H H H F H	
	1785		*a* D. Read		
	A63	E♭	*a*	416	VICTORY
	A63.2	E♭	*a*	416	VICTORY
	A80	E♭	*a*	416	VICTORY
	A98	E♭	*b*	416	VICTORY
	A109	E♭	*b*	416	VICTORY
	A114	E♭	*a*	416	VICTORY
	A119	E♭	*a*	416	VICTORY
	A80.4	E♭	*a*	416	VICTORY
	A114.B	E♭	*a*	416	VICTORY
	A121	D		416	VICTORY
	A124	E♭	*a*	416	VICTORY
	A137	E♭	*a*	416	VICTORY
	A145	E♭	*a*	416	VICTORY
	A147	E♭	*a*	416	VICTORY
	A158	E♭	*a*	416	VICTORY
	A80.5	E♭	*a*	416	VICTORY
	A160	E♭	*a*	416	VICTORY
	A163	E♭	*a*	416	VICTORY
	A167	E♭	*a*	416	VICTORY
	A168	E♭	*a*	416	VICTORY
	A170	E♭	*a*	416	VICTORY
	A172	E♭	*a*	416	VICTORY
	A175	E♭	*a*	416	VICTORY
	A181	E♭		416	VICTORY
	A182	E♭		416	VICTORY
	A190	E♭	*a*	416	VICTORY
	A181.5	E♭	*a*	416	VICTORY
	A195	E♭	*a*	416	VICTORY
	A198	E♭	*a*	416	VICTORY

b Mann

1132. 5 5 5 5 6 7 1 7 6 5 5 5 5 4 5   1 2 3͡ 4͡ 4
           CM   4v   F H E F F
           c. 1757
               P166   F   492
               D15   F   *b*   204   SOUTHWARK NEW

           _____

           b H [ill?]

           See also **467**.

1133. 5 5 5 5 6 7 6 5 5 4 5 3 2 1 2   1 2͡ 3 4
           LM   3v   H H F O
           1794   *a* Dupuis
               P297   A   *a*   819

           5 5 5 5 7 1 1 6 2 7 5 3 2 3 2:   *soprano of* **18**

1134. 5 5 5 6 1 1 1 7 5 5 7 7 6 5 5   1 1 2 3 3 4 4 4
           CM   4v   H F F F H F F O
           c. 1785   *a* Tremain
               P256   D   *a*   581

1135. 5 5 5 6 1 2 1 7 1 7 5 1 7 1 7   1 2 3 4
           LM   4v   H F C H
           1798   *a* Loder
               P310   D   *a*   384

1136. 5 5 5 6 1 6 6 5 7 7 1 1 6 7 1   1 2 3 4
CM   4v   F H F H
c.1752   *a* Knapp

P148	D	*a*	483	CORFE-MULLEN
P148.2	D	*a*	483	CORFE-MULLEN
P148.3	D	*a*	483	CORFE-MULLEN
P148.4	D	*a*	483	CORFE-MULLEN
P148.5	D	*a*	483	CORFE-MULLEN
P204	D		481	TENTERDEN
P220	D		481	SANDWICH

1137. 5 5 5 6 3 4 2 5 5 5 1 5 5 5 1   1 2 3 4 5 6 7 8
CMD   4v · H H F H F H F H
c.1790   *a* M. Cooke

P274	E♭	*a*	439

1138. 5 5 5 6 4 4 6 5 1 1 1 1 1 1 1   1 2 2͡ 3͡ 4 4
CM   4v   H H H F F H
1791   *a* Jomelli

P291	E♭	*a*	161

1139. 5 5 5 6 5 4 3 2 3 5 5 5 7 5 1   1 2 3͡ 4
CM   3v   F E F F
1790   *a* Cooper

A98	f	*a*	775	CONSOLATION
A109	f	*a*	775	CONSOLATION
A114	f	*a*	775	CONSOLATION
A114.B	f	*a*	775	CONSOLATION
A137	f	*a*	775	CONSOLATION

5 5 5 6 5 4 3 4 5 5 5 4 4 4 3:   *soprano of* **693**

5 5 5 6 5 6 7 1 7 1 7 6 5 5 3:   *alto of* **121**

5 5 5 6 6 4 4 5 5 6 6 5 5 4 4:   *soprano of* **697**

5 5 5 6 7 3 7 1 7 5 4 3 4 3 5:   *see* **743**

5 5 5 6 7 3 7 1 7 6 5 3 4 3 5:   *see* **743**

1140.	5 5 5 6 7 6 7 6 7 1 7 6 5 1 1			1 2 3 4 3 4	
	CM		4v	F H E H H E	
	c.1757				
	P166	G	483		

1141.	5 5 5 7 1 5 4 3 2 1 3 4 5 4 3			1 2 M M 4 3 4	
	CM		4v	H E F O H H H	
	1797		*a* Belknap		
	A166	g	*a*	677	NEWMARK
	A192	g	*a*	677	NEWMARK

1142.	5 5 5 7 1 7 7 7 7 5 5 4 3 4 5			1 2 3 4 4	
	CM		3v	H H H F H	
	c.1776				
	P231	g	362		

1143.   5 5 5 7 4 5 7 7 7 5 3 4 5 6 5   1 2 3 4 4
CM   3v   H E H F H
c.1776
    P231   a   673

1144.   5 5 5 7 7 1 7 1 2 3 2 4 3 5 4   1 2 3 4 5 6 7 8 9 X Y Z
888888²   3v   O O O O O O H H F O H H
1794   *a* J. S. Smith
    P297   D   *a*   783

1145.   5 5 5 7 7 5 3 2 1 2 3 4 5 7 7   1 2 3 4 4 4
LM   4v   F H H F F F
1783   *a* Strong
    A51   e   *a*   548   SUNDERLAND
    A62   e   *a*   548   SUNDERLAND
    A62.3   e   *a*   548   SUNDERLNAD

    5 5 5 7 7 5 5 5 5 5 6 7 5 1 7:   *alto of* **199**

1146.   5 5 6 5 1 2 1 7 6 7 1 7 6 1 3   1 2 3 3 3 4 4 4
CM   4v   F F E A H F F H
c.1776
    P231   C   277

Phrases 3-8 are in E .

    5 5 6 5 1 7 6 5 4 5 5 1 2 3 4:   *soprano of* **701**

1147. 5 5 6 5 3 1 4 2 2 2 2 3 2 1 7   1 2 3 4 5 6 6

      666688   4v   H H H H F C H

      1798   a Loder

        P310   F   *a*   805

1148. 5 5 6 5 4 3 5 1 1 1 7 6 5 1 5   1 2 3 4 5̑ 6 7 8

      CMD   4v   H H H H F F H H

      1786

A68	F	797	OCEAN
A92	F	693	OCEAN
A92.2	F	693	OCEAN
A101	F	693	OCEAN
A103	F	693	OCEAN
A106	F	797	OCEAN
A110[1]	F	860	OCEAN
A106.4	F	797	OCEAN
A111[1]	F	797	OCEAN
A114	F	693	OCEAN
A119	F	693	OCEAN
A114.B	F	693	OCEAN
A121[1]	F	797	OCEAN
A124	F	693	OCEAN
A130	F	797	OCEAN
A131	F	*b*	797	OCEAN
A111.3[1]	F	797	OCEAN
A137	F	693	OCEAN
A145	F	693	OCEAN
A146	F	693	OCEAN
A147	F	693	OCEAN
A111.4[1]	F	797	OCEAN
A148	F	797	OCEAN
A158	F	693	OCEAN
A111.5[1]	F	797	OCEAN
A103.4	F	693	OCEAN
A160	F	693	OCEAN

---

[1] 5 5 6 5 4 3 6 1 1 1 7 6 5 1 5

b Swan   *1148 continued*

A163	F		693	OCEAN
A111.6[1]	F		797	OCEAN
A103.5	F		693	OCEAN
A146.5	F		693	OCEAN
A168	F		693	OCEAN
A170	F	c	693	OCEAN
A172	F		693	OCEAN
A174	F		693	OCEAN
A175	F		693	OCEAN
A181	F		693	OCEAN
A103.6	F		693	OCEAN
A189	F	b	693	OCEAN
A190	F		693	OCEAN
A181.5	F		693	OCEAN
A198	F	b	693	OCEAN
A200	F		797	OCEAN

[1] 5 5 6 5 4 3 6 1 1 1 7 6 5 1 5

b Swan

c Morgan

1149.   5 5 6 5 4 3 5 6 5 4 3 2 1 5 1   1 2 3 4
    CM   4v   F F F H
    c.1755   a Pratt
       P158   G   a   14

5 5 6 5 4 3 6 1 1 1 7 6 5 1 5:   *see* **1148**

5 5 6 5 4 5 6 5 5 5 7 1 1 7 5:   *soprano of* **455**

1150. 5 5 6 5 5 4 2 3 5 6 7 1 6 7 5   1 2 2 3 4 4
      CM   3v   H H H F H H
      1791   *a* Callcott
         P291   G   *a*   843
         D15[1]   G   531   TILBURY

      ———————

[1] 5 3 4 2 3 6 7 1 5 6 7 1 2 3 7

      5 5 6 5 5 4 3 2 3 4 3 5 5 6 5:   *soprano of* **702**

      5 5 6 5 5 5 1 2 3 2 1 7 1 1 5:   *soprano of* **698**

1151. 5 5 6 5 6 5 4 3 6 3 4 5 3 5 6   1̑ 2̑ 3̑ 3̑ 4̑ 4
      LM   4v   F F O O F O
      c.1776
         P231   G   748

1152. 5 5 6 6 5 5 1 7 5 6 1 3 2 1 1   1 2 3 4̑ 4̑ 4
      SM   4v   E F F O O F
      1791   *a* Callcott
         P291   A   *a*   102

      5 5 6 7 1 2 3 2 1 7 1 1 2 5 3:   *soprano of* **707**

1153. 5 5 6 7 5 6 7 1 2 7 5 2 1 7 1   1̑ 2 3̑ 4
      CM   3v   O F F F
      1791   *a* Handel
         P291   A   *a*   287

5 5 7 1 1 1 2 3 7 7 6 5 5 5 4:   *soprano of* **24**

1154.   5 5 7 1 1 7 5 1 1 5 4 3 7 5 3   1 2 3 M͡ M͡ 4
       CM   4v   H H F F O H
       1799   *a* Jenks
         A187   e   *a*   388   WOODBRIDGE

5 5 7 1 2 1 2 3 4 3 3 2 1 2 3:   *soprano of* **737**

1155.   5 5 7 1 2 1 7 5 4 5 3 4 5 7 7   1 2 3 4͡ 5͡ 6 4 5 6
       888888   4v   H H H F F F H H H
       1800
         A200   e   241   LIVONA

1156.   5 5 7 1 5 3 2 3 4 5 1 7 7 6 5   1 2 3 4 4
       LM   4v   H H F F H
       1797   *a* Belknap
         A166   f♯   *a*   539   SOUTHBOROUGH
         A192   f♯   *a*   539   SOUTHBOROUGH

1157.   5 5 7 1 5 4 3 2 4 3 1 3 4 5 7   1 2 3 4͡ 4͡
       SM   4v   H H F F O
       1797   *a* Willcox
         A167   e   *a*   291   ESSEX

5 5 7 1 5 5 6 5 5 5 7 1 7 6 5:   *soprano of* **358**

5 5 7 1 7 1 6 5 7 1 7 7 7 7 1:   *soprano of* **95**

1158.	5 5 7	2 4 5	5 5 4	4 3 3	4 5 5	1 2 3 4 5 6 7 8
	LMD				4v	O H F H O H H H
	1791			*a* S. Arnold		
	P291		g	*a*	119	

5 5 7 7 7 1 7 6 5 5 5 5 7 6 5:   *soprano of* **272**

1159.	5 6 1	2 3 2	1 7 6	5 1 7	6 5 6	1̂ 1 2 3̂ 3 4
	CM				3v	O O F O O F
	1799					
	D15		D		30	GRANCHESTER

1160.	5 6 1	7 6 5	5 5 5	6 5 6	7 1 1	1 2 3 4 3 4 5 6 7̂ 8̂ M̂ 8 7 8
	SMD				4v	H H H H H H E E F F F F H H
	1778			*a* Wood		
	A41	F	*a*	200		WORCESTER
	A43	F	*a*	200		WORCESTER
	A47a	F	*a*	200		WORCESTER
	A54	F		200		WORCESTER
	A56	F		200		WORCESTER
	A60	F		200		WORCESTER
	A70	F	*a*	200		WORCESTER
	A84	F	*a*	200		WORCESTER
	A85	F		200		WORCESTER
	A89	F		200		WORCESTER
	A91	F	*a*	200		WORCESTER

1160 continued

A92	F	*a*	200	WORCESTER
A95	F		200	WORCESTER
A92.3	F	*a*	200	WORCESTER
A98	F	*a*	200	WORCESTER
A101	F		200	WORCESTER
A103	F	*a*	200	WORCESTER
A106	F		200	WORCESTER
A108	F	*a*	200	WORCESTER
A109	F	*a*	200	WORCESTER
A106.4	F		200	WORCESTER
A113	F	*a*	200	WORCESTER
A114	F	*a*	200	WORCESTER
A119	F	*a*	200	WORCESTER
A114.B	F	*a*	200	WORCESTER
A124	F	*a*	200	WORCESTER
A131	F	*a*	200	WORCESTER
A132	F	*a*	200	WORCESTER
A146	F		200	WORCESTER
A147	F	*a*	200	WORCESTER
A148	F	*a*	200	WORCESTER
A158	F	*a*	200	WORCESTER
A103.4	F	*a*	200	WORCESTER
A160	F	*a*	200	WORCESTER
A163	F	*a*	200	WORCESTER
A103.5	F	*a*	200	WORCESTER
A146.5	F		200	WORCESTER
A168	F	*a*	200	WORCESTER
A170	F	*a*	200	WORCESTER
A175	F	*a*	200	WORCESTER
A181	F		200	WORCESTER
A103.6	F	*a*	200	WORCESTER
A189	F	*a*	200	WORCESTER
A190	F	*a*	200	WORCESTER
A181.5	F	*a*	200	WORCESTER
A195	F	*a*	200	WORCESTER
A198	F	*a*	200	WORCESTER

5 6 5 4 3 2 1 2 3 6 5 1 7 1 7:   *soprano of* **222**

1161.   5 6 5 4 3 2 1 7 6 4 5 4 3 2 1   1 1 2 3 4
       CM   4v   E F H F H
       c.1746

P129a	G	557	
P148	G	557	HAM WORTHY
P148.2	G	557	HAM WORTHY
P148.3	G	557	HAM WORTHY
P182a	G	557	
P148.4	G	557	HAM WORTHY
P148.5	G	557	HAM WORTHY
P220	G	562	SOUTHFLEET
P228	G	557	

       5 6 5 4 3 2 3 5 4 3 2 1 5 5 5:   *soprano of* **716**

1162.   5 6 5 5 5 5 3 3 4 5 6 6 5 5 4   1 2 3 4 4 4
       CM   4v   F F F O O H
       1791   *a* Callcott

P291	E♭	*a*	120

1163.   5 6 6 5 1 1 7 6 7 4 5 6 5 6 7   1 2 2 3 3 3 4 4
       CM   4v   F F O F F O F O
       1791   *a* Handel

P291	e		25

1164.   5 6 7 1 1 2 1 7 6 5 5 1 7 1 5   1 2 3 4 5 6 7 8 8 8
       LMD   4v   H H H H H H H O F H
       1781   *a* W. Billings

A91	E	*a*	293	MANCHESTER
A108	E	*a*	293	MANCHESTER

1164 continued

	A119	E	*a*	293	MANCHESTER
	A147	E	*a*	293	MANCHESTER
	A168	E	*a*	293	MANCHESTER

The first printing of this tune in **A44** is not fuging due to a different text underlay.

5 6 7 1 2 5 3 2 1 5 6 6 6 7 1: *soprano of* **1165**

1165. 5 6 7 1 2 5 3 2 1 7 1 2 1 7 5   1 2 3̂ 3 3 4 4
          CM   4v   F H H O H F F
          1784   *a* Greatorex

	P253	B♭	*a*	661	BIRMINGHAM
	P253.2	B♭	*a*	661	BIRMINGHAM
	A79	B♭		661	BIRMINGHAM
	A87	B♭		661	BIRMINGHAM
	A117	B♭		661	BIRMINGHAM
	P253.4	B♭	*a*	661	BIRMINGHAM

5 6 7 1 3 2 1 7 2 3 4 5 1 4 3: *soprano of* **1031**

5 6 7 1 5 5 6 7 1 2 7 1 1 3 1: *see* **709**

1166. 5 6 7 1 5 6 5 4 3 2 1 5 5 1 5   1 2 3̂ 4
          CM   4v   H H F O
          1793   *a* Stone

	A131	F	*a*	507	HARRISBURGH

1167. 5 6 7 1 5 6 5 4 3 4 3 2 1 2 3   1 2 3 4
      CM   4v   F H F H
      1789
        P266   E♭   436   REDBRIDGE

1168. 5 6 7 1 6 2 2 5 1 5 3 1 1 1 7   1 2 3 4 5 6 7 8
      LMD   4v   H H F F F F F H H
      1759   *a* French (*E*)
        P170   D   *a*   556

1169. 5 6 7 1 6 2 3 4 3 1 1 7 6 5 4   1 2 2 3 4 3 4
      LM   3v   H H F F H H F
      1789   *a* Randall
        P269   F   *a*   345   ANGLESEY
        P269.2   F   *a*   345   ANGLESEY
        P269.3   F   *a*   345   ANGLESEY

1170. 5 6 7 1 6 7 1 2 7 1 2 3 1 1 7   1͡ 2 3 4
      LM   4v   F F H H
      1786
        P258   D   *b*   356   SANDWICH

---

b "Latter part from H.Y Purcel."

5 6 7 1 7 1 2 3 4 3 2 1 7 6 5: *see* **1227**

1171. 567 171 321 766 534   1 2 3 4 3͡3 4 4
LM   4v   H H E H F F F H
1786   *a* Mann

A70	D	*a*	344	LANCASTER
A74	D		344	LANCASTER
A84	D	*a*	344	LANCASTER
A85	D		344	LANCASTER
A91	D	*a*	344	LANCASTER
A108	D	*a*	344	LANCASTER
A110 [1,2]	D	*a*	811	LANCASTER
A119	D	*a*	344	LANCASTER
A170	D	*a*	344	NO. 1

[1] 1 2 3 4 5͡6 7 8
     H H E H F F F H

[2] LMD

1172. 567 171 345 671 755   1͡ 2͡1 2 M M 4 5 M͡M 8͡6 7 8
66664444   4v   F F H H F F H F F F F O O H
1791   *a* Handel

P291	E♭	*a*	802

1173. 567 176 655 354 325   1 2 3 4 4 5 6 7͡8 7 8
CMD   4v   H H H F H H H H F O H H
1793   *a* Wood

A132	E	*a*	699	ASPIRATION

567 654 342 333 443:   *soprano of* **925**

1174. 567 671 212 321 333   1 2 3͡4
CM   4v   F F F F
1754

P151	C		483
P157	C		483
P198	A		483

1175. 5 7 1   2 1 2   3 4 3   2 1 7   1 2 3   1 2 3 4
CM   4v   H E H F
c.1746

P129a	C	391
P135	C	391
P145a	C	391

1176. 5 7 4   3 4 5   5 7 7   5 1 1   5 4 3   1 2 3 4 5 6 6
XXXXXX   4v   H H H H A F H
1795   *a* N. Billings

A150	e	*a*	39	LAST DAY

1177. 5 7 5   1 1 3   2 1 7   2 1 7   1 6 6   1 2 3 3 4 5 6 7̑ 8
CMD   4v   F H H H F H H F F
1770

P200	B♭	608

1178. 5 7 5   1 2 3   2 1 7   1 2 3   2 1 6   1 2 3 4
CM   4v   H H H F
1760   *a* Stephenson

P171	d	*a*	690
P171.4	d	*a*	690

1179. 5 7 5   1 2 3   2 1 7   2 1 7   1 6 6   1 2 3 3 4 5 6 7̑ 8
CMD   4v   F H H H F H H F O
c.1770-5

⁺P204	C	31	ELTHAM
⁺P220	A	31	NORTH CRAY

1180.   5 7 5   1 7 1   1 5 6   5 4 3   2 3 5   1   2   3͡   M   4
SM   4v   H   H   F   O   H
1790   *a* Edson

A96	e	*a*	16	LAINSBOROUGH
A111	e	*a*	16	LAINSBOROUGH
A111.3	e	*a*	16	LAINSBOROUGH
A111.4	e	*a*	16	LAINSBOROUGH
A111.5	e	*a*	16	LAINSBOROUGH
A111.6	e	*a*	16	LAINSBOROUGH
A189	e	*a*	16	LAINSBOROUGH

1181.   5 7 5   1 7 5   4 5 3   2 1 2   3 4 5   1 2 3 4 5 6 7 8 8
SMD   4v   H H H H F H H E H
c. 1790-6

A102	d	574	SAINTS COMPLAINT
A110	d	574	SAINTS COMPLAINT

5 7 5   4 3 1   7 7 3   5 5 3   1 3 1:   *see* **1182**

1182.   5 7 5   4 3 1   7 7 3   5 5 3   5 3 1   1 2 3 4 5 6 7 8
CMD   4v   H H H H H H H F
1790   *a* Swan

A96	e	*a*	178	EGYPT
A111	e	*a*	178	EGYPT
A132[1]	e	*a*	178	EGYPT
A111.3	e	*a*	178	EGYPT
A111.4	e	*a*	178	EGYPT
A111.5	e	*a*	178	EGYPT
A111.6	e	*a*	178	EGYPT

[1] 5 7 5   4 3 1   7 7 3   5 5 3   1 3 1

1183.   5 7 5 4 3 2 1 2 1 2 3 4 5 5 7   1 2 3 4 5̑ 6
      888888   4v   O H H H F F
      1793   *a* Bruce

A132	f	*a*	100	BRAINTREE
A150	f	*a*	100	BRAINTREE

      5 7 7 1 2 3 2 2 1 7 1 5 7 7 2:   *see* **1219**

      5 7 7 1 5 4 3 1 6 4 5 1 7 6 5:   *see* **1184**

1184.   5 7 7 1 5 4 3 1 6 4 5 1 7 7 6   1 2 3̑ 4
      CM   4v   H H F F
      -1793   *a* Goff

[+]A121	f♯		534	SUTTON
[+]A131[1]	f♯	*a*	534	SUTTON
A158[2,3,4]	f♯	*a*	534	SUTTON
A163[2,3,4]	f♯	*a*	534	SUTTON
[+]A164[1]	f♯		534	SUTTON
A174[1]	f♯		534	SUTTON
A175[2,3,4]	f♯	*a*	534	SUTTON
A181[2]	f♯		534	SUTTON NEW
A182[1]	f♯		534	SUTTON
A181.5[2,3,4]	f♯	*a*	534	SUTTON

---

[1] 5 7 7 1 5 4 3 1 6 4 5 1 7 6 5

[2] 5 7 7 1 5 4 3 7 6 4 5 1 7 6 5

[3] 3v

[4] 1 2 3̑ 4 4
   H H F F H

      5 7 7 1 5 4 3 7 6 4 5 1 7 6 5:   *see* **1184**

1185.   5 7 7   1 7 6   5 1 7   7 1 5   4 3 5   1 2̂ 2 3 4
         CM   4v   H O O F F
         1759

	P169	d		777	KEGWORTH
	P169.2	d		777	KEGWORTH
	P198	d		777	
	A43[1]	e	b	777	SALEM
	A47a[1]	e	b	777	SALEM
	A56[1]	e		777	SALEM
	A57[1]	e		777	SALEM
	A57.2[1]	e		777	SALEM
	A74[1]	e		777	SALEM
	A84[1]	e	b	777	SALEM
	A85[1]	e		777	SALEM
	A91[1]	e	b	777	SALEM
	A98[1]	e	b	777	SALEM
	A106[1]	e	b	777	SALEM
	A106.4[1]	e	b	777	SALEM
	A109[1]	e	b	777	SALEM
	A114[1]	e	b	777	SALEM
	A114.B[1]	e	b	777	SALEM

[1] 1 2̂ 2 3 4
    H O F F F

b J. Arnold

1186.   5 7 7   5 3 4   4 4 3   5 7 7   6 7 5   1 2 3̂ 4̂ 4
         CM   4v   H H F O F
         1794   a Belcher

	A135	d	a	754	TRANSITION

6 4 3   7 5 5   4 3 3   3 3 3   3 3 3:   *soprano of* **967**

6 5 4   3 2 1   1 2 3   4 2 5   6 7 7:   *soprano of* **625**

1187.   7 1 1   1 1 1   7 1 3   3 3 4   3 2 1   1 2 3 4
        LM   3v   H H F F
        1791   *a* Callcott
           P291   A   *a*   58

1188.   7 1 1   1 7 5   6 7 1   7 7 7   1 2 1   1 2 2 3 4 4 4
        LM   3v   F O O F F F H
        1791   *a* Graun
           P291   A   *a*   585

1189.   7 1 1   7 1 7   1 7 5   2 3 1   7 1 1   1 2 3 4 4 5 6 6
        888888   4v   H H H H H H O F
        1791   *a* Handel
           P291   G   *a*   152

1190.   7 1 2   3 4 5   3 4 3   2 1 1   7 1 2   1 2 3 4
        LM   3v   H F H H
        1794   *a* M. Cooke
           P297   e   *a*   573

        7 1 5   3 2 1   6 5 4   3 2 3   4 5 4:   *soprano of* **640**

1191.   7 1 7   1 1 6   5 5 3   6 7 1   2 3 7   1 2 3 4 5 6 7 8
        CMD   4v   H E C H O H F H
        c.1790   *a* M. Cooke
           P274   D   *a*   6

717 122 343 217 332:   *soprano of* **139**

1192.   717 654 545 671 765   1 2 3 4 5 6 7 8
         LMD   4v   H O F F H H H F
         1791   *a* Callcott
             P291   F   *a*   746

722 343 211 145 432:   *soprano of* **206**

727 321 275 171 237:   *soprano of* **267**

756 712 321 712 321:   *soprano of* **937**

1193.   766 532 175 152 571   1 2 3 4 4 5 6 5 6 7 8 8
         CMD   4v   H F H F C C H C H E F E
         1798   *a* Cantelo
             P310   B♭   *a*   311

1194.   777 155 452 525 677   1 2 3 4 4 3 4 4
         CM   4v   H H H F E H H H
         1789-91
             P264   D   193

428

Note: The following tunes are out of numerical order.

1195.   1 3 3   2 2 1   6 5 5   1 1 2   7 1 5   1 2 3 4 3 4
CM   4v   H H F F F H
1800
     A181.5   C   204   SPRINGWATER

1196.   1 5 4   3 5 1   3 2 2   3 3 2   1 2 1   1 2 3 M 4
CM   4v   H H F O H
1800
     A181.5   C   207   NORTHFIELD

1197.   1 3 4   5 3 4   3 2 2   3 4 5   4 3 2   1 2 3 4 3 4
CM   4v   H H F F H E
1798   *a* A. Munson
     A180   A   457   ARMENIA

1198.   1 5 5   6 7 1   5 3 1   6 5 4   3 5 5   1 2 3 4 3 4
LM   4v   H H F F F H
1798
     A180   E   839   DOMINION

1199.   5 3 5   1 2 1   1 3 1   3 2 1   7 6 5   1 2 3 4 5 6 7 7 8
SMD   4v   H H F H H H H H H
1798   *a* A. Munson
     A180   C   *a*   283   NEWBURGH

1200. 1 7 6 4 3 2 1 2 3 3 6 7 1 2 1   1 2 3 4
CM   3v   H H H F
1754-
    D2   G   829   MILE END
    D3   G   829   MILE END

1201. 1 3 1 2 5 1 7 1 3 2 1 2 3 4 3   1 2 3 4͡ 4
LM   4v   H H H F F
1798   *a* Leach
    D14   C   *a*   845   INFANCY

1202. 1 3 4 5 6 5 1 2 3 2 1 6 5 4 3   1 2 3 4 5 6
887887   4v   H H H A H F
1798   *a* Leach
    D14   D   *a*   846   MOUNT ZION

1203. 1 5 3 4 5 3 2 1 3 2 7 1 2 3 4   1 2 3 4 4
CM   4v   H H H F H
1798   *a* Leach
    D14   a   *a*   847   NEW WINDSOR

1204. 1 5 4 3 4 6 5 4 3 2 3 5 3 6 5   1 2 3 4 4
CM   4v   H H H F H
1798   *a* Leach
    D14   A   *a*   386   TABERNACLE

1205. 3 2 1 2 3 5 1 5 4 3 3 2 6 5 7   1 2 3 4
7777   4v   H H F A
1798   *a* Leach
    D14   F   *a*   848   LEBANON

1206.   5 4 3 6 7 1 3 2 1 3 5 1 7 1 2   1 2 3 4
       CM   4v   H H F H
       1798   *a* Leach
           D14   F   *a*   849   SMYRNA

1207.   1 1 2 1 5 1 2 3 5 3 2 1 2 3 4   1 2 3 4
       LM   4v   H E F H
       c.1791-6
           A110   A   215   RIPLEY

1208.   1 3 3 3 4 3 4 5 1 7 7 5 4 3 1   1 2 3 4 5 6 7 8 8
       SMD   4v   F H H H F H E H E
       c.1791-6
           A110   e   423   PS. 32

1209.   1 3 3 4 4 6 5 1 7 1 3 2 7 5 7   1 2 3 4
       SM   4v   H H F H
       c.1791-6
           A110   d   291   PS. 55

1210.   1 3 3 6 5 6 7 1 5 6 5 6 5 4 3   1 2 3 4
       LM   4v   H H F E
       c.1791-6
           A110   F   854   PS. 91

1211.   1 5 3 6 4 3 2 1 5 1 2 3 2 1 6   1 2 3 4
       CM   4v   H E F E
       c.1791-6
           A110   D   855   BERLIN

1212. 156 536 715 356 555   1 2 3 4 5 6 7 8 9 X Y Z Y Z
LMT   4v   H E H E H H H H F H H H H H
c.1791-6
    A110   E   856   PS. 65

1213. 512 161 231 217 655   1 2 3 4 4
CM   4v   H H F H H
c.1791-6
    A110   d   857   PS. 132

1214. 512 353 121 711 121   1 2 3 4 5 6 7 8
CMD   4v   H H H H H H F H
c.1791-6
    A110   A   331   PS. 4

1215. 512 354 321 543 176   1 2 3 4
SM   4v   H H F E
c.1791-6
    A110   G   52   PS. 19

1216. 532 176 567 125 432   1 2 3 4 5 6 7 8 8
LMD   4v   H H H H H H F F F
c.1791-6
    A110   D   841   TEMPEST

1217. 532 177 115 345 511   1 2 3 4
CM   4v   F H E H
c.1791-6
    A110   e   457   REPENTANCE

1218.   5 3 5   1 6 5   6 5 4   3 2 1   1 3 3   1   2   3   4   4
       SM   4v   H   H   F   F   H
       c. 1791-6
         A110   F   858   PS. 48

1219.   5 7 7   1 2 3   2 2 1   7 1 5   7 7 2   1   2   3   4   5   6   6
       XXXXXX   4v   H   E   H   E   F   H   E
       c. 1791-6
         A110   c   859   EDENTON

1220.   1 3 2   1 3 2   2 5 4   3 2 1   5 5 5   1   2   3   4   5   6
       666688   4v   H   H   H   H   F   H
       1799   *a* Jenks
         A187   a   *a*   174   PROTECTION

1221.   1 5 5   4 3 2   7 5 5   4 3 2   1 3 5   1   2   3   4
       SM   4v   H   H   F   H
       1799   *a* Jenks
         A187   a   291   CONTENTMENT

1222.   5 5 5   1 1 7   7 1 1   5 5 3   3 4 6   1   2   3   4   M
       LM   4v   H   H   F   F   F
       1799   *a* Jenks
         A187   e   *a*   834   SOLEMNITY

1223.   3 5 5   4 3 4   5 3 2   1 2 3   4 3 2   1   2   3   4   3   4   5   6   5   6   5   5   6   5   5   6
       878747   3v   H   H   H   E   H   H   O   H   F   H   H   H   H   H   H
       1795   *a* Holyoke
         A153   A   *a*   861   SANDUSKY

1224. 1 2 4 5 3 4 6 4 2 3 1 6 1 2 2   1 2 2 3͡ 3 4͡ 4
CM   4v   F H H F F F F
1763   *a* Barnes or Carpendale
  P186a   G   549

1225. 1 3 7 1 2 3 2 1 2 7 1 7 6 1 2   1 2͡ 2 3͡ 3 4
CM   4v   F F F F F O
1763   *a* Barnes or Carpendale
  P186a   A   *a*   599

1226. 3 4 2 3 1 2 7 1 4 3 5 4 3 2 1   1 2 3 3 4 4
CM   4v   F F F H F H
1763   *a* Barnes or Carpendale
  P186a   g   *a*   322

1227. 5 6 7 1 7 1 2 3 4 3 2 1 7 6 5   1 2͡ 2 3 4 4
CM   4v   F F F H F H
1763   *a* Barnes or Carpendale
  P186a   c   *a*   862

1228. 5 1 2 3 4 3 2 1 3 2 1 7 6 5 7   1 2͡ 2 3 3 4͡ 4
CM   4v   H F F H H F F
1763   *a* Barnes or Carpendale
  P186a   C   *a*   278

1229. 1 3 2 1 7 1 6 2 1 7 7 5 6 7 1   1 2 3 4͡ 4
LM   4v   F F F F F
1763   *a* Barnes or Carpendale
  P186a   C   *a*   475

1230. 5 1 2 3 1 6 6 1 2 3 4 3 5 4 3   1 2 2 3 4 4
CM   4v   F F H F F F
1763   *a* Barnes or Carpendale
    P186a   B♭   *a*   863

1231. 1 7 5 6 5 4 5 6 7 5 1 7 6 7 6   1 2 3 4
LM   4v   F F F F
1763   *a* Barnes or Carpendale
    P186a   d   *a*   720

1232. 5 3 1 2 3 3 4 3 2 1 7 1 2 5 3   1 2 3 4 5 6
888888   4v   F H F F H F
1763   *a* Barnes or Carpendale
    P186a   A   *a*   864

1233. 5 1 6 7 5 6 7 1 1 3 1 2 7 5 5   1 2 2 3 4 4
LM   4v   F F H F F F
1763   *a* Barnes or Carpendale
    P186a   E♭   *a*   435

1234. 1 7 5 6 7 1 6 4 6 5 1 2 7 1 6   1 1 2 2 3 4 4
LM   4v   O F F F O F H
1763   *a* Barnes or Carpendale
    P186a   D   *a*   518

1235. 1 2 7 5 7 1 3 2 1 6 7 1 7 3 2   1 2 3 4
LM   6v   F O F O
1763   *a* Barnes or Carpendale
    P186a   B♭   *a*   585

1236.   1 3 4 5 3 4 5 6 5 4 3 2 7 1 6   1 2 2 3 3 4
        CM   4v   H F F H H F
        1763   *a* Barnes or Carpendale
            P186a   G   482

1237.   1 3 2 3 4 3 4 5 4 3 2 1 3 4 3   1 2 3 4 4
        LM   4v   F F H F F
        1763   *a* Barnes or Carpendale
            P186a   B♭   *a*   865

1238.   1 5 5 4 3 2 1 4 3 2 3 2 1 5 3   1 2 3 4 5 6
        886886   4v   H H H F F F
        1763   *a* Barnes or Carpendale
            P186a   C   *a*   19

1239.   1 5 4 3 2 3 4 3 5 1 4 3 2 1 1   1 2 3 4 3 4 M
        CM   4v   H H E H F F O
        1790   *a* W. Billings
            A97   *g*   *a*   550   THE BIRD

BIBLIOGRAPHY OF SECONDARY SOURCES

Barbour, J. Murray. *The Church Music of William Billings.* East Lansing, 1960.

Benson, Louis F. *The English Hymn: Its Development and Use.* Richmond, Va., 1915. Reprint, Richmond, Va., 1962.

Britton, Allen P. "Theoretical Introductions in American Tunebooks to 1800." Ph.D. dissertation, University of Michigan, 1949.

Buechner, Alan. "Yankee Singing Schools and the Golden Age of Choral Music in New England, 1760-1800." Ph.D. dissertation, Harvard University, 1960.

Chase, Gilbert. *America's Music from the Pilgrims to the Present.* New York, 1955.

Crawford, Richard. *Andrew Law, American Psalmodist.* Evanston, 1968.

———. "Connecticut Sacred Music Imprints, 1778-1810." *Notes* 27 (1971): 445-52, 671-79.

———. *The Core Repertory of Early American Psalmody.* (Forthcoming.)

———. "Psalmody. II. North America." *The New Grove Dictionary of Music and Musicians,* ed. Stanley Sadie (London, 1980), 15: 345-47.

———, ed. James Lyon, *Urania* (New York, 1974).

———, et al. *A Bibliography of Sacred Music Printed in America Through 1810.* Worcester, [1983?].

Evans, Charles. *American Bibliography.* 14 vols. Chicago, Worcester, 1903-59.

Julian, John. *A Dictionary of Hymnology.* 2nd edn. London, 1907. Reprint, New York, 1957.

Keller, Kate Van Winkle, and Carolyn Rabson. *The National Tune Index.* New York, 1980.

Kroeger, Karl. "The *Worcester Collection of Sacred Harmony* and Sacred Music in America." Ph.D. dissertation, Brown University, 1976.

———, ed. William Billings, *The New-England Psalm-Singer.* The Complete Works of William Billings, no. 1. [n. p.], 1981.

Lindstrom, Carl E. "William Billings and His Times." *The Musical Quarterly* 15 (1939): 479-97.

Lowens, Irving. *Music and Musicians in Early America.* New York, 1964.

————. "The Origins of the American Fuging Tune." *Journal of the American Musicological Society* 6 (1953): 43-52.

MacDougall, Hamilton C. *Early New England Psalmody.* Brattleboro, 1940.

McKay, David P., and Richard Crawford. *William Billings of Boston: 18th-Century Composer.* Princeton, 1975.

Nathan, Hans. *William Billings: Data and Documents.* Detroit, 1976.

Patrick, Millar. *Four Centuries of Scottish Psalmody.* London, 1949.

Perry, William S., ed. *Historical Collections Relating to the American Colonial Church.* 5 vols. Hartford, 1973.

Routley, Erik. *The English Carol.* London, 1958.

Schnapper, Edith B., ed. *The British Union-Catalogue of Early Music.* 2 vols. London, 1957.

Sonneck, Oscar G. T. *Francis Hopkinson and James Lyon.* Washington, 1905. Reprint, New York, 1967.

Stéphan, J. *Adeste Fideles.* Buckfast Abbey, 1947.

Stevenson, Robert. *Protestant Church Music In America.* New York, 1966.

Stigberg, David K. "Congregational Psalmody in Eighteenth Century New England." M. M. thesis, University of Illinois, 1970.

Temperley, Nicholas. "John Playford and the Metrical Psalms." *Journal of the American Musicological Society* 25 (1972): 331-78.

————. *The Music of the English Parish Church.* 2 vols. Cambridge, 1979.

————. "The Origins of the Fuging Tune." *Royal Musical Association Research Chronicle* 17 (1981): 1-32.

————. "The Old Way of Singing: Its Origins and Development." *Journal of the American Musicological Society* 34 (1981): 511-44.

Wilson, Ruth Mack. *Connecticut's Music in the Revolutionary Era.* Hartford, 1979.

Worst, John W. "New England Psalmody 1760-1810: Analysis of an American Idiom." Ph. D. dissertation, University of Michigan, 1974.

INDEX OF TEXTS

The first lines of all texts underlaid or designated for use with the fuging tunes in any source are listed below, in alphabetical order ("The" and "A" included). Spelling and punctuation have been modernized. Following each first line in parentheses is either a verified text source, an attribution in a stated source, or a tentative suggestion of the source with question mark—or nothing, if nothing can be said about the source. Full names and dates of authors cited can be found in the Index of Persons. An obelisk sign (†) means that the first line of the text differs from its original form. Text numbers which appear in brackets were not used; tune numbers to which the text was set appear in boldface on the right.

Abbreviated Text Sources

Abbreviation	*Source*	*Method of Reference*
Huntingdon 1780	[Selina, Countess of Huntingdon,] *A Select Collection of Hymns to be Universally Sung in All the Countess of Huntingdon's Chapels* (London, 1780)	Hymn number
Merrick Ps	James Merrick, *The Psalms of David Translated or Paraphrased in English Verse* (London, 1765)	Psalm number: line of paraphrase
NV Ps	Nahum Tate & Nicholas Brady, *A New Version of the Psalms* (London, 1696)	Psalm: verse of psalm
OV Ps	Thomas Sternhold, John Hopkins and others, *The Whole Book of Psalms* (first complete edition, London, 1573)	Psalm: verse of psalm
Watts Hy	Isaac Watts, *Hymns and Spiritual Songs* (3 vols., London, 1707)	Volume number, hymn [:verse if other than verse 1]
Watts Ps	Isaac Watts, *The Psalms of David Imitated in the Language of the New Testament* (London, 1719)	Psalm, [part, if any, in lower-case roman numerals]: verse of paraphrase

Index

No.	Text and Source	Tune
72	Buried in shadows of the night (Watts Hy I, 97)	475
73	But, Lord, thy mercies, my sure hope (NV Ps 36:5†)	402
74	But there's a dreadful God (Watts Ps 36:5)	41
75	By thy unwearied strength upheld (Merrick Ps 21:1)	145
76	By what means may a young man best (OV Ps 119:9)	1130
77	Cast me not, Lord, out from thy sight (OV Ps 51:11)	475
78	Cease awhile, ye winds, to blow	174
79	Come, children, learn to fear the Lord (Watts Ps 34ii:1)	1071
80	Come forth and hearken here full soon (OV Ps 66:16)	1042
81	Come hither, and I will thee teach (OV Ps 32:8)	619
82	Come Holy Ghost, Creator, come (Tate & Brady, *Supplement,* 1700)	649
83	Come, let our voices join to raise (Watts Ps 95:1)	187
84	Come, let us join our cheerful songs (Watts Hy I, 62)	129, 307, 312, 380, 389, 932
85	Come, let us sing unto the Lord (W. Billings, A40)	86
86	Come, my beloved, haste away (attr. Watts in A136)	496, 908
87	Come near to me, my children, and (OV Ps 34:11)	273
	Come on, my partners in distress. *See* 846	
88	Come saints, adore Jehovah's name	190
89	Come, see the wonders of our Lord (Watts?)	130
90	Come, sound his praise abroad (Watts Ps 95:1)	413, 633, 774, 813, 815
91	Compose a hymn of praise, and touch	455
92	Consider all my sorrows, Lord (Watts Ps 119:153)	855
93	Consider my affliction, Lord (NV Ps 119:153)	1065
94	Dark dismal thoughts and boding fears (Watts Ps 102i:6)	185
95	Day of judgment, day of wonders (Newton, *Olney Hymns* II, 1779, no. 77)	1053
[96]		
97	Dearest of all the names above (Watts Hy II, 148)	33
98	Death is to us a sweet repose	420
99	Death, with his warrant in his hand (W. Billings, A40)	767
100	Deep in a cold and joyless cell (Hart, *Supplement,* 1762)	1183
101	Deep in our hearts let us record (Watts Ps 69:1)	101, 204, 225, 602, 804, 873
102	Defend me, Lord, from shame (NV Ps 31:1)	31, 1152
103	Did Christ for sinners weep? (attr. Beddome in Rippon, *Hymns,* 1787)	497
104	Down headlong from the native skies (Watts Hy II, 96)	441
105	Draw us, O God, with sovereign grace	1087
106	Early, my God, without delay (Watts Ps 63i:1)	303
107	Earth, tremble on; well mayst thou fear (NV Ps 114:7)	197
108	Ere the blue heavens were stretched abroad (Watts Hy I, 2)	565
109	Erect your heads, eternal gates (NV Ps 24:7)	106, 393, 452
110	Erect your heads, ye gates, unfold (NV Ps 24:7†)	106

No.	Text and Source	Tune
111	Eternal power, whose high abode	74
112	False are the men of high degree (Watts Ps 62:3)	254
113	Far as thy name is known (Watts Ps 48ii:1)	1089
114	Far be thine honours spread	384
115	Father of all, enthroned above	42
116	Father of all, my soul defend (Merrick Ps 16:1)	635
117	Firm was my health, my day was bright (Watts Ps 30ii:1)	64, 278, 610
118	Fly me, riches, fly me, cares	570
119	For thee, O God, our constant praise (NV Ps 65:1)	714, 1158
120	Forever and forever, Lord (NV Ps 119:89)	1162
121	Forever blessed be the Lord (Watts Ps 144:1)	256
122	Forever blest be God the Lord (NV Ps 144i:1)	118
	From all that dwell below the skies (Watts Ps 117:1†). *See* 123	
123	From all who dwell below the skies (Watts Ps 117:1)	187, 807
124	From day to day we humbly own	1060
125	From ill recede, to good incline (Merrick Ps 37:93)	657
126	From my youth up, may Israel say (NV Ps 129:1)	549
127	From out thy unexhausted store (NV Ps 65:9)	625
128	From the cross uplifted high (Haweis, *Carmina Christo*, 1792)	952
129	From the third heaven where God resides	223
	Give ear, thou judge of all the earth (NV Ps 55:1). *See* 862	
130	Give laud unto the Lord (OV Ps 148:1)	293, 447, 860
131	Give me the wings of faith to rise (Watts Hy II, 140)	375
132	Give praise unto the God of Gods (OV Ps 136:2)	567
133	Give praises unto God the Lord (OV Ps 105:1)	679, 748
134	Give thanks to God most high (Watts Ps 136:1)	15
135	Give thanks unto the Lord our God	737
136	Give to our God immortal praise (Watts Ps 136:1). *See also* 137	241, 709
137	Give to the Lord immortal praise (Watts Ps 136:1†). *See also* 136	601
138	Give to the Lord, ye potentates (OV Ps 29:1)	768
139	Gnashing his teeth the fool prepares (Merrick Ps 37:41†)	669
140	God, as with fervent lips I pray (Merrick Ps 55:51†)	1050
141	God counts the sorrows of his saints (Watts Ps 56:6)	300
142	God from his cloudy cistern pours (Watts Ps 104:9)	28?
143	God in his earthly temple lays (Watts Ps 87:1)	631
144	God in the great assembly stands (NV Ps 82:1)	199, 606
145	God is gone up, our Lord and king (NV Ps 47:5)	19
146	God is our refuge in distress (NV Ps 46:1)	58, 337, 443, 681, 716, 962
147	God moves in a mysterious way (Cowper?, *Gospel Magazine*, 1774)	899
148	God, my supporter and my hope (Watts Ps 73ii:1)	272
149	God of my life, look gently down (Watts Ps 39iii:1)	44

No.	Text and Source	Tune
216	How pleasant is thy dwelling place (OV Ps 84:1)	477, 616, 914
217	How pleasant 'tis to see (Watts Ps 133:1)	
		85?, 194, 250, 355, 417, 608, 902
218	How pleased and blest was I (Watts Ps 122:1). *See also* 219	
		30, 84, 355, 435, 533, 867, 1068, 1080
219	How pleased, how blest was I (Watts Ps 122:1†). *See also* 218	194
220	How shall the young preserve their ways (NV Ps 119:9)	942
221	How vast must their advantage be (NV Ps 133:1)	237, 290, 449
222	I am a stranger on the earth	1018
223	I am the Saviour, I th'almighty God (Watts Ps 50ii:6)	511
224	I did in heart rejoice (OV Ps 122:1)	160, 325
225	I in the burying place may see	438
226	I lift my heart to thee (OV Ps 25:1)	344
	I lift my soul to God. *See* 833	
227	I love the Lord, because the voice (OV Ps 116:1†)	521, 843
228	I love the volumes of thy word (Watts Ps 19:5)	795
229	I love thy habitation, Lord (attr. Watts in A196)	83
230	I send the joys of earth away (Watts Hy II, 11)	498
231	I set the Lord still in my sight (OV Ps 16:8)	422
232	I to the Lord will pay my vows (OV Ps 116:14†)	1095
233	I waited long and sought the Lord (OV Ps 40:1)	531, 1005
234	I waited meekly for the Lord (NV Ps 40:1)	618, 1001
235	I waited patient for the Lord (Watts Ps 40i:1)	38, 267
	I will give thanks to thee, O Lord. *See* 832	
236	I will regard and think upon (OV Ps 77:11)	1060, 1081
237	I with my voice to God did cry (OV Ps 77:1†)	1060
238	If angels sung a saviour's birth (anon. in P51.2)	653, 1002
239	If up to heaven I take my flight (NV Ps 139:1)	586
240	I'll lift my banner, saith the Lord (Watts Hy I, 29†)	1054
241	I'll praise my maker with my breath (Watts Ps 146:1)	
		277, 337, 414, 921, 957, 1003, 1155
242	I'll search the land and raise the just (Watts Ps 101:5)	501
243	I'll speak the honours of my king (Watts Ps 45:1)	213
244	Ill tidings never can surprise (Watts Ps 112:5)	539
245	I'll trust God's word, and so despise (NV Ps 56:10)	677
246	Important news arrive	929
247	In all my vast concerns with thee (Watts Ps 139i:1)	524
248	In deep distress I oft have cried (NV Ps 120:1)	702
249	In God the Lord I put my trust (OV Ps 11:1)	47, 105
250	In God's own house pronounce his praise (Watts Ps 150:1)	73, 648, 1002
251	In the cold prison of a tomb (Watts Hy II, 72)	723

No.	Text and Source	Tune
401	No burning heats by day (Watts Ps 121:1)	464
402	No change of times shall ever shock (NV Ps 18:1)	243, 281, 604
403	No more beneath the oppressive hand	1099
404	No more shall atheists mock his long delay (Watts Ps 50i:1)	67
	No sleep nor slumber to his eyes. *See 857*	
405	No victims, Lord, in solemn rite (Merrick Ps 51:55)	730
406	Not all the blood of beasts (Watts Hy II, 142)	394, 479
407	Not from the dust affliction grows (Watts Hy I, 83)	553
408	Now in the heat of youthful blood (Watts Hy I, 91)	347, 1056
409	Now is the hour of darkness past (Watts Hy I, 58)	805
410	Now let a spacious world arise (Watts Hy II, 147)	104
411	Now let our lips with holy fear (Watts Ps 69ii:1)	605
412	Now let our mournful songs record (Watts Ps 22:1)	807
	Now let our souls' immortal powers. *See 840*	
413	Now let our voices rise (Doddridge, *Hymns,* 1755)	344
414	Now let the Lord my Saviour smile (Watts Hy II, 50)	248
415	Now sable clouds from western skies	792
416	Now shall my head be lifted high (Watts Ps 27i:5)	205, 308, 1131
417	Now shall my inward joys arise (Watts Hy I, 39)	336, 353, 382, 532, 561
418	Now to the Lamb that once was slain (Watts Hy I, 1:5). *See also* 835	600
	Now to the Lord that once was slain. *See 835*	
419	O all ye nations of the world (OV Ps 117:1)	911
420	O all ye nations, praise the Lord (Watts Ps 117:1)	778
421	O all ye people, clap your hands (NV Ps 47:1)	34, 378, 402, 458, 941
422	O bless the Lord, my soul (Watts Ps 103i:1)	208
423	O blessed souls are they (Watts Ps 32:1)	1208
[424-432]		
433	O come all ye that fear the Lord (NV Ps 66:16)	864
434	O come, let us with one accord	411
435	O come, loud anthems let us sing (NV Ps 95:1)	
		187, 242, 279, 451, 519, 983, 1070, 1233
436	O for a shout of sacred joy (Watts Ps 47:1)	218, 303, 1167
	O for an heart to praise my God. *See 849*	
437	O for an overcoming faith (Watts Hy I, 17)	233
438	O for this love let earth and skies (attr. Watts in A171)	134
439	O God, how joyful is the king (OV Ps 21:1†)	1137
440	O God, my God, I early seek (OV Ps 63:1†)	440, 971, 1083
441	O God, my God, O tell me why (Merrick Ps 22:1†)	165
442	O God, my gracious God, to thee (NV Ps 63:1)	317, 724
443	O God, my heart is fixed, 'tis bent (NV Ps 57:7)	88, 178, 365, 856, 993
444	O God, my heart is fully bent (NV Ps 108:1)	381, 688, 690, 997

No.	Text and Source	Tune
630	The name and glory of the Lord (NV Ps 102:15)	27
631	The saints shall flourish in his days	1094
632	The Saviour calls: let every ear (Steele, *Poems,* 1760, I, p. 162)	761
633	The shining worlds above (Watts Ps 148:3)	773
634	The singers go before with joy (OV Ps 68:26)	246
	The sorrows of my heart. *See* 851	
635	The spacious firmament on high (Addison, Ps 19:1, *Spectator,* 1712)	802
636	The spirits of the just (Hart, *Supplement,* 1762)	437, 840
637	The states, O Lord, with songs of praise (NV Ps 21:1†). *See also* 510, 599	196
638	The time of our abode on earth (OV Ps 90:10†)	603
639	The voice of my beloved sounds (Watts Hy I, 69)	310, 315, 891
640	The watchmen join their voice	883
641	The wondering world inquires to know (Watts Hy I, 75)	484, 607
642	The words that from my lips proceed (Merrick Ps 5:1)	164
	Thee I will bless, my God and king (NV Ps 145:1†). *See* 838	
643	Thee, Lord, our king, and thee alone (Merrick Ps 44)	710
644	Thee we adore, eternal name (Watts Hy II, 55)	127, 1060
	Thee will I bless, my God and king. *See* 838	
645	Thee will I laud, my God and king (OV Ps 145:1)	221, 246, 326
646	Thee will I praise with my whole heart (OV Ps 138:1)	642, 1045
647	Then in the Lord let Israel trust (Watts Ps 130:7)	330
648	Then jointly all the harpers round	1088
649	Then open wide the temple gate (NV Ps 118:19†)	20
650	Then to thy throne, victorious king	416
651	There is a house not made with hands (Watts Hy I, 110)	298, 442
652	There is a land of pure delight (Watts Hy II, 66)	485, 782, 869
653	There is no God, do foolish men (OV Ps 14:1†)	1116
654	There was an hour when Christ rejoiced (Watts Hy I, 11)	870
655	There's joy in heaven and joy on earth (anon. in Rippon, *Selection,* 1787)	363
656	They that do place their confidence (OV Ps 125:1†). *See also* 667	402
657	They that in ships with courage bold (NV Ps 107:23)	1112
658	Think, mighty God, on feeble man (Watts Ps 89:1)	
		57, 331, 337, 518, 598, 786, 850
659	This day is God's: let all the land	75
660	This God is the God we adore (Hart, *Hymns,* 1759†)	166
	This is the day, the blessed morn. *See* 865	
661	This is the day the Lord hath made (Watts Ps 118iv:1)	1165
662	This is the glorious day (Watts Ps 118:4)	961
663	This life's a dream, an empty show (Watts Ps 17:4)	587, 1103

INDEX OF TUNE NAMES

Names referring to psalms, e.g. 20TH PSALM, *have been standardized as* PSALM 20, *etc. Original spellings are retained; the definite or indefinite article has been omitted.*

VERMONT 511 838
VERNON 382
VERONA 884
VESPERS 788
VICTORY 872 1131
VIENNA 72
VOICE OF NATURE 802
WALLINGFORD 833
WALLINGSFORD 833
WALPOLE 268
WALTHAM 578
WARD 524
WAREHAM 63
WARREN 252
WARWICK 118 1002
WASHINGTON 10 123 377 963 1102
WASHINGTON-STREET 561
WATERFORD 84
WATERTOWN 579
WATFORD 990
WEATHERSFIELD 270
WELLS 993
WENDOVER 184
WENHASTON 125
WESTBOROUGH 93
WESTERHAM 736
WESTFIELD 588
WESTMINSTER 113 573
WESTPOINT 815
WETHERSFIELD 709 835

WEYMOUTH 369
WHEELERS POINT 474
WHITES TOWN 550
WHITSTABLE 374
WIGAN 30 31
WILLIAM 180
WILLIAMSTED 991
WILLIAMSTOWN 126
WILLINGTON 384
WILMINGTON 781 931
WILTON 193 410 491
WILTSHIRE 302
WINBORNE 466
WINBOURN 73
WINSOR 945
WINTERINGHAM 941
WINTHROP 361
WITTON 365
WOBURN 64
WOODBRIDGE 1154
WOODHOUSE 517
WOODTHORPE 733
WORCESTER 192 1160
WORKSOP 921
WRENTHAM 551 1060
WROTHAM 125
YARMOUTH 286 690 799 911
YORK 1042
YOXFORD 62
ZION 13 69 147 255 355

This Index includes all compilers of collections, composers of tunes, authors of texts included in the Census, and other persons of contemporary importance mentioned in the Historical Account, pages 3-54. After each name, given in parentheses where known, are the dates and countries of birth and death (E = England, S = Scotland, A = America), or of activity (fl. = flourished), followed by any sources of which the person was the compiler, (referring to the List of Sources on pages 55-81). Next are listed, in boldface type, the tunes which the person is reliably believed to have composed, or which were adapted from his music. Texts of which he/she was the author (referring to the Index of Texts on pages 439-63) follow in roman type. Finally, numbers in italics refer to pages in the Historical Account. Spellings of names have been standardized. Incorrect or improbable composer attributions (designated b, c, etc. in the Census) have not been indexed.

Adams (?A fl.1800)
 − **655 862**
Adams, Abraham (E fl.1752)
 − P174
 − **344**
 − pp. 21 23
Addington, Rev. Stephen (E 1729-96)
 − D6 D15
 − pp. 19 25 27
Addison, Joseph (E 1672-1719)
 − texts 603 616 635 736
Adgate, Andrew (A 1762-93)
 − A92, A103
Alcock, Dr. John (E 1715-1806)
 − P126
 − **567**
 − p. 11
Allin, W. (?A fl.1793)
 − **981**
Arne, Dr. Thomas (E 1710-78)
 − **108** (adapted)
Arnold, John (E c.1720-92)
 − P117 P163 P169 P233
 − **246**
 − pp. 10 20 23 24 34n. 35 42

Arnold, Dr. Samuel (E 1740-1802)
 − P291
 − **9 10 17 111 151 154 658 716 863 1039 1041 1052 1113 1127 1128 1158**
 − pp. 30 31 42 50
Ashton, John (E fl.1786)
 − **598 692**
Ashworth, Rev. Caleb (E 1722-75)
 − P175
 − p. 25
Atterbury, Luffman (E d.1796)
 − **4 21 150 650 651 669 706**
 − p. 30
Atwell, [?Richard] (A fl.1793)
 − **209 584 831**
Atwell, Thomas H. (A 1795)
 − A148
B., A. (?S fl.1800)
 − **1038**
Babcock, Samuel (A fl.1795)
 − A149
 − **75 93 177 252 392 551 1115**
Baird, [?T. D.] (A fl.1793)
 − **578 901**

Shield, William (*E* 1748-1829)
— **53 675**
— *p. 30*

Shumway, Nehemiah (*A* fl.1793)
— A131
— **113 156 201 309 334 393 398 512
534 536 554 958 1053**
— *pp. 38 48 49*

Skinner, Thomas (*A* fl.1796)
— A164 A182

Slater (*A* fl.1797)
— **486**

Smart, Christopher (*E* 1722-71)
— P191
— texts 198 523
— *p. 30*

Smith, Benjamin (*E* fl.1732)
— P105

Smith, Isaac (*E* fl.1755-80)
— P246
— *pp. 25n. 27 28n.*

Smith, John (*E* fl.1755)
— **193**

Smith, J[ohn?] S[tafford?]
(*E* 1750-1836)
— **701 1144**

Smith, Rev. William (*S* 1727-*A* 1803)
— *p. 33*

Smith, [?William] (?*A* fl.1796)
— **316 504 898 964**

Spicer, Ishmaih (*A* b.1760)
— **101**

Sreeve, John (*E* fl.1740)
— P118

Stanley, John (?*E* 1713-89)
— **609**
— *p. 30*

Steele, Anne (*E* 1716-78)
— texts 363 632 762

Steffani, Agostino (1654-1748)
— **20 649 994** (all adapted)

Stennett, Dr. Samuel (*E* c.1727-95)
— texts 186 697

Stephenson, Joseph (*E* fl.1760)
— P168 P171 P227
— **42 220 240 244 262 269 281 282
302 366 367 443 448 452 488
489 492 521 555 592 790 794
1001 1126 1178**
— *pp. 19 20-21 35 36n 41 42 45*

Sternhold, Thomas (*E* d.1549)
Hopkins, John (*E* fl.1549-62),
and others
— texts, *passim* (OV)
— *pp. 4 33n. 38n.*

Stevens, Richard John Samuel
(*E* 1757-1837)
— **163 652 738**

Stevenson, Dr. John Andrew
(*E* 1761-1833)
— **258 853**

Stickney, John (*A* 1744-1827)
— A39 A54
— *pp. 35 36 44*

Stone, Joseph (*A* fl.1793)
— A132
— **32 110 233 283 322 346 361 414
421 434 490 495 524 542 566
573 574 579 593 612 771 791
840 965 1166**
— *p. 48*

Storm, J. P. (*A* fl.1795)
— **507**

Strong, Rev. Joseph (*A* fl.1783)
— **311 834 985 1145**

Swan, Timothy (*A* 1758-1842)
— **91 300 483 571 760 807 1029
1182**
— *pp. 41 49*

T., J. (*S* fl.1800; James Thomson?)
— **1038**

Tans'ur, William (*E* c.1700-1783)
— P142 P155 P210; A28 A30 A31

TUNES IN MODERN EDITIONS

Tunes are listed in numerical order, as in the tune census. After each tune number is an abbreviated reference to a modern edition or dissertation, referring to the list of sources below, pages 489-93. Editions of post-1800 psalmody collections are not included.

14	Wor₂		130	Bil₁ Van₇
15	Cra Kro₂ Low₃ Mac Mar Pie Ste Van₄ Wor₂		136	Dan₂
			141	Lyo
22	Bel₂ Dan₁ Owe		165	Tem₂
29	Bil₁		187	Cra Gle Low₃ Smi Wor₂
33	Owe		191	Wor₂
40	Nat₁		204	Doo
41	Cra Wor₂		205	Kro₂ Owe
43	Bel₂ Owe		214	Bil₁
45	Bel₁ Van₇		217	Tem₂
50	Wor₂		219	Tem₂
63	Bil₃		221	Kro₁
64	Dan₂ Fis Kro₂ Mar Wil		223	Cra Wor₂
73	Fis		235	Bel₂ Owe
74	Fis Wor₂		238	Cra Wor₂
76	Bel₂ Owe		254	Cra Doo Gle Low₂ McK₁ Pie Ste Wor₂
80	Gen Wor₂			
94	Smi		256	Wor₂
96	Cra Wor₂		260	Bil₁ Cra McK₁ Pis
106	Tem₁		267	Tem₂
117	Wor₂		268	Ben Doo Wor₂
124	Low₂ McK₁ Pis Van₆		274	Bil₁
125	Lyo		277	Gol Mar
126	Rey		292	Gen
128	Nat₁		302	Cra Low₃ Wor₂

303	Beh Cra Fis Mar Van$_4$ Wor$_2$	561	Bil$_1$ Bil$_2$ Van$_5$
307	Nat$_1$	563	Wor$_2$
308	Bil$_3$ DeC	571	Cra Wor$_2$
312	Wor$_2$	576	Bel$_2$ Owe
337	Cra Ell Hit Wor$_2$	581	Bel$_2$ Owe
345	Lyo	585	Bel$_2$ Owe
347	Beh Mar	591	Cra Mac Wor$_2$
351	Bel$_2$ Owe	595	Bel$_2$ Bel$_4$ Owe
355	Kro$_2$ Wor$_2$	607	Gen
360	Bil$_1$ Van$_6$	608	Wor$_2$
364	Gen	611	Ben
369	Bil$_1$	613	Bar Wor$_2$
380	Bel$_2$ Owe	626	Bel$_2$ Owe
381	Mar	665	Gen
382	Doo	698	Dan$_2$
388	Gen	715	Bel$_2$ Owe
403	Dan$_2$	728	Kro$_2$
405	Cra Nat$_1$ Wor$_2$	736	Fis Gle Mar
412	Bel$_2$ Owe	743	Kro$_2$
428	Bil$_1$ Pis Van$_6$	749	Kro$_2$
430	Wor$_2$	756	Nat$_1$
431	Gol Kro$_1$	757	Wor$_2$
433	Bel$_2$ Bel$_3$ Dan$_1$ Owe	759	Bil$_1$
438	Gen	760	Beh Cra Kro$_2$ Smi Wor$_2$
464	Wor$_2$	761	Kro$_2$
481	Dan$_3$ Van$_6$	765	Doo
482	Nat$_1$	766	Bil$_1$ Gar Pie Wor$_2$
493	Kro$_1$	772	Ben
494	Beh	773	Wor$_2$
496	Bel$_2$ Owe	775	Lan Tem$_1$
506	Bil$_1$ Van$_7$	779	Bel$_2$ Owe
514	Doo	784	Doo Kro$_2$
517	Lyo	790	McK$_1$
525	Bil$_1$ Bil$_2$ Fis	798	Doo
528	Doo	799	Wil
534	Wie$_1$	807	Cra Fis Web Wor$_2$
538	Gol	813	Low$_1$
540	Kro$_2$	819	Gen
545	Bel$_2$ Owe Wor$_2$	820	Wor$_2$
546	Nat$_1$ Wie$_3$	821	Gen
553	Dan$_2$ Gol	825	Bil$_3$
560	Wor$_2$	827	Bil$_1$ Rey Van$_7$

838	Mar	968	Ben Bor Bus Cra Hit Wor_2
842	Beh Mar	990	Tem_1
843	McK_1	1002	Cra Kro_2 Van_1 Wor_2
844	Bel_1 Bel_2 Gol Mar Owe	1003	Wor_2
845	Cra Wor_2	1011	Bil_3
849	Bil_1	1021	Mar
866	Bel_2 Owe	1026	Gen
870	Gen	1030	Bel_2 Owe
872	Bil_1 Van_3	1054	Gen
875	Wor_2	1057	Cra Doo Fis Kro_2 Wor_2
887	Bil_1 Van_7	1060	Hit Lyo Wor_2
890	Wor_2	1088	Bel_2 Owe Van_1
891	Bel_2 Owe	1091	Bel_2 Owe
892	Gen	1101	Nat_1 Wor_2
893	Kro_2 Nat_1 Nat_2 Wor_2	1102	Beh Kro_2 Nat_1 Wie_3
908	Dan_2 Fis Mar Wil	1112	Kro_2
917	Doo Wor_2	1131	Fis Wor_2
926	Gle Gol	1148	Cra Kro_2 Wor_2
930	Doo	1160	Cra Fis Kro_2 Mar McK_1 Van_1
935	And Dan_3 McK_1 Nat_1 Pis		Woo Wor_2
	Rey Van_2 Wor_2	1164	Kro_2
936	Wie_1	1171	Wor_2
938	Ben	1182	Wor_1
943	Kro_2 Wor_2	1184	Cra Wor_2
945	Doo	1185	Kro_2
947	Ben Pat Wie_2	1186	Bel_2 Bel_3 Owe
948	Lyo	1196	Ben Low_1 Mar Met Pie Rey
956	Kro_2		Van_4
957	Bel_2 Owe	1199	Wor_2
961	Kro_2	1223	Ben Pat
962	Bel_2 Owe	1239	Dan_3 Wie_1

Modern Editions Cited

And   Anderson, Gillian (ed.). *The Christmas Music of William Billings (1764-1800).* Washington, 1973.

Bar   Barbour, J. Murray. *The Church Music of William Billings.* East Lansing, 1960.

Beh   Behrend, Jeanne (ed.). *Choral Music of the American Folk Tradition: Fuguing Tunes.* Philadelphia, 1954.

Bel₁   Belcher, Supply. *Blow Ye the Trumpet,* ed. Leonard Van Camp. New York, 1975.

Bel₂   Belcher, Supply. *The Harmony of Maine.* Facs. edn. with an introduction by H. Wiley Hitchcock. (Earlier American Music, 6.) New York, 1972. [A135]

Bel₃   Belcher, Supply. *Welcome to Spring,* ed. Leonard Van Camp. New York, 1975.

Bel₄   Belcher, Supply. *While Shepherds Watched Their Flocks,* ed. Leonard Van Camp. New York, 1975.

Ben   Bennett, Lawrence (ed.). *The Western Wind American Tune-Book.* New York, 1974.

Bil₁   Billings, William. *The Continental Harmony.* Facs. edn. with an introduction by Hans Nathan. Cambridge, Mass., 1961. [A136]

Bil₂   Billings, William. *Now Shall My Inward Joys* and *Time, What an Empty Vapor 'Tis,* ed. Herbert Colvin. San Antonio, 1969.

Bil₃   Billings, William. *The Psalm-Singer's Amusement.* Facs. edn. with an introduction by H. Wiley Hitchcock. (Earlier American Music, 20.) New York, 1974. [A44]

Bor   Borroff, Edith. *Music in Europe and the United States: A History.* Englewood Cliffs, 1971.

Bus   Bushnell, Vinson. "Daniel Read of New Haven (1757-1836): The Man and His Musical Activities." Ph.D. diss., Harvard University, 1978.

Cra   Crawford, Richard. *The Core Repertory of Early American Psalmody.* (In press.)

Dan₁   Daniel, Oliver (ed.). *Deep North Spirituals, 1794.* New York, 1973.

Dan₂   Daniel, Oliver (ed.). *Down East Spirituals.* New York, 1973.

Dan₃   Daniel, Oliver (ed.). *William Billings (1746-1800).* New York, 1970.

DeC   DeCormier, Robert (ed.). *Robert DeCormier Choral Series.* New York, 1968.

Dic   Dickinson, Clarence. *William Billings: Three Fuguing Tunes.* New York, 1940.

Doo   [Doolittle, Amos, and Daniel Read.] *The American Musical Magazine, Vol. I.* Scarsdale, 1961. [A72]

Ell   Ellinwood, Leonard. *The History of American Church Music.* New York, 1953.

Fis   Fisher, William Arms (ed.). *Ye Olde New-England Psalm-Tunes.* Boston, 1930.

Gar   Garrett, Allen. "The Works of William Billings." Ph.D. diss., University of North Carolina, 1952.

Gen   Genuchi, Marvin. "The Life and Music of Jacob French." Ph.D. diss., State University of Iowa, 1964.

Gle   Gleason, Harold. *American Music from 1620-1920.* (Music Literature Outlines, Series III.) New York, 1955.

Gol   Goldman, Richard Franko, and Roger Smith. *Landmarks of Early American Music.* New York, 1943.

Hit   Hitchcock, H. Wiley. *Music in the United States.* 2nd edn. Englewood Cliffs, 1974.

Kro₁   Kroeger, Karl (ed.). *The Complete Works of William Billings.* Vol. I.: *The New-England Psalm-Singer.* N.p., 1982. [A33]

Kro₂   Kroeger, Karl. "The Worcester Collection of Sacred Harmony and Sacred Music in America." Ph.D. diss., Brown University, 1976.

Lan   Landon, H. C. Robbins. *Haydn: Chronicle and Works.* Vol. III: *Haydn in England 1791-1795.* Bloomington, 1976.

Low₁   Lowens, Irving (ed.). *The Arthur Jordan Choral Series.* New York, 1953.

Low₂   Lowens, Irving (ed.). *Early Colonial Classics.* New York, 1956.

Low₃   Lowens. Irving. *Music and Musicians in Early America.* New York, 1964.

Lyo   Lyon, James. *Urania.* Facs. edn. with a preface by Richard Crawford. New York, 1974. [A17]

Mac   Macdougall, Hamilton C. *Early New England Psalmody*. Brattleboro, 1940.

Mar   Marrocco, W. Thomas, and Harold Gleason. *Music in America*. New York, 1964.

McK₁   McKay, David P. (ed.). *Choruses from 18th Century New England*. Delaware Water Gap, 1975.

McK₂   McKay, David P., and Richard Crawford. *William Billings of Boston: Eighteenth-Century Musician*. Princeton, 1975.

Met   Metcalf, Frank J. *American Writers and Compilers of Sacred Music*. New York, 1925.

Nat₁   Nathan, Hans (ed.). *The Complete Works of William Billings*. Vol. II: *The Singing Master's Assistant (1778)* and *Music in Miniature (1779)*. N.p., 1977. [A40]

Nat₂   Nathan, Hans. *William Billings: Data and Documents*. Detroit, 1976.

Owe   Owen, Earl, Jr. "The Life and Music of Supply Belcher." D.M.A. diss., Southern Baptist Theological Seminary, 1968.

Pat   Patterson, Relford. "Three American 'Primitives': A Study of the Musical Style of Hans Gram, Oliver Holden, and Samuel Holyoke." Ph.D. diss., Washington University, 1963.

Pie   Pierce, Edwin Hall. "The Rise and Fall of the 'Fugue-Tune' in America," *Musical Quarterly,* 16 (1930): 214-28.

Pis   Pisano, Richard C. (ed.). *The Best of Billings*. New York, 1968.

Rey   Reynolds, William J. (ed.). *Early American Fuguing Tunes*. New York, 1969.

Rit   Ritter, Frédéric Louis. *Music in America*. New edn. New York, 1890.

Smi   Smith, James G. (ed.). *The New Liberty Bell*. Champaign, 1976.

Ste   Stevenson, Robert. *Protestant Church Music in America*. New York, 1966.

Tem₁   Temperley, Nicholas. *The Music of the English Parish Church*. Cambridge, 1979.

Tem_2 Temperley, Nicholas. "Psalmody: I. England," *The New Grove Dictionary of Music and Musicians* (London, 1980), 15: 337-45.

Van_1 Van Camp, Leonard (ed.). *Christmas Music from Colonial America*. New York, 1975.

Van_2 Van Camp, Leonard (ed.). *The Christmas Story*. Saint Louis, 1974.

Van_3 Van Camp, Leonard (ed.). *A Cry for Freedom*. Carol Stream, 1974.

Van_4 Van Camp, Leonard (ed.). *Favorite Hymns of Early America*. Macomb, 1975.

Van_5 Van Camp, Leonard (ed.). *Meet America's William Billings*. Champaign, 1974.

Van_6 Van Camp, Leonard (ed.). *The Passion and Resurrection of Our Lord*. St. Louis, 1974.

Van_7 Van Camp, Leonard (ed.). *Sacred Choral Music from Colonial America by William Billings*. St. Louis, 1973.

Web Webb, Guy. "Timothy Swan: Yankee Tunesmith." D.M.A. diss., University of Illinois, 1972.

Wie_1 Wienandt, Elwyn A. (ed.). *The Bicentennial Collection of American Music*. Carol Stream, 1974.

Wie_2 Wienandt, Elwyn A. (ed.). *Three Early American Anthems*. New York, 1973.

Wie_3 Wienandt, Elwyn A. (ed.). *William Billings: Two Fuging Tunes*. Carol Stream, 1973.

Wil Wilcox, Glenn. "Jacob Kimball, Jr. (1761-1826): His Life and Works" Ph.D. diss., University of South Carolina, 1957.

Woo Wood, Abraham. *Hymn XXXII. For Worcester. On Peace,* ed. Gillian Anderson. Washington, 1975.

Wor_1 Worst, John (ed.). *Four Psalm Tunes from "The New England Harmony."* New York, 1972.

Wor_2 Worst, John. "New England Psalmody." Ph.D. diss., University of Michigan, 1974.

EXAMPLE:

To look up the piece found on page 59 of Andrew Law's *Select Harmony* (1779)—
reproduced on pages x-xi of this book:

1. Is it a "tune"? (A tune is a piece of music intended for strophic
   repetition with a sacred metrical text.)

   Yes.

2. Is it "fuging"? (In at least one phrase, two or more voice parts enter
   non-simultaneously, with rests preceding at least one entry, in such
   a way as to produce overlap of text.)

   Yes.

3. Is it in a printed source published before 1801? (Then it should be
   in the Tune Census.)

   Yes.

4. Determine the keynote of the tune.

   The last bass note: A.

5. Call this note 1. A = 1

6. Write down the numbers representing the first fifteen notes of the
   tenor part (the second stave from the bottom).

   (Disregard octave register, accidentals, rhythmic values, rests,
   grace notes, and ornament signs. If the part divides into two or more
   "choosing notes," choose the upper one.)

7. Now you have a string of fifteen digits. 1 1 2 3 2 1 7 1 5 3 2 1 7 1 2
   Look it up, in numerical order, in the Tune Census. (*See opposite.*)